THE REMAKING
OF
A CULTURE

BOOKS BY THEODORE BRAMELD

Cultural Foundations of Education—An Interdisciplinary Exploration

Patterns of Educational Philosophy—A Democratic Interpretation (revised and re-published as two volumes):

   Philosophies of Education in Cultural Perspective

   Toward a Reconstructed Philosophy of Education

Ends and Means in Education—A Midcentury Appraisal

Minority Problems in the Public Schools

Design for America—An Educational Exploration of the Future of Democracy

Workers' Education in the United States (Editor and Co-Author)

A Philosophic Approach to Communism

THE REMAKING
of
A CULTURE

Life and Education in Puerto Rico

By THEODORE BRAMELD

Visiting Professor, University of Puerto Rico

with the assistance of
Ona K. Brameld and Domingo Rosado

Foreword by Oscar E. Porrata
Dean, College of Education
University of Puerto Rico

HARPER & BROTHERS PUBLISHERS, NEW YORK

To Kristin

CONTENTS

CONTENTS

FOREWORD

AT THE beginning of the present century a public educational system, embracing the principal types of institutions from the elementary school to the university, was established in Puerto Rico. This system was and is strongly influenced by traditional forms of school organization prevailing in the continental United States. Its chief agencies of control were determined by Congressional action in Washington. Until recently—to be exact, in 1947, when Congress approved the Butler-Crawford Reform Act—the executive head of the Puerto Rican public school system was appointed by the President of the United States, with the advice and consent of the federal Congress. The most important duties of this Presidential appointee were, among others, those of superintending public instruction and of preparing courses of study for all schools of the Island.

In consequence, the main characteristic of the administration and control of the Puerto Rican school system has been a centralized system of authority. Policies and orders have come directly from the top. Local participation has been little encouraged and parents have had but a feeble voice in the organization of the schools, in methods of learning, or in the development of curricula.

After five decades of experience with such a system it is proper that research be conducted to determine how the public schools have performed and should perform the acculturative role which is expected of them. Are educational philosophy and the school program responding adequately to the needs and aspirations of the Puerto Rican people, especially in this historic period when, as the author of this study points out, "change is the fulcrum around which all other events and facts revolve"?

The College of Education of the University of Puerto Rico, being aware of the need to examine and interpret public education in the setting of the Puerto Rican culture, invited Professor Theodore Brameld to serve as Visiting Professor of Educational Philosophy.

We knew that he had served as a staff member of the Center for Human Relations Studies, New York University, and that he had carried out research projects in various parts of the United States. One of these, supported by the University of Minnesota, was a curriculum experiment published under the title, *Design for America*. Another, a nationwide study of school policies governing Negro and other minority groups, was sponsored by the Rosenwald Fund and published under the title, *Minority Problems in the Public Schools*. Dr. Brameld's background as an author of several other volumes in political, anthropological, and educational theory qualified him to conduct a distinctive type of research that could bring the culture and the schools of Puerto Rico into closer and more vigorous association.

This book is the consequence of his efforts extending over nearly three years, together with the efforts of his research associates and of many other persons in Puerto Rico who cooperated with him. Its chief purpose is to interpret the culture of today in comprehensive scope, with continuous regard for education as a focal institution of Puerto Rican culture. The method of research is primarily anthropological, but Dr. Brameld has not hesitated to utilize exploratory techniques that reflect his knowledge of other behavioral sciences, as well as of philosophy and education.

As the author emphasizes, his book is controversial. It should provoke discussion and constructive criticism abroad as well as in Puerto Rico, and should lead to further studies that explore more fully the many issues that it raises. The College of Education and the University of Puerto Rico do not, of course, assume responsibility for the plan of research or the specific content, nor would Dr. Brameld wish us to do so.

We hope that the many proposals arising from this book will lead to experimentation. We firmly agree with Dr. Brameld that the primary value of his endeavor will be measured by the extent to which it is translated into "action research." *The Remaking of a Culture* must not remain merely another "paper" study.

These proposals, most of which come directly from Puerto Rican citizens themselves, constitute a challenging agenda for the years ahead. New designs for curricula on all levels of education, including teacher training; much better ways of learning and teaching; more democratic policies of organization and control—all of these and more are discussed and recommended.

This book builds a two-way bridge between the living culture and education in Puerto Rico. For it demonstrates that each is indispensable to the welfare and growth of the other.

Oscar E. Porrata
Dean of the College of Education
University of Puerto Rico

PREFACE

THIS BOOK is addressed to two audiences. The first is the citizens of Puerto Rico. The second is the people of other countries concerned with how a frontier culture seeks to remake itself, and especially with how it wishes to enlist education in that remaking.

The first audience will, I hope, include not only social scientists, educators, and other Puerto Rican leaders dedicated to the remarkable cultural program now under way, but classroom teachers, students, parents, and other typical residents who constitute the main subject of study. The second audience will, I equally hope, include not only representatives of other so-called underdeveloped countries in Latin America and elsewhere, but of countries such as the United States.

For, in myriad ways that these pages describe and interpret, Puerto Rico has at least as much to teach as it has to learn. With all its differences, the character of its culture and the effort it exerts to build a strong program of public education are rewarding, even exciting, lessons to countries that in some respects may be richer or more experienced.

This work, moreover, attempts to approach the interrelations of Puerto Rican culture and education through methods of research and appraisal that could operate just as effectively elsewhere in the world —including a community in Kansas or Connecticut as well as in Mexico or India. Granting that these methods could be improved and that modifications of detail would be necessary in terms of local circumstances, nevertheless the essential framework of theory and practice is applicable to many cultures.

This framework may be described as interdisciplinary. It proceeds from the assumption that any critically synoptic interpretation of the role of education in culture requires the cooperative and constant utilization of several disciplines.

Precisely how we have sought to develop such an interdisciplinary approach to Puerto Rican culture may be left for Chapter 2 and, supplementally, "Notes on Methodology" (Appendix, I). I restate only one fact from those pages: the present work is based squarely upon my preceding work—*Cultural Foundations of Education*. The theoretical substructure developed in that volume is accordingly presupposed here.

Because in a number of respects both volumes utilize hitherto little-tried techniques and venture into cultural domains, such as values, where relatively few explorations have been made in comparable ways, many questions can and should be raised about the research design as well as its results. Anthropologists and philosophers will assuredly find grounds for criticism—some of which may be anticipated in Chapter 19 and the Appendix, I. This book makes no pretense of being what it is not, however. Especially, if for no other reason than that it views its findings from an explicit viewpoint in educational philosophy, it is not to be judged by conventional canons of social science research.

Puerto Rican citizens will also wish to take issue with some of the contents. This is good, for no claim to finality is made. What we must have next are parallel studies of this and other cultures that succeed in probing further and more skillfully than we into the complex spheres of attitude and practice that our work encompasses.

Nowhere are such opportunities more abundant than in attempts to draw education directly into the jet stream of culture itself. One reason why formal schooling seems desultory and feeble in its impact upon cultural change, for example, is its absorption in routines that are often sterile, often cut off from socioeconomic and similar forces at work all about it. Even in the energetic culture that we study, this kind of absorption is so commonplace that I confess an intentional touch of irony in the dualistic implication of the subtitle: "Life *and* Education in Puerto Rico."

The irony is compounded, if anything, by the devotion *to* education that one encounters everywhere on the Island. The friendly interest and generous support provided in carrying through our investigation testify to this devotion. In Chapter 2 and the Appendix, I, are listed many individuals who contributed labor, time, and thought; my indebtedness to them is great indeed. Here I wish to add the names of my two research associates: Ona K. Brameld, Lecturer in Education, and Domingo Rosado, Associate Professor of Education, University of Puerto Rico. Their share in this undertaking has been so large that without them it could not have been achieved.

Boston University   THEODORE BRAMELD

PART I
THE CULTURAL LABORATORY
OF PUERTO RICO

CHAPTER ONE

PUERTO RICAN PROFILE

FLY OVER Puerto Rico and peer down through your plane window. Far below, you behold a crazy quilt of fields and groves of infinite shapes and sizes, in subtle hues of green, brown, yellow, red. Graceful mountain slopes are dotted with thousands of tiny cottages. Villages nestle in the valleys and high up on the labyrinth of roads and paths. Yet never far away on your horizon is some large city, the greatest of which still seems to be guarded by a grim, impregnable fortress. The blue-green of the Caribbean provides a lovely framework of contrast.

If Puerto Rican culture could be pictured, it too would reveal designs and patterns of irregular but definite color, shape, and altitude. But one never actually "sees" a culture. All that is visible are some of its products—its fields, its towns, its arts. One cannot see its history, for example, nor its future. Yet what has already happened and what people hope or expect will happen are both essential to the present culture—to what is happening. Similarly, one cannot literally see the attitudes and feelings of people; at best, one can approach somewhere near them through such symbolic media as music or words. Yet, like the fruits of memory and imagination, these too are part and parcel of cultural experience.

For culture embraces the total environment that man has in any way affected. What he has fashioned with his hands; what he learns from others to do, so that he may be accepted by them; what he and they have organized in the form of institutions so that they may live together; what he creates and celebrates to honor himself, his fellows, and his world—all these and more, much more, fall within the meaning of this encompassing concept.

We are concerned with the whole of but one culture—with its

3

customs, beliefs, events, organized behaviors, tribulations, and achievements. Particularly we are concerned with those multiple aspects that defy direct perception—that is, with aspects that must be inferred rather than observed in the way that ceremonials, say, may be observed. Even more directly than many other studies of culture, ours is a study of symbolic meanings—or, still more precisely, of the ways in which Puerto Ricans speak of themselves and of their entrancing Island.

In order to undertake this task (one which we shall, of course, only partially complete), we must first have a framework of essential facts. Here we shall leave much out; it is not our aim to present a detailed picture; this has been well done by others several times.[1] * Later chapters, moreover, will often fill in. We wish only to provide a "map" by which we may be guided more sure-footedly toward the complex life of the people.

Puerto Rico is at the eastern end of a chain of high mountains largely submerged by the Atlantic Ocean on the north and the Caribbean Sea on the south. It lies about 1,500 miles southeast of New York, five and one-half hours away by plane (reduced by jets to less than three). It is about the size of Long Island—105 miles from west to east and 35 miles from north to south.

The Island is rimmed with plains, most of them covered with rich sugar-cane fields. One need drive only a short distance inland, however, to reach increasingly rugged terrain. Only a little farther, one travels up steep, winding roads over mountains reaching some 4,000 feet in height. The temperature cools as one ascends, yet for the country as a whole the average is only about 75° Fahrenheit in winter, 80° in summer—less than the variation between night and day. Rainfalls in the mountainous and northern regions are often torrential, but the southeast coast enjoys so little rain that one wonders, as he travels southward across desertlike wastes toward the irrigated rim, whether he is still on the same Island.

The graceful curvatures of the terrain remind one of New England. But in other respects differences are striking. Unlike the endless lonely miles of pine and other woods that cover the White and Green Mountains, only a fraction of the Island's surface now contains forests. Even

* References can be found beginning on page 457.

steep slopes are likely to be occupied by families of farmers and their helpers who miraculously manage, despite gutting erosion and the apparent danger of falling out of their fields, to produce rich tobacco, coffee, and other crops.

For it is in the rural areas that a majority of the more than two and one-quarter million Puerto Ricans continue to live. The density of population is one of the highest in the world among agricultural societies: well over 600 per square mile, an 18 per cent increase in only ten years between 1940 and 1950. Even more incredible is the estimate that nearly 1,500 persons occupy each square mile of *arable* land as compared with only a little more than 200 in the United States proper. If all the people on earth were packed within the boundaries of the United States, the population density would be about the same as Puerto Rico's today.

Overpopulation is, indeed, often considered to be the Island's foremost problem. With almost no natural resources except people and soil, the task of finding ways to feed, clothe, house, educate, and in general to raise the standard of living to the minimums of more advanced countries is, to say the least, herculean. Even in times of relative prosperity, such as the midfifties, unemployment remained serious: 84,000 in 1957, for example, or 13 per cent of the total labor force. Many more than this percentage were employed only part of the time, for much of the work is seasonal. Little wonder, then, that the per capita personal income in 1957 was $468, as compared with about $2,000 in the United States and about $850 in the poorest state, Mississippi. Despite minimum-wage laws, factory workers received an average of 76 cents per hour, as compared with $1.98 in the United States, and $1.29 in Mississippi.

And yet, were it not for migration, the situation would be much worse. As United States citizens since 1917, Puerto Ricans—when they can find the fare—are free to come and go. Thus in 1956 alone, the net migration was over 61,000, in 1958 over 27,000. But such an outlet depends upon job opportunities on the Continent:* when these decline, as during recessions and depressions, unemployment on the Island accordingly increases. Indeed, since Puerto Ricans abroad often

---

* In accordance with Puerto Rican usage, the terms "Continent" and "Continentals" refer to the United States and its inhabitants.

hold the least secure jobs (in terms, say, of seniority and skill), they are among the first to be released, to go on relief, and, if possible, to return to their homeland, where they add still more to the unemployed ranks.[2]

Color is a factor, too. Puerto Ricans, with minor exceptions, are a mixture of European, African, and native Indian stocks. Of the European, the Spanish strain is by far the strongest (the Spanish language is, of course, the Island's mother tongue), but Corsican, German, French, Portuguese, Scandinavian, and other strains have also intermingled. To be sure, only 40 per cent recently classified themselves by census as *trigueño* (mixed), compared with 54 per cent as white and 5.5 per cent as Negro. But these distributions are far from accurate. Actually, the proportion of mixed blood is higher, with important economic results: even in Puerto Rico, where prejudice is relatively weak, the correlation between low income and dark pigmentation remains disquietingly high.

Yet to attribute the struggle for existence on the Island solely to overpopulation would falsify the facts. Actually the trouble reaches much farther back—across more than four centuries of colonial exploitation. The history of Puerto Rico, unless one includes the unrecorded aboriginal centuries of Indian occupation, begins on November 19, 1493, when Columbus landed and claimed the Island for Spain. But Ponce de León and his soldiers were the first foreign occupants: in 1508 they came to conquer the Indians—an easy enough victory—and to begin a colony. Negro slaves arrived as early as 1513, but other islands, such as Santo Domingo, proved more profitable for development. Ponce de León himself went on to discover Florida and to die in Cuba.

For nearly three centuries, Puerto Rico served chiefly as an important military outpost. Its gigantic fortress, El Morro, begun in 1540 and finished three-quarters of a century later, not only guarded the whole Caribbean from enemy fleets but, supported by other fortresses, successfully repelled Sir Francis Drake and subsequent invaders. Population and economic growth, however, were slow indeed, with San Juan and the rest of the Island living in almost separate worlds. The former, a walled city, contained its coteries of soldiers, priests, politicians, and their followers. The latter consisted of a thin, rustic residue of pauperized farmers largely ignored by the city. Only later did two other cities—Mayaguez and Ponce—assume limited importance.

The nineteenth century marked a period of momentous change. The Spanish crown began to take more interest in the Island's welfare and its possibilities for agricultural wealth. Immigrants by thousands, some of them well-to-do, arrived from nearby countries torn by civil strife, and thousands of slaves were imported for work on sugar plantations. The government remained autocratic, making reluctant concessions in taxes and other privileges, but still for the most part indifferent to disease, ignorance, and malnutrition. Yet the population rose to nearly a million. Public interest in civil rights increased as the effects of British, French, and especially American democracy were felt. Slavery was abolished in 1869—after its abolition in the United States. Trade with the latter also grew apace, and a few North American farmers began to establish themselves in the coastal areas.

The great climactic event of the nineteenth century was the Spanish-American War of 1898, which resulted in the acquisition of Puerto Rico by the United States. For more than thirty years thereafter, colonialism continued with its typical spawns of exploitation: company towns, mechanized mills, huge landed estates often under absentee ownership, and grinding poverty. (A law passed by Congress in 1900 prohibiting single ownership of more than 500 acres was not enforced for over thirty years.) But agricultural production rapidly expanded, with sugar replacing coffee as the principal crop, so that the condition of the majority of common people did not, at least, worsen. In fact, by comparison with Spain, the United States showed far greater social responsibility: schools, public health programs, roads, tariff-free trade—these and other improvements were, relatively speaking, momentous.

But profits by millions were still taken overseas, and what remained was absorbed by such heavy costs as that of importing the bulk of consumable goods. (Even today 60 per cent of all food is imported.) Thus the standard of living for most of the population remained low: as late as 1929 the average weekly wage of a working-class family was $6.47, or 12 cents per day per person. Meanwhile, governors were still appointed by the President of the United States—some of whom had either little capacity to govern or little sympathy with the people of the Island. Insular politics, indeed, was controlled mainly by and for those with vested interests. No wonder that, despite a considerable amount of nominal self-government, men workers who earned 10 cents an hour for backbreaking toil in the hot fields, and women who earned 3 cents a dozen for hemming handkerchiefs, commonly sold their votes for $2 each.

If 1898 was a milestone in the history of Puerto Rico, 1940 was a year of destiny. During the 1930's, the Roosevelt administration in Washington had encouraged the mood of social change in Puerto Rico, and Rexford Tugwell, a leading New Dealer, had served as vigorous Governor. In 1940, the Popular party, with its slogan of "Bread, Land, and Liberty," achieved its first limited success at the polls—a success which paved the way for overwhelming victories in all subsequent elections down to the present time. Luis Muñoz Marín, the leader of the Popular party, rose from President of the Senate to become in 1948 the first Governor elected by the people; since then he has been re-elected twice. His party stands for liberal reform and is responsible for the present status of Puerto Rico as a "Free Associated State" or Commonwealth.

Under this policy, the benefits of free trade continue, so that sugar particularly can be exported without ruinous tariff barriers. Since Puerto Ricans cannot vote for U.S. senators or representatives (its Resident Commissioner in Washington has no vote), they are relieved of federal income taxes, while the Commonwealth treasury retains all excise taxes collected on rum, tobacco, and other local products. At the same time, federal services, such as financial aid to public housing and the school lunch program, are allocated to Puerto Rico on terms often similar to those in the states. Most of the millions of dollars paid to Puerto Rico in federal grants-in-aid are, however, returned in the form of indirect taxes on imported consumer goods.

The Commonwealth of Puerto Rico has its own constitution, adopted in 1952. (Some of the original human-rights provisions were considered too radical by Congress and were accordingly weakened, but it is still impressively democratic.) Under this constitution, an elected legislature passes and provides for enforcement of all Puerto Rican laws. The latter are, of course, subject to review by the federal courts, as is true of any state of the union. But to a great extent the operation of the country rests in the hands of its people, within the limits noted: young Puerto Ricans, for example, are subject to military service though they have no direct legal voice in determining American military and foreign policy.

The attainment of power by the Popular party was by no means an easy one, and opposition to it remains vocal and vigorous today. Its opponents include the illegal Nationalists who have hurt the Island's reputation in the United States by their sporadic resort to violence. Then there are those who continue to favor the achievement of independence by parliamentary means, and still others who want Puerto Rico to become a state. The two latter opposing groups hold legislative posts by virtue of a law guaranteeing representation to minority parties. But the great majority of the population remain Popular supporters, especially the rural and urban lower classes who were first persuaded by Muñoz Marín not to sell their votes.

We return now to such vexing problems as overpopulation. The Commonwealth today is engaged in a militant effort to meet and overcome these problems by an ingenious, many-sided program.

The effort most publicized in the United States is that of the Economic Development Administration, which has successfully promoted or assisted in the establishment of over 500 enterprises since 1947. Many of these enterprises are branch factories of large Continental firms engaged in light industry—their products ranging from garments to cigars to fountain pens to electronic equipment to baby shoes. The chief inducements are a ten-year moratorium on Insular taxes and lower wage rates than prevail in the United States. Net profits have been substantial (30 per cent or even more is not unusual), with the result that income is still being drained off the Island to a degree that disturbs many citizens. Also, a sizable fraction of the new factories have failed. Yet it is estimated that 80,000 year-round jobs have resulted from the EDA program. Frequently, too, factories, luxury hotels, and other establishments have been built for prospective occupants as a government investment.

The EDA is not, of course, solely responsible for economic progress. Early in the forties, several plants (glass, cement, paperboard, and others) were established and owned by the government, but later sold to private enterprise. All utilities except the telephone are still publicly owned. The "Five Hundred Acre Law" has been restored to life. Profit-sharing farms and cooperatives are active. Thousands of landless workers have been given plots of land. Organized labor, though still beset by conflicts and feeble bargaining power, has grown to the stage where about half the total working force is unionized. Publicly authorized gambling (chiefly horse racing, casinos, and a government lottery) provides additional revenues. And industries and banks controlled primarily by Puerto Rican businessmen have also grown—in fact, the economy has now lost its predominantly agricultural status in the respect that, in 1956-57, net income from manufacturing exceeded that of farming by 40 per cent. Devastating hurricanes have been an added factor in the recent decline of agricultural income.

Wages rose during the same brief period by 18.5 per cent, a rate of increase over three times faster than in the United States. Thirty-seven industry divisions were meeting a minimum wage of $1 per hour, but sixty-nine other divisions, such as home needlework trades, were still paying 70 cents or less. Meanwhile the cost of living has risen almost as much as on the Continent.

The government of Puerto Rico is itself a major employer—indeed, the proportion of its budget earmarked for public services, by comparison with the United States, is much higher on a per capita basis. The number of civil employees rose from 34,000 to 40,000 between 1953 and 1957, and during the latter year alone government expenditures rose from $189 million to $230 million. The largest single expenditure was for public education: about one-fourth of the total budget. Health was next with 18 per cent. Resettlement of rural and urban slum dwellers in housing developments has been a major public endeavor—federal funds here aiding Commonwealth funds. Thus in 1956, forty-five different projects, involving 20,000 families, were under way. Between private and public enterprise, some 50,000 new housing units have been provided since 1940, and slum clearance alone has been proceeding at the rate of about 6,000 units per year. In the rural areas, whole new villages of little concrete homes are being built, many of them through the cooperative labor of their future owners—at a total cost per home of about $300! But the magnitude of the housing problem is illustrated by the fact that, according to one estimate, 100,000, or one-fourth of the population of San Juan, still live in slums.

The health program is equally impressive. Malaria has been wiped out, while other parasitic and infectious diseases are declining. A recent sample of families showed two-thirds utilizing the free services of government medical care. Nearly half of these family members were drinking one pint or more of milk every day—almost double the consumption of ten years earlier—and improvement in protein diet was even more marked. Municipal health centers and hospitals operate throughout the Island. Private practice, however, remains expensive, and there is still only one physician available for every 2,000 persons. A plan called "Operation Regionalization" is now under way to decentralize health services; it is considerably in advance of Continental plans in this important field.

As is always true when health improves, the death rate drops. Today, life expectancy—sixty-eight years—slightly exceeds that of the Continent, an increase of fourteen years since 1940. In the same period, the birth rate, due partly to a publicly sponsored birth-control program, has dropped from thirty-nine per thousand to thirty-three per thousand. This does not, however, offset the increasing longevity and the rapid decrease in the rate of infant mortality, so that the total population is still increasing: there were 400,000 more births than deaths between 1950 and 1956. But when one notes that over 300,000 left the Island in the same six years, the total increase is now less than 3 per cent per year—lower than in the United States proper.

Meanwhile, organized prostitution—almost always a barometer of political corruption and indifference to human welfare—has radically declined. By comparison with a country like Cuba, where prostitution has been conducted as a "big business," the practice that remains in Puerto Rico (and it does remain, especially in the larger cities) is trivial.

Of special interest to us is the major emphasis placed upon education. In 1956, over 700,000 (nearly one-third of the entire population) were attending some kind of school, an increase of over 30,000 in a single year, including 96 per cent of the children between six and twelve years of age. Also, vocational and adult programs are both zealously encouraged. Teachers increased by about 1,000 during 1957, to a total twelve times that large. Fifty thousand students were in private schools—many of the latter understandably Catholic, since about 80 per cent of the people are classified as members of this church. The University of Puerto Rico, including several professional schools, such as medicine and law, attained a combined enrollment of over 15,000. Scholarships are provided to help needy children continue in elementary and secondary school, and to the more promising young adults for higher and professional education. In 1957-58, about $1,500,000 was awarded to 10,000 students, and no one is denied who proves his worth. Many, including teachers, are sent abroad for advanced training at government expense. Literacy is rising rapidly: in 1898, 80 per cent of the population were classified as illiterate; in 1957, 17 per cent over ten years of age were so classified. Yet thousands in the mountain areas still do not attend classes at all because they are too far away, while some 60,000 others must walk about two miles to the nearest school.

One additional example of the Island's extraordinary efforts to face its tasks with audacity and foresight is the Puerto Rico Planning Board in the Office of the Governor. With an annual budget approaching $2 million, this agency accepts one major principle—that it is both possible and desirable to estimate patterns of social growth and to plan accordingly—and one major purpose: to eliminate poverty. Economic planning is, of course, primary, but the entire culture is included in its agenda of responsibilities. For example, its most recent six-year program, extending to 1963, makes recommendations embracing (among other areas) agriculture, recreation, health, housing, industry, electrification, communication, and education. Perhaps its single most audacious goal is an annual per capita income by at least 1975 equal to that in the United States in 1958. Already per capita income is the highest in the Caribbean—unless one excepts Venezuela.

The Board's analysis of educational needs illustrates its approach. Predicting that the demand for an educated and skilled labor force will expand rapidly, specific measures are proposed to improve transportation for school children, to increase the number of classrooms and teaching resources, to maintain better records, to provide more scholarships, and to improve the quality of instruction.

The precision of its planning operations is illustrated by the Board's estimate that, by 1975, 6 per cent of all positions should be filled by college graduates and 51 per cent by senior or junior high school graduates, while only 12 per cent of all positions will require less than six years of education. To meet the demand there must therefore be a prodigious increase in educational goals—100,000 graduates at the high school level, more than 100 per cent at the college level, and a tenfold increase at the adult level. Already only about one-third of those complying with requirements can be accepted by the over-crowded University.

A culture engaged in metamorphosis provides incredibly rich opportunity for creative research of many kinds. In the remainder of this book we propose to grasp such an opportunity.

CHAPTER TWO

FOCUSING ON THE PUERTO RICAN CULTURE

THE IMMEDIATE problem that any interpreter of a culture faces is that of constructing instruments that will focus on the material and immaterial human experiences that provide his subject matter. As every scientist and artist of culture knows, the refinement of such instruments is half the battle. In Puerto Rico, the problem is compounded by several factors: the fluid condition of its life in the mid-twentieth century, the meager research that has thus far occurred on the Island in cultural fields, the even more meager research in education considered as an institution of culture, and the inadequate instruments that have been constructed by anthropologists and allied experts for their analyses of any kind of contemporary, "nonprimitive" cultures.

Partly for these reasons, but also partly because of our own limitations and proclivities, we do not propose to adopt the conventional assumptions or methods of anthropology without considerable deviation. Rather, this study is based upon and utilizes a triumvirate of disciplines: anthropology, education, and philosophy. It borrows much from all three fields and relates them to one another.

Readers interested in evaluating some of the more technical and controversial aspects of our methodology are referred to the Appendix, I.* Here we shall confine ourselves to a description of, first, the theoretical framework; second, the research areas; third, respondents in the subcultures; fourth, national leaders as respondents; fifth, interviewing and other techniques of investigation; and sixth, our over-all plan of interpretation.

* See pp. 423–442.

THE THEORETICAL FRAMEWORK

Every study of a culture proceeds from tacit or carefully enunciated principles concerning the phenomena under investigation. In our case, we have tried to be explicit as to the nature of these principles. With the guidance of research experts in the behavioral sciences, and of theorists in anthropology, history, education, and allied fields, we intend to approach the culture of Puerto Rico in terms of three inclusive cultural categories called *order, process,* and *goals,* each of which is considered as a theoretical problem, each of which is divided into numerous subcategories and subproblems, and each of which is shown to have abundant educational implications.

In studying a culture by means of such categories, we assume that its typical members hold many beliefs about it which they may not have expressed in these terms but which are nevertheless implicit in their attitudes, customs, and practices. These beliefs may be called *metacultural*—that is, beneath or beyond the level of their overt, explicit, formal language and behavior. They constitute the inherent "philosophy of life" of a people.

The meaning of the three categories should become clear as we operate with them upon the concrete situation described in Chapter 1. Theoretically inclined readers will, however, wish at this point to consult our companion volume,[1] which provides the foundation of this study and in which each category is analyzed at length. Meanwhile, we hope that others will be patient enough to consider a minimum of preliminary working definitions.

By cultural order, we mean the relations of culture both internally and externally—that is, the relations within a given culture and the relations among cultures. Order is both "spatial" and "temporal." Spatial order refers to the ways in which the parts of a culture do or do not fit together at any given time. Thus one may look at the structure of culture on a kind of "horizontal" plane—that is, as a series of widening concentric circles, beginning in the center with the relations of a few parts (such as the members of a family), and extending outward to great encompassing circles as suggested by the concept of "national character" or of the "whole culture."

The order of culture is also "vertical," revealing different kinds of strata or levels—for example, that of economic classes or social groupings with varying degrees of ascending and descending prestige and power. To obtain anything like a full picture of spatial order, it is essential to bring the horizontal and vertical dimensions into relationship. But every culture also possesses historical and temporal dimensions—that is, it evolves from the past into the present and toward a future which continuously affects its spatial structure.

Turning now to the second category, process, the problem centers in the dynamics of culture—that is, in the infinite ways that its parts change and affect themselves and one another. The process of culture cannot, in fact, be separated from order, especially temporal order, any more than the horizontal and vertical dimensions can be separated. Nevertheless, for purposes of analysis it is useful to focus on culture through one or another category of process such as acculturation, assimilation, and innovation. All of these concepts are treated as operating instruments by which a culture may be examined as it undergoes slow or rapid modifications of its ordered or disordered structures.

Such modifications are inseparable from the personalities who are the constituent members of any culture. For personalities, too, are affected by innovations, crises, and all other processes; in turn, personalities affect these processes. The personality-and-culture movement, as it is often called, may therefore be examined in relation to cultural dynamics. Here such fruitful concepts as learning and modal personality require interpretation. Learning is considered by culture theorists as the central psychological process by which cultures are perpetuated and modified from generation to generation. The problem of modal personality deals with whether or not cultures tend to produce definable modes or types of character structure that vary as cultures themselves vary.

The third of our major categories—cultural goals—gravitates toward the difficult but crucial problem of the values, purposes, and ends of culture. In this area, anthropologists and other behavioral scientists are only beginning to work systematically; yet they would agree with philosophers and educators that the problem is of paramount importance. For example, are all cultural values relative to a given culture or are certain empirically ascertainable values cross-cultural, perhaps even universal? Again, can the behavioral sciences provide a deeper, more meaningful conception of human freedom as a cultural goal than has been provided thus far by the more speculative, unverified views of philosophers and other theorists?

Each of the three dominant categories is significant for educational theory and practice. The frame of reference is that education, properly understood, is a central cultural phenomenon—that all cultures maintain some kind of educational program even when not dignified by formal schools or by professional personnel. To approach education in this context, then, is to provide it with a deeper and wider import than would be possible were it more narrowly defined. The concepts of order, process, and goals throw light upon the meaning and role of education—upon both its deficiencies and opportunities in our time. We shall find that all of them, together with their many subcategories, are applicable to our interpretation of Puerto Rican education in its cultural context.

Our theoretical framework is not "objective." While respectful of "facts" and of the "real world" as depicted by physical and social science, this framework is also shaped by frankly normative (that is, evaluative) judgments concerning the character of the age in which we live. Our theory of culture is inextricable from our philosophy of life and of education, and so again we are compelled to refer interested readers to preceding works which affect our analysis and appraisal of Puerto Rican culture.[2] Inevitably, the kind of evidence we have selected has itself been influenced by our philosophic outlook.

The core of this outlook is based upon two premises. The first is that we live today in one of the greatest periods of crisis in history. Granting that all history consists of recurrent crises, this one is unprecedented in several ways, the most monstrous of which is the fact that man has achieved the capacity to destroy civilization overnight. Yet granting that destruction by nuclear war is the most horrifying fear of our time, only a little less horrifying are the insidious disintegrations threatened by radioactive fallouts.

Add to these the record of two bloody intercontinental wars within a quarter-century, the rise of a mighty totalitarian system that already jeopardizes America's position as the foremost industrial power, and now the looming conquest of space with its portents of evil as well as good. For the educational system of Puerto Rico or anywhere else not to give these events priority, for it not to provide every possible opportunity to diagnose their causes and to consider how the growing generation may cope with them while time remains, is for that system to shirk its most urgent responsibility.

The second premise is that, just as the physical sciences have recently passed through a revolution which was, indeed, partly responsible for the crisis itself, so today the behavioral sciences are entering upon a revolution of their own. This revolution is already awakening those familiar with it to the realization that mankind is now approaching the opportunity to achieve a world civilization of abundance, health, and humane capacity that is as life-affirming as the crisis symbolized by sputniks and hydrogen bombs is life-denying. This revolution also requires education to re-examine its whole conventional structure and to consider new ways of (1) ordering its subject matters, (2) engaging in the processes by which they are taught and learned, and (3) formulating the purposes of school and society.

Not one of the three imperatives would have been realizable before the emergence of such young sciences as cultural anthropology and psychiatry, or the interrelating of these with such older ones as economics, sociology, and history. None of them depends upon metaphysical or otherwise speculative doctrines. All of them, while open to a great deal of further clarification and verification, are potentially demonstrable and defensible in the same way that all science is demonstrable and defensible.

Let us illustrate each of the imperatives in educational terms.

1. Up to this time, the structure of the typical school and college curriculum has been a jumble of discrete subject matters that, for the average student, have little or no meaningful relations to one another —languages, mathematics, social science, natural science, and others— each of which is often again subdivided into further discrete units. The behavioral sciences are now demonstrating that, so far at least as all the areas having to do with biopsychological experience are concerned, these divisions and subdivisions are less and less tenable. Concepts such as organism, connoting relationships between parts as much as the parts related, are replacing the older atomistic concepts. Human life, individually and culturally, is increasingly seen in terms of patterns and configurations.

Programs of general or integrated education, recognizing that something must be done to give meaningful unity to the curriculum structure, have sometimes been tangentially affected by this interdisciplinary view of human behavior. Unfortunately, however, they have also been plagued by the same confusions in theory and practice that are chronic to other educational programs. Some general educationists, for example, take their cue from the physical sciences, others from Neo-Scholasticism. Few regard the tasks and goals of human beings as the first and most important concern of vital education in an age such as ours. Or, for that matter, in any age.

This is not to say that the physical sciences, any more than the humanities, should be neglected by the needed new framework. It does mean that they are encompassed by it. A theory of unified man, both derived from and contributing to our experimental knowledge of human behavior in its multiple perspectives, not only should integrate all other fields of knowledge; it should provide them with a fresh and potent significance.

2. The required rebuilding of teaching and learning processes is heralded by a great body of recent behavioral research, only a fraction of which has begun to permeate educational practice. Perhaps the one point where permeation has occurred at all fruitfully thus far is in the methodology of "group dynamics." Yet even here, as so commonly happens in educational circles, this methodology has oftener acquired the earmarks of a superficial fad than of a profound process dependent upon a widening range of discoveries about the "fields of forces" that constitute the interactions of human beings in their multiple roles.

Even more promising is the personality-and-culture frontier. Here anthropologists and psychologists are joining hands. And they are demonstrating that learning, for example, involves polaristic dimensions of inner and outer experience, some of it unconscious, that have been neglected by the orthodox formulations underlying classroom routines.

Again, the problem of how to enlist education in the processes of institutional change so that it functions, not merely to transmit but to modify and reconstruct outmoded arrangements, can now be attacked with the aid of substantial knowledge. The concept of crisis itself exemplifies this opportunity. Citing outstanding authorities in the behavioral sciences, we have elsewhere pointed out that

There is no good reason, except timidity or irresponsibility, that prevents high schools and colleges from encouraging young people to analyze both the meaning of crisis theoretically and its manifestations overtly. Leaders ought accordingly to clarify their orientation here: they ought to face the issue of whether education is to be regarded as capable of sharing importantly in the control and resolution of crises, or as a pawn of overpowering material or spiritual forces beyond control and resolution.[3]

3. The shaping of new purposes for education and culture is also becoming feasible in ways that could hardly have been conceived even three or four decades ago. In other words, the behavioral sciences are beginning to prove, really for the first time in history, that it is possible to formulate human goals, not for sentimental, romantic, mystical, or similarly arbitrary reasons, but on the basis of what we are learning about cross-cultural and even universal values. Though studies in this difficult field have moved only a little way, they have moved far enough so that it is already becoming plausible both to describe these values objectively and to demonstrate that most human beings prefer them to alternative values.

Freedom is an example. By analyzing drives and motivations, by determining what human beings in many different cultures most deeply need and want, freedom both as fact and norm undergoes something of a metamorphosis of meaning. Yet it preserves the rich kernel of significance intuited by Jefferson and other geniuses of a prescientific age.

This way of constructing educational purposes rests, too, upon an expanding inventory of research evidence. Human resources for a happy life on earth are greater than, hitherto, we have ever dreamed possible—resources that we have hardly begun to tap because we are so often blinded by the destructive forces of conflict, ignorance, and fear. Building out of the characteristics of any and all cultures, a truly goal-centered education could contribute more than any other agency to displacing these destructive forces by scientifically ascertainable and testable hopes for the future of mankind.

SELECTING THE RESEARCH AREAS

The task of dredging a channel between a theoretical interpretation of culture and the concrete experience of an ongoing culture has involved a good deal of trial and error, immersion in the life of Puerto Rico, conferences with everyday citizens as well as with leaders of many sorts, visits to various projects and institutions, investigations of the Puerto Rican literature in such fields as social science and education, consultations with Continental anthropologists, and direct contact with several other cultures in the Caribbean area with which Puerto Rico might be compared.

Always presupposing our theoretical framework, the first concrete problem to be solved in building a research design was that of selecting the areas to be studied. This task has been facilitated by the elaborate research study of a team of anthropologists engaged by the Social Science Research Center of the University of Puerto Rico. The study was under the direction of Professor Julian Steward of the University of Illinois, and published under the title *The People of Puerto Rico*.[4] Unfortunately, over six years elapsed between field and library research and actual publication—a period during which perhaps the most rapid changes in the history of the Island were taking place. A consequence is that many details in the volume are already obsolete or in need of qualification. Nevertheless, despite this and other weaknesses, the work is the most comprehensive and exhaustive anthropological interpretation of Puerto Rico published thus far.

The rich material in the historical section of the Steward work is presupposed by our study, equally with the material which comprises the main body of that work—namely, the firsthand examination of five subcultures. These are as follows (the names are fictitious): (1) "Tabara: Subcultures of a Tobacco and Mixed Crops Municipality"; (2) "San José: Subcultures of a 'Traditional' Coffee Municipality"; (3) "Nocora: The Subculture of Workers on a Government-Owned Sugar Plantation"; (4) "Cañamelar: The Subculture of a Rural Sugar Plantation Proletariat"; and (5) "The Prominent Families of Puerto Rico." All of these five subcultures (or more than five in that "Tabara" and "San José" are each defined pluralistically) are interpreted in a roughly parallel way. No claim was made, however, that they are exhaustive of all types of subcultures in Puerto Rico or even that they are the most representative.

Partly for lack of time, partly because it appeared doubtful that enough benefit would accrue to justify returning to all five for intensive re-examination, our own study is limited to three subcultures. In addition, by adapting Steward's concept of levels, it gives consideration to the cultural-educational outlook of a selected group of national-level leaders. Before choosing the three subcultures, however, all five were visited for a brief period. It was then decided to select two of the same ones studied by the Steward group—namely, Cañamelar and San José—for the reason that, of the rural subcultures, these offered greatest opportunity to view the cultural patterns relating to and emerging from the two most important agricultural technologies of the Island—sugar and coffee, respectively.

Our third subculture is only partly represented in the Steward work. It seemed to us that more advantages might accrue from studying an urban middle-class subculture than from the urban upper-class subculture represented in that volume. For one thing, the latter section of the study is considered less satisfactory to various critics than the others. The middle class, for another thing, is more typical of urban life than are "the prominent families." It is also expanding rapidly by comparison with the upper class. Finally, despite its importance, little anthropological analysis has thus far been made of the urban middle class in Puerto Rico.

After consultation with the superintendent of schools of one of the three largest cities in Puerto Rico, a neighborhood was chosen within which are found both a senior high school and an elementary school, surrounded by a large proportion of homes that could be considered roughly in the middle cost bracket. That is, they are neither of the slum type nor of the expensive type to be found in the upper-class section of San Juan studied by the Steward group. Although the choice was far from scientifically made, no better way presented itself. We have given the name "Hermosa" to this urban neighborhood, and later we present evidence to show that it is predominantly middle class.*

SELECTING RESPONDENTS IN THE SUBCULTURES

The next problem was that of selecting subcultural respondents to serve as primary resources. In consulting with educational leaders from both the national level and the selected communities, four groups came to mind: teachers, students, parents, and school administrators.

The subculture chosen for initial field work was San José (a municipality or "county" consisting of a town and surrounding country *barrios* or "townships"). A series of meetings was arranged with the faculty of the junior and senior high school, the faculty of the ele-

* See pp. 373–378.

mentary school, the student officers of the senior high school, and the parent-teacher association of the town. At each of these meetings, the project was described at length, with emphasis upon the contribution that the community could make to Puerto Rican education through its participation.

In nearly all cases, following questions and clarifications, the group then nominated several persons to serve as respondents. Their qualifications were discussed informally during a brief recess. Finally, one was elected by secret ballot. Usually the winner received a large majority of the votes cast. Only one of the five respondents in the town of San José was chosen by us rather than elected—the representative of the administrators, a lifelong resident. Another respondent, a parent in the rural area, was chosen by the owner of a coffee *hacienda* (plantation) who had participated in the Steward project. Still another parent in the same area was chosen by the teachers of the rural school, since there was no PTA to elect them. Altogether, the seven respondents in San José consisted of two women (secondary and elementary teachers) and five men (a high school senior, an elementary school principal, the owner of a furniture store, the owner of a small mixed-crop farm, and a coffee plantation worker). In general, the same methods of selection were utilized in Cañamelar and Hermosa.

Of the twenty respondents in the three subcultures, fifteen were men and five were women. Their age range was from seventeen to about sixty, the average age being near forty. Five of the twenty respondents were of predominantly Negroid stock, although two others of lighter skin might be so classified. Five were Protestants; fifteen were Catholics. All were born in Puerto Rico and have lived there most of their lives. Two have been abroad with the American armed forces; six others have spent brief periods in the United States; two have studied there. The range of their education has extended from one respondent with a third-grade education to one with a master of arts degree. Four had only an elementary school education; four were approaching high school graduation (one of these was a parent); eight had bachelor's degrees; the remainder had pursued some study beyond high school. Occupationally, three were high school students of the top two years; two were farmers (although a dozen others came from families of farmers or of farm workers); three were school administrators who had been teachers; two were merchants; one was a Protestant minister; one was a civil service employee; one was a union leader; the remaining seven were teachers. The father of one student respondent was the owner of a television repair shop; the father of a second was an irrigation worker on a sugar plantation; the mother (a widow) of the third was a worker in a tobacco factory. Four held political office, all elective: one was a Representative in the Commonwealth legislature; two were presidents and one was vice-president of their Municipal Assemblies.

Using Lloyd Warner's categories of "social class" (in which people of a community rank each other primarily according to prestige on six strata from upper-upper to lower-lower),[5] it is likely that the twenty respondents could now be classified roughly as follows: three, lower-lower; two, upper-lower; nine, lower-middle; six, upper-middle. It should be remembered, however, that self-ratings vary from sub-culture to subculture. Thus a person who might be rated upper-middle in a small town, such as San José, might be rated lower-middle or even upper-lower in a large city, such as San Juan. If income is re-garded as one of the variables, this fluctuation becomes especially probable; thus a person with an income of $3,000 per year in Cañame-lar might rate considerably higher than a person with that income in San Juan.

On an Insular basis, one could assume that the majority of the respondents were lower-middle. This seems likely if one considers that the highest annual income of any grassroots respondent was about $5,000 (although the total *family* income of two was around $10,000), while three headed or belonged to families with total annual incomes below $1,000. The average income of subcultural respondents (or their families, in the case of students) was estimated as between $2,000 and $2,500.

The question may be asked whether the process of selecting sub-cultural respondents was defensible. We examine this question, too, in the Appendix, I. Here it may be pointed out that whatever the preferred anthropological technique, it is primarily a qualitative rather than a quantitative one. That is, it aims to obtain knowledge of a culture more by a process of "depth analysis" than by statistical sampling or other more objective techniques of investigation. The results have the limitations of this method—for example, it is much more selective—but they have the advantage of probing further, if successful, than is often possible in more standardized sociological types of research.

SELECTING NATIONAL LEADERS AS RESPONDENTS

The study of any culture is invariably one of perspectives. In addition to approaching Puerto Rican culture from three subcultural levels (from "below," as it were), it was approached also from the national level, that is, from "above"—a perspective which the Steward study recommended but did not utilize in the way that we attempt.

The problem of selecting a group of leaders for this purpose was met through a "jury" of eight national-level educators chosen by the staff for their familiarity with Puerto Rican leadership and with the general character of the research project. (Two of the jurymen were also elected as respondents, and a third was a close relative of one; therefore their names are withheld to avoid possible embarrassment.) Each juryman was briefed in the general purposes and methods of the project. He was then asked to nominate about ten national leaders representing a variety of fields, such as government, literature, and education itself.

One interesting result was the divergence of agreement in the choice of nominees—over thirty-five being on the original total list. Those nominated only once were eliminated, leaving twenty persons, with most of whom personal appointments were arranged for the purpose of explaining the nature of the project. Of these, sixteen not only accepted but covered most or all of the same cultural territory embraced by the interviews.

Each leader respondent was also provided with a letter which stated the purpose of the project and included the following paragraph:

The information you supply me will be treated confidentially. In preparing my document, I shall under no circumstances quote or identify you. The judgments obtained will be pooled with those of the other leaders and integrated in such a way as to represent a cross-section rather than judgments of any one person, with due regard for minority judgments. Also, I shall submit to you a copy of the notes of the interview for any corrections or amendments that you may care to make. Unless you direct me otherwise, I shall make public your name along with the names of the other leaders interviewed, but I reiterate that your personal opinions, judgments, and criticisms will at no time be identified as your own.

. In accordance with this understanding, and since no objection was raised, the list of national-level leaders who participated is indicated in alphabetical order together with their titles at the time of the study (several have changed since):

1. Ronald Bauer, President of Inter-American University (San Germán).
2. Ramón Colón-Torres, Director of Cooperative Development, formerly Secretary of Agriculture (San Juan).
3. Rafael de J. Cordero, Auditor of Puerto Rico (San Juan).
4. Sol Luis Descartes, Director of the Puerto Rico Water Resources Authority (San Juan).
5. Eugenio Fernández Méndez, Associate Professor of Anthropology, University of Puerto Rico (Rio Piedras).
6. Luis Ferré, President of Ferré Industries, 1956 candidate for Governor on the ticket of the Republican party (Ponce).
7. Enrique A. Laguerre Velez, novelist and essayist, Professor of Spanish Studies, University of Puerto Rico (Rio Piedras).
8. Miguel Meléndez Muñoz, essayist, formerly an officer of the Department of Education (Cayey).
9. Teodoro Moscoso, Director of the Economic Development Administration (San Juan).
10. Pedro Muñoz Amato, Dean of the College of Social Sciences, University of Puerto Rico (Rio Piedras).
11. Luis Muñoz Marín, Governor of Puerto Rico and Chairman of the Popular Democratic party (San Juan).
12. Rafael Picó, Treasurer of Puerto Rico (San Juan), formerly Director of the Puerto Rico Planning Board.
13. Angel G. Quintero Alfaro, Dean of General Studies, University of Puerto Rico (Rio Piedras).
14. Marcos Ramírez, lawyer, 1956 candidate for Resident Commissioner in Washington on the ticket of the Independence party (San Juan).
15. José C. Rosario, Professor of Sociology, retired, University of Puerto Rico (Rio Piedras).
16. Fred Wale, Director of the Division of Community Education, Department of Education (San Juan).*

A summary of the publicly known background of these leaders is enlightening. Four of the sixteen were formerly on the faculty of the University of Puerto Rico (Cordero, Descartes, Picó, and Ramírez).

---

* At his request, Mr. Wale was joined by his wife, also an official of the Division, in two of the three sessions covering this interview.

Included with those now on the faculty or retired, a total of nine, or slightly above half, have had or now have academic posts at this University, while two have taught in other universities (Bauer and Wale). Six of the leaders hold political positions warranting membership in the Governor's Cabinet: besides Muñoz Marín himself, these are Colón-Torres, Cordero, Descartes, Moscoso, and Picó. All three of the recognized political parties are represented by top-ranking leaders: Muñoz Marín, Ferré, and Ramírez. Two of the outstanding writers in the field of Puerto Rican literature are Laguerre and Meléndez Muñoz, while Muñoz Marín is often considered to be, first of all, a poet. Other fields in which the leaders have professional training include education (Bauer, Quintero, and Wale), agriculture (Colon-Torres), economics (Cordero, Descartes, and Ferré), anthropology (Fernández Méndez), pharmacy (Moscoso), political science (Muñoz Amato and Ramírez), geography (Picó), sociology (Rosario), and law (Ramírez and Rosario). It will be seen that background in the social sciences is exceptionally strong, with education, literature, and law each represented by two or more leaders. At the same time, a number of important fields are conspicuously absent, and there are other weaknesses, to be noted in the Appendix, I.

All sixteen of our leaders have spent considerable time in the United States, one being a Continental by birth and rearing (Bauer) and one being a native of Bermuda though a long-time Continental resident and citizen (Wale). A number have traveled extensively in other countries, one having spent years in England and South Africa (Bauer). A large majority have studied in Continental schools and universities, including Harvard, Chicago, Columbia, Clark, Cornell, Michigan, Georgetown, and the Massachusetts Institute of Technology. A few hold doctorates, including honorary ones received by Governor Muñoz Marín. Several come from families of farmers, although the majority come from urban backgrounds.

In terms of Warner's categories, all the leaders would probably now be classified as upper-middle or above. The family backgrounds of perhaps a fourth of the group have such high prestige as to warrant their inclusion in the lower-upper and upper-upper category, while another fourth come from families that could be considered to be of lower status. It is difficult to estimate average annual income since one of the respondents is a millionaire, but the average income of the remainder of the leaders is roughly four to five times higher than that of the average grassroots respondent. Religiously, it is also more difficult to classify the panel of leaders than the subcultural panel, since a number of them—about half—no longer identify themselves with any organized religious body. A minority are active Catholics; the remaining minority are either Protestants or more or less nominal Catholics.

INTERVIEWING AND OTHER TECHNIQUES OF INVESTIGATION

Each of the series of sessions with each subcultural respondent required about an hour. This schedule was usually maintained in all three subcultures. Thus, in the town of San José, each day of interviews with the five respondents required about five hours. (Interviews with the two San José countrymen were concentrated in much longer single periods over two consecutive days.) In Hermosa, six interviews per day of one hour each were maintained. In Cañamelar, the same schedule prevailed except in the case of the labor leader, with whom meetings were intermittent. Only rarely did any other participants miss their appointments. The average time spent with each respondent reached about ten hours, for a total of about two hundred hours. This does not include social gatherings, conversations with other members of the community, visits to classes, local industries, and churches, and frequent luncheon meetings with school administrators and teachers. Most subcultural interviews were held in schools and homes.

Meetings with leaders were arranged according to their convenience. Often, a session occurred on a week end or in the evening, when several consecutive hours could be set aside. A majority of leaders were interviewed partly or wholly in their own homes. One meeting was held in a hotel room, another on a roadside in the mountains, a third at Luquillo Beach, a fourth in an oceanside cottage. The shortest time given by a national leader totaled just under five hours; the longest time was nearly twelve; the average time per respondent reached between seven and eight hours. No respondent attempted to answer all the questions in a continuous session. The total time required to complete the sixteen interviews was about 120 hours, without allowing for many unrecorded conversations.

The problem of communication with both groups of respondents was not merely that of two languages but of meanings—a problem complicated by the fact that the kind of beliefs, opinions, and attitudes most sought after were difficult to express unambiguously. In the subcultures, Spanish and English were both used freely. Among national-level leaders, all but one of the interviews were conducted in English. The technique of interviewing varied between the two groups of respondents, although in both our role was partly that of "participant observer." The considerable difference in average formal education was enough in itself to anticipate that the symbols required for communication should be more concrete and graphic for grassroots informants than for leaders likely to be habituated to more abstract thinking. Thus, while the scope and subject matter of the study were essentially the same for both groups, homely examples were utilized on the subcultural level more often than on the national level. (The guiding questions are given in the Appendix, II,* but *there were many deviations and restatements in the course of each interview.*) Also there was less structuring of the interviews on the grassroots panel, although on both panels an effort was made to prevent rigidity and to keep the discussion "open-ended." It is fair to say that no interview on either level was devoid of free expression; and in every interview the answers to certain questions would pose a series of new questions not generated by other respondents. One result is a considerable body of data unanticipated by the study in advance. Answers to a single question varied greatly in length—from less than a minute to more than an hour.

Three additional research sources were utilized. They were (1) a sociological survey of the three subcultures, with special regard for the middle-class character of Hermosa; (2) a questionnaire submitted to the superintendents of schools of the three subcultures; and (3) a critical examination of other research studies with which our own might be compared.

These resources were only supplementary to our principal interest —namely, the qualitative evidence obtained from our respondents. Looking at both panels together, we must recognize that this evidence is confined to what thirty-six persons, far from perfectly representative, were able in limited time to reveal both of themselves and of

* See pp. 443–450.

others. That they often claimed to speak for many people besides themselves, and that the evidence they provided is often supported in Part V by other research findings, is the most that can be affirmed from the evidence as such.

But we shall not hesitate to draw inferences that extend further. That is, we shall utilize our theoretical framework to criticize and evaluate whatever we learn from our informants. We shall always try to distinguish, however, between the two functions—the first, to present our research evidence in its own right and with as little distortion as possible; the second, to interpret its significance from our point of view.

PLAN OF INTERPRETATION

Let us restate our central purpose. It is to describe and interpret Puerto Rican culture and education with the hope both of increasing our understanding of the relations of each to the other and of providing constructive opportunities through which the culture may clarify and improve its educational philosophy and program. In this double purpose, the project is an example of "applied" rather than "pure" research.

Some issues that might be fruitful if our interests were different are not given detailed attention. For example, one of the chief preoccupations of the Steward study—to determine how far genuine distinctions as well as uniformities exist between Puerto Rican subcultures—matters less to us than it would if our objectives were similar to those of that study. Likewise, differences and similarities between subcultural and national levels are of subordinate interest. We shall pay attention to these questions where they have relevance, but they are not our dominant concern.

The aim is to view and appraise our evidence comparatively, that is, as related to partial or total consensuses or lack of consensuses. We accordingly try to bring the data together as more or less of a composite, but also with continuous regard for individual and minority reactions. Indeed, we shall find that these reactions constitute much of the substance—if not the distinctiveness—of our research. *While generalizations and summarizations are frequently included, they are no substitute for the ways in which particular respondents or small groups of respondents both on the grassroots and national levels deal*

*with particular questions in the context of the particular culture or
subculture.* We have endeavored to give full recognition to these ways.
They symbolize the "individual differences" of this as of every culture.
However, since there are no direct quotations (except occasional non-
identifiable phrases), no participant would probably state his beliefs
or other reactions in exactly the form that we state them.

At the same time, let us be clear that our frequent use of terms
such as "majority" and "minority" or "few" and "many" do not convey
exact, measurable reactions. Such terms are only intended to suggest
tendencies toward strong or weak consensuses among our respondents
—or no consensuses at all. We reiterate that our study is primarily
qualitative in character. The only quantitative evidence is in the form
of subsidiary data.

Our unifying and guiding concepts are those earlier defined as
cultural order, process, and goals, always utilized in the framework
of our own educational philosophy. With these as instruments of
analysis and interpretation, we wish to depict and to evaluate how a
selective but by no means completely atypical group of Puerto Rican
citizens look upon their culture—with special concern for one of its
most important institutions as they see it functioning both in present
actual forms and in potential future forms.

Part II deals with problems of cultural order in Puerto Rico, Parts
III and IV with similar interpretations of process and goals. Part V
evaluates all our evidence and recommends next steps for Puerto
Rican education, together with our own critical reactions. In each of
the chapters of our next three parts, we usually follow a parallel plan:
first, an encapsulation both of the chapter as a whole and of our
viewpoint toward the central problem; second, a presentation of our
research findings covering that problem; third, consideration of its
educational significance as seen by our respondents; and, finally, an
appraisal in terms of our own outlook.

Let us recapitulate the principal points both implied and explicated
by this chapter. They include a number of hypotheses to be partially
tested in the course of our investigation.

1. Culture is a concept designed to explain the total environment
made by and for man.

2. Formal and informal education, being an institution created *by*
culture to perpetuate and modify its customs, habits, practices and

beliefs, is subject to analysis and interpretation as an institution *of* culture. Accordingly, the latter may better be understood when examined through the lens of education in the same way that education may better be understood when examined through the lens of culture.

3. Culture can be dissected into a series of fundamental concepts which, in turn, may be utilized to operate upon any existing culture, including any of its institutions such as education.

4. Culture must be perceived in several perspectives in order to attain any complete or near-complete picture. Among these perspectives, those of representative subcultures and of the national level may both be indispensable, although seldom if ever exhaustive of all perspectives.

5. Education, whether organized formally or not, is so fundamental and universal to culture that representative members of this institution can provide subcultural resources for analyzing and interpreting, though never completely, any given culture on a wider scale. Such representatives embrace students, teachers, parents, and school or college administrators. All of these must accordingly serve as resources if education is to be studied as a cultural institution.

6. National leaders tend to regard their culture, and hence such institutions as education, in wider and more inclusive scope than do members on subcultural levels. Thus they can contribute to any cultural interpretation by adding perspectives to it that supplement or modify subcultural perspectives.

7. Because the data of anthropological research are often more selective than those of certain other social sciences—e.g., economics or sociology—any generalizations and inferences that the research affords are more qualified, at least in certain respects, than are those of more objective and extensive inquiries. But this limitation is partially counterbalanced by the intensity with which such data may be pursued and analyzed.

8. This limitation is further reduced in the degree that care is exercised in the choice of institutions for examination and of the informants that represent them. Especially if time is limited within which to become familiar with the culture or subcultures to be investigated, more reliable and fruitful results may accrue if all or part of the respondents are carefully selected by the groups to which they

belong and to whom they are better known than to professional investigators.

9. Every culture contains a large body of beliefs, customs, attitudes (sometimes called "implicit" or "metacultural") which are only partially articulated in any systematic or formal manner as codes, doctrines, or philosophies. To a large although usually unmeasured degree, they influence and probably often determine the official or semiofficial policies of a culture as expressed in the charters and programs of its political, religious, educational, and other institutions. Metacultural data are discoverable in all subcultures as well as on the national level of every culture. Many, however, may be expressed in the form of opinions that have not been verified and probably are not verifiable by standard research methodologies.

10. Culture and therefore education are characterized by various dimensions of *order* which, when understood, serve to provide clearer policies and programs by which that order could be strengthened, modified, or changed.

11. Culture and therefore education are characterized by various forms of *process* which, when understood, serve to provide clearer policies and programs by which those processes could be strengthened, modified, or changed.

12. Culture and therefore education are characterized by various types of *goals* which, when understood, serve to provide clearer policies and programs by which those goals could be strengthened, modified, or changed.

13. The order, process, and goals of culture and hence of education are interdependent. All three must be understood and utilized as operating concepts if any one is to be understood and utilized.

14. Equally, the three concepts are to be regarded as integral to a philosophy of culture and education which is world-wide in scope. The framework of this philosophy centers in an interpretation of our age as one of both shattering crisis and magnificent opportunity for cultural reconstruction. It is, at the same time, a philosophy that recognizes as crucial to its own character the necessity of building upon the resources available in any given culture. It is in principle opposed to both superimposition and indoctrination.

15. While the aim is to achieve and evaluate whatever consensuses these resources permit, full recognition must also be given to "indi-

vidual differences"—that is, to the deviations of attitude, habit, belief, and practice abundant in this as in every culture.

16. The consensuses or lack of consensuses, as well as the criticisms and recommendations, that emerge from this study do not necessarily express the judgments of any one respondent in precisely the form that he would approve. Equally, the beliefs and attitudes of any individual respondent may or may not meet with the approval of others. *No one respondent necessarily subscribes fully to any one of the findings or interpretations stated in the following pages.*

PART II

THE PROBLEM OF CULTURAL ORDER IN PUERTO RICO

INTRODUCTION TO PART II

WHEN WE speak of the "order" of Puerto Rican culture, we are thinking of the network of relations that constitute its whole. These relations are multiple: they include the interpersonal sharings of husband, wife, and children; the interclass and interracial patterns of groups; the interworkings of state, school, industry, church, and other institutions; the subtle crosscurrents of attitude, belief, habit, and practice; and finally the connections, official or unofficial, between this culture and many others both nearby and remote.

Of the numerous ways by which it is possible to approach our problem, we propose to do so in terms of space and time. The former concerns the orders one may discover when one examines Puerto Rico on horizontal planes and in vertical layers. The second concerns the kinds of order discernible in its historical development.

In treating the family "spatially," we mean to be chiefly concerned with the present relations of its members to each other in a unified structure—its "horizontal" aspects being illustrated by the phenomenon of the extended family. That it possesses "vertical" aspects (e.g., in the hierarchical relations of parents to children) as well as "temporal" aspects (e.g., the kinship system of descent) is sufficient indication that none of our organizing categories can be utilized without keeping the others at least in the background of our minds—a rule that applies equally to all other areas to be treated in this study. Thus, when we turn next to the class structure viewed as a vertical dimension of spatial order, we do not ignore even when we subordinate the horizontal dimension, nor do we do so when we deal with the temporal approach in our chapter on history. The final three chapters of Part II interfuse the respective phases of cultural order by means of the spatiotemporal concepts of configuration and national character—the latter, concerned as it is with the "whole" of Puerto Rican culture, thus serving as a unifying concept par excellence.

In attempting to cope with these topics, let us keep in mind the important rule laid down at the close of Part I: no statements to be made at any point in this work necessarily express the views of any single respondent in the precise form that he would himself choose to express them. In many cases, he might completely reject a particular statement.

CHAPTER THREE

THE ORDER OF THE PUERTO RICAN FAMILY

THE FAMILY is the most universal of cultural institutions. In a real sense, it is the core of culture. From it radiate other institutions of widening scope. Its order or structure, however, varies tremendously from culture to culture.

The Puerto Rican family, too, is a fascinating cultural phenomenon, and already a number of research studies* go farther and deeper than our own limited inquiry. Yet, in attempting as we do to portray the culture in panoramic fashion, it would be impossible to omit consideration of the family's general features or to disregard its significance for any educational program that aims to deal with the urgencies of Insular life.

In the following sections we propose to elicit from our two panels of respondents their views as to, first, the nature of the family in a period of unusual change; second, such deep-seated traditions as the double standard and consensual marriage; third, the status of women; fourth, how they evaluate the over-all family situation; and fifth, what the schools are doing and ought to do about the problems that this situation generates. Some of these topics will receive additional treatment in later contexts.

In accordance with the plan of presentation hitherto outlined, readers should remember that our treatment is partially reportorial of how our informants view their own families, in particular, and the Puerto Rican family, in general. We do not, until our concluding paragraphs, attempt to pass judgment upon what we describe. Rather, we

* See pp. 360–363. The evidence provided by respondents in this and subsequent chapters is placed against and compared with other recent research studies summarized in Chapters 18 and 19.

are concerned to learn what we can from those to whom we have turned in three subcultures and on the national level about this pivotal institution. The facts and judgments thus provided are not ours, though of course they are affected by the kinds of questions we have asked in terms of our own philosophic, educational, and cultural point of view.

By way of anticipation, this point of view may be characterized as one of deep concern that traditional family life in Puerto Rico, admirable though it surely has been in various respects, cannot and indeed should not survive without a substantial degree of re-examination and even reconstruction. Its chief weaknesses have resulted from its unduly hierarchical, paternalistic, and self-centered structure. Its chief strengths are rooted in profound loyalties and affections that reach far beyond its immediate members. What must be undertaken is the restabilization of family life by capitalizing upon its inherent strengths, while at the same time democratizing its internal relations and harmonizing these with its external responsibilities to the wider dimensions of the emerging cultural order.

STRAINS AND STRESSES

In general, as our informants have interpreted the family today, it is grounded in mores and customs that reflect its European and especially Spanish past; but it is also beginning to acquire attitudes and habits that resemble certain types of North American families. One consequence is instability and conflict, particularly between older and younger members.

On the one hand, the family as it is now developing continues to reveal its internal solidarity. One leader tried to underscore this solidarity by contending that the tradition is "too strong to break." Typically, children remain respectful and obedient. Our student correspondents, for example, implied that their parents had every right to make the rules concerning their own behavior at least through the high school years.

Family loyalties extend further than parents and children. They include kin that may be only remotely related by blood or marriage and that include, also, religious ceremonial relations symbolized by the term *compadrazgo*—a pattern that has exercised much more than sentimental or casual influence. For centuries, it has provided reciprocal aid and protection of many kinds through what has been called the "extended family." The *compadre* or godparent is the key figure: often he is completely accepted as a family member with a deep mutual sense of affection and obligation.

On the other hand, though intrafamilial solidarity is still cohesive, it is being modified by such events as migration which may separate its members by thousands of miles and by long periods of time. An immediate effect is the decline of the *compadrazgo* institution itself. While it continues as a formal ritual in the overwhelming majority of families, no dissent was heard from the common opinion that the singular responsibility and devotion earlier characterizing godparent-godchildren relations are less pronounced than even a decade or two ago. This is by no means always true, of course: even in the cities, though more so in the country, the *compadre* may remain a member of the extended family with very close ties. One rural respondent, to take an instance, was helping his godson financially to study for the priesthood. But the genuine, often sacrificial service that the *padrino* (godfather) formerly rendered by way of security and affection—service that actual parents could not always equally render—has tended to diminish as their own economic condition has improved and group solidarity has in general weakened.

Similarly, the opinion was prevalent that lines of authority within the family are being gradually modified. With minor exceptions (two leaders who implied that the Puerto Rican family is basically "matriarchal," two others who hesitated to generalize at all), both panels agreed that the father traditionally has been the dominant authority—the chief rule-maker and rule-enforcer—hence that the term "patriarchal" is loosely appropriate. As one spokesman half-facetiously put it: Puerto Rico has suffered historically from three tyrannies—the church, the state, and the father! Certainly, at any rate, patriarchy still appears largely typical of all areas as well as all classes, although perhaps most strongly in the rural population. To cite a few examples, one rural respondent, a father, insisted upon approving his children's choice of marriage partners; another refused to permit his son, a high school senior, to have "dates" under any circumstances; a third was unequivocal in his conviction that the wife's tasks are to cook, wash, and care for the children; a fourth held that many young people have married at an early age mainly to escape from their fathers' domination. One leader familiar with recent research pointed out, however, that the patriarchal order is less pronounced in the sugar than in the coffee areas.

Yet, everywhere it is an order that has been shifting progressively if slowly through the decades since 1900. Two subcultural respondents of middle age spoke of their fathers as "all-powerful" by comparison with their own more qualified roles. Another mentioned that his younger children were less respectful toward him than his older, grown-up ones. A number on both panels even expressed anxiety over too far a swing of the pendulum in the opposite direction. In many families, but especially urban, it was held that children have too much "freedom": there is too little discipline, too little respect, too little supervision. Women also are becoming independent to a degree that often jeopardizes the stability of their homes. Thousands of fathers go to the States for as much as six months of each year; sometimes they never return. The ease of travel not only between Puerto Rico and the United States but, as roads improve, within the Island itself tends to encourage mobility of family members and thus to invite cultivation of outside interests which the father finds difficulty in sharing or directing. The home was depicted as less the center of holiday festivities, for example, than it used to be. At least equally significant is the fact that many children are now acquiring more education and better jobs than their parents, with the double consequence that the older forms of authority are neither as easily accepted nor as confidently exercised.

Nevertheless, the mother's role was viewed as important. Our resource persons stressed that a division of authority as well as labor has been customary—the father being primarily concerned with the "external" relations of the family, the mother with the "internal." Thus the father hitherto has provided most or all of the income and has decided how it should be spent. (He, rather than his wife, has done most of the family purchasing.) Likewise he has established schedules of work and play for his children outside the home, with especially strict rules for their teen-age relations with members of the opposite sex. Yet, inside the home, the mother has often been the more salient influence—so much so that the term "matriarchal" is not as surprising as one might at first suppose. One grassroots informant in Cañamelar epitomized the structure there: the father makes the rules, but the mother is still the "policeman" who enforces them.

"Overprotection" was also used a number of times to describe the role of the mother, particularly toward her sons even well into their twenties. This practice may partly result, one leader thought, from unsatisfactory relations with her husband. Also, according to another leader, girls tend to be more secure and more reliable than boys—perhaps because they are less protected by their mothers. This contention is, however, weakened by the "virginity cult" to be discussed below.

Corporal punishment continues to be commonly exercised by the father. Yet, again, the mother has habitually if less severely exercised it for infraction of rules that she, more than her husband, has established for the household.

In any case, the patriarchal order has been limited further, we were told, by a degree of family hierarchy. Older children are not only assigned the task of caring for younger ones; it has ordinarily been taken for granted that the oldest child is next in authority with almost the same right as his parents to enforce family discipline.

EXTRAMARITAL RELATIONS AND CONSENSUAL MARRIAGE

One of the complex features of traditional families described by various informants has been the widespread though far from universal practice of extramarital relations by the father. Several also agreed that the father, above all in country areas, has usually tried not only to treat the children born of these relations with affection but to assume economic responsibility for them. Such responsibility, however, has often been less pronounced than toward those of his immediate family, if only because his income has usually been too low to provide enough even for them.

Various factors have contributed in recent years to some weakening of this tradition. Among them are laws requiring the father to provide support for all of his children whether legally sanctioned or not; increasing birth control; growing disapproval of concubinage as an institution, especially by the middle levels; and, related to the latter, a subtle infiltration of different moral standards from customary ones. But the problem was considered still severe in its effects not only upon children themselves but in the anguish suffered by wives, who, though they recognize the double standard and often accept the children of extramarital unions into their own homes, are seldom if ever as emotionally reconciled to the practice as are their husbands. We return to this topic in Chapter 6.*

A second cultural phenomenon of primary importance to the family pattern is the consensual or common-law marriage. In one of the rural *barrios* studied, respondents alleged that over half of all marriages were consensual and that over 60 per cent of the children in the rural school were the issue of such marriages. Although both Catholic and Protestant churches as well as the government have sought with considerable success to reduce the number of consensual alliances, the families resulting from them are viewed by the local community as no less moral or conventional than from civilly or religiously sanctioned marriages.

This attitude was supported by a grassroots consensus that "illegitimate"† children should have the same respect and the same share in community life as any other children—indeed, they are rarely regarded in this light at all. The difficulty is not, according to most respondents, one of stigmatization, but of instability. Not being bound by formal or legal commitments, it is easier for one or the other mate, oftener the father, to leave or establish a new relationship than it would be otherwise. Partly offsetting such instability, however, is not only the protection customarily provided by the mother and her extended family to the children, but the fact that parents cannot receive social security or other state financial aid until their marriages are legalized.

THE STATUS OF WOMEN

The status of women is weakening the patriarchal order—in the terms of one leader, the "Roman type" of family which Puerto Rico inherited from southern Europe. What we have not clarified is a principal cause of this changing status as seen by our panels, namely, the industrialization program with employment openings in factories, most of which specialize in light industry, such as garment manufac-

---

* See pp. 107–109.

† This term is seldom applied to the Puerto Rican children of consensual marriages, although in the literal, legal sense (at least according to a speaker on an Insular radio program) one-third of all Puerto Rican children are "illegitimate."

ture. Many thousands of young women not only for the first time receive as much education as men; they often earn much more. When they get married, this almost inevitably means a stronger demand to be heard in family affairs, a sharper sense of autonomous rights, and a consequent loosening of the older lines of authority. It also means more opportunity for women to meet other people, including men, and to discover that the circumscribed life ordained by Puerto Rican mores is not the only kind available to them.

Children are also affected, of course. Working mothers must be gone during the day, with the result that protective habits are disturbed. Children remain at home with maids of little education or with relatives such as grandparents; or, because of "double sessions," they are left without any supervision during the half-days that the majority are out of school. (Some elementary-age children, one informant reported, "stay around" after class hours simply because they have nowhere else to go. In one subculture, three neglected tots below five years of age spent many hours daily in the corridor of the school superintendent's office during our visits. No one sent them away.)

And yet, granting unanimity of judgment that the woman's functions in the family are being affected by cultural and especially technological conditions, in one respect, at least, any change in her role is thus far minimal. Except perhaps among a small minority of sophisticated urbanites, the "cult of virginity," as it is sometimes called—the deeply rooted belief that a woman must have had no sexual relations before her marriage—was said to be entrenched as firmly as ever. Many stories are told of grooms sending their brides home upon the suspicion of nonvirginity, although nothing like comparable disapproval results from premarital sexual relations by young men, frequently with prostitutes.

The double standard thus prevails before marriage also. It is exemplified by the tradition of chaperonage, which, though weakening, is still far commoner than not. No grassroots respondent could remember having gone to a movie, while unmarried, with a member of the opposite sex unless accompanied either by a chaperon or, less often, by parent-approved groups of young people. As one young informant put it, his father would forbid unescorted moviegoing for fear of what others would say. Only rarely does a girl attend a dance unchaperoned or without a group as escort. Moreover, almost no respondent, even among the younger, dated at all except under similar escort until they were publicly engaged, although one has continued to meet his girl friend in secret rendezvous.

Frequently, a young woman is considered engaged after one or two dates, especially in the interior rural areas. Her reputation was said to be so easily damaged by dating with several young men that a number of other cases were cited of inability as a result to marry at all, unless perhaps consensually. Even holding of hands in public (a practice now common on the campus of the University) would still be considered "sinful" in many rural communities, one respondent said.

Our panels were not united on the extent to which chaperonage is diminishing. Nor did they deny that movie dates without escorts sometimes occur. They did agree that chaperonage is weaker in urban than in rural areas, but they also agreed that the guardianship of young women by parents of all classes and regions remains much more stern than in the average North American community.

One result of this venerable practice has been, we were told, that most women still marry with meager opportunity to know other men than their husbands through courtship experiences, and with relatively little knowledge of erotic behavior directly or even verbally.

EVALUATIVE JUDGMENTS OF THE FAMILY

Thus far we have been drawing together the main descriptive evidence obtained from our respondents concerning the family. What do we find if we turn to their normative judgments?

The principal judgment is anticipated by our introductory statement that the order of the family, being decreasingly if still heavily traditional, is passing through an uneasy transition with accompanying uncertainties and gropings as yet far from resolved. Kinship solidarity, for example, which one leader described as Puerto Rican "familialism" (in his opinion, much more prevalent than "nationalism"), has produced ambivalent loyalties between the state and the family—one immediate and chronic result of which is a form of "nepotism," of bureaucratic job-passing among members of extended families, including *compadres*.

The fact of this ambivalence is supported by a question (clarified, of course, with examples) addressed to our grassroots respondents:

"If you were faced with a conflict in your ambitions, which would you want to do most: advance yourself, serve your family, or serve your community?" None answered "myself," although one answered "all three equally." Three answered, "the family and the community equally." The rest were sharply divided between the two latter choices.

On both the grassroots and national panels, most informants were convinced that the father has been overdominating, and that the shift toward more participation and less division of labor in family affairs is desirable. Several fathers indicated that they were attempting to encourage such participation and were even assisting their wives in household chores.

But several others in the subcultures admitted that they were and ought to be firmly in control of their families, with the wives solely responsible for work in the home. As one respondent put it, women should not take outside jobs because then they might not always agree with their husbands. As another put it, speaking of controlling his own children and quoting what he called the "Masonic Code," children from one to ten years of age ought to "fear you," from ten to twenty they ought to "respect you," and from twenty on they ought to "love you." He would no doubt lament a symptomatic shift mentioned by one of his peers: children today increasingly use the informal second personal pronoun *tu* in addressing their fathers, rather than the formal *usted* of his own boyhood.

Only a single national leader would apparently agree with the authoritarian dictum just cited. He alone among his peers favored the historic forms of discipline and dominance by the father, although rather inconsistently he, too, recognized the right of children to share in family decisions. Another advocated vigorous spanking, expressing considerable skepticism over the undue influence and perhaps superficially grasped theories of Freud and Dewey for their condemnation of "frustration" and their advocacy of "self-expression" for children. Two grassroots respondents made a somewhat similar point in asserting that, while more self-expression may be desirable, psychologists have not yet clarified its proper function, its limits, or its range. Thus, opposition to patriarchy was modified by what, for most respondents, may be considered a "middle-road" position: a more democratic family with more rational rule-making than has been customary, yet

one with considerably stronger control over its members than would
be typical of American families influenced by liberal ideas and
practices.

As to the status of women, consternation was expressed in different
ways at the damage being done both to husband-wife relations and
to children as the result of a radical shifting from confinement in the
home to outside opportunities. One subcultural respondent bemoaned
the neglect of housework. Conceding that the problem was not yet
serious, a leader feared that, unless Puerto Rico finds a way to build
heavy industry (a difficult problem in a relatively isolated country
with few natural resources) so that men can be employed as often
and at least as remuneratively as the average woman, a matriarchy
will emerge. For as young women workers marry, they may displace
their husbands as heads of their households. An example: in Cayey,
a large interior town, a sweater factory was reported to employ 675
workers, of whom 600 are women, many of them still in their teens
and twenties.

Immorality and increasing divorce were blamed as evils resulting
partly from woman's changing position in the economy. Juvenile
delinquency was also attributed by several to the fact that so many
children are left uncared for. Nearly all subcultural respondents dis-
approved of women working if they have children. One, however,
believed the primary cause of juvenile delinquency to be lack of
religion, while one leader insisted that a still deeper cause is the
continued prevalence of illegitimacy with accompanying deficient or
totally absent parental responsibility.

Few respondents on either level chose to criticize sharply the
dependent and subordinate position that they admitted women have
hitherto occupied in the family and community. No grassroots respondent and only two leaders did so, one of the latter attributing part
of what he termed the "servant" role of women to the influence of
the Roman Catholic Church. Two other leaders did, however, call
attention to the "passivity" of the Puerto Rican woman—a characteristic which they found to be related to her habit of relinquishing
erotic activity as much as possible to the *machismo* (aggressively
virile) male. Perhaps for comparable reasons, only a small minority
were frankly critical of the custom of chaperonage with its cluster
of attitudes tied to the ideal of virginity. A few, to be sure, made the

point that it would be better if young women could become acquainted with several young men before marriage.

It is, then, impossible to say that Puerto Ricans, at least as represented by our respondents, are on the whole pleased with emerging female roles in family and community. More education for women than in the past is approved, without doubt. Expanding positions in professional and political life, the right to vote, and greater opportunities to travel abroad also met with wide approval on the two panels. Nor was the fact denied that women have, through employment, raised the living standards of thousands of homes and thereby also gained more respect from their husbands. Yet the question remains unanswered whether, when a balance is struck, the temporary gains outweigh what appeared to nearly all of our respondents to be heavy losses to family life.

Curiously, the absence of many thousands of migrant fathers for months of each year during the slack seasons in Puerto Rico, especially in the sugar areas, was not considered to be a grave problem. That mothers and children may even feel relieved by a temporary relaxation of patriarchal rule was not suggested. One informant did contend that vandalism, including stealing, in his school has increased during these periods. The point that was underscored by most spokesmen, however, was that families are so much better off as a result of pay checks mailed to them from the States that any negative consequence is more than offset.

A word should be said also about the size of families and the question of limiting them to the number desired by parents. We shall consider the issue of birth control at a later place,* only noting here that a majority on both panels favored it not only for reasons of family health and welfare but because of the supersaturated population.

The size of families represented by respondents is perhaps an index to the Insular situation as a whole. On the grassroots level, the children of married respondents ranged from none to fourteen. The unmarried belonged to families of two to ten children—one respondent's mother, forty-eight years of age, having given birth to twenty-four children, nine still living. The average number of living and deceased children of married grassroots respondents was approximately

* See pp. 305–310.

five; the average number in families of the unmarried was approximately eight (the parents of these families being, as a rule, somewhat older than the married respondents who were parents). The urban subcultural group, taking the married and unmarried together, belonged to families with an average number of living or deceased children totaling between two and three. The two rural subcultural groups represented families of between eight and nine children— the age range of children of married respondents being from five to thirty-four. On the national level (all respondents now being urban), the average number of children per family was close to three. Thus our respondents are cross-sectional in the following regards: rural parents have more children than urban parents, well-educated parents have fewer children than the poorer educated, and the parents of today's generation have fewer children than yesterday's.

In these and other respects, customary family patterns, while resembling those of other Spanish-speaking cultures, are not limited to the latter either in fact or meaning. Yet it would probably be difficult to prove that any of the aspects noted are strikingly unique, although they are not merely imitative either. What is more important for our study is that the resistance of these patterns to drastic modification, combined with indisputable evidence that they nevertheless face the necessity of such modification, produce disturbing problems but also constructive opportunities.

Thoughtful citizens are far from cynical in mood. They are searching for a rationale that can produce a healthy and happy family life for a new period of their history. If they have not yet found that rationale, one can only say that the family in Puerto Rico mirrors, in various respects, the emerging character of the whole culture.

TASKS AND OPPORTUNITIES FOR EDUCATION IN FAMILY PROBLEMS

Although some notice is paid by the schools to problems of family life, our respondents approached a consensus in their emphatic opinion that much more could and should be accomplished as rapidly as possible.

Perhaps the most sustained educational attention to the family today is found in home-economics courses on the junior and senior high school level. Since these courses are largely limited to girls and then do not deal with wider cultural aspects nearly as much as with modern practices of homemaking, it cannot be said that the majority of young people finish their secondary educations with informed sensitivity to the disturbing issues of family life.

When subcultural respondents were asked whether they would approve of offering home economics to boys so that they too could learn about child care, cooking, and other household responsibilities that, traditionally, have been assigned to women, the proposal met with general approval from men as well as women. Two pointed out that limited attempts have been made in second-unit schools (rural junior high schools combining agricultural and vocational with liberal-arts training) to include boys in these courses, so that the proposal is not without precedent. In the eighth and ninth grades, some schools even provide for boys to elect home economics for two or three weeks in exchange with girls who elect shopwork during the same period.

Also, "Community Problems" in the elementary school and "Social and Economic Problems of Puerto Rico" in the secondary school include units on the family. In both courses, teachers are urged to deviate from the syllabus and to include family problems of the local community. Yet, little evidence could be discovered of any critical thoroughness with which such problems are attacked by the typical teacher, or of any resource materials supplied by government agencies, although some teachers are more concerned and prepared to deal with them than are others.

It would be misleading to assert that most teachers are indifferent to the family backgrounds and problems of their students. Some are earnestly concerned with the emotional disturbances that result from broken homes, and with illegitimacy, malnutrition, or similar evils. Moreover, women elementary teachers often play a strongly maternal role; gestures of affection such as kissing, for example, seem to be taken for granted to a much greater extent than between American teachers and their small charges.

But it remains problematic as to how far such admirable concern is augmented by accurate information or understanding of the tensions and conflicts now developing. Nor, in the judgment of one leader, is the habit of "mothering" by teachers necessarily desirable: it may encourage passivity and postpone maturity in the same way that actual mothers, in his opinion, tend to prolong immaturity by overprotecting their own children.

The fact that a large percentage of teachers do not live in the communities where they teach (this is especially true of rural teachers, but by no means limited to them) makes it more difficult to know local family problems intimately. Partly for this reason, partly because of abnormally large classes, and partly because many teachers hold other jobs during their free hours, the majority apparently do not visit the homes of their children unless an emergency such as illness arises, and often not then. This responsibility, we were informed, is left primarily to the "visiting teacher," who appears to be a combination truant officer and social worker and who, if available at all, is normally assigned to so many schools that it is impossible to establish familiarity with the great majority of families. But home-economics teachers, especially in second-unit schools, do spend part of their schedules in visiting homes and encouraging better sanitation, food habits, or other improvements. And in the town of San José a plan was being developed whereby many teachers would be given free time to visit families as part of their regular schedule.

Some opportunities for parents to meet teachers in the school itself were likewise reported. Many schools have parent-teacher associations, but many others do not. Meetings of those that do have them are not normally attended by a majority of teachers if only because they live too far away to return for an evening meeting—the same obstacle applying to numerous principals and superintendents. While the liveliest PTA's were said to function in private schools, several public schools visited during the present study hold from one to seven or eight PTA meetings per year. Some raise money for clothing, shoes, library books, and other projects, or are otherwise active in school affairs. Others have almost no general meetings but leave the organization chiefly in the hands of officers. Still others have active parent groups organized by individual classes of children.

Yet in none of the PTA's described by our respondents were family problems considered as a central topic for parent-teacher discussion. In none were outside counselors such as social workers invited to confer with parents in a regular program. Respondents could not agree as to whether many parents would attend if meetings were devoted to the kind of issues raised in this chapter. One spokesman did report that meetings on family problems have been well attended when conducted by a local church; he was confident they would also succeed if well planned by the schools.

Stress was placed on the need for more vigorous attack upon family problems by adult education in Puerto Rico. Here the Division of Community Education was said to be accomplishing more than any other adult-education agency. For example, it has published a widely discussed pamphlet, *La Familia,* which raises such issues as paternal authoritarianism. Films bearing upon family problems have also been prepared and used in many communities.

But the Division thus far has concentrated much more heavily in rural than in urban areas, with the result that thousands of families, recently uprooted from long-accustomed country environments and resettled in a metropolis such as San Juan or New York, have not yet been reached by any kind of competent guidance. For that matter, its own staff would be the first to agree that family problems are dealt with meagerly even in the limited number of rural areas where they have been able to serve. The recommendation of another leader not connected with the Division that it be granted a budget at least twice its present size, so that its staff could be enlarged especially for intensive urban work, was motivated primarily by his concern for the family problem.

Leaders warned, however, that education alone cannot cope with this problem, even when it is as informal and functional as the Division's program. (One spokesman was sure that social-work agencies should have the heaviest burden.) An original recommendation was that a "Secretary of the Family" be added to the Governor's Cabinet, with the responsibility of drawing upon social and educational resources more systematically and efficiently. Another of his responsibilities could deal with overpopulation by attacking illegitimacy. (In the opinion of another leader, overpopulation is largely the effect of moral laxity and neglect of duties that accompany this evil.) The need for clinics and laboratories conducted by sociologically and psychiatrically trained experts, and for carefully prepared television and radio programs on the family, could be still another responsibility of the new Secretary. All of these ideas are, of course, profoundly educational in the cultural rather than merely formal sense.

Further recommendations relate more directly to the schools. One of the most important, since it cuts through many problems besides that of the family, will be reported again: curricula should become less verbal and bookish and more involved in the actual life of people. Students and teachers should oftener leave the artificial climate of their classrooms in order to know by direct contact the habits and difficulties of families belonging to other classes, statuses, and subcultures than their own. Moreover, they should become familiar with family life in other countries, not only through films and novels, but through student travel and cultural exchange projects.

One of the most disturbing of all problems, we noted above, is the decline of parental supervision caused by absentee fathers and, increasingly, mothers also. The suggestion of one subcultural respondent that the Commonwealth experiment with a carefully supervised nursery school program under the Department of Education would therefore seem noteworthy. The few nursery schools that now operate are private or run by other agencies and severely limited in both trained personnel and facilities. Yet the experience of several other countries (Australia is one) undergoing comparable technological development would seem to show that investment in publicly financed nursery schools produces rich dividends in diminished parental anxiety and happy children.

Another proposal by a grassroots respondent (though judged impractical by a peer) was that supervised playgrounds and social centers be developed for children during the mornings and afternoons that the majority are not in school. School yards could also be opened under supervision during evenings, week ends, and summers, with swings and other equipment for children of different ages, including those in their teens. Trips to various institutions and other social experiences could be included in the program.

Like so many others, this proposal is far from easy to implement either financially or in man power. Yet, with the cooperation of the Departments of Recreation and Education, it would not seem impractical to attempt a pilot project in at least two or three communities and to measure its effects upon the adjustment of children. The experience of the rural community of Castañer, where supervised activities, such as handicrafts for children, have already been carried on by Protestant groups as a part of their remarkable program of service, would be one example from which other communities could learn.

Money might be provided in a municipality such as Cañamelar partly or wholly by local funds which were said to be available for extra projects.

Part of the personnel could be enlisted from the ranks of teachers as a means of increasing their income. Such teachers should be carefully chosen and receive special training in workshops during the summer "activity month" established by the Department of Education as a way to strengthen the professional competence of its teaching personnel. (This "activity month," incidentally, would also provide excellent opportunity, in the opinion of another grassroots respondent, to develop pilot projects in local family problems to be conducted for high school students, or parents, or both.)

We conclude our survey of educational reactions to the family, viewed as the heart of cultural order, by noting a profound observation by two leaders. The single most urgent task in coping with this problem, they insisted, is that of developing a clear, defensible conception of what the cohesive Puerto Rican family ought to be as it undergoes modification.

That security, affection, and responsibility must not only be preserved but revitalized and intensified would surely meet with the opposition of no respondent on any level. More difficult is the question of how to prevent the two extremes of family authoritarianism and family anarchism, both of which were held to be almost chronic phenomena, both of which were largely repudiated. The positive conception of a democratic family which avoids these extremes by ensuring adequate controls harmonized with adequate expression as well as participation among all its members is the difficult, as yet uncrystallized norm to which many of our respondents would wish the schools of their culture to be dedicated.

THE FUTURE OF THE PUERTO RICAN FAMILY

Up to this point we have tried to exclude, though surely not with total success, our own evaluation of the picture sketched both from the negative or positive reactions provided mainly by our resource persons, and more briefly from our observations while in the field. Since the present chapter sets the pattern for most of those to follow, let us reiterate our plan to provide such a picture before we attempt to appraise it in terms of our philosophy of culture and education.

This philosophy, we have also said, includes the principle that any normative judgments in the form of criticisms or recommendations must always draw upon the inherent resources of the culture under consideration. Therefore we begin our appraisal by reviewing the limited evidence that we have been able to obtain thus far.

The traditional family, which includes the important *compadrazgo* relationship of ceremonial kinship, has been characterized by a powerful cohesiveness. Slowly but steadily since at least 1900, however, the effects of such forces as urbanization, industrialization, and intercultural relations are detected in a diminution of this cohesiveness. Simultaneously, the structure of hierarchical authority, though still very strong, has been modified in the direction of greater participation in family affairs by the wife and mother, by a somewhat diminished authoritarian discipline over children, and by relatively new wage-earning roles on the part of adult female members. The double standard, exemplified by the practice of concubinage, is also diminishing—faster, apparently, than consensual marriage, though this too is less prevalent than earlier as a result of legal obstacles and of such influences as organized religion. At the same time, the habit of protectiveness of children even into young maturity remains pronounced—unmarried females, for example, having considerably less freedom to associate with males than is found in the cultures of North America.

In evaluating the contemporary family, our respondents themselves tended to reflect this mobile situation, both in the size and structure of their own families and in their attitudes. Thus, while the majority were critical of the patriarchal order, a decided minority clearly continued to favor it. Even more significant, perhaps, was the vehement disapproval of the changing role of women which accompanied the admission that their status has, in various ways, nevertheless improved.

Yet, judged by their educational proposals, both panels recognized that much more effort is needed than at present to cope with family problems. The inclusion of boys in home-economics courses, the enrichment of social studies in this area, association by teachers with the home life of students, the vitalizing of parent-teacher associations and adult programs, the establishment of experimental nursery schools and playground programs, the appointment of a "Secretary of the Family" in the government itself, and direct contact with family experience—these were the chief proposals.

All of them deserve earnest consideration. We would go further, however. Much better coordination of the several agencies concerned with family life is one imperative if education is itself to be effective. Again, forthright study of such practices as consensual marriage is needed both in classrooms and in parent groups.

But, with the two leader respondents cited at the conclusion of our survey, we find that the most pressing issue lies on a more elusive level. Whatever instabilities the family suffers from today are enmeshed with those of the wider culture. The key to these instabilities lies in the conflict between what one respondent called the allegiance to "familialism," on the one hand, and Island-wide tasks and goals, on the other hand. Like other conflicts that we shall have occasion to examine, this one is by no means exclusively Puerto Rican. It is virtually world-wide—indeed, one symptom of the crisis in human affairs to which we have already called attention.

More concretely in terms of the Puerto Rican family, the conflict may be induced chiefly by the fact that the comparative autonomy of an agrarian family no longer serves the needs of an increasingly interdependent socioeconomic order. For related reasons, the authority of the father and husband who rather efficiently controlled his simple realm is challenged by the growing interests, activities, and skills of other members of his household. While he recognizes and even approves some of these changes, he is also disturbed by them: thus he cannot, as many of our respondents could not, readily concede that the woman's changing role is a beneficial one; to do so is to relinquish something of his own inherent place of dominance and thus something of his own pride and security. His case is strengthened, too, by the difficulties and confusions which that role undoubtedly engenders.

Yet, even were it possible, we think it undesirable to urge the preservation of the old familial order. Undesirable because, in terms of the values of democratic living, the patriarchal structure permits too little sharing, too much arbitrary power. Undesirable, too, because we are dubious of the effects upon personality development from, say, the overprotection of children or from the circumscribed, inequalitarian privileges accorded the female sex.

At the same time, a desirable future for the Puerto Rican family does not lie in repudiation of its historic virtues. Certainly it is not to be found in the anarchic permissiveness that many Continental families have recently substituted for the overstrictness of earlier generations. The solution to the problem of too much discipline is not to discard all discipline. Nor is the solution to the problem of introverted family loyalty no family loyalty at all. Precisely because the typical Puerto Rican family has more firmly retained respect for the importance of both discipline and loyalty, it is in some ways better equipped to achieve an amalgam with the newer, more democratic trends in its culture than is the kind of North American family which too often swings to the other extreme.

The task of achieving such an amalgam—by no means a simple or rapid task, and certainly by no means adequately clarified—is the greatest that confronts Puerto Rican education in this first and crucial sphere of its cultural order.

CHAPTER FOUR

THE CLASS STRUCTURE OF PUERTO RICO

BEFORE CONSIDERING further the horizontal relations of spatial order in Puerto Rico, we wish now to look at some of its vertical dimensions. That is, we propose to slice, as it were, the culture from the top down in order to expose its human strata of statuses and classes, and to subject these to brief analysis and interpretation.

It may be well to recall at the outset that our two panels of respondents probably represented all six of the social status levels postulated by Warner in terms chiefly of degrees of prestige—from the upper-upper "aristocrat" to the lower-lower "peasant" (both terms being used by various spokesmen). More strictly in terms of economic class (that is, position in the vertical order as determined primarily by one's relations to the productive system—e.g., whether manager or worker), they ranged from a top-rank industrial employer down through professionals, small businessmen, and government employees to propertyless bottom-level families on sugar-cane and coffee *haciendas*.

Parenthetically, we may note that a number of our subcultural respondents—five, at least—came from families who had once owned farms but had lost them in hard times. Now, after a generation or more of poverty, these individuals were once more "on the way up." In their case, as indeed of many individuals, it is sometimes difficult to separate "social status" from "economic class." In our case, however, we distinguish operationally between the two terms while granting that they often overlap.

Reactions to the stratification problem in Puerto Rico were even more diverse than in the case of the family—perhaps a partial consequence of the fact that, until very recently, little research has been carried on in this important field. Surely even more responsible are the historic events noted in Chapter 1. A culture subjected to centuries of colonial, semifeudal rule with its typically rigid class structure of the ruling minority and the ruled majority has found itself, almost overnight, confronted with the opportunity to reverse this order of authority. That it has sometimes stumbled in the act of grasping so vast an opportunity, and that its citizens have not always comprehended or acted skillfully in the face of the breathtaking events that accompany new political and economic alignments, is surely normal enough. Nor is it surprising that, since these alignments are still shifting, citizens may be far from agreed either as to what they mean or how they will shift in the future.

We shall try to get inside the problem by raising a number of questions as to where in the vertical order power is concentrated; how people of various classes tend to appraise each other; what the significance of race may be in terms of stratification; how we are to view the middle class that is now emerging; and what bearing all of these questions have upon education.

In the light of such evidence as we have been able to obtain, our concluding evaluation must be negative as well as positive. Upward mobility, with its accompanying equalizations and expanding opportunities, is surely commendable in many respects. Much less commendable is an insufficient consciousness both of the significance of actual and potential class alignments, and of the directions in which present mobile trends should lead if they are not to produce dangerous new class divisions and powers. In terms that we have used elsewhere,[1] the "forces of expansion," now on the march in Puerto Rico, must continue to expand if they are not to be captured by the "forces of contraction."

WHERE IS POWER CONCENTRATED?

The diversity of opinion was at once exemplified by two minority answers and a third representing the majority on the issue of power, considered here in terms of control over people.

One small group argued that it lies, as it always has, in the top moneyed class which ultimately dominates the chief institutions of the culture even when its lines of influence remain concealed. A more substantial minority took just the opposite view: they insisted that greatest power centers today in the poorest people, for it is they who control the most votes and it is they who have overwhelmingly decided to put the Popular Democratic party in power as their government and to keep it there. (Only one spokesman—a subcultural resident—took the pains to distinguish here between political and economic power: the latter, he said, still rests in the top economic class; the former rests in the bottom classes.)

The largest group, while agreeing that power is vested heavily in the political franchise of the party now in office, held that its important leaders are not themselves and have never been members of the lower socioeconomic strata. Rather, they are predominantly men and women of upper-middle status, many of them professionals and intellectuals of moderate means, who have obtained a mandate from the great majority of workers and countrymen by establishing a program that benefits this majority more than any minority. The program is accepted because its leaders have been honestly concerned with the general welfare rather than because it is the creation of the common people.

The issue is complicated further by the contention that even the leadership of the Popular Democratic party is by no means exclusively middle class. Many minor leaders—members of the legislature, mayors, and others—were said to have won office from the poorest strata of their communities. Also, according to several respondents, citizens of the top economic level are no longer leaving Puerto Rico as they did earlier because of opposition to the government; instead, if they do not support the Republican (or Statehood) party, they may try to infiltrate the Popular party and to affect its policies from within. And though they by no means exercise power in the same degree that Republicans do in the United States, the fact that they continue to hold a monopoly over the most widely read Insular newspapers as well as the most widely heard and watched radio and television stations means that they can often exert considerable pressure on the government by shaping public opinion in behalf of their interests. Moreover, some members of the highest class are, according to one leader, "just too rich" for the good of the country.

When respondents referred to members of the top level, they were usually careful to distinguish between present economic position and older standards of prestige. True, some top-level groups such as contractors, physicians, and industrial managers are rapidly acquiring a new kind of prestige based partly on economic status, partly on Continental educations, proficiencies, and habits of living. True, too, some families are both upper-upper in status and in the highest economic class. But the point was emphasized that, prestige-wise, upper-upper groups still consist quite largely of old families of direct Spanish ancestry. A number of them made agricultural fortunes in the pre-American era, but they pride themselves less on their money (often quite limited) than on their devotion to Spanish traditions, their fervent Catholicism, their white skins, and not infrequently their love of Spain, which they like to visit when they can.

One informant was sure that more families of this type reside in or near the south coast city of Ponce than anywhere else in Puerto Rico. The statement was given some credence by two great portraits, each several feet in height, hanging in its upper-class *casino* (social club) at the time of our visit: one, a painting of King Alfonso; the other, a huge photograph of Franco. But such families are also to be found elsewhere in Puerto Rico. Thus a number were reported to live in the coffee subculture of San José (where church bells rang when Franco won the Spanish Civil War). With few important exceptions, however, they were said no longer to exert substantial political or even economic power upon the culture as a whole. No respondent identified himself with this upper group. Indeed, two leaders who would probably be regarded by many Puerto Ricans as top level were careful to dissociate themselves and to insist that they were really "middle-class citizens."

Most *americanos* who hold high status were said to be admitted today even to the most exclusive Puerto Rican *casinos,* business and country clubs. There is more and more rapprochement between both upper-ethnic groups as each accepts the other with dwindling invidious feelings. Here is an instance, we were told, of a radical change from earlier decades of the century when, perhaps partly because they felt unwelcome and partly because they themselves wished to remain aloof, North Americans much more often formed their own cliques. Even separate drinking fountains, not to mention separate *casinos,* were reputedly maintained by United States-owned sugar companies. The "vicious circle" of ethnocentric behavior on the part of both upper groups was an inevitable consequence.

HOW DO UPPER AND LOWER CLASSES APPRAISE EACH OTHER?

The impossibility of picturing the vertical order in pure black and white is further exemplified by how upper and lower classes appraise each other. A sizable minority on both panels held that neither class regards the other as superior or inferior in any conspicuous way but rather as equals. The majority disagreed: they held that most upper-class Puerto Ricans, probably because of their colonial and feudal heritage, still regard the lower classes as their inferiors either socially or intelligently or both. Conversely, about as strong an opinion was expressed that lower-level Puerto Ricans, although possibly less often, regard the top levels as their superiors again in either or both ways.

But qualifications were introduced by various respondents. One leader saw a marked difference on this question between rural and urban groups: feelings of both superiority and inferiority are much stronger in the rural than in the urban upper and lower classes, respectively. This is due mainly, he held, to the fact that working people in the cities are today often manually skilled as, say, mechanics and carpenters and therefore command respect from the unskilled upper classes as well as pride in their own abilities.

Another made the insightful point that the attitudes of lower-level people, particularly countrymen, toward a member of the upper groups—including the *americano*—depend primarily upon how he approaches them. If there is any display of haughtiness or of dislike toward their customs, or if upper-level people lack warmth and unaffected friendliness, the reaction is likely to be one of suspicion and withdrawal. (The attitudes of Army personnel were cited as too often conducive of this kind of reaction.) The point was further supported by two lower-status rural respondents: in their communities, they said, feelings toward individual *mayordomos* (managers) and other plantation officers such as *capataces* (foremen) varied from bitter hostility to occasional mixing and even affection. A young respondent of a sugar worker's family, incidentally, had never been inside the home of any *mayordomo;* yet one was his *compadre.*

A third leader, disagreeing with the predominant opinion that the lower strata look up to the top strata as their superiors, contended that it all depends on the qualities of the upper-class person: no matter how wealthy he might be, if he is "ignorant," he will receive meager respect indeed. Several respondents noted a related point when they differentiated between the kinds of superior and inferior feelings that prevail: it is widely assumed that lower-class people, including students, are potentially just as competent as any others, but that they have lacked opportunity to prove it. Consequently, these attitudes were said to derive from socioeconomic differentiation much more than from any sense of inherent inequality of intelligence or ability among either upper or lower strata. (The claim that the scholarship program has helped to reduce invidious status feelings was offered by another leader in support of this contention.)

More strictly in terms of economic class rather than status, no dominant opinion emerged as to whether, how much, or what kinds of conflict between employer and worker now prevail. No one argued that class hostility is as severe as in some other parts of the world. (Japan was mentioned by an Army veteran.) One was sure it was much more severe fifty years ago than it is now. Several held that in recent years it has been reduced to a minimum by relatively few strikes, by wage or other laws protecting labor groups, by the upward mobility of lower levels, and by the equalitarian mood of the country. A few on both panels, however, contended that class conflict does manifest itself—the strongest contention coming from one top-level leader, and from several respondents in Cañamelar where unionism among sugar-cane workers is strong. The weakest union consciousness, incidentally, was manifested in San José, where, despite attempts, no workers in the coffee *haciendas* have thus far been organized. Nor are they organized in either of the two local factories.

No respondent on any level expressed impassioned opposition to organized labor—on the contrary, the attitude was on the whole sympathetic. A young middle-class respondent, for example, thought that unions properly reduce the employer's power at the same time that they increase the worker's self-respect, and that the right to strike is justified. Again, an upper-status leader contended that unionization is needed to rebuild the old securities now being liquidated by the waning of traditional paternalistic employer-worker relations. A number of others, however, emphasized that more governmental regulations over unions ought to be established so that "duties" are better balanced against "rights," particularly on the waterfront.

Some doubt was also revealed toward the quality of labor leaders. Most of them were said to be middle-class professionals, such as lawyers, rather than members of the working classes with a labor philosophy. Several respondents at the grassroots were also skeptical of the power held by local labor leaders: while no accusation of dishonesty was heard, the point was made in one community that welfare funds amounting to tens of thousands of dollars have not been properly audited and that there is discouragement of democratic participation and criticism by rank-and-file members. Yet it was apparent that these local leaders were admired—almost revered—by many workers, especially by those who remember the relatively great improvement in wages, hours, and other benefits that have followed both unionization itself and the achievement of political power by the labor-backed Popular Democratic party.

A number on both levels also held that labor and management are cooperating more and more effectively, although it was emphasized several times that organized labor is still so badly divided into such a welter of conflicting factions that it has yet to function as a cohesive force. The fact that some unions are affiliated with the Continental AFL-CIO (the United Packinghouse Workers, which represents more sugar workers than any other union in Puerto Rico, claims about 30,000 members) may hasten the process of unification that must be attained before organized labor can act effectively on the Island as a whole. As one leader put it, labor today is not so much "organized" as woefully "disorganized."

Employers also received sharp criticism. Two leaders emphasized that, although improving, Puerto Rican employers have shown less "social responsibility" and have been less concerned on the whole with the interests of their workers than have North American employers. This phenomenon was attributed to the persistence of colonial or at least hierarchical attitudes. By contrast, one spokesman commented on the pleasant, clean cafeterias and rest rooms often to be found in North American-owned factories.

Even more emphatic was the hostile feeling of certain grassroots respondents, especially in the coffee areas, toward *hacienda* owners and businessmen known as first-, second-, or third-generation Spaniards. Repeatedly the point was made that they are less well liked than Continental employers, that they are even "feared," that they are more interested in making money than in the welfare of their workers, and that, too often, they hold "superiority attitudes" toward countrymen.

The chief exceptions to this feeling came from subcultural respondents of upper-middle status who were themselves closely related to Spanish families, and from one lower-lower respondent who had not only been born and raised on the largest *hacienda* in his *barrio* but whose father, grandfather, and great-grandfather had been also. His attitude seemed to be one of genuine loyalty and devotion to the owner, who, he said, often helped him with loans, provided medical assistance, and visited his home with the same welcome that he felt when he visited the owner's. That this kind of relationship is one of the most authentic remaining symbols of a feudal heritage would perhaps be disputed by no respondent. The assertion of one leader that the feeling toward individuals known more as "Spaniards" than as "Puerto Ricans" is now an "academic" question (because the former can no longer immigrate to the Island in any substantial numbers) would, however, be questioned especially in a subculture such as San José. One informant there, for example, suggested that ambivalence still prevails among his fellow citizens as a result of their "hatred" of Spanish-born exploiters, on the one hand, and their "love" of Spanish traditions, on the other hand.

HOW DO RACES FIT INTO THE CLASS STRUCTURE?

Any inspection of "vertical" order in Puerto Rican culture would be incomplete without attention to race relations. If the not quite unanimous judgment of our respondents was correct, attitudes toward people of color (and the infinite shadings of skin range from black through brown to white) are primarily attitudes derived from socioeconomic divergences rather than from the kind of race consciousness that one finds in South Africa or the Southern region of the United States. Though one leader was sure that race prejudice is virulent under the surface, the preponderant opinion was otherwise: the average colored person is likely to have lower status and lower class position than the average white person, not because he is considered to belong to an inferior race, but because he is likely to have a poorer job and hence less of the amenities that money affords. After all, it must be remembered that in Puerto Rico, too, the Negro achieved his freedom much later than the white, and that he had less opportunity to obtain property in the long period when Spanish and other colonists were consolidating their economic gains.

Let us for the moment assume this viewpoint. If we recall that superiority-inferiority feelings apparently remain strong between upper and lower strata, it follows that these feelings would apply to colored people if for no other reason than that many more of them are to be found in the lower than in the middle or upper levels. Thus a person of dark skin may be more or less automatically relegated to an inferior socioeconomic position by the casual observer. As one spokesman remarked, color may be a more effective badge than money, for at least you "can't see into a man's pocket."

Several white respondents did speak proudly of fellow citizens of dark complexion who hold prominent positions in the government, and of others who are successful business and professional people. A subcultural spokesman knew of a dark-skinned family that inherited a plantation from a Puerto Rican of Negroid stock who had himself once owned slaves. But class and status stratifications within the colored population have not produced anything like a caste system such as one finds in the Continental South, or in Chicago and New York. According to one leader, this could partly be explained by the fact that there are simply too few upper-level Negroes in Puerto Rico to make such a system workable.

So many citizens, moreover, reveal some pigmentation that, as another leader pointed out, light-brown color is seldom considered a mark of racial difference as it would be in the American South. Whether still another leader would be considered correct in his opinion that almost all are of mixed stock whose families have lived on the Island for several generations was not determined. Nor was the view explicitly supported by more than one leader that a major reason for the dearth of virulent racial prejudice in Puerto Rico, by comparison with the American South, is that there is a much smaller proportion of "pure" Negroes—only about 10 per cent—and thus less occasion to fear their potential power. This figure, as well as his contention, is of course debatable: the proportion of "pure" Negroes in either place is probably smaller than laymen unversed in anthropological evidence tend to assume.

What is scarcely debatable is the pronounced difference between the way Puerto Ricans and white-supremacy Southerners view the color problem—a difference exemplified by several respondents in the words *blanquito* and *negrito*. The former, although literally meaning "little white," sometimes implies disdain toward the well-dressed person of any color; while the latter, literally meaning "little black," may be a term of endearment for a person of any color. But both terms were said to vary in their shades of meaning according to the degree of friendship involved; the situation in which they are used affects their positive or negative connotation. Similarly with the word Negro: it is often resented by the dark Puerto Rican as connoting prejudice—almost akin to the North American word "nigger"—yet it may be applied by a friend to any person, black or white, to suggest a feeling of happy regard.

Several subcultural respondents of deep skin color had other revealing comments on this problem. In Cañamelar, where the percentage of colored people is higher than in most subcultures, whites (especially women) often intermarry with them—particularly, it was held, if thereby they are upgraded in status or class or both. Likewise, dating and dancing between racial groupings were reported as commoner than in either of the other two subcultures. (Two colored respondents said they had regularly dated whites.) A number at the grassroots also expressed the same opinion as most national leaders that whatever race prejudice remains tends to intensify with the rising status level.

The relatively minor importance attributed to race differences as a problem of vertical order may be suggested by the fact that only one respondent—himself the darkest of the entire group—thought that the improved condition of colored people should be counted as a major advancement of the last twenty years. By way of support, he pointed to laws against discrimination which have resulted, for example, in the wide employment of colored policemen. Interestingly, they were reported to marry teachers frequently, partly because the two professions are as yet considered relatively equal in status.*

WHAT IS THE SIGNIFICANCE OF THE MIDDLE STRATUM?

But it is not only those of substantial Negroid strain that have more expectation than earlier in their history of rising from lower to higher

* For further discussion of race, see pp. 103–105, 112–113.

levels in the vertical order of their culture; many citizens of all colorations have such an expectation. A large majority of respondents agreed that the middle groups are the fastest growing of all groups in the culture. A minority, themselves lower-stratum respondents, insisted that theirs is still the fastest growing.

But the question was not asked with sufficient precision. In terms of sheer numbers, the minority is probably right, but in proportional terms it seems probable that the middle levels, although by no means an entirely new phenomenon in Puerto Rico, have recently expanded most rapidly. Such expansion, however, was held to be faster in its own lower echelons than in its higher. That is, many more people have climbed to the lower-middle rung of the socioeconomic ladder (to white-collar jobs, especially) than to the upper-middle rung.

This booming middle group already acquires dramatic significance. It is demanding and getting more education and a higher standard of living than ever before. One leader thought that the influence of migration in developing equalitarian attitudes was partly responsible for its growth. Others held that it is beginning to question governmental policies more freely than a few years ago—not only their "socialist tendencies," as one respondent put it, but increased taxes. To paraphrase another respondent, the party in power has taught voters how to be intelligently critical, and they are—increasingly so. To paraphrase still another, the lower classes are taxed very little for the abundant services, such as public housing, which have been provided by the government in power; the upper classes can afford and ought to pay heavier taxes than they do; but the middle classes, though they still have relatively meager incomes by Continental standards, suffer severely in proportion to their capacity to pay.

Several informants were certain that the heaviest vote for the Republican party in the last election was a protest vote of citizens on the middle levels. Yet it would be incorrect to say that the majority of such citizens have turned away from the Popular Democratic party. For example, nearly all of our lower-middle and upper-middle subcultural respondents were as devoted supporters as the majority of the national panel. But a number on both panels expressed sharp reservations perhaps symptomatic of a freshly critical mood toward the government which, several would also probably admit, has boosted their recent upward climb.

Three further qualifications suggested by a discerning leader help to underscore the difficulty of generalization about any stratum in Puerto Rico, middle or otherwise. One was that different people tend to emphasize different factors in considering the problem of stratification. Thus, while he found at least four factors at work in Puerto Rico—namely, family, education, wealth, and color—no one factor may invariably be placed ahead of another in any judgment about who belongs where. Social status and economic class, for example, may coincide in a particular individual or group, but not necessarily. In Puerto Rico, according to another leader, they frequently do not.

The second qualification was that, because of numerous subcultures, it is often difficult to ascertain that a vertical classification appropriate to one part of the Island would be appropriate to another. Take an example or two. The "richest man in town," according to Cañamelar respondents, owned less than two hundred acres of land—a small amount indeed by comparison with, say, the *hacienda* owners of San José, but large in the eyes of the propertyless "rural proletariat" who are predominant. Even he, however, was regarded as enjoying less social status than his son (the municipal doctor) despite the latter's reputedly smaller income. Again, two rural Cañamelar respondents, both elementary teachers, considered themselves of middle status; yet, if judged by color and caliber of home, it is quite likely that they would be classified as upper-lower in a large urban center such as San Juan. It is worth adding that only a few persons in their community, unless we include plantation officials, were said to earn more than they: the owner of a small grocery store, a *publico* (bus) driver, and several women factory workers.

The third qualification was that not only the vertical order itself but the criteria of status and class evaluation are shifting. As one respondent put it, "clean hands" are no longer so important a token of one's position as the kind of skill a person has acquired. This is only to say that older attitudes toward work and leisure as marks of status are decreasingly important in a culture increasingly influenced by technology and democratic attitudes.

HOW DOES THE CLASS STRUCTURE BEAR UPON EDUCATION?

By comparison with the range of reactions to various other questions on the problem of stratification, informants were remarkably harmonious on the question of the teacher's place. They agreed that the great bulk of teachers cluster in the middle range, with slight variation upward and more so downward. University professors, for example, gravitate upward even as high, according to one leader, as lower-upper. (This opinion was opposed by another leader who held that even they are chiefly lower-middle.)

Moreover, though elementary teachers were said to enjoy higher prestige in rural communities than urban teachers do in theirs, nevertheless within the profession itself urban high school teachers enjoy the highest professional prestige. The "single salary scale," to be sure, applies to all teaching groups of parallel qualifications. But secondary teachers often receive higher pay because of more education, more experience, or both—their status being higher for all of these reasons.

On an Insular basis, the profession would be regarded as mainly lower-middle by our panels. Only one respondent held that the bulk of teachers are on the upper-lower level, while another emphasized that teachers tend to rate themselves considerably higher—that is, upper-middle—than would other citizens on this or higher levels. Moreover, as men and women from the lower levels move into the educational profession from still lower levels—and many do, including a larger ratio of colored than of white citizens—the traditional prestige of the profession was said to diminish.

Finally, the point made above that subcultures may differ sharply in their estimation of class and status levels would seem to apply to teachers. Thus, in a rural subculture one respondent, a high school teacher, was sure that he would be ranked as upper-middle by the community, most citizens of which have markedly less education and less income than he. Yet that he would be ranked above the lower-middle level by an urban middle-class community is not at all certain.

If we assume that teachers cluster mainly in the middle range, the question arises whether this has influenced their attitudes toward children in their classrooms, many of whom in the public schools are still on class and status levels somewhat below them. The point is important because, according to studies made in the United States, the middle status of the great majority of teachers affects their reactions to the intelligence, habits, and values of lower-level students—often more negatively than positively—and thus tends to generate emotional biases and misjudgments of ability or character. Respondents were, as a rule, unable to answer the question succinctly, partly perhaps because no careful examination of the matter has thus far been undertaken in Puerto Rico.

A number did offer the conjecture that the problem would tend to be less serious than on the Continent because a larger proportion of Insular teachers have themselves risen from the level of their students; therefore they can understand them from their own comparable experience. Quite an opposite inference, however, was drawn by one leader: he cited graphic examples of teachers who, though they had come from lower-stratum families, revealed intense hostility to lower-level habits and attitudes, as though in rebellion against them.

Another leader was fearful that a profession with such strong middle-status aspirations would indoctrinate children too narrowly in these aspirations. But his concern would be doubted by the rather caustic view of still another: it is impossible for teachers to indoctrinate their own attitudes and values, for the simple reason that both of the latter as yet are too amorphous, too uncongealed.

At present, problems of class and race, although by no means totally ignored, were said to receive much too limited attention in the schools and colleges. Young citizens require more informed views on the relation of the tax program to the class structure, for example. There is need, too, for a more sensitive policy of wide interstatus and interracial representation in administrative posts of the Department of Education. Slower upgrading of colored than of white teachers was also charged by one leader. An educational philosophy that transcends all class allegiances was urged by another. But only one member of either panel took occasion to note the requirement of similar school dress as an equalizing policy already in effect.

The middle-level orientation of the profession is further indicated by responses to this question: Should the teachers of Puerto Rico continue to endorse the policies of their present organization, which not only includes both teachers and administrators but appears to be largely controlled by the latter group? Or should they follow the example of some 50,000 Continental teachers and affiliate with the American Federation of Teachers, itself attached to the joint American Federation of Labor and Congress of Industrial Organizations, and controlled entirely by teachers? The chief intent of the question was to determine further whether or not Puerto Rican teachers regard themselves as essentially white-collar workers, with problems and obligations so closely related to those of other wage earners as to require the common interest and support of organized labor.

Many respondents replied, in one way or another, that the teaching profession would consider labor affiliation a downgrading of their status. In Cañamelar, the subculture with more labor strength than the other two, a substantial number of teachers refused to attend a party given to them by the local union during our field work, although their motives were not made clear. One respondent there estimated, however, that about half the teachers of the municipality could be persuaded to join a labor-affiliated teachers' union. But a much smaller proportion of our two panels endorsed such a move: a quarter of the national panel (one hoped that the leadership of organized labor would also be improved thereby) and less than that fraction of subcultural respondents. Of these, but one respondent from each group was hopeful of such a step in the near future.

Opposition was based on several arguments, none of them unanimously supported. One: no government employees should organize as a union or have the right to strike. (A strike of teachers some years ago is still recalled with conflicting emotions.) Two: fully granting the need for substantially better remuneration than the present average of about $2,000 per year, teachers who used the techniques of organized labor to gain higher salaries would badly upset the economy. Three: teachers should not, on principle, identify themselves with any one section of the population, however admirable organized labor may be as an instrument of economic democracy. (One other leader took the anomalous position that, while teachers should have the right to strike, they should not affiliate with labor.) A number of respondents on both levels also expressed admiration for achievements of the Puerto Rican Teachers Association—its medical plan was especially praised—but they were critical of what they regarded as narrow, politically slanted leadership.

Organized labor is sufficiently important, at least in some parts of Puerto Rico, that it also seemed desirable to a few grassroots respondents to provide curricular units in the functions and duties of, say, the sugar-cane unions, which children have opportunity to observe first-hand. As far as could be learned, even schools in strongly unionized communities pay no concerted attention to these matters, despite the fact that many students may follow their fathers into the unions.

For similar reasons, it was suggested that the adult-education program of these communities give more attention to workers' education —that is, to discussion courses and projects for local union members. At present, union meetings (some of which are held in Cañamelar at five A.M. before the sugar-cane cutter's day begins) deal with a variety of problems affecting not only union but civic welfare. But little organized workers' education has thus far been attempted. (One series of meetings has been held in Cañamelar.) And even where local unions have rendered support to their public schools, labor leaders, we were told, are rarely if ever utilized as resource persons in studying labor's role in the community.

Several respondents on both panels also pressed for more and better vocational and commercial courses. Progress has been made in meeting such needs. But, if the respondents who discussed them are correct, none of the present efforts begins to fill one of the greatest gaps— namely, vocational preparation integrated with a modern liberal-arts program on the senior high school level, with adequate facilities (such as modern office equipment in commercial courses) for preparing young people to meet growing demands for technological proficiency. The point is pertinent because, as many high schools are now organized, students have no choice but a liberal-arts curriculum. This may encourage upper-class economic ambitions. It may even be suitable for upper-status social life. But it is not, we were informed, necessarily adapted to young people better qualified to become electricians, mechanics, stenographers, and similar types of skilled workers on upper-lower or lower-middle levels.

One other educational issue was raised in connection with vertical order—whether or not private schools are more of a divisive or a cohesive force. The majority of those to whom the question was addressed agreed that private schools tend to divide classes because they encourage the middle and upper classes to separate their children from those of the lower classes who cannot afford tuitions. Indeed, as one grassroots spokesman put it, the public school population is becoming more and more heavily concentrated in the lower classes.

Yet it is noteworthy that many of our respondents with sufficient incomes send or plan to send their children to private schools. Others said they would like to do so if they could afford the tuition and if oftener available in small towns. Their principal reason was that the overcrowded condition of the public schools, added to "double sessions" and teaching staffs with meager training, reluctantly forced this choice upon them.

To be sure, several leaders spoke praisingly of their own education in the public schools of an earlier day when, they said, standards and learning conditions were better than now, and when children of every class mingled freely with every other. All of them hoped that in time (perhaps ten years, according to one estimate) the public schools will provide classes of moderate size, full-day sessions, well-trained teachers, abundant books and other materials. Even now, at least one leader would, on principle, send his children to public schools if they provided busses for transportation—a service normally offered by the private schools.

But the picture is distorted until it is pointed out that private schools were favored for other reasons than the limited facilities of public ones. Several respondents asserted that more and more people even of lower-middle income are sending their children to private schools, especially in the urban areas, because opportunity is thereby provided for upgrading through social intercourse with children of the upper levels. Others contended that standards of instruction are measurably higher, especially in the teaching of English, which, in some, is the first language—a contention which, it was said, can be supported by the higher ratings that private school graduates attain upon entering the University.

Almost no one argued that another advantage of the private schools is that, since most of them are parochial (a few Protestant, the rest Catholic), religious instruction is added to their curricula. Nor was the point strongly emphasized by most respondents, although it was made by a small minority of leaders, that private schools, especially if nonsectarian, could offer richer opportunities for experimentation with frontier methods of learning and teaching than the uniform Insular policies of the public schools.

Dissenting opinions on this issue reveal it to be controversial. Some spokesmen questioned whether, by and large, the educational quality of private schools is higher than the public schools; in support of their skepticism, they pointed out that Catholic parochial schools are often staffed by nuns trained in highly traditional, if not outmoded,

European methods of rote learning and rigid discipline. One grass-roots respondent mentioned that by no means all private schools provide all-day sessions; they may even be partly staffed by fatigued public school teachers who bolster their meager incomes by working in them during their "free" hours.

On the positive side, others pointed out that private schools are beginning to provide scholarships for children of low-income families in order to spread the class representation of their student bodies. It is a practice which, however, was said to be as yet extremely limited and, if one respondent is correct, even circumvented for a time by at least one private school which set up segregated quarters for students from the lower strata. One leader insisted that the charge of class divisiveness is invalid in the case of Catholic University, to which students of all classes are welcome.

The single most controversial argument in favor of private schools was that they provide more opportunity for discussion of opposing political and economic viewpoints than do the public schools. According to the leader who offered this argument, the Popular Democratic party has utilized such organs as *Escuela* and *Semana* ("School" and "Week")—publications of the Department of Education circulated as a reading aid and current-events resource—as a sounding board for its own program, and that it has minimized and even excluded the viewpoints and information offered by minority parties. (This criticism had the support, though less vehemently, of a second leader.) Private schools on all levels, including higher education, therefore have the important role to play of encouraging dissent, and of offering opportunity for present minorities to develop into new majorities.

As for educational recommendations that emerged from the dispute over private and public schools, several should be recorded. Scholarships more generously provided by private schools would tend to equalize class representation in their student bodies. Regularly planned opportunities for students and teachers of private schools to visit public schools, and vice versa, would help to break down barriers based on stereotypes and lack of information. The need for experimental private schools would seem to require serious attention, since none as yet operate in any systematic way. Such schools might well be encouraged and supported by the Department of Education or by teacher-training institutions as laboratories for the testing of proposals that could, if proved effective, then be adopted on an Insular scale.

The most crucial of all recommendations is obviously hardest to implement—to build the best possible public school system that the education-dedicated people of Puerto Rico can possibly provide. No other answer to the issue of private schools began to compare with it in importance among our respondents. And no other gained more vehement support.

THE CLASS PROBLEM IN NORMATIVE PERSPECTIVE

Keeping in mind the many deviations and disagreements, let us highlight the greater or lesser consensuses that have appeared in the course of this chapter. In seeking to answer the question "Where is power concentrated?" our panels inclined toward the judgment, though by no means unqualifiedly, that it rests chiefly in the hands of the leadership of the Popular party—leadership characterized more by upper-middle status than by comparable middle-class economic power.* No one disagreed, however, that the majority of lower-status and lower-class citizens have given the party a clear mandate to exert its authority—economically and otherwise.

Top-level groups are also to be distinguished by status and class. Those of highest prestige were said to consist largely of old conservative, often pro-Franco families of proud Spanish background, some of them much less wealthy than *nouveaux riches* professionals, industrialists, and others. *Americanos* among the latter groups are now often accepted socially by these old families. Superiority attitudes of top-level groups toward low-level groups were said to be common—at least as much so as inferiority attitudes on the part of the latter toward the former. Apparently, however, both sorts of attitudes are being tempered by equalitarian and other democratic values which the party itself has sought to inculcate in people of all levels.

A striking lack of agreement prevailed as to whether and how far class conflict or consciousness of such conflict is prevalent. Organized labor, to be sure, was widely approved, despite criticisms of its leaders and of labor's internal divisions. But such approval seemed to emanate more from the present conciliatory tactics of unions than from any

* The Governor's salary, according to *Time,* is $10,000 a year. "His wealth, as itemized before the 1956 election, consisted of $562 and a house with 16 years yet to go on its FHA mortgage; when he went to New York recently, he bought tickets on a fly-now-pay-later basis."[2]

manifestations of militancy. If anything, employer groups, especially expatriated Spaniards, were more severely criticized—especially for their alleged callousness toward farm and factory workers.

One of the few questions able to evoke near unanimity concerned the relation of race to stratification. Nearly all respondents agreed that, while people of dark complexion tend to fill lower positions than those of light complexion (though there are many exceptions), public attitudes toward them are rarely the effect of race prejudice. If a Negro is regarded with inferiority feelings, it is probably because of the supposition that he is low in the socioeconomic scale.

An almost equally large consensus prevailed that the middle groups are now growing rapidly in size and influence. As they do so, they tend to be increasingly critical of the Popular party for its tax and other programs that favor lower-income groups. The largest protest vote comes from the middle levels.

Turning to education, teachers, we were told, cluster predominantly in the lower-middle range, a fact that probably helps to account for doubts shared by the majority of both panels that the profession would welcome affiliation with organized labor. Awareness of class, race, and labor issues by both teachers and students, however, was held to be deficient, as were adult programs for workers and vocational programs in liberal-arts high schools. The spread of private schools, meanwhile, was felt by some though not all spokesmen to have intensified class divisiveness by tending to separate children of the middle and upper levels from those of the lower. But all of these problems were considered remediable in time through enriched curricula in problems of stratification, better teacher training, and equalization of educational standards and privileges for children of all levels.

How shall we appraise these findings? The fluid quality of vertical order, with its relatively rapid shifting of levels, is essential to the development of socioeconomic democracy in Puerto Rico. Strata are by no means rigid, and opportunities for those of the lowest classes and statuses to climb at least one or two rungs up the social ladder are one of the primary achievements and hopes of the day. The remarkable scholarship program is perhaps as fine an index to the present situation as any that could be named.

And yet, again in terms of the theory of culture and education

governing this study, certain doubts are inescapable, some of which—
the race question is one—are better left for later comment. Here we
limit our concern chiefly to the inability of our panels to reach any
kind of consensus on the disturbing issue of conflict between classes.
Superiority-inferiority feelings affected by levels were, to be sure, admitted rather freely. Also, especially in the Cañamelar area, some
awareness of class conflict was perceptible. For the most part, however,
neither the meaning of this phenomenon nor any precise estimate of
how prevalent it might be could easily be inferred.

The point is important because, granting that class conflict is not
acute in any *overt* way (strikes, we recall, have recently been few),
still in Puerto Rico no less than in many other countries *covert* forms
of conflict may be quite another matter. Consider as an example the
tremendous profits made by North American-owned businesses established on the Island in the past few years, and compare these with
the wages paid to their workers who have, to a high degree, made
these profits possible. The persuasive argument that such a program
has been necessary to provide employment is not, for the moment,
apropos. Let it, indeed, be granted. What is apropos are two basic
questions. First, can this disparity mean that employer and employee
enjoy a completely common interest, or does it mean that their deeper
interests, however often inarticulate, are in opposition? Second, do
the workers in these and other factories have opportunity to consider
in any guided way what the former question involves or how it might
be dealt with?

The second question is easier to answer than the first. With meager
exceptions at most, and despite commendable efforts of a special
agency (the Labor Relations Institute of the University), workers'
education that deals with controversial issues of this kind—or indeed
of any kind—has reached as yet but a minute fraction of the adult
working people. For that matter, we are doubtful from the evidence
provided us that such issues are considered forthrightly even in the
social-studies courses open to their children.

Returning to the first question, many will of course insist that employer and employee do enjoy a common interest. Certainly this is
the proper answer for those who accept the historic assumptions of a
competitive enterprise system. Leaders of any educational program devoted to fair inquiry rather than to indoctrination of official or other-

wise dominant policy will admit, however, that these assumptions are open to debate. Indeed, according to, say, the theory of a public enterprise system or, for that matter, of the Rochdale type of cooperative system now growing in Puerto Rico itself, the answer to the question is that employer-employee interests in privately owned and controlled factories fundamentally conflict.

The important point at the moment is not who does or who does not have the soundest answer to this far from simple question. Rather it is that, according to our evidence, the whole significance of class conflict and class interests in Puerto Rico—their causes and effects— remains in an amorphous state. Such lack of clarity is, we think, dangerous. Recognition of legitimate class interests and of organized action, especially by the working people to protect and promote those interests, is essential to achieving any kind of industrial democracy worthy of the name.

The issue we have raised may be pursued in another direction with the example of the class and status attitudes of teachers—attitudes which, we have found, are oriented primarily toward middle-level roles. One consequence is that their own standards of, say, correct behavior may run counter to those of public school students who remain predominantly influenced by lower-status backgrounds. Despite the inclination of most respondents to minimize this problem, we suspect (in the light of Continental studies[3]) that another respondent was more nearly right in attributing invidious if not insidious status feelings to many Puerto Rican teachers in their attitudes toward students. The question needs probing by means of careful educational research, for, if the suspicion is confirmed, different kinds of conflict than those merely between economic classes—emotional kinds, primarily—are sure to result.

Another consequence of middle-stratum values among teachers is the incompatibility that may result, consciously or not, between their desire to enjoy prestige as middle-level citizens (many teachers, we recall, have risen from lower levels) and their equal desire for remuneration commensurate with the imperative services they render. In the latter desire, they are more like than different from others who work for wages. In the former, they permit nonmaterial satisfactions obtained from sharing in upward mobility to dim their perception both of their economic interests and of how to act concertedly so that those interests could be properly rewarded. One result is, of course, that the earnings of teachers are frequently less than those of, say, organized mechanics.

Granting all the obstacles in the way of an adequate salary scale, it has not apparently occurred to most teachers to consider their *class* position. Their Insular organization reveals little of the philosophy or strategy of a democratic union geared to the present dynamic program of the total culture. At the least, then, more discussion of the pros and cons of labor affiliation for teachers would seem to be called for. Whether they are properly defined as white-collar workers, for example, and whether they should "take sides" for or against so important an institution as organized labor, are questions that cannot be answered satisfactorily until they are much more often critically examined—especially by those responsible for professional teacher training.

Back of these and other issues is the question of what kind of vertical order the culture should aim to achieve. The belief of some—perhaps many—citizens besides teachers that middle-stratum standards and practices are the best of all possible norms is clearly an appealing one. Yet, as we shall have further occasion to observe,* such a goal already disturbs some of the most thoughtful leaders. Should the historic attitudes and habits of the countryman and his urban cousin of the lower strata then be submerged? Is the North American middle class the model to be emulated? And, as middle groups grow and consolidate their strength, what of the program of social reform that the taxes of these groups have helped so greatly to promote?

By contrast with a middle-level norm, the conception that we believe is closer to the spirit of many Puerto Ricans and (despite its own middle-range propensities) of the vested political authority is one which, while embracing all levels, first of all assures that the working and farming people share increasingly and proportionately in all cultural resources. For them this really means, of course, not weaker but stronger and clearer organized power, not lower but higher progressive income taxes, not narrower but wider experimental public enterprises and cooperatives, not feebler but more vigorous social reforms.[4] And education's role in implementing this conception can be nothing short of crucial—an education that not only attacks every problem germane to the nature of class relations, divisions, conflicts, and objectives, but shares throughout in their solution.

* See pp. 166–167, 169–171, 189, 202–204.

CHAPTER FIVE

HOW DO PUERTO RICANS LOOK UPON THEIR HISTORY?

PUERTO RICO, like every culture, has a past, a present, and a future. It lives and grows in time as well as in space. Even the preceding two chapters, though they deal primarily with spatial order, are compelled to recognize how previous events condition current patterns and anticipate things to come. The temporal dimension of cultural order has, however, been subordinated thus far so that we might view some of its features as they look to us in space.

The present chapter aims to correct this one-sidedness, with particular regard for historical relations. We are not concerned to write a history of the Island; this could not be accomplished in brief compass even were we competent to attempt it. Rather, we are interested in a few of the fundamental ways that citizens view the temporal dimension as integral to understanding of the culture to which they belong and upon which they exert influence by virtue of their belonging.

In order to focus upon this large problem, four issues must suffice: first, how significant the past may be to the shaping of the culture's present and future; second, whether it is possible to decide upon the most powerful causes that have operated in the Island's history; third, what progress means to Puerto Ricans and, related to this question, how legitimate it is to predict events ahead; and fourth, the significance of temporal order for the school program.

On the whole, we support the dominant judgments of our panels on these issues where they approach consensuses. In essence, they incline to be more hopeful about the emerging culture than adulatory toward its long record—a hopefulness that they would like education to share more enthusiastically. For our part, we would insist even more strongly than they upon a future-oriented policy—certainly in education. The more clearly that such a policy is crystallized, the greater the possibilities that present predictions will prove to be future realities. For agreement upon the kind of ends that the Puerto Rican people want to win tomorrow is imperative to their agreement upon the kind of means that they must fashion and exercise today.

THE IMPORTANCE OF THE PAST

Through well over four centuries, Puerto Rico was a country subjugated by colonial powers which made most of its rules from abroad and determined how most of its people should live and die. Like all summary statements this one must of course be qualified: many fascinating events have been recorded by historians.[1] What historians cannot deny, however, is that Puerto Rico, unlike some other countries in the Caribbean or Central or South America, never achieved a major revolt against its oppressors. Although there were abortive attempts, no social cataclysm, no upsurge of the masses such as occurred in Haiti, for example, is described in its archives. Even its capture by the United States was accompanied by a minimum of bloodshed or resistance. It has even been argued, though not without strenuous objection, that the spirit of romance which fires a people proud of their story of courage and sacrifice against tyrannical foes has been difficult to kindle in the typical Puerto Rican heart.[2]

Would a more vivid history be an important asset to the order now evolving? This question, like others in this chapter, was not raised as persistently with subcultural as with national-level respondents. Fewer of the latter, at any rate, agreed that it would be such an asset than those who believed it would not. While at least one leader felt that a more "authentic" culture could have emerged had its history been richer, and another held that a weak history tends to reduce Insular resistance to Mainland influence, most respondents were unconvinced that a past marked by civil wars or revolutions, by traumas and violence—however heroic the story might have been—would necessarily have produced a finer culture than the comparatively prosaic past that has been alleged. The commonest reason offered for satisfaction, however, was not so much the cost in destruction and suffering that would have been paid as the lack of fanatical fixation on bygone glories. A consequence is more resilience, readier adaptability, to the far-reaching reconstructions that now preoccupy the majority of people.

Still, it is one thing to contend that an unexciting history may be advantageous and another thing to dismiss as unimportant whatever history there is. None of the leaders did dismiss history in this way. Where they disagreed was on the issue of *how* important—how far it is to be taken into account in the remaking of their culture. One spoke of a temptation to overindulge in Puerto Rican history to "compensate" for its actual thinness. Another held that the greatest weakness in its pacifistic past is its lack of experience with crisis situations. Several, however, insisted that the Island, granting that its career has been less colorful than some of its neighbors', does nevertheless have a record of significant events that needs to be known and appreciated as integral to its character. After all, how could it be otherwise for a nation with so long a history?

Spanish traditions, it was pointed out, have played a tremendous role. Nor are legends and folklore as meager as some critics have contended. Moreover, even if relatively little might be said for the sixteenth to eighteenth centuries, the nineteenth and early twentieth centuries developed distinguished figures (to mention only Ramón Power, Ruíz Belvis, Acosta, Quiñones, de Hostos, de Diego, and Muñoz Rivera) who were forefathers of the present democratic leadership in demanding better education, a clearer voice in government, and—perhaps most successfully—the peaceful freeing of some 30,000 slaves. The strains and suspicions that prevailed between the urban population concentrated in San Juan and the rest of the people scattered in smaller towns and rural areas were also noted as conditioning factors in shaping the Island's course.

The very fact of Puerto Rico's isolation was held to be historically pertinent. It became a haven for thousands of people trying to escape the chaos of other Latin American countries torn by revolutions—a partial explanation, one leader held, for the nonviolent attitudes of past generations and thus largely for those of the present generation. Combined with other immigrants from Corsica, Mallorca, the Canary Islands, and elsewhere—most of whom were hard-working people who sought only to build modest homes for their families and to live in peace—these refugees from turmoil helped to produce a relatively more stable population than was typical of adjacent cultures.

To this could be added the intriguing observation of a Cañamelar respondent. While he did not speak of other parts of the country, he was convinced that in that subculture, at least, the contributions of

European families to the "precorporation" period were invaluable. Not only Spanish but French, English, and German families settled there and brought with them many trades and skills—blacksmithing (one of the old blacksmiths of that period still lives in the town), tailoring, and saddlemaking, among others. These artisans trained apprentices who, in turn, contributed to the industrious, patient habits of life which so many respondents stressed.

What of the arts in Insular history? Little if anything, all leaders agreed, can be discovered in music, painting, or literature that deserves to be ranked with the works of modern European masters. The first book by a native writer, one recalled, was published hardly more than a century ago. There has never been a definitive "school" of Puerto Rican painting. Nor can it be said that a folk art ever developed that could be compared with, say, that of Mexico, where—granting unparallel conditions—the Indians survived and managed to preserve more than a little of their aboriginal genius. True, admiration was expressed particularly for one writer and one composer of the past—de Hostos and Campos, respectively—and several mentioned dance and dramatic contributions. On the whole, nevertheless, the estimate was a humble one.

Yet even here some leaders were readier than others to highlight the historic place of the arts. As one argued, the United States has not produced a Shakespeare either, but this is far from meaning that it has been aesthetically moribund. In the same way that Puerto Rico's political background, though less brilliant than some might wish, still deserves attention and appreciation, so too does its artistic background.

In general, however, there was more concern to assure sufficient attention to historic influences other than those of the arts. One leader even considered the lack of indigenous architectural forms to be advantageous, because the design of modern buildings (there are already a striking number) need not be encumbered by customary notions of what beautiful buildings should be. The same opportunity may emerge in other arts—indeed, there are signs that it is already beginning in music, the dance, literature, and painting. Even new centers of craftsmanship—fiber weaving is one, pottery another—are taking hold and showing signs of creative expression that could be all the fresher for being less imitative than in a culture harnessed to traditional craft practices.

All in all, the commonest position was probably well stated by a spokesman for the "golden mean" toward Puerto Rican history. It must neither be inflated out of proportion to its real importance nor deflated less than it deserves. Even the new Institute of Puerto Rican Culture must be as much concerned, another leader said, to preserve and esteem recent achievements in, say, industrial development as more venerable monuments such as churches and forts. To relegate the Island's history to an insignificant footnote or to suppose that it has "sprung from a vacuum" is to run the risk of losing all sense of cultural self-consciousness. But to exaggerate or sentimentalize that history is to run the opposite risk of being enslaved by a past which, if our informants have assessed it soundly, is entitled to respect but scarcely to adulation.

THE CAUSES OF PUERTO RICO'S HISTORY

The issue here is the elusive one of whether it is possible to decide on the most fundamental cause or causes that brought Puerto Rico to its present stage of evolution. As would be true among philosophers of history as well as anthropologists, leader respondents were far from any consensus on this issue. Formal education, with emphasis by some upon the University and its research program especially in social science, was selected slightly oftener than others as the primary cause. But leadership and economic-political forces were selected almost as often. One argued that occupation by the United States should be placed first, while two others held that several causes were so intertwined that to select any as dominant would be indefensible. Six related causes were mentioned by these "historical pluralists": the Hispanic background of Puerto Rico, the French and American revolutions, economic factors, climate, African immigration, and the American political, economic, and educational systems.

It is evident from this compilation that many respondents were thinking more of the twentieth century than of the span of nearly half a millennium—an understandable limitation in view of the fact that the most dramatic transformations have occurred in this brief period. Formal education, for example, could hardly be regarded as a primary cause before 1900, since the overwhelming majority up to and even beyond that date were illiterate.

Among the few who replied to the question with a longer time span in mind, only two—both social scientists—could be said to approach "economic determinism" (the familiar doctrine that the instruments of production are more crucial than any other forces in shaping human history); yet even they modified their preference by citing other factors. Nor did most respondents appear to support the ecological hypothesis of the Steward research team. True, several admitted that productive forces are exceedingly important, but the most they would concede was that at least one other cause—namely, leadership—should be placed on a par with the economic environment. In view of the predominantly Roman Catholic background of the Island, it is also striking that no one took the contrasting view from economic determinists—namely, that it is spiritual forces in the universe that determine the course of history. Only one informant might have implied it.

The exceptional importance attached to leadership by both panels receives further attention shortly.* In connection with the problem of historical causation, a few respondents were inclined to place leadership first, though only one held that it was the primary force in the nineteenth as well as the twentieth century, and another generalized further by insisting that the very existence of civilization today depends upon less than one hundred leaders. A large majority did hold that leadership in the past two decades—most prominently represented by the present Governor—has been a potent influence.

But the majority could not agree on the precise extent of this influence. Some pointed out that the Popular party, although bolstered by the experience of able leaders in the socialist and other political movements out of which it grew, came to power at a time when President Roosevelt and the New Deal were prepared to support Puerto Rican reforms with vigor and money. Also, technological development was accelerating—a development that was radically altering many other undeveloped regions but that enabled Puerto Rico to move more swiftly than most because of North American backing and prosperity. Moreover, mass migration would have occurred anyway: overpopulation and underemployment have forced it upon many thousands. Even the "liberalization" of human rights, such as political participation, would have come to the Island, it was argued, if for no other reason than that this was "in the air" and could scarcely have by-passed a country so immersed in the democratic climate of the age.

Such minimizations of leadership as a major cause of recent history

* See pp. 100–101.

were counterbalanced by more generous estimates. Granting that the Governor and his associates had the advantage of "lucky breaks," the fact that they were ready and available was also a "lucky break." The exhilarating mood of the culture, several felt, must be attributed in no small measure to the talent of its foremost leader to express in everyday language the needs and rights of common people, and to encourage them to think matters out for themselves.

And even granting that the broad features of the Commonwealth program would have come about regardless of particular leaders, there is no certainty whatever that its timing would have been similar; on the contrary, a considerable period might have elapsed before anything like the present stage were reached. Nor should we forget the encouragement and financial support provided able young men and women to prepare both there and in Continental universities for political and administrative service on the Island. One informant, indeed, went so far as to contend that "intellectuals" have been more influential than any other cause of its renascence.

The fact that some other countries have had rather similar advantages by way of outside economic support as well as a similar ecology and colonial background, and yet have failed to develop their democratic potentialities to anything like a comparable stage or in as spectacular a way, was cited by two respondents in support of the heavy impact that leadership has exerted. For them, it could be regarded as the single most decisive variable in accounting for the difference in recent history between Puerto Rico and, particularly, Cuba.*

THE PROBLEMS OF PREDICTION AND PROGRESS

Closely related to the problem of causation is that of prediction— of whether in the light of what Puerto Ricans know about their past and present they can go one step further and predict their future. One would suppose that the differences of opinion that prevailed about the causes of what *has* happened would produce comparable differences as to what *will* happen. This was not quite the case, however. While a minority of the leader panel rejected the possibility of any defensible predictions, and while even the majority were reluctant to

---

* It is likely that the 1958-59 revolution in Cuba will eventually justify a less negative comparison. That most people in Puerto Rico welcomed the overthrow of the Cuban dictatorship can be taken for granted.

anticipate the course of events with absolute assurance, many did express confidence that the decades ahead would be marked by expanding opportunity and a fuller, happier life for the masses of citizens.

This optimism was by no means merely wishful thinking. Several cited studies of trends in Puerto Rico that showed how, on the basis of recent growth, the standard of living will approximate present Continental standards at least by 1975. The amount of manufacturing capital invested per worker will be equal to that of the United States by 1965. And the income of the average worker will be double his current income in another decade.

At the same time, some respondents spoke of contingencies—depression and atomic war, worst of all—that could upset all calculations. Also, the future policies of Congress were considered by one leader as another serious contingency—especially with regard to whether these policies promoted, as he hoped, still closer ties with the United States or encouraged a resurgence of nationalism. Yet even the more cautious respondents seemed ready to emphasize strong probabilities. They held, for example, that serious depressions and inflation can now be controlled, and that atomic war is most unlikely because of mutual fear on the part of all nations that no one could win.

Several were willing to go further in their predictions. One respondent had no doubt that the rural population will continue to decline, a trend that he welcomed while also hoping for a more equitable balance between agricultural and industrial production than has thus far been attained. Comparably, another was sure that, regardless of what might happen to the political structure, industrialization would continue to expand, and as it does the cultural mores are bound to be modified further.

On a profounder level, still another respondent firmly predicted a more humane and democratic life for the Puerto Rican people because, he said, this is in accord with what we already know of their deepest natures and aspirations—an expectation that might be delayed but never destroyed by adverse circumstances. Equally provocative was the conviction of a peer that the present period of cultural experimentation, and the correlative habits of adaptability that develop in such an environment, make reasonably certain that the people can learn to adjust even to emergencies. Thus they can learn to protect themselves from the dire consequences that often result when a culture is too brittle or too static.

In view of the confident tone of well over half the leaders' replies to the problem of prediction, it is worth comparing replies at the grassroots. Of those who were asked the question, over twice as many questioned the legitimacy of prediction for Puerto Rico as accepted it. Significantly, to such contingencies as war they added the danger of earthquakes and hurricanes. The fact that these respondents or their families had probably more often than national leaders suffered directly from such devastation may help to explain their greater skepticism.

Related to prediction though by no means identical is the problem of progress—of whether it is reasonable to contend that the culture has been developing in fundamental ways from a worse to a better order of life. That human evolution has been, on the whole, melioristic or progressive has been, of course, a classical view in anthropology —that is, cultures are supposed to have evolved, granting many setbacks, from "savagery" through "barbarism" to "civilization." In presenting the problem to our leaders, however, they were reminded of the theory of Toynbee and other philosophers of history who sharply question the classical view when civilizations are studied in broad range. Nevertheless, as we might anticipate, answers were much more strongly affirmative than they were negative.

They supported their answers with a multitude of examples. Progress has occurred in economic expansion and family security; in human relations between races; in life expectancy; in sanitation and health; in tolerance and sympathy; in education and the development of talent; in transportation and housing; in social security for the young, the ill, and the aged; in nonsectarian Christian principles such as equality and concern for the weak and poor; in better and more abundant food; in service, cooperation, and participation; in political honesty and trust of government; in morality and art as these are affected by other progressive forces.

Such diverse examples are sufficient to reveal that progress was regarded both in "material" and "spiritual" terms. Only a small minority of leaders were inclined to divide one from the other in order to argue that, while the former kinds of progress are admirable enough, the latter are weaker if not at points regressive in Puerto

Rico—in the qualities, for example, of responsibility, aesthetic creativity, and family loyalty. And only three leaders were unsure whether it was possible to believe that progress is occurring when their culture is seen in the setting of modern world history, although one of these did go so far as to declare his confidence in the long-range progress of the Western Hemisphere. Against these doubts should be placed the outright repudiation, by another leader, of Toynbee's thesis that all known civilizations have passed through cycles of birth, growth, and decay.

Several respondents also sought to measure progress by more definite criteria. One contended that the first test (which he believed Puerto Rico meets) is the capacity of any culture to relate itself to other cultures without thereby either isolating itself or being "swallowed up" by the rest of the world. Others considered the test to be psychological and ethical: the increasingly free affirmation and enjoyment of human life in all its dimensions. Still another would add to this affirmation the growth of democracy as marked, above all, by widening participation in all kinds of institutional life—familial, educational, political. If applied to Puerto Rico such a criterion could mean that for him, and perhaps for other respondents, too much optimism prevails of the kind one notes in the United States with its notoriously naïve faith in the "inevitability of progress."

Even so, despite this possible frailty, it was impressive to observe the extent to which the concepts of prediction and progress were connected with the future dimension of time. As one leader expressed it, the absence of a thrilling revolutionary tradition may be compensated by the opportunity to create a unique kind in the decades ahead—an effort in which the Popular party today serves as the democratic but revolutionary vanguard. Such a conception would probably meet with the approval of at least two others who held that the history of Puerto Rico contributes to the total order only in so far as it is a forward-looking tool. It is a way of preparing for the future through perceiving the errors and achievements of dead and living generations.

WHAT ROLE SHOULD HISTORY PLAY IN EDUCATION?

The intriguing view just noted, that history should point ahead as well as behind, raises the practical question of how education ought to cope with the temporal perspective upon cultural order.

Subcultural respondents, many of whom we remember were closer to school practice than most national-level respondents, answered this question directly. A majority agreed that the urgencies of the current scene rather than the future should be the central interest of the educational program. In this preference, they tended to reflect the dominant philosophic orientation of progressive education on the Continent.[3] The view of one student respondent was thus perhaps typical: study of the future would be wasteful, since it would deprive the curriculum of time for study of present problems.

Nevertheless, a sizable minority were emphatic in holding that the future should be the educational focus—a viewpoint suggestive of what is sometimes called the reconstructionist philosophy of education.[4] Said one rural respondent: to teach for the future is the single most serious obligation of the elementary school, for the past of Puerto Rico is "no longer good." According to an administrator respondent this philosophy is already tacitly influential in the sense that about 20 per cent of the curriculum is now concerned with the past, 30 per cent with the present, and 50 per cent with the future— a distribution which, although debatable in fact, he thoroughly endorsed. Two others preferred an equal balance between present and future, but only one wished all three dimensions of time to receive the same attention. And only one, another rural respondent, reflected the essentialist philosophy of education[5] in its stress upon teaching the social heritage as the most solemn of the school's responsibilities.

We must not convey the impression that education of the Puerto Rican past had no importance for most of our grassroots panel. Their awareness of the meaning of science, to which we give attention in a subsequent place,* was indicated by several when they rightly noted that the method of experimentation—e.g., in medicine or social science—requires careful diagnosis of past events leading up to any present problematic situation. More than this, prediction itself demands such diagnosis; without it, no one can plan intelligently for what lies ahead.

Whether for this reason, or whether these respondents were simply inconsistent with their predominant concern for the present and future, a large majority advocated more study of Puerto Rican history in the schools than is presently the case. One elementary teacher re-

* See pages 117–130.

spondent wished to see carefully prepared units introduced into his own courses, where, he said, meager attention is paid except during special days that celebrate the birthday of de Hostos or other historical events. A high school teacher recommended that the present offering of one semester in North American history and one semester in Puerto Rican history be, in each case, expanded to a full-year course. His principal reason for the second half of his recommendation was that few migrants to the United States are prepared to explain to their new neighbors how Puerto Rico came to be the kind of culture it is. A student respondent urged wider study of world cultures and Puerto Rico's relations with them.

Before proper attention can be paid to the past, more satisfactory textbooks and other materials must be provided. While new texts were reported to be under way, and while better teaching of Insular history was said to be discernible than in years gone by, sharp criticism was heard on both levels of the most widely used textbook: it was written by a North American who knew too little and treated what he did know superficially. A higher appraisal was given a recent anthology of Latin American, including Puerto Rican, writers prepared by the Department of Education.

More attention, also, should be given to movements and forces in the Island's past rather than to individuals and isolated events. Too often, moreover, the stress has been upon Latin American history, with Puerto Rico treated incidentally. The need for a philosophic framework through which temporal aspects of the culture could be seen in perspective was stressed by one leader respondent, while another urged that Puerto Rico be studied as a "chapter" which has both influenced and been influenced by the whole story of Western culture. Several others wanted the contributions of the arts to be woven into the story —one leader urging that a historic survey of literature and other arts be provided not later than the third year of secondary school. But, again, caution was apparent: the danger of "fictionizing" by exaggerating Puerto Rican art and history must, at all costs, be avoided.

Ways of integrating the past with present-centered and future-centered education were suggested by a number of leaders. Radio and television programs could be prepared to inspire the adult population and develop clearer understanding and greater pride in its history. Such programs, as well as courses for school children, would be more challenging if current problems were the point of departure and return. Again, taking children out of the classrooms and into the community could help to develop historical-mindedness—especially so if teachers themselves were made more aware of the long chain of causes and effects always being forged in culture as in nature.

One final question: Are high school students capable of grasping such abstruse problems as historical causation, prediction, and progress? Or must these be left till later—till the University years, and even then perhaps confined to a few outstanding students?

The answer to the first question by the leaders' panel was, without exception, "yes," and so to the second, "no." But several went further. The earliest years of education—the nursery school is none too soon—should begin to weigh these problems, couched obviously in language appropriate to levels of maturation. Unless they are, the likelihood that high school or college can do so is accordingly reduced.

The difficulty, several insisted, is not that students are not intelligent enough. If one leader is right, many adolescents are at least as capable as persons he knows who have won Ph.D.'s. The difficulty rather is that too little opportunity is available for them to exercise or extend the intelligence they have. The causes of Insular history, for example, are as rarely examined carefully as is the question of prediction or progress even raised. The mass system of education forced upon the people by the circumstances of their impoverished past has neither thus far encouraged critical-mindedness and nonconformity among students, nor has it trained teachers to be keenly aware that historical issues prevail even when they know how to stimulate interest in such issues.

For one leader, therefore, the most pressing task is to provide teachers—especially in social studies—with more historical *substance*. Methods of teaching are important, to be sure, but these were alleged to occupy an already disproportionate place in the training program. It is not so much a question of the amount of history that is taught; in the opinion of another leader, this may already be quite ample. Rather the task is to assure skill and sensitivity combined with quality.

THE TEMPORAL DIMENSION OF PUERTO RICAN ORDER— A REAPPRAISAL

Although unanimity was once more rare, the following limited agreements have emerged from our four questions:

First, granting that Puerto Rican history may be less dramatic than that of countries with more violent or romantic pasts, this is an asset principally because it allows citizens to concentrate more of their energies on present tasks and future objectives. Respondents did not dismiss historic achievements in political, aesthetic, or other fields; they did usually try to keep them in modest perspective.

Second, no common conviction as to the central cause of Insular history thus far prevails. Education, leadership, and economic-political forces were oftenest stressed, though no one denied that all of these causes, as well as others, have had some effect.

Third, while prediction of Puerto Rico's future course is far from foolproof, careful studies by planning agencies were among the reasons advanced for confidence that the course of development now under way is not only likely to continue but rightly deserves to be called "progress"—a confidence, however, shared less enthusiastically by subcultural than by national-level spokesmen.

Fourth, education should concentrate its attention more on present problems of the culture than on either its past or future. At the same time, neither of the latter dimensions of time can properly be ignored. More effective and thorough treatment of history is essential; so too is study of all other basic problems of time-in-culture exemplified by the few we have raised.

As mentioned in our introduction, many of these judgments meet with our approval. We do, however, hold certain reservations. Let us proceed in the same order as above, with special regard for education.

The question of the importance of Puerto Rico's history to its present character is unlikely to be settled by polemical dispute—however intellectually provocative. We doubt, moreover, whether either the interjection of more and more history courses in the curriculum or of efforts by the Institute of Puerto Rican Culture to glorify traditions (by no means its only purpose, to be sure) is the most effective way to develop legitimate concern with the temporal dimension.

Rather, the need confronting education on all levels is to provide constant opportunity—there is little at present—to bring the past to bear upon present and future tasks. This can seldom be accomplished by walling off historical resources into separate bodies of subject matter; it can best be done when these resources are utilized in virtually every phase of the curriculum. The point implied by several respondents that scientific prognosis first requires diagnosis, and that diagnosis in turn requires historical analysis, applies to problems of a culture just as well as to organic disease. That specialized courses in Puerto Rican history, and even more in its relations to Latin American and world history, also have a place especially in the higher learning is undeniable. But for the average student this is not the primary requirement. Though he, too, needs not less but more awareness of the Island's past, he will best obtain that awareness only as he perceives its relevance to his own life and therefore to his own and others' interests.

As to the issue of historical causation, the wide range of views indicates not only that the issue is as difficult to resolve in Puerto Rico as it is in, say, the United States; it likewise indicates a need for much more critical attention to the conflicting claims of alternative explanations. The causal influence attributed to "education," for example, appears to us naïve unless education is more comprehensively defined as a universal instrument of cultural permanence and change. Likewise, the heavy stress placed by a minority of leaders upon a kind of "great man theory of history" is open to grave doubt—much more so, we believe, than the contrastingly feeble stress placed upon the power of socioeconomic forces. The Steward type of ecological hypothesis, for example, has not apparently influenced our panels as much as it deserves. Without going so far as to assert that geographic-productive patterns are the sufficient cause of Insular history (our sympathies here are with the pluralistic views of several respondents), we would insist that they are a necessary condition of that history.

Consider next the concepts of prediction and progress. We applaud the caution with which resource persons usually reacted to the questions these concepts raised. But we would urge even greater caution. Understandably enough, the prevailing mood was an optimistic one; yet, though it noted such contingencies as depression and atomic war, it failed to stress sufficiently the almost complete dependency of the Island's plans upon vastly more powerful outside forces.

To put the point in another way, our panels did not in our terms squarely enough face the planetary crisis in human affairs—a crisis which could, if we are right, lead even in our lifetime as easily to the destruction of whole civilizations as to an unprecedented age of plenty and peace. The possibilities of progress both in a "material" and "spiritual" sense are, we agree, genuine indeed. But whether they will actually be realized is entirely beyond any mortal's capacity to know.

Thus we are led to the final issue. To say that we are unable to predict with any certainty is not to say that we should not project our cultural imaginations. On the contrary, one of the reasons why the future is now so precarious may be laid to pragmatic, shortsighted, trial-and-error, quick-buck policies on the part of such great powers as the United States. It is often said, and justifiably, that we Continentals have no idea of where we really want to go. Thus, lacking long-range plans, we are often buffeted about by other nations—the Soviet Union, most notoriously of late—that certainly do not lack them.

Granting, then, that the best laid plans of Puerto Rico are jeopardized by the relative planlessness of the nation upon which it so heavily relies, yet we must applaud the extraordinary efforts to combat that jeopardy to the limits of its own frail strength. The Puerto Rican Planning Board—though even it appears to us overtinged by the pragmatic kind of Continental premises[6]—is at least future-centered and committed to the achievement of definite if circumscribed goals.

The fact that grassroots respondents could not agree as to whether education should be similarly committed is one indication that it is even more strongly tinged by such pragmatic premises—an indication supported further by the influence, ideologically at least, of the largely present-centered progressivist philosophy. It will be recalled, however, that a minority of these respondents, as well as several on the national panel, expressed the belief that the future should now become the focal point of all public education. While of course no temporal dimension can be ignored by the curriculum, we back this minority. We do not say that even the most careful yet audacious planning for the future will guarantee achievement. We do say that this kind of planning affords the best available investment within the capacity of the Puerto Rican people.

CHAPTER SIX

EXPLICIT AND IMPLICIT CULTURE IN PUERTO RICO: DEMOCRACY, RELIGION, AND MORALITY[1]

LIKE ALL cultures without exception, the Puerto Rican is saturated with a vast array of attitudes and beliefs about its own way of life. These attitudes and beliefs, we have said, are called metacultural because, much of the time, they lie beneath the surface of daily experience. They are absorbed into the "blood stream" of the people with little awareness that the absorption is occurring steadily from the earliest to the latest years of every normal person.

Theorists have various terms to describe this elusive level of culture, but the one we shall adopt is *configuration*, the underlying pattern of order that harmonizes—and sometimes disharmonizes—the deepest meanings, the "style of life," of a culture. Anthropologists have found difficulty in delineating very precisely the configuration of any culture they investigate precisely because, by definition, it is never fully, accurately expressed in the formal or official language of government, religion, education, or other institutions.

To put the matter in a different way, metacultural beliefs are seldom if ever exactly equated with the *ideology* of a culture—that is, its symbolic self-portrait as conveyed through such typical agents as journalists, politicians, priests, and teachers. Yet, despite the difficulty of comparing an ideology with a configuration, no culture can be understood until the metacultural level is probed and interpreted. For here, more than anywhere else, the pervasive philosophy of a people living together in a society is to be discovered. In a genuine sense, it is the key to cultural order.

As anyone will perceive who has followed our interpretation thus far, the configuration of Puerto Rican culture is not now to be considered for the first time. It loomed in our discussions of the family, of class structure, and of historical development. This is only to say that configuration embraces and pervades all dimensions of cultural order—spatial and temporal alike. In this and the next chapter, however, we propose to highlight the question by asking our resource persons how far in their judgment the *explicit* or ideological level on which Puerto Ricans, like all people, publicly communicate their attitudes, policies, and doctrines to one another is or is not compatible with their *implicit* or metacultural level of experience.

We shall not exhaust the question. It will arise again many times in relation to process and goals. Here we hope only to become more conscious both of its significance and of its ubiquity by viewing three important areas of belief encompassed by the terms democracy, religion, and morality. The following chapter considers science, at the conclusion of which we present our evaluative judgments concerning all four areas.

Foremost among them will be the judgment that Puerto Rican schools and colleges are confronted with a rare opportunity not only to make educational history for themselves but to set an example for other cultures. For they could, if they so chose, attempt consciously, deliberately, to close existing gaps (and they are wide indeed) between explicit and implicit levels of belief—to make of democracy, religion, morality, and science genuine related events of everyday life with maximum compatibility between verbal and behavioral expression.

DEMOCRACY

Puerto Rico is a democracy-conscious culture. Many of its citizens, despite their memory of North American colonialism, proclaim their pride in sixty years of association with a nation which, since the eighteenth century, has been admired by the world as one of the greatest of democracies. The influence of English and French democracy was also frequently noted by respondents as was the Hispanic-Christian conception of human worth.

The Commonwealth constitution, moreover, is considered a model of democratic principles. The government formally operates according to these principles, and constantly expounds them. All religions are free to worship. Race discrimination is unlawful. The public schools are modeled upon the North American pattern far more than any other, and children are taught the rights and duties of citizens living in a democratic country. Finally, other instruments that shape the citizen's mind, such as newspapers and radio and television stations, enunciate this ideology as loudly as they repudiate alternatives. The syndicated columnists in *El Mundo,* for example, are for the most part the same ones that are read in Continental newspapers, while the magazines most widely circulated are also Continental. Explicitly, Puerto Rican culture is overwhelmingly devoted to the slogans of democracy, and all of our respondents professed this ideology themselves.

Is it equally so on the implicit level? The answer here, as it would be in the parent democracy, is far more equivocal. According to most respondents, the bulk of the people have not yet learned the meaning of such devotion nearly as completely as they should in one major respect at least—namely, in their tendency to idolize their present leaders (particularly one, the Governor), and to leave too much by way of policy and implementation to those they have elected.

Many voices were heard at the grassroots to the effect that Puerto Ricans trust their highest leadership too abjectly for the good of their democracy. Only a small minority, one a respondent habituated to the pseudo-feudal life of a coffee *hacienda,* felt that it was a proper habit to encourage. The majority held that other types of leaders—notably, labor and religious—are also accepted too abjectly. The degree of acceptance varies, however. Two respondents pointed to the landslide election as senator of a well-known Protestant who had been publicly opposed by the Catholic Church; this illustrated, they said, that political leaders have a stronger grip on the people than do religious leaders. A comparable point was made by a leader-respondent who reported that the Bishop of Ponce has repeatedly shown hostility toward the Popular party, with little effect. Labor leaders were also said to have greater influence than religious leaders, but they have been closely affiliated with the dominant political leadership. Even local mayors, if a militant Catholic respondent was correct, are usually "listened to" much more than local priests.

National-level respondents, although they usually supported this general opinion, were more inclined to qualify it. Whether or not they were influenced by the fact of their own positions of sometimes high authority, several pointed out that respect by the people for strong political leadership is not necessarily inconsistent with democracy. The real question is whether such leadership represents the public's wishes—also, whether citizens have sufficient opportunity to criticize and, if they so choose, to repudiate those they have elected.

Stated this way, no respondent on any level contended that present government leaders are unrepresentative of what the great majority have thus far considered to be their best interests, and no one questioned the integrity of the top leadership. The point was also made that this leadership has performed a democratic function in motivating the people—in helping them to understand their own problems, needs, and rights. In this sense, even though it has often had to move more slowly than it might have wished or might have attempted if less democratic, the government in power has played a tremendous educational as well as a strictly political role.

Nevertheless, even at the national level considerable concern was manifested by the gap between ideological and underlying attitudes concerning the leadership issue. The habit of relying heavily on leaders, several pointed out, derives from a mixture of Hispanic, religious, and colonial traditions—a habit symbolized by the term *personalismo,* and connoting the great respect for persons in authority observed previously in the patriarchal family. Thus, while a larger proportion of adults were said to go to the polls every four years than in any state of the Union, they tend to assume that their duty is then over and that it is up to the chosen leaders to work out a program for their benefit until the next election. One subcultural respondent estimated that 80 per cent of the citizens—the least educated majority—think the leader should decide all crucial questions once they have approved him.

Concern arose, also, over the question of minority dissent to majority rule—another central democratic principle. Several leaders were convinced that Puerto Ricans already respect this principle, as indicated by their tolerance of unpopular ideas. One mentioned how difficult it is to keep Nationalists in prison for extended periods, not because of widespread approval of their views, but because of respect for their right to oppose the majority. For the same reason, it would be more difficult to imprison Communists convicted under the Smith Act than in many North American states. Likewise, if another leader is correct, most Puerto Ricans, unlike most Mainlanders, are not frightened by "socialist" or equally unorthodox economic and political proposals; indeed, they often accept them not only in words but in housing, agricultural, and other practices. The reasonableness and tolerance of ideas even suggested to one leader that the *personalismo* tradition, with its spirit of arbitrary and sometimes violent authority, is nowhere nearly as influential as some have tried to argue.[2]

The fact that the American Civil Liberties Union was engaged by the government to study minority rights in Puerto Rico and to recommend means of strengthening them—a quite unprecedented step among democratic countries—would support further the explicit acceptance of the majority-minority principle. It would not, however, prove that no incompatibility with the implicit level prevails. Criticism of the Department of Education for "censoring" certain of its publications was cited earlier. Several respondents mentioned the refusal of a large majority of Popular mayors, despite the Governor's plea, to grant minority parties an official voice in municipal affairs. Repeatedly, too, comments were made at the grassroots to the effect that dissenters are "afraid" to make themselves conspicuous—especially if they hold jobs that depend on the good will of party officers or government bureaucrats. Finally, according to one leader, agencies set up to serve the people are too often staffed by persons who lack understanding of such methods of democracy as criticism and participation.

But respondents disagreed as to where the greatest compatibility or incompatibility between democratic ideology and configuration lies in terms of class and region. Some were certain that the lower socioeconomic strata manifest the most compatibility—their argument being that because ideological beliefs are of minor concern to people with little education and little guided opportunity to reflect about so profound a concept, their tendency is to be democratic simply because it is their "way of life." One leader made an intriguing distinction: lower-strata groups especially in the rural areas are more democratic in their individual relations (for example, their respect for one another as persons) than in their institutional behavior (for example, their careless regard for traffic rules).

A few maintained that the middle urban strata are more consistently democratic than the lower. The former have thought more than the latter about democracy, and so they try harder to equate practice with professed belief even in the face of insecurities that sometimes result from such conscious effort. The fact that in the last election they were more critical than other classes, judging by the size of their vote against the party in power, could be offered in support of this contention. No respondent argued that the greatest compatibility is to be found in the highest stratum of Puerto Rican vertical order.

Further comment is required with regard to the problem of race relations, viewed now in the context of democratic beliefs. Chapter 4 examined this problem as it pertains to the class structure, and found that equality among races is not only supported by law but is widely accepted both ideologically and in overt conduct. One leader was sure that one finds as little prejudice in areas where few Negroes live as in areas with many. But it was also noted that prejudice and discrimination are admitted to exist and that, while most respondents considered these practices to be socioeconomic rather than racial in motivation, this view did not go undisputed.

In any case, respondents did not deny that a limited kind of segregation occurs in Island restaurants, hotels, swimming pools, and other places where tourists and the well-to-do gather. Segregation, however, does not result from official rules established by the management (such rules would be illegal) but rather from the fact that the average colored citizen cannot afford luxury prices. That he might also feel uncomfortable for fear of being unwelcome in such surroundings may likewise be an intangible factor, as it would be in many northern cities of the Continent. At the same time, a few Negroes do appear in the most expensive establishments. More serious in terms of our problem is the fact that they were reported to be excluded by membership qualifications from most if not all upper-class *casinos,* from certain businessmen's clubs, and from such religious organizations as the Catholic Daughters of America.

Still more serious were the discrepancies between ideology and configuration that appeared in the personal feelings of some resource persons. As anyone knows who has looked into the matter, one of the most revealing tests of such feelings is that of attitudes toward marriage between races. Only one of the "white" respondents on the subcultural level would have no serious objection to racial intermarriage for his own children. Three "white" fathers insisted they would do all they could to prevent it. Reasons were diverse: one respondent said that it would "lower the race"; another said that "white is for white" and "black for black"; still another feared that his daughter would be boycotted by her friends and that his grandchildren would suffer if they went to the United States. The question was not asked of all leader respondents, but it was possible to infer from related questions that their attitude was typically more liberal. Among all respondents, only one revealed the kind of extreme inconsistency common on the Continent: while unusually vocal in professing the egalitarian ideology and insisting that he was not "against" Negroes, he was hostile not only toward miscegenation but interracial dancing in high school; he spoke of the "trash," largely colored, that inhabited nearby slums; he thought that Negroes should be excluded from hotel swimming pools; he wanted them to "keep their distance" in social affairs.

The fact that Puerto Ricans who migrate to the States often experience discrimination would lead one to suppose that Insular concern over the problem might be intense, particularly since so many travel back and forth. The two Army veterans both admitted they had experienced discrimination, one at the hands of a private, the second from a Negro officer! Three other grassroots respondents said they had heard of prejudiced treatment against Puerto Ricans. Yet no respondent, even among leaders, volunteered much concern over this problem.

Nor was anti-Semitism (which often develops in North American cities, especially among lower-class people who seek a "scapegoat" for their troubles) discernible in the interviews. This is interesting in view of the fact not only that many thousands of Puerto Ricans are employed in the New York garment industry, which is manned predominantly by Jewish workers and managers, but that they live in Harlem tenements where anti-Semitism is often rife because of alleged Jewish landlords. The only evidence of anti-Semitism observed on the Island was in the form of stereotypes and prejudiced attitudes on the part of some University students in an educational psychology course.

Looked at together, both panels were nevertheless convinced that democracy, racially as well as politically, is far from a mere shibboleth to most Puerto Ricans—hence that an impressive compatibility is already revealed between their explicit allegiance to its principles and their implicit acceptance of them. Such compatibility, we were told, has increased rapidly in less than twenty years, although understanding of important aspects of democracy is still to be achieved. All in all, the degree of synthesis between the two levels was generally considered greater, certainly in democratic political beliefs, than in any other country south of the United States.

RELIGION

One of the paradoxes in Puerto Rican culture is the disparity between formal affiliation with the Roman Catholic Church (between 80 and 85 per cent of the population, according to most estimates) and meager concern for its religious ceremonials and dogmas. The fact noted above that, in the judgment of several respondents on both levels, the recommendations of political leaders are followed more fully than those of religious leaders is one index of this disparity. The fact that services of the Catholic Church are attended regularly by a much larger proportion of women than men (one leader was sure this was largely due to the *machismo* tradition: it is unmasculine to be seen too often in church), and that the most ardent Catholics, classwise, are members of the upper stratum, helps further to sharpen the paradox.

Its significance for the problem of this chapter is obvious. If the religious ideology is predominantly Catholic, and yet if only a fraction of the population (10 to 15 per cent, according to some informants) are sufficiently devout to follow the mandates and rituals of Catholicism with any regularity, can it not then be said that another type of incompatibility appears between the explicit and implicit levels of belief?

Respondents were largely agreed upon a degree of incompatibility, but they were equally agreed upon the importance of distinguishing between the theological routines of the Catholic Church, on the one hand, and the core tenets of Christianity, on the other hand. If one leader was right, only a tiny handful of citizens could be considered freethinkers: virtually all believe in God; probably as many believe in immortality. Yet, several others placed the Christian belief in human brotherhood and sanctity of personality even higher in importance for most Puerto Ricans. And it is worthy of note that the lower strata were regarded by two leaders as more harmonious religiously than the upper strata, their reason being the same as in the case of democratic beliefs: though there is the least ideological sophistication on the lower levels, there is consequently the greatest implicit sincerity.

Another distinction was stressed by both groups of respondents, including Catholics themselves. The degree of incompatibility between ideological creed and deeper religious attitudes is strikingly less among Protestants in Puerto Rico. In other words, the 15 to 20 per cent of the population belonging to one or another of their numerous denominations (the Baptist, to mention but one, was said to maintain about fifty churches on the island) are more successful in relating creed to behavior than is the Catholic majority. This is demonstrated not only in a higher ratio of church attendance by both Protestant men and women, not only in the greater zeal with which they participate in ceremonials, but in their development of social services such as rural hospitals and agricultural projects. These services were said to dramatize the nonsectarian, nontheological, and democratic aspects of the Christian faith.

Several explanations were given for the greater gap between the two kinds of belief among Catholics. One was the "clerical" reputation of the Church, meaning the close affiliation of a politically minded hierarchy with the colonial rule of earlier centuries—a fact true of other Hispanic cultures. Such a reputation has lingered long and helps to explain the continued support of the Church by the top status level of the population. Also, at least partially, it accounts for a half-conscious suspicion if not an outright hostility with which many people of lower and even middle status tend to look upon the Catholic clergy. These attitudes, which were noted in several subcultural respondents, have been reinforced by its reputed indifference to the personal and social welfare of the common people—an indifference related again to the "clerical" habits of a priesthood imported, hitherto, largely from Spain itself. But the situation is now changing, it was reported—indeed, one Protestant informant went so far as to assert that Catholics are already surpassing Protestants in social-welfare programs.

Traditionally, at any rate, the use of Latin rather than the Spanish vernacular in Catholic rituals, the remoteness from churches of many rural settlements, the expense of ceremonials such as Church marriages, and the difficulty of living up to the stern principles of Catholicism (most notably, in sex relations)—all were regarded as further contributing factors to the disparity.

This last point is underscored by the growing numbers who practice birth control despite bitter opposition of the Catholic hierarchy; by the thousands of women, who, though they may attend church regularly, have also visited one of the many birth-control clinics established by the Department of Health; and by the fact that both sterilization and divorce are on the increase. Only one of the fifteen subcultural respondents who were Catholics expressed opposition to all forms of birth control as well as divorce (except for infidelity). This same respondent, a lifelong rural resident, was also the only one who expressed a wish that only Catholics would live in his *barrio*. But even this lone wish was countered by another Catholic respondent in the same *barrio* who said he would welcome Protestants as friends equally with Catholics.

MORALITY

The problem of morality, which was confined in our research mainly to standards of sex conduct, is closely related to religion for the reason that the ideological code is profoundly influenced by Christian doctrine, especially the Sixth Commandment. This problem is complicated by the traditional practices of concubinage, consensual marriage, and the double standard. Although these practices were said to be decreasing—most rapidly in the urban middle strata—no one contended that they are negligible.

Here, then, a conflict even in explicit beliefs inevitably occurs. The Christian ideology completely repudiates both premarital and extramarital sex relations; the secular cultural ideology tolerates if it does not openly condone these relations. Moreover, while it could not be argued that most women approve, it did appear evident from several responses that even they tend to regard the double standard with considerably greater forbearance, albeit a reluctant one, than might be true in cultures such as the United States. To cite two examples: one young woman respondent thought it proper for boys to learn more than girls about "the facts of life"; another reported that upper-class mothers of illegitimate children in her community were fully accepted

EDUCATION'S ROLE: THE EXAMPLE OF DEMOCRACY

In the opinion of a respected leader, one of the most important tasks of education in Puerto Rico is to close the gaps between its explicit and implicit culture—a task which cannot, of course, be left only to formal institutions but must be undertaken by all kinds of groups concerned with building a unified culture—economic, religious, political, and others.

Can such a complex undertaking "get off the ground" in any deliberate, organized way? Limiting ourselves chiefly to democracy, the most far-reaching of all respondents' recommendations was that the schools and colleges learn how to become democratic by *experiencing* its principles—by teachers and administrators learning the difference between autocratic and democratic leadership in their own performance, and by students discovering in classrooms that the right to participate in planning is just as important as the duty to accept the plans that are made.

The official ideology would endorse these proposals. At the same time, its own educational leadership would probably admit that they have not as yet been implemented in everyday practice except to a limited extent. The centralized system has not been conducive to wide democratic sharing in the formulation or operation of policies. Curricula, teaching methods, and most rules have been established in the central office for Island-wide adoption. The personnel of local schools have been habituated, in turn, to following prescribed routines with minimum deviation.

Few grassroots respondents were unduly disturbed. The majority, on the contrary, seemed to accept this situation as a matter of course. Thus it had not occurred to most parents that in their PTA's they might seriously consider matters such as the curriculum of their local schools. When the question was raised, some admitted that cooperative study and recommendations by parents might be beneficial, but others held that all such matters should be left to officials. Nor was the question of whether teachers and students might also participate in curriculum planning, in formulating rules of discipline, and in offering constructive criticisms apparently one which had received much previous consideration by subcultural respondents. Thus when they were asked to make specific recommendations, only a small minority thought to include the strengthening of democratic processes in their own institutions.

This minority did suggest that more decentralization in policies and programs ought now to be attempted. It objected to the frequency with which syllabuses, for example, are prepared at the top with little help or guidance from teachers at the base. Particularly, it criticized some supervisors for imposing their own will arbitrarily upon principals and teachers who had deviated even slightly from their own directives.

Principals and teachers were also criticized by the same minority for deficient concern with democratic principles on the plane of daily practice. In the estimate of one administrator respondent, considerably less than half of the principals in charge of local public schools attempt in any significant way to encourage such practice—a habit that would tend to be reinforced by their own subjection to rules imposed from above. The more common orientation was thus perhaps typified by another administrator respondent, who, though emphatic in explicitly opposing "traditional methods," also opposed student councils with authority to make any rules except for parties, who felt that students ought not to criticize, who was content to have curricula made entirely at "headquarters," and who would insist on the right to "veto" any suggestions that parents might make.

The same critical estimate was roughly applied to the body of teachers, although in their case the fact that they are in charge of abnormally large classes of children (more than sixty were counted in several of the schools we visited) could help to account for their frequently rather authoritarian roles. It hardly accounts entirely, however: insecurity and fear of "higher ups"; the teacher's traditional "matriarchal" role; youthful habits of passivity acquired in family relations; the still chronic practice (despite an official ban) of mild corporal punishment by elementary teachers; finally, on the university level, the hierarchical structure of administrative authority and the European-influenced custom of professorial dignity—these were noted by various respondents as other contributing factors.

Such examples by no means imply that democracy in Puerto Rican education remains up to now wholly an affair of words. While the gap is still a wide one, it is slowly narrowing—a fact supported by the sensitivity of at least a subcultural minority to such incompatibilities as we have just listed. Also, in the opinion of some leaders, the gap is closing rapidly in two fields, both of them concerned primarily with informal and functional rather than formal instruction: first, in the program of community education on the adult level; second, in the consumer cooperative movement. The latter, moreover, is reaching into the public schools themselves.*

Nor should we forget that individual schools and individual teachers vary markedly in their application of the democratic ideology. Thus, in one of the three subcultures, participation by teachers in limited curriculum planning, the operation on the secondary level of a student council with some authority, as well as group methods of learning, were becoming accepted in a few schools of the municipality. Also, the fact that many grassroots respondents were willing when asked to endorse more participation and other democratic processes for parents, for teachers, and even for children might indicate a potential readiness that has not yet found opportunity for actual expression. The fact, too, that several of these same respondents, including teachers, were unsure whether to admire or to condemn Franco as a leader might indicate lack of sophistication in democratic political principles rather than reasoned opposition to them.

Perhaps most revealing, the explicit concept of equality of races has moved far in education toward complete achievement as an implicit cultural pattern. Although one leader admitted that colored college students sometimes cluster in groups, this "self-imposed" segregation is much less noticeable than in schools even of northern cities on the Continent. Colored teachers are as commonly observed in charge of classes of predominantly white children as white teachers are observed in the converse situation. A great preponderance of all public schools contain some mixture of colored and white students as well as teachers —a phenomenon so taken for granted that school people showed surprise when it was called to their attention. As noted in our study of vertical order, many though not all respondents would consider a more serious discrepancy between ideology and configuration to be the divisions that arise between classes due to the rapid growth of private schools—divisions that have the effect also of tending to separate racial stocks in so far as light-skinned children in larger proportion than dark-skinned children belong to the upper classes that

* See pp. 278–279.

can afford private school tuitions. Nevertheless, the racial situation when appraised by democratic standards probably reveals less discrepancy than in any other comparably sized area under the American flag, unless it be Hawaii. No respondent on either panel expressed the slightest opposition to racial integration in the public school system. Rather, it was wholeheartedly accepted.

Much of the evidence presented thus far concerning education as a configurational expression of democracy has been derived from the three subcultures. National-level respondents agreed with many of the same points, but they both limited and enriched them. One leader insisted that a wider gap exists between the explicit and implicit levels in formal education than it does in most other institutions—a weakness he attributed more to ononverbalization and middle-class biases operating in professional teacher-training programs than to any other cause.

Two other leaders differed almost diametrically from each other on the proposal that one way to narrow the gap would be to remake classrooms into miniature laboratories of democratic living and learning, with special regard for experience in majority rule-minority dissent. The one who opposed was afraid that children would learn the meaning of democracy in a superficial manner. Maturity, he argued, must be attained first—especially the capacity to reason—an argument he supported by reference to classic thinkers in political philosophy. The respondent who as strongly favored the proposal would avoid superficiality by giving teachers and children opportunity to learn democratic principles through daily practice.

We postpone examination of educational issues that arise from the second and third examples of belief—religion and morality—because these were considered more fully by our respondents in connection with the problem of cultural goals.* We anticipate only enough to assert that incompatibilities between explicit and implicit beliefs were discernible here also—most conspicuously in religion, where the ideological principle of separation of church and state is neither strictly manifested in daily school activities nor supported on the implicit level by the beliefs of many respondents. As for morality, the fact that sex instruction is only slightly touched upon by most curricula, hence that sex morality is not as yet widely regarded as a fit subject for formal learning, makes it doubtful whether the gaps be-

* See pp. 291–301, 305–310.

tween ideological and metacultural beliefs that we have observed in the broader culture would be less pronounced in education.

One leader did insist that cheating is widespread on the college level and that this is symptomatic of a deeper moral challenge than the evils of the practice itself. Cheating is due, he contended, to the "artificiality" of much Puerto Rican education—to the stress upon paper work, verbalization, and grades, and hence to the separation between these and the real interests of typical learners. Cheating will cease to be a problem when students become excited by the intrinsic importance and worth of what they are learning—a prediction that would be equally relevant to education in other cultures.

His point, however, is germane to the problem of sex morality as well. If the failure of many students to respect in conduct a code of honesty which they accept as ideology is much less of a reflection upon the code itself than upon the lack of functional relationship between it and the education they continue to receive, then perhaps deceits and other effects of customary sex morality are traceable to relationships that are equally dichotomous. One implication surely is that education should afford no less opportunity for scrupulous examination of disruptions caused at least partly by incompatibilities between explicit sex codes and implicit sex attitudes and conduct than it affords for any other cultural behavior—the political, say. Just as cheating will diminish, this leader believed, when Puerto Rican education is vitalized in terms of such behavior, so will the tragic effects of inharmonious relations between men and women also diminish.

What are the principal opinions and inferences obtained from our panels thus far? As would be true of all cultures, inconsistency prevails in all three areas of belief. As to the first, the widest gap was attributed largely to the stubborn persistence of the *personalismo* tradition, although inadequate appreciation of the principle of minority dissent —the polar principle to majority rule—was considered by some as, in long range, even more serious a deficiency. Grassroots respondents were perhaps more incensed at their fellow citizens for relinquishing too much authority and responsibility to leadership than they were at leaders for accepting it. Also, they seemed less concerned with the problem of minority dissent than were most national-level repondents, who, interestingly enough, seemed less concerned in turn with the problem of overconcentrated leadership.

While strata and regions were considered unlike in the extent to which they have achieved a democratic configuration that harmonizes with their political and social ideology, it is a commentary on the unsettled nature of the problem that respondents also differed as to which groups have attained the greatest harmony thus far. They did imply that the upper stratum is the least harmonious.

In race relations, something of a gap between the explicit principle of equality and implicit attitudes was also discernible. Perhaps because the problem of race relations does not loom large on the Island, little indignation was revealed toward discriminatory treatment suffered on the Continent. When tested by questions that touched personal sensitivities, however, prejudiced feelings toward persons of conspicuously Negroid stock were found to be acute.

We round up our evidence concerning the second example chosen to focus upon cultural configuration by asserting that incompatibility between ideological and metacultural beliefs may be wider at least with regard to formal religion than in the case of political democracy. If, however, one means by explicit religious beliefs the kind that would be accepted by earnest Christians almost everywhere, even though such beliefs may seldom be expressed in ecclesiastical doctrines or articulated as dogmatic creeds, then in this sense the degree of compatibility was regarded by our respondents as extremely high.

Our third example, sex morality, is complicated even on the explicit level by inconsistency between secular custom and religious ideology—an inconsistency limited almost exclusively, however, to the male sex. This secular custom of polygynous activity, though it was said to produce strains and hypocrisies in marital and even premarital relations, was nevertheless regarded by many respondents with greater tolerance than would probably be true of cultures which lack customary sanctions for such activity.

Perhaps the over-all configuration of Puerto Rican culture and education can now be perceived with slightly greater clarity. Negatively, this configuration, according to our data, is decidedly less democratic, less religious, and less moral than we should expect were we to be guided by typical ideological formulations such as those taught by the schools. Positively, it may be more implicitly democratic than other Central American or South American cultures; it is manifestly more religious in universal Christian attitudes than in ecclesiastical allegiances; and it is more consistently moral according to its secular traditions than its religious ones. Also, we may fairly assume that much the same congruities and incongruities that prevail in the cultural configuration prevail in education. This, of course, has been an assumption from the beginning of our study, but it is now supported by cumulative evidence.

CHAPTER SEVEN

EXPLICIT AND IMPLICIT CULTURE IN PUERTO RICO: SCIENCE[1]

THE PROBLEM discussed in the preceding chapter—of how much and what kinds of compatibility are discernible between explicit or ideological and implicit or metacultural beliefs—is pursued further here with special regard for beliefs about science. But now we shift the focus. Instead of examining science parallel with democracy, religion, and morality, we wish to inquire how consistently and consciously Puerto Ricans believe they are capable of shaping their own lives in the general sense of scientific control.

Let us approach this guiding question by asking two others as bluntly as possible: Do many citizens implicitly believe that culture determines what they are, or do they rather believe that they make the culture whatever it is? (Or is there some third alternative?) Though few if any would raise these questions in precisely our terms, yet we may hope to discover some attitude toward them if for no other reason than that, in many different expressions, they are to be found probably in all cultures among people of widely different ranges of sophistication.

More technically, to assume that culture has, as it were, an independent existence and that it is governed by objective forces which you and I must learn to accept, to obey, perhaps even to revere, is to believe implicitly that it has a kind of external, overpowering reality of its own with dominant laws of its own. In a variety of forms, this orientation is often associated with great metaphysical or pseudo-religious views of the world, although it is also defended by many who consider themselves scientists.

Contrasted with such an outlook is one which, again in technical terms, regards culture as an intellectual tool for understanding and coping with the relations of people living in society—a concept that enables us to examine and interpret these relations and that often leads to various sorts of controlled action for solving human problems. We call this the *operational* approach. It is part and parcel of the scientific method, by which we mean, as simply as possible, the method of confronting and resolving a difficulty through operating upon it in the way that a physician, for example, operates: analyzing its elements, formulating a corrective proposal, and then actively testing it in order to see whether the difficulty is thereby removed.

Whether the problem be physical, biological, social, or personal, the operational way is at heart the same. It does not, of course, deny that various types of ordered relations are recognizable in all realms of nature, and therefore culture, but it considers these not so much to accept them or revere them as to control them by operating with and upon them. The scientific approach to culture is thus essentially creative—indeed, it has many subtle connections with creative art. It presupposes a confidence in man's capacity to direct himself and his environment, while having full regard for obstacles and limitations.

"ACTIVISTIC" AND "DETERMINISTIC" ATTITUDES

Now when we ask how far and in what ways Puerto Ricans tend toward one or another, or both, of these deep-seated attitudes toward culture, a strong consensus emerges in favor of the operational way. It is a consensus which like many others is neither unanimous nor unqualified. Two leaders, particularly, held that a "passive" attitude toward the culture is still dominant; three others, that both attitudes are held about "fifty-fifty." The remainder on both panels, speaking for their fellow citizens, contended that they are increasingly the makers and shapers of their way of life; that through patient and reflective deliberation they are finding ways of coping with such troubles as malnutrition, disease, and ignorance. Therefore they believe that, through planning and social experimentation, they can gradually lift themselves by their own bootstraps. This metaphor, significantly, has been adopted by the government for its famous program of economic development: "Operation Bootstrap."

An equally strong consensus, however, revealed that the *activistic* orientation (as we shall now call it) is comparatively recent. The year 1940 and the start of a new political regime were mentioned several times as the date from which this orientation began to supersede the *deterministic* orientation (as we may now call the alternative belief).* The point was punctuated by one informant who called attention to an optimistic campaign song of the Popular party which had been rewritten from an older Puerto Rican song filled with pessimistic lines.

This is not to say that only in 1940 did the activistic attitude appear for the first time. One respondent maintained that, through the influence of a few great leaders on the Island (some of them Spaniards, others Puerto Ricans), the belief that men are "the masters of their own destiny" began to take hold vigorously in the mid-nineteenth century—that before this time the people just "drifted along" with an abject sense of dependency upon outside powers. Others implied that its roots extend still deeper into Insular economic and political history and into a Spanish heritage which is itself highly complex. (For example, one leader was sure that the Catalonians of northern Spain are more activistic than the Andalusians of the South. Another held that the activistic attitude was already becoming dominant in the eighteenth century.) Still more is it traceable, other respondents held, to the period beginning in 1898 when the United States, "the most scientifically advanced country in the world," began to permeate its new charges with something of its own spirit as a "young, daring country." In recent years, when thousands of young citizens have served in the armed forces and other thousands have known the Continent firsthand, this spirit was said to have quickened.

One may also make certain qualifications by class and location. Countrymen, according to our evidence, appear to lean toward the deterministic orientation more than do urbanites—to believe, as one leader put it, that "hurricanes or the Lord or government" determine everything for them. Yet it is impossible to draw any sharp line, both because many urbanites were only recently countrymen themselves and because the latter have been exposed directly or indirectly to urban influence. Nevertheless, countrymen oftener than urbanites were said to accept the adage *sentarse a esperar* ("sit down and wait"), for God will take care of us—an attitude said to be partly the effect of long-

---

* "Determinism" is utilized here to suggest a pervasive attitude toward the dominance of culture over men rather than the common philosophic meaning that all events have antecedent causes. Some respondents also introduced the term "fatalism" at points in this discussion. But fatalism, more strictly defined, is considered later. See pp. 343–346.

ingrained feelings of hopelessness or at least powerlessness. The fact that urbanites of the lower classes also share this attitude more prevalently than the middle and upper classes would logically follow, since a large proportion of those of menial and unskilled status not only come from rural areas but continue to suffer from more insecurity and poverty.

Several respondents also implied a correlation between upward mobility and the activistic attitude: the higher the class and status, the more it prevails, although one alleged that the consciousness that "men make themselves" is filtering down especially from leader to follower groups. For not wholly unrelated reasons, many individuals, especially of the less privileged areas and levels, were portrayed by the subcultural panel as believing strongly in "luck" as the best way to get ahead (one reason, doubtless, for the popularity of both legal and illegal lotteries). And they tend even more strongly to deny that they are to blame for their own troubles.

There is still another reason for the continued, if lessening, influence of the deterministic attitude. If we are willing to grant that the operational and hence scientific way of utilizing the culture concept is, in turn, inherent in the activistic approach to culture, then it follows that this approach (rarely expressed in formal terms, of course) would tend to be held more clearly and consistently in the degree that the operational-scientific way is clearly understood. But uncertainty prevails as to the extent of this sort of understanding. The fact, it was argued, that Puerto Ricans were said to admire and support the growth of technology, or that they have moved farther in this direction than most Latin American peoples, does not necessarily prove that they have grasped the meaning of science as it functions in relation to technological enterprise.

On the contrary, some respondents were of the opinion that there is still relatively feeble grasp of such a relationship. Indeed, according to one spokesman, even industry—though it lags less than agriculture in Puerto Rico—is by no means sufficiently "technologized." For example, the number of competent technicians available for laboratory-type positions where scientific techniques are required was described as woefully short of the current demand. In a different sphere, some local political leaders perhaps unconsciously perpetuate deterministic attitudes because they suspect that thereby it is easier to retain power and control over their constituents. Even many experts in fields of social welfare and social service, if they are not also deterministic, were adjudged unskillful, impulsive, or domineering in training people to deal activistically with community needs.

Part of the difficulty, in the judgment of several, is that Puerto Ricans are more aesthetically minded than they are scientifically minded. They prefer the arts and humanities with their warm emotional qualities more than they do the coldly precise, surgical kind of thinking and behavior that science demands. This contention, however, was disputed by others who argued that Puerto Ricans are just as amenable to technological and scientific proficiency as are, say, *americanos*. The reason they are less proficient thus far is not so much the effect of cultural preference for aesthetic experience as of limited opportunity and practice. One leader gave the example of time clocks: many workers, when they begin their first factory jobs, have never owned a clock or watch; the experience of "punching in" and "punching out" on schedule is totally new to them and requires the formation of new habits.

As another argued, the fact that so many inhabitants have dared to go forth from their long-familiar surroundings, to migrate to strange new worlds (nearly 20 per cent in less than ten years from San José alone), is itself an indication of the kind of exploratory, adventurous attitude that is an essential ingredient of the scientific spirit. Another indication is the fact that the great bulk of the people have supported experimental undertakings that were unheard of twenty years ago.

THE INFLUENCE OF RELIGIOUS ATTITUDES

Nevertheless, since the deterministic attitude remains influential, we must inquire whether religious attitudes may not also encourage it. Certainly a common corollary of such attitudes is a belief that the ultimate powers of the universe—and thus of the culture as a part of the universe—lie beyond the scope of scientific explanation and control. To be sure, we noted earlier that our leader respondents overwhelmingly rejected a "spiritual interpretation of history" in favor of a more naturalistic if also eclectic theory. Yet there appeared to be considerable confusion at least on the grassroots panel as to which of the two attitudes, in a conflict situation, is to be preferred.

For example, informants by no means wholly agreed as to whether, if a child in the family were seriously ill, they should resort to prayer first or call a doctor first. One active Protestant was sure that most Puerto Ricans would send for the minister before they went for the doctor, but a Catholic was sure that the reverse order is more common. Only a minority supported the Protestant's view (certain sects maintain that "Jesus is their doctor"), but nearly all grassroots respondents insisted that prayer will help also—prayer, be it noted, to a divine lawgiver who will finally decide whether or not the child shall recover.

For similar reasons, a minority had confidence that the *rogativa* (an outdoor religious procession with the image of a saint) will bring rain to parched crops. So effective is it, indeed, that one rural respondent reported an instance in his *barrio* of having to organize a second *rogativa* to pray for the rain to stop!

While a majority might not go as far as this, few on our subcultural panel revealed any sense of possible inconsistency between medical science and religious supplication. Both ways for them were considered "activistic," although one opposed praying for better crops, while another was sure that the only value prayer may have in the case of illness is that is provides psychological "release." One respondent pinpointed the prevalent viewpoint (acceptable by implication also to some national-level respondents) by quoting a Spanish saying: *A Dios rogando y con el mazo dando* ("Pray to God but still keep hammering")—a saying reminiscent of one popular in the United States during the Second World War: "Praise the Lord and pass the ammunition!"

The extent to which long-established religious beliefs, implicit or explicit, interfuse with and bolster the deterministic orientation, or vice versa, cannot be measured by this study. It is only fair to note, however, that a few leaders doubted that organized Catholicism (for such reasons as were noted in our preceding chapter) or even the whole Hispanic tradition plays any potent role today in perpetuating that orientation. It is also worth noting one opinion among them that the expansion in recent decades of Protestant churches, with their stress upon religious liberty and social service, has accompanied the expansion of activistic attitudes. Nevertheless, as was implied in our examination of religious beliefs, deterministic tendencies remain strong in Protestants also, in so far as faith in an all-powerful "God as Lawgiver" is implicit in those tendencies.

In this connection, a substantial proportion on our grassroots panel —both Protestant and Catholic—agreed that, if one were compelled to choose, one should obey the laws of God rather than the laws of man. A minority, however, found no conflict between the two "if understood" (one even cited du Noüy's *Human Destiny*[2] in support); two said that each kind of law belongs in its own sphere (for example, moral troubles must be solved by God's laws, socioeconomic problems by science); one held that it is sometimes necessary to break a law of God ("Thou shalt not kill" is one) even when one knows it to be wrong; and one felt unqualified to answer.

A final qualification should be noted to the generalization that the activistic orientation is increasingly accepted from year to year. This was a national-level dissenting opinion as to the recent influence of the government. Within the party itself, so he contended, a "counter-current" has been at work since about 1945 to resist the trend toward what some members fear is emerging—a technological, commercial-ized, supermarket kind of miniature of the United States. The rele-vant point is that critics of such resistance see in it a part-way reversion to the nonactivistic orientation because closer to the mores and customs of the Spanish-influenced, theocratic era of Puerto Rican history.

This dissenting opinion, while supported by several other respond-ents in the respect that a mild reaction to North American influence was conceded to be developing (we examine this matter below*), caused little consternation. To a far greater extent, Puerto Ricans, we were told, are for the growth of technology and scientific method, and for the kind of pragmatic, experimental approach to cultural control that is often associated with the United States culture.

HOW SHALL EDUCATION COPE WITH THE ISSUE OF DETERMINISM VERSUS ACTIVISM?

To put the issue in these terms may fail to convey any sense of educational urgency. Yet, though the relationship between theoretical formulations and their practical fruits are not always obvious, virtually all respondents sooner or later recognized this relationship and ex-pressed concern that it be faced.

Perhaps the most serious weakness in education that bears upon the issue is the limited extent to which the operational-scientific method

* See pp. 161–164.

seems to have been grasped by students. Although a few respondents were uncertain, a fairly strong consensus was apparent that even on the university level many students cannot define science clearly, much less demonstrate that they have incorporated its meaning into their thinking and behavior. One leader was sure that Puerto Rican students, by and large, are more deterministic than those in North America, but not more so than those in South America or southern Europe. In the judgment of two others, one cause is insufficient attention to the natural sciences when balanced against the humanities and less precise social sciences. In the judgment of another, almost no attention is paid to the history of science. Still another held that university students are naïvely optimistic about technological progress, but often ignorant of the role of scientific method in making such progress possible.

On levels below the higher learning, the proportion of students who understand and utilize scientific method was considered to be still weaker. One estimate was that more than half the student population on the secondary level seriously follow horoscopes (published daily in Insular newspapers) and are otherwise superstitious. Certain teachers known to one respondent are spiritualists who attend séances regularly; others go to fortunetellers. At least two grassroots respondents have been attended for little or no fee by *santiguadoras* (women who claim special healing powers through such rituals as prayers and anointments of oil). This custom is still familiar especially in rural areas. One respondent, who insisted that "witchcraft" is common in his municipality and that sick persons are often considered "bedeviled," knew about ten *santiguadoras*. He also reported a rather ironic practice: local drugstores do a thriving business in native herbs and oils which are sold for higher prices than scientifically tested prescriptions.

One of the reasons why elementary and secondary students do not comprehend the scientific method more adequately is the limited facilities available for experimental practice. On the elementary level, science is incorporated intermittently in Community Problems, but it is considered mainly in a "bookish" manner, we were told, with few if any materials for demonstrations, and almost no opportunity for children to deal either with meaningful problems through direct laboratory experience or with Island flora and fauna. On the high school level, courses in physics, chemistry, biology, and the social studies offer more opporunity; considering that here, too, laboratory facilities and teacher skills are meager, science study was said to have an important effect upon activistic attitudes among young people.

The elected student respondents in this study, for example, were all science majors with high scholastic averages and with ambitions to continue in pure or applied scientific fields. Yet the alternative attitude remained influential even with them. One insisted that he would never permit himself even to consider whether there might be reasons for conflict between his religious and scientific beliefs; hence he would refuse to study philosophy in the University. Equally revealing was his belief that the *rogativa* is a useful way to bring on rain but that "seeding clouds" would be still better. Another reported approvingly that his physics teacher takes frequent opportunity to emphasize how the laws of nature (the equalizing of gas pressures was given as an instance) reveal the wonders of God's work. All three were devout Catholics.

Thus, according to our evidence, many of the same deviations from a consistently activistic attitude in the sense defined are to be found in the school proper as in the wider culture. Though the propensity was usually to suppose that education is encouraging this attitude more than the deterministic, respondents were far from unanimous as to how far it is really influential even among school superintendents. Yet, on two levels, growth of the activistic orientation was recognized by some as relatively rapid: the university and the adult. The program of the Division of Community Education was selected to exemplify the broadly operational way of dealing with human problems that are meaningful to the experience of participants. As two spokesmen argued, countrymen, despite their deterministic habits, can and do learn to think and act scientifically together; nothing inherently prevents such learning. Also, television, radio, and the newspapers are popularizing science, at least superficially. Vocational education, which was praised for its commendable strides in changing the alleged Hispanic dislike of manual work, contributes still further—increasingly so as its program is widened to include firsthand experimentation as well as learning of skills. At the same time, one leader was sharply critical of the Schools of Agriculture and Engineering of the University; they fail, he said, to develop scientific-mindedness; indeed, they are lagging by nearly thirty years! Meanwhile, the training of teachers in science was described as improving. But the bulk of elementary teachers (most of whom are without college degrees) were said to retain strong, though largely implicit, deterministic attitudes which help to reinforce their passive habits of instruction. These are in turn inculcated and reinforced in their pupils along with a mixture of activistic attitudes.

Let us turn to recommendations for education derived from this discussion. One leader held that the activistic mood should permeate the whole curriculum rather than be taught directly. Perhaps what he had in mind was implied by another suggestion that close attention be paid to the culture concept itself. For teachers to have a clear understanding of the role of culture—for them to perceive by concrete examples the implications and distinctions between, say, the deterministic and activistic orientations—is prerequisite to clear understanding by their students and thus to reduction of the ambivalences now detectable. Courses in the history of science and of technology in its relations to modern civilization were also urged for all high school and college students. Moreover, the University should invite at least as many leading natural scientists for lectures and consultation as it does humanists and social scientists.

Another recommendation was that Community Problems in elementary schools be revamped to give much more attention to scientific experiences that are meaningful to children—and to develop *latent* interest, not merely to satisfy interests already aroused. How to create attention-getting, imagination-stirring problems from the resources of the immediate physical, biological, and social environment; how to encourage lively questioning; how to build, manipulate, and measure (mechanical toys would be one effective stimulus, "do-it-yourself" shops another); how to develop skills in native crafts, as is done in Mexico—these were noted as needs of teachers and students that cannot be met quickly. Yet until they are met (first of all in teacher-training programs) science as a revolutionary way of looking at and dealing with life's problems will not deeply affect the attitudes or behavior of children. One leader epitomized the demand thus: in addition to the "three R's," public education needs the "three C's," too: Cooperation, Creativeness, and Curiosity. Another put it more fundamentally for the level of higher education: what is required "at least for a while" is more solid understanding of the experimental method as expounded by John Dewey—and less of the classical humanists.

But several others issued a sharp warning. They feared that superficial or exaggerated stress upon the activistic orientation would produce too much of the individualistic, competitive, "go-getting" kind of ambition that Mainland education tends to inculcate. They feared, also, too blind a faith in technology as a panacea, too little patience, too little regard for the potent influence that cultural forces exert in shaping the lives of human beings. After all, as one expressed it, some things can be changed and some cannot. For these leaders, the most serious task is to keep the deterministic and activistic orientations in balance rather than to discard either in favor of the other. The correct view, another leader held, is that culture both determines and is determined by men: the relation is reciprocal.

We return, however, to the stronger note. Granting all the qualifications we have recorded, granting even the dangers in oversimplified solutions of the problem, it is impossible from our evidence to deny that this culture expresses with increasing zest the activistic orientation. That confusions prevail, that many citizens have not thought through the implications of their expanding preference, that they often fail to translate explicit or ideological endorsement of scientific method into consistent educational and other institutional kinds of implicit belief or behavior, would be true of them as it is true in lesser or greater degree of all peoples of the world—certainly the North American. For those who prefer the deterministic orientation in its various manifestations, the present trend is unfortunate. For the greater number who choose to be primarily activistic, the trend is one of the most inviting features of the Puerto Rican laboratory in human development.

CONFIGURATION AND EDUCATION— SOME TASKS AHEAD

On one proposal, both panels would tend to agree: education has great responsibility toward all four areas of belief examined and reviewed in the present chapter and the preceding one. On this proposal, we too agree. Yet it is one which, in any consciously deliberate way, is so seldom attempted anywhere in education—not just in Puerto Rico —that a pioneering opportunity awaits the several kinds of action proposed by our respondents.

In some sense, to be sure, any education that encourages forthright analysis of ideological attitudes and practices is already on the road toward this kind of opportunity. But even in the limited degree that such study occurs, it is likely to be piecemeal and dependent upon the whim of unusual teachers or the even rarer educational administrators who happen to be versed in, say, philosophy and anthropology. Moreover, in terms of the kind of philosophy of education required for an age of crisis, the need to attack the conflicts prevailing almost everywhere between explicit and implicit levels of belief and conduct is far from merely academic; it is equally a social and psychological need that touches everyone. Cultural and personal health both depend upon its satisfaction.

The most vital of all proposals, in our judgment, was that the schools provide much more abundant ways to examine and experience their democratic ideology. The more often they do so as a day-by-day affair, the more will students, teachers, parents, and administrators become acclimated not only to the disparities between that ideology and deeper attitudes but to the corrections in policy and practice that must be made if these disparities are to be reduced. The *personalismo* tradition, for example, which one notes so plainly in the line-staff structure of school authority, is not likely to be modified from any amount of merely verbalized awareness of overdependence upon leadership. It will be modified in behavior only as and if constant and widespread participation in educational and social planning occurs all the way from the humblest rural school right up to the Department of Education and the University themselves.

The same principle applies to each of the other three areas. Nontheological aspects of the Christian and other world religions—social service is one—can and should permeate the whole curriculum by providing ways for children and adults to contribute to the program of human welfare that now preoccupies so many in the culture. To become a part of, say, the housing program is entirely practicable by relating Community Problems and other courses directly and actively to that program. The Division of Community Education has already pointed the way; it remains for the schools and colleges to emulate its example in terms appropriate to their own resources and responsibilities.

Nor can problems of morality be "parked" outside the classroom.

We thoroughly agree with the leader respondent who drew an analogy with cheating. Explict codes of moral conduct of whatever kind will remain in acute conflict with the implicit level just as long as students fail to harmonize such codes with their overt actions. We do not say that prevailing moral dichotomies even on the explicit level will magically disappear as such harmonizing occurs; the moral life is notoriously resistant to change. We do say that by far the most effective way to increase compatibility is certainly not by the sort of "character education" that indoctrinates by exhortation, but by enabling young people to face and share their moral problems with utmost honesty and frankness.

The interdependence of all four of our exemplary areas is underscored by the fourth. To develop the scientific attitude toward life is, at the same time, to deepen and widen the scope of democratic, moral, in some ways even religious attitudes. Accordingly, the view of one or two subcultural respondents that morality is a matter for religion, while socioeconomic and other problems are a matter for scientific treatment, seems to us mischievous; it perpetuates the same dichotomies and thus the same evils of hypocrisy and conflict. Democracy, too, is the ally, not the enemy, of science: in both, the approach to all issues of life—including moral issues—is critical and self-correcting, cooperative and public, rather than arbitrary or authoritarian.

As elsewhere in the world, these interdependencies have not been achieved in Puerto Rico. The gaps and inconsistencies, not only between them, but between each of the four areas in its explicit and implicit levels of meaning and behavior, remain, in many instances, alarmingly wide. Indeed, our own observations would lead us to conjecture whether—in the matter of race prejudice, say, or in the degree to which the scientific method is actually grasped, or even in the extent to which democratic methods are desired in education—our panels have been anything like critical enough. Theologically influenced deterministic attitudes, moreover, seem to us often at odds with activistic attitudes even though we recognize, as do various respondents, that the issues here are anything but simple—indeed, that some aspects of the religious mood are not necessarily inimical to the latter kind of attitudes.*

At the same time, the plea of several spokesmen that Puerto Rican

* For further discussion, see pp. 284–291.

culture seek for a balanced view between "contentment" and "discontentment" (and thus, in some respects perhaps, between the "religious" and "scientific" orientations) points toward a configuration that may supersede the one-sidedness of either by fusing the virtues of both. Further consideration of the possible meanings of this and related fusions is the theme of our concluding chapter on the nature of cultural order.

can students easier to "understand" than Continentals—and not merely because of language.

Other respondents on both levels chose to deal with the Spanish-North American amalgam in terms of location, age, or status. Thus it was held that people of lower status still tend to be more Spanish than people higher in the scale; people in the coastal regions tend to be more North American than those in the interior; the younger generation is more so than the older. One grassroots respondent made a striking, if arguable, point to the effect that the lowest status groups are much more loyal to the United States politically than they are in their customary habits of living, whereas just the reverse is true of the highest status groups: they are likely to be Continentalized in their external manner of living (among them one often finds the largest North American automobiles, the latest North American appliances, and the most fashionable North American clothes), but they are often lukewarm in their regard for the political relations of Puerto Rico with the United States. This respondent, supported by a few others, would qualify his paradoxical observation in certain respects, and particularly in one: men of both the lowest and highest groups are most likely to practice the Hispanic tradition of concubinage —the lowest, because economic considerations enter directly into such a relationship only a little, if at all; the highest, because economic costs are no obstacle: they can best afford the "luxury."

The answer to our question—"Is Puerto Rico a syncretic culture?" —was also challenged by a minority of leaders on the ground that a national character was already well developed before the intrusion of the United States. Although opposed by those who, we remember, were skeptical of the creative importance of Puerto Rico's history, two leaders were sure that a clear national character emerged near the middle of the nineteenth century. According to one, the appearance of several great leaders in the fight against slavery and in the promulgation of a liberal political-social ideology was the primary cause. Indeed, development of the Island's ethos, which had been well under way by the beginning of the twentieth century, was retarded for a time by the disrupting impact of the United States. The second leader (he was not entirely consistent with other of his comments that seemed to favor the syncretic view) appeared convinced that North American influence has not as yet fundamentally altered "the feeling special regard for their heroic opposition to slavery and exploitation. Another suggestion favored a large-scale exchange program, financed by the federal government, so that hundreds of Puerto Rican teachers could spend many months each year acclimating themselves to the North American way of life at the same time that Mainland teachers were serving on the Island.

One leader recommended concentrated attention to rural patterns, including opportunities for students to live with rural families. Puerto Rico has been, after all, essentially agrarian and it cannot afford to sacrifice the positive virtues of these patterns if its character is not to be emasculated. A supporting commentary on this recommendation was the answer of grassroots respondents to the question of whether, if they had the choice, they would rather live in the country or in the city: a larger proportion preferred the former than the latter, including several urban residents.

Another leader pointed out that Puerto Rico has an unusual educational responsibility in a broader sense. Precisely because it is developing its own syncretic culture, it can serve as a "bridge" between South and North America—helping to interpret each to the other in ways that neither one is equally equipped to do. The Point Four program is already performing something of this function; for this, among other reasons, it should be expanded.

But perhaps the most fundamental recommendation was that prolonged, scholarly investigation be made of the whole question of this chapter and that the knowledge thus attained be slowly and carefully enfused through the curricula of all Island schools. With this end in mind, courses in political science, economics, geography, sociology, and anthropology should be added and enriched. For teachers in training, it was proposed that the cultural foundations of education be introduced, with special attention to the problem of Puerto Rico's syncretic character.

Once more we conclude our interpretation both with a review and a critical evaluation of our own. To consider the former first, the national character of Puerto Rico, however resistant to precise articulation, acquires at least one kind of fertile meaning when it is perceived as a cultural "mutation"—that is, as a creatively syncretic product of

PART III

THE PROBLEM OF CULTURAL
PROCESS IN PUERTO RICO

INTRODUCTION TO PART III

GO WITH US to a *colonia* (large sugar plantation) a mile or two east of the town of Cañamelar. There, in the middle of the field, a tremendous red machine, imported from the United States, is clattering across the charred stubble. A tentacle-like arm protrudes horizontally from its side into the rows of standing cane, ruthlessly cutting them down and pulling them back into piles in the wake of the machine. Three men operate its controls; others follow behind to cut and pile up the stalks that evaded the revolving knives.

A hundred or more workers stand watching the operation, some with expressions of anger and worry, others with inscrutable stares. We approach a worker and ask him what he makes of it. He answers sharply: *"¡Al diablo a ese monstruo. Neustros hijos necesitan comer!"* ("To hell with the monster. Our children must eat!")

The machine and its masters ignore him. Intermittently the loud clattering stops and the young mechanical engineer in charge tinkers with one or another wheel or chain. We speak to him next. "This is a tryout," he replies in adequate but typically accented English. "Thus far, it costs more to operate than hand-cutting would cost, and it cuts only about half the amount in the same time. We are trying to perfect it so that it will cross irrigation ditches without getting stuck. Also, we expect to reduce the size of clean-up squads from thirty to four or five. It will take a while yet. But we'll perfect it all right."

Near the cutting machine is a mechanical loader. It lifts the piles of stalks neatly and efficiently from the field and deposits them in a string of tractor-drawn trailers. The loader has been in operation about two years and has itself replaced many workers in that brief time.

The union leader who has driven us to the field is also worried. The men threaten to strike, he tells us. He is trying to dissuade them against hasty action, although he points to a clause in the printed contract which he carries in his pocket and which states that mechanization of cutting or other operations is subject to negotiation between employers and workers. He admits that mechanization cannot be stopped, but he insists that any such changes must be made gradually in order to prevent wholesale unemployment. Factories must be brought to Cañamelar to absorb displaced cane workers. The union is prepared to invest $100,000 from its reserves in a single factory.

The next day two hundred men go on strike. The roads leading to the *colonia* are guarded by dozens of policemen, but there is no violence. Nearly all respondents in this subculture are sympathetic with the strikers. Like the workers who spoke in the field, they fear the era of automation, of which the huge machine is for them the worst of all warning signals. They remind us that in the few short years since Cañamelar was studied by anthropologists, so many steps toward automation have been taken that, among major processes, only cutting remains a hand operation. It is therefore upon this job that the bulk of cane workers and their families still depend. For this backbreaking, blackening toil they receive a little more than $5 per eight-hour day. And this is time and a half, won for them by their union when most *colonias* instituted the practice of burning off the superfluous fibers and leaves of a cane crop just before harvesting —a practice which does not reduce sugar content but certainly does make the labor still more arduous. And now even this reward is threatened.

The cutting machine—this "monster" of the technological age— is thus a graphic symbol. No characteristics of Puerto Rican culture are more conspicuous or more dramatic than those of change. In more than one sense, change is the fulcrum around which all other events and facts revolve.

In the present part we examine some of these characteristics in terms of the problem of process, one of the major concepts we have adopted by means of which any culture may be examined and interpreted. Like the problem of cultural order, process in Puerto Rico has many aspects, only a few of which can be considered.

Of course, problems of process have already received attention. No one can examine such questions as the nature of the family, class structure, history, configuration, and national character without constantly observing that almost every facet of the Island's cultural order is affected both directly and indirectly by swift events of the present period. Nevertheless, granting the interdependence of order and process, and of these in turn with goals, we propose to single out various problems that arise when the dynamics of the culture are systematically approached.

These problems may be grouped around several large overlapping questions, to each of which a chapter is devoted. First, what are some of the main dimensions of the cultural process now in operation? Second, in what ways do and should culture and education cope with these dimensions? Third, how do the dynamics of the culture affect personality? Fourth, how do and should people deal with cultural processes through their capacity to learn? And fifth, how do and should culture and education in Puerto Rico meet the problem of two languages?

It would be well to recall that, as in Part II, we have a double responsibility toward these questions: on the one hand, to report the evidence obtained primarily from our resource panels and secondarily from our obervations; on the other hand, to criticize and evaluate this evidence in the light of our own cultural-educational-philosophic theory.

CHAPTER NINE

A CULTURE IN DYNAMIC FLUX

ANTHROPOLOGY HAS shown us that cultural processes are complex and multiple. A number of concepts have therefore been developed that prove to be fruitful ways of unifying, explaining, and sometimes controlling an otherwise bewildering mass of human activities—activities that often, on the surface, seem to clash with one another and to reveal no meaningful arrangement.

Two such concepts were anticipated by Chapter 5: *causation* and *prediction*. Another, which surely relates to both of these as well as to others, was that of *progress*. Still others have been implied. Hitherto we have not, however, explicitly referred in this volume to the following familiar concepts of cultural process:

Innovation—the recombining of cultural traits and complexes so as to produce a qualitatively different form and thus original effect.

Diffusion—the spreading of specific cultural traits and complexes from one culture to another, oftener inferred from various kinds of records than directly perceived.

Acculturation—the ongoing processes of observable contact by two or more cultures upon one another, resulting in observable modifications of one or more of the cultures in contact.

Force—the imposing or depriving of cultural traits and complexes with varying degrees and types of coercion that often if not always accompany acculturation.

Assimilation—the process by which, through observable contact, greater or lesser parts of a culture are absorbed by another to such an extent that these parts can no longer be distinguished between the two cultures as significantly different in quality.

Nativism—a collective reaction against assimilative and other processes that have threatened to alter indigenous cultural forms.

Conflict—the manifestation of disharmony between cultures or within a single culture that may range all the way from hidden tension to open warfare.

Focus—the tendency of a culture to express greater variability and resilience in some of its practices and institutions than in others.

Still another important concept of process—*crisis*—we defer until a later place.* Meanwhile, let us note that the definitions just stated, while they epitomize our understanding of what experts incline to accept as the core meanings of the respective concepts, would doubtless be modified by many. Also, these concepts are interdependent. It is often difficult, for example, to decide in a given case where to draw the line between diffusion, acculturation, and assimilation. Nevertheless, as in the case of others thus far utilized, the group of concepts just defined can assist us in operating upon several important phases of culture and education in Puerto Rico that highlight the stirring events of recent years.

In this chapter our panels, supplemented by occasional observations of our own, look at the processes occurring today. In the next chapter, they relate these processes directly to the schools, after which, again, we react normatively to what both chapters report together.

Our chief reaction to this report will be that the overwhelming sense of cultural movement in Puerto Rico carries with it unbounded potentials both dubious and promising in worth. This reaction is scarcely astonishing. Indeed, the numerous conflicts and disturbances already observed in Part II are integral with the processes now to be considered. But, just as in their case it appeared to us that opportunities for resolution were abundant, here too we shall find them abundant. The most needed of these opportunities and one of the most neglected thus far is to draw education into the mainstream of cultural change—to make of it, in the strict sense, a *focal* institution.

WHAT IS ORIGINAL IN THE PUERTO RICAN CULTURE?

When two cultures are in contact, they thereby modify the nature of one or the other or, probably oftener, of both. In this sense, degrees of innovation always result from diffusion and acculturation even when striking novelty does not. The question is apropos in the case

* See pp. 311–317.

of Puerto Rico because, as "the crossroads of the Caribbean," it has been influenced by four great caravans of culture—the Indian nations, Spanish colonists, African slaves, and North American capitalist-democrats. In addition, it has of course been deeply affected both directly and indirectly in other ways—for example, by immigrants from South America and Europe. (The smattering of English, Scandinavian, German, French, and Italian along with Spanish names in the population attests to such infiltration.) In the light of what we have learned from our panels and other sources, these four caravans, however, have been the most impressive and direct.

The diffusion of Indian traits over many centuries by way of other Caribbean, Central, and South American cultural areas and beyond can be taken for granted. Many fragments of their culture, such as stone images, pottery, and arrowheads, have been discovered and preserved that confirm this observation. More extraordinary is the fact that little if anything of unique importance from the pre-Spanish epoch of the Island can be singled out as a trait or complex of its living culture. Unlike areas where the Indian culture was not virtually liquidated by invaders, no innovations that could be credited directly to the aboriginal culture were noted by our respondents.

(We do raise a question whether careful research by physical anthropologists would not disclose that Indian facial and other bodily features continue to be inherited as genetic characteristics by parts of the population with a long Insular ancestry. This is an entirely amateur opinion that was formed from observing thousands of Puerto Ricans, but it has since been confirmed.[1])

Whether the African people who were forcibly brought to Puerto Rico beginning early in the sixteenth century have contributed striking innovations is equally doubtful from our evidence. That the *santi-guadora* and her healing rituals are African-influenced along with certain carvings and other artifacts, and that these have been modified since their origin, is indisputable. But they are not, apparently, any more indigenously Puerto Rican than they are Dominican or Cuban or Jamaican. Nor is the religious rite of "possession," as practiced by several Protestant sects such as the Defenders of the Faith, culturally distinctive of Puerto Rico. To be sure, ethnological research conducted recently in Loíza, a village made up largely of dark-skinned inhabitants, may have demonstrated that ceremonials dramatized by its *fiesta* have created a novel aesthetic fusion of African and Spanish-Catholic traditions.[2] Also, two respondents (though not without disagreement by their peers) mentioned the *bomba* and the *plena* as original dances that resulted from this fusion. Yet when one views the Island as a whole, one is as much struck by the contrast between it and Haiti in terms of the creative impact of African culture as by the contrast between it and Central American countries in terms of the Indian culture.

Turning to the two remaining caravans of culture—the Spanish and North American—the case for originality in the process of Puerto Rico's evolution becomes stronger. Recalling the modesty with which leader respondents tended to appraise the importance of art in the Island's history, nevertheless a number of them insisted that some original contributions have been made. Most frequently mentioned was the Spanish-influenced music of the *danza,* although one respondent insisted that even this was imported from Venezuela. Other musical and dance forms for which originality (though with Spanish derivations) was claimed by one or more informants were the *seis* and *mapellé,* while others mentioned three musical instruments: the *cuatro, tiple,* and *requinto.*

No one claimed that Puerto Rico has as yet made any very distinctive contributions to the plastic or graphic arts, but several were prepared to argue that within the last five or so years a group of painters have been maturing who, though still strongly influenced by artists such as Picasso and Orozco, herald a rich and quite unprecedented period of creative achievement. Literature, while it too was admired by a few, generated less enthusiasm either for achieved or anticipated originality than did the field of painting. Still, according to one informant, there is no reason why all the fine arts should not flourish in the future. Especially is this possible if promising young innovators can have the benefit of exposure to the great art centers of the world—New York, Paris, Rome—in the same way that other citizens have benefited by travel and education abroad. A sound economy could make this possible.

What of inventions or other innovations in scientific, social, economic, and similar areas where North American influence is strong? No one mentioned any in pure or applied natural science, but a substantial group did agree that, since about 1940, a number of unprecedented accomplishments should be recognized in industrial, governmental, and welfare practices. At the same time, no unanimity could be discerned as to how far or in what ways even these could claim to be innovations in a precise cultural sense.

Fomento (improvement) is the name popularized by the government for the program of the Economic Development Administration briefly described in Chapter 1. Is *Fomento* an innovation? Several respondents at the national level were prepared to call it so. But a larger number agreed that it had been transplanted in its basic policies primarily from Chile.

Informants were divided more evenly on the question of whether the "mutual aid" housing program directed by the Department of Agriculture could be called an Insular invention. The central technique of this program is the teamwork provided by owner-builders: by contributing and sharing their labor they have been able to construct thousands of small, tidy concrete houses in many rural communities at an extremely low cost. Those who doubted the uniqueness of this program said that Puerto Rico had acquired it from Sweden. Moreover, the practice of cooperative labor through the *junta* (group) came by way of Spain and has long been a custom during coffee-picking and other busy times.

One leader chose the "proportional benefit farm" to exemplify an economic invention—a system whereby the government provides land and other facilities to individual farmers in exchange for a share of the income. In contending, however, that more countries had learned from Puerto Rico how to conduct such farms successfully than the other way around, he was also admitting that this plan had much in common *with* that of other countries.

The closest approximation to a consensus on the question of innovation was reached, not in the economic sphere, but in government and politics. While by no means every respondent volunteered this opinion, all but two who did so were sure that the institutionalization of the "Commonwealth" or "Free Associated State" is original. One of the dissenters was doubtful that the concept has been clarified; it is still a "question mark." The other simply held that the concept is not original at all. The large majority also recognized similarities to the British Commonwealth of Nations.

But they were equally quick to point out differences, particularly in

the growth of what, in Chapter 8, was called the non-nationalist attitude. This attitude, in the present context, was described by one
leader as a new concept of political relations in which cultural identity
is not only retained but reinvigorated without retreat into a fictitious
because unworkable isolationism. The Popular Democratic party as
the archexponent of the non-nationalistic concept is, according to another leader, unique not only in this respect but in its lack of
resemblance to any Continental or other Latin American party—in
its pragmatic flexibility, for example, and in its exceptional honesty.
Still other ingredients that strengthen the claim of governmental and
political originality are, first, the combination of Anglo-American and
Spanish principles of law and public administration; and, second, the
policy of representation by minority parties in the Insular legislature.

The more general views of further respondents on the present
issue may serve to tie several loose strands. The question of just when
a work of art or an institution deserves to be called an original creation or invention was considered at least as difficult to answer in the
case of Puerto Rico as it would be of other cultures. Often it becomes a matter of degree so that, while the basic plan of, for example,
Fomento may have come from Chile, or the mutual-aid housing
program from Sweden, the way that elements have been recombined
and adapted still may produce an effect not duplicated elsewhere.
After all, since the Island is made up of human beings who are
different as well as like other human beings, its culture would inevitably generate some originality. Indeed, as one leader put it, the
very fact that it has an infinitesimal amount of natural resources per
capita, and yet that it has managed despite this gigantic handicap to
raise its standard of living to a level roughly equal to that of the two
richest countries south of the United States—Argentina and Venezuela—this in itself is no meager innovation. Perhaps it is the most
impressive of all.

THE PROBLEM OF CULTURAL FORCE

A second question of process is whether and, if so, how far other
cultures have imposed themselves, violently or passively, upon Puerto
Rico. The question is important because, for one thing, it helps to
anticipate correlative questions of whether and, if so, how far resistance and conflict have developed against any such imposition.

No respondent chose to stress the exercise of force during the pre-American colonial-theocratic period, either in the original conquest of the Island or in the subsequent treatment of Indians, Negro slaves, and immigrant peons. Yet, as noted in our discussion of the temporal dimension, so little vigorous resistance by people on the Island was said to occur during the four long centuries of Spanish domination that the term, rebellion, would scarcely fit any of the abortive incidents that have been recorded.

But when we come to the great moment of invasion by the United States, the role of force was explicitly considered. No one denied that the occupation was itself achieved by the exercise of superior power. Yet very few seemed anxious to believe that force has operated since then except in one important respect—in the early imposition of the English language upon Puerto Rican schools. In economic matters, no one singled out the rapid development early in the century of huge North American-owned sugar plantations as an instance of force. On the contrary, two respondents recalled that Puerto Rican farmers were free to sell or not; most of them sold their land not because they were compelled to do so but because they were offered exceptionally high prices.

Several others did point out that a kind of inadvertent force operates whenever people have no choice but to accept what is offered to them. In this sense, migration to the Continent of vast numbers of workers, for example, is not an action that most of them choose to take; rather, they must take it in order to be employed at all. Likewise, the consumption of Continental food, clothing, appliances, movies, and thousands of other products that shape minds as well as sustain bodies in exchange for earnings is not a choice that Puerto Ricans freely make among alternative choices. However much they may feel satisfied, most of them *have* no alternative.

By comparison with early decades of the U. S. regime, to be sure, choices in some ways were said to have widened. The first imported Governors were diligent in trying to superimpose not only language but wholesale customs and practices. Unlike the United States, where a democratic ideology gradually developed concurrently with democratic institutions, Puerto Rico found itself suddenly compelled to accept both. One Governor in particular was described as "a 150 per cent American" so bent upon transforming the Island almost over-

night that he exercised unremitting "missionary zeal." One tragic consequence was the bloody "massacre" (as it is often termed) of a
number of Nationalists in the city of Ponce. Another consequence was
the habitual practice of gubernatorial and congressional favoritism in
appointments and promotions of Puerto Ricans regarded as strongly
pro-American. These types of coercive acculturation have now been
superseded by freedom to elect political leaders and to select among
different political programs.

And yet, as one spokesman contended, perhaps the almost acquiescent willingness of so many citizens to follow the cultural lead of the
United States becomes in itself a subtle kind of coercion. The fact
that no "naked, brute force" is exercised in propagandizing for North
American standards of living, for conformity with North American
notions of proper behavior, or for North American economic or
educational practices does not necessarily mean that force is nonexistent. Since 1898, the United States has "called all the major
plays." If today its calls seem more muted, they are still audible
enough, he said, to those who care to listen.

ACCULTURATION AT WORK—A SAMPLING

As in the case of other processes thus far considered, and as particularly anticipated by our preceding chapter, acculturation in Puerto
Rico is the effect chiefly of its relations with Spain and the United
States. Other cultures, however, have had their influence both directly and, still more richly, indirectly by way of the latter two
cultures. When, for example, we talk of Spanish-Puerto Rican acculturation, which of course has been tremendous, we refer to a process
that derives from at least the whole of Europe and South America.
Similarly, the influence of the United States is really transcultural,
since the latter has been profoundly affected by a great variety of
cultures. In this and later sections, we shall take these facts for
granted, and concentrate on the more direct kinds of acculturation
that are now occurring between the Island and the Continent.

The picture drawn a few pages back of the sugar-cane cutting
machine in a testing operation is a typical picture of the impact of
technology on an agrarian economy where the resulting acculturation
is largely in one direction. Continental technology, in this respect,
produces many more changes in the receptive culture than the latter

does upon the country from which these machines come. Thus far there is relatively little acculturation between the two.

But when one considers more than technology—that is, if one includes other dimensions of Puerto Rican and North American culture—then the process is more reciprocal. Consider the cultural inroads of over a half-million Puerto Ricans upon New York City alone. A large fraction of this half-million have permanently departed from municipalities such as Cañamelar because technological unemployment and other insecurities offered them no option. They carry with them, of course, not only their language but a whole assortment of other baggage that cannot be weighed on the airport scales— feelings, habits, customs, and beliefs. At the present rate of population increase, one well-informed respondent predicted that New York in ten years or less will contain more Puerto Ricans than any other nationality (not excepting the Irish) and that, perhaps even sooner than this, a mayor of Puerto Rican origin will preside in its City Hall. Already the culture of the third largest metropolis on earth is being affected in multiple ways—witness the Broadway hit *West Side Story,* or the well-attended exhibits by Puerto Rican artists and clothing designers. Nor should we overlook the more pervasive though less glamorous results of daily social and business contacts, intermarriages, religious affiliations, classroom interminglings.

That Puerto Ricans generate negative as well as positive reactions upon New York life—juvenile delinquency, most notoriously—no respondent denied. Several at the grassroots did remind us that only a tiny proportion of migrants have been responsible for much sensational and damaging publicity. (This judgment is corroborated, incidentally, by New York statistics showing that the percentage of Puerto Ricans with police records is little if any higher than that of the city's population as a whole.)

The constant absorption of U.S. culture by Puerto Rican migrants has, moreover, prodigious retroactive effects upon the Island. Virtually every resource person in this study mentioned close relatives— brothers, sisters, fathers, mothers, uncles, aunts, sons, daughters— who live somewhere on the Continent, many of whom return for visits and who, in turn, are visited. In addition, the cyclical flow of migratory workers carries with it a variety of fresh learnings—speech, clothing styles, work skills, food habits, courtship and recreation practices. All this leaves a permanent deposit upon Insular patterns after the workers have, once again, flown away from home.

Easy communication as well as transportation also accelerate the acculturative process. While three grassroots respondents took no magazines or newspapers (in the home of a rural middle-class respondent with several children, not a single book or magazine was anywhere to be seen), the majority subscribed to one or more— among them, the Spanish or English edition of *The Reader's Digest, Life,* and *Time,* as well as *The National Geographic, The Saturday Evening Post, Glamour, Popular Mechanics,* and, of course, *Imparcial, El Mundo,* or both. Homes of several national-level respondents (not all were visited) contained hundreds of books, many more in English than Spanish, as well as the air edition of *The New York Times.* Privately owned radio and television stations, though their programs are mostly in Spanish, copy the conventional U.S. format as far as possible, and incessantly advertise a polyglot of Continental products, from Schaefer beer to Chevrolet cars. It is estimated that, although the first station is but half a decade old, some 150,000 television receivers already operate.

Moreover, North American holidays and modes of entertainment are fast encroaching upon traditional Puerto Rican ways. *Beisbol* (baseball) is probably the most popular sport, although cockfighting, racing, the lottery, and public gambling casinos more directly reflect traditional recreations.

All grassroots respondents also agreed that, though the Hispanic-Christian *fiesta* of Three Kings Day continues to be more widely celebrated than Christmas Day in rural areas, the latter holiday (complete with real Christmas trees imported from New England and Canada) has taken priority in typical urban neighborhoods. Even many rural homes boasting of a brother, uncle, or father who has lived on the Continent now celebrate both days with comparable zest. The tradition-weighted town of San José again is revealing: during our stay there, one merchant for the first time in a career going back half a century had placed a miniature, illuminated Santa Claus in his display window for the Christmas season. Like hundreds of other merchants in Puerto Rico, he was preparing for *two* profitable times. Unlike the haggard, depleted stores that one finds in Mainland towns on December 26, Island stores quickly become crowded all over again in preparation for the second great holiday on January 6. And children increasingly expect toys on both festive occasions.

Other U. S. holidays besides Christmas Day that are now recognized more or less officially are something of an index to the wider process: Valentine's Day, Washington's Birthday, Thanksgiving Day, Memorial Day, and the Fourth of July. Special Puerto Rican days are Discovery Day, Abolition of Slavery Day, de Hostos Day, Muñoz Rivera (the father of Muñoz Marín) Day, Three Kings Day, Barbosa Day, Constitution Day, and de Diego Day.

To claim that citizens celebrate both sets of days with equal enthusiasm would not, however, be accurate. One San José respondent maintained that two popular Continental holidays—Thanksgiving and the Fourth of July—are barely noticed in her community. On the other hand, while Easter Week has always been honored by both cultures, even here North American acculturation begins to operate: toy bunnies and gaily colored Easter eggs now give quite as great delight to thousands of Puerto Rican children as to their Mainland cousins.

One of the most traditional celebrations—the annual *fiesta* held to honor the local community's patron saint—has also been affected. Cañamelar is no doubt a good example, where a ten-day celebration is held each July. In the past two decades, we were informed, activities have shifted largely from private homes, where clustering by class and status was customary, to the town *plaza,* where people of all levels mix together, dance to Spanish, Latin, and Continental music, and patronize mechanical rides and games manufactured in the United States. The originally religious character of the *fiesta* has been overshadowed by practices increasingly like those of the North American or European country fair.

Nor should we overlook modifications in dancing itself. Latin American rhythms, such as the calypso and rumba, remain popular. But large dance halls on San Juan's outskirts advertise "rock-'n-roll" as their main attraction, along with all the other Continental styles that alternate with Spanish tunes from hundreds of blaring juke boxes in town and country stores and bars. Also, the manner of holding partners was noted by one disapproving woman respondent: whereas only a few years ago it was thought improper for a couple to dance in close embrace, and while it is still frowned upon by many of the older generation, today the practice at almost any public dance is rather commonplace.

Even swimming may be influenced by U.S. customs. Until quite recently, it was said, only a small proportion of Puerto Ricans regarded their lovely warm sea and its golden beaches as places for recreation. A result is that, though no statistics are available, one physical-education authority estimates that less than 20 per cent of all adults of either sex have learned how to swim at all. Most of the younger generation still apparently fail to enjoy the sport with anything like the gusto of young Continentals. During many months, beaches are usually quite empty of Puerto Ricans. Though the figure has been disputed, thousands of children in the coastal city of San Juan were said never to have visited the oceanside. One student respondent confessed that, though he had occasionally swum in a pond, he had never once been swimming in the sea—less than a mile from his own home. And an older respondent recalled that not very long ago the sexes were always kept two hundred yards apart if they did venture to immerse!

Nevertheless, here too taboos are weakening—perhaps a consequence, in part, of the zest with which *americanos* indulge in swimming as a sport. Women who, until a few years ago, would refuse to be seen in bathing suits now wear the latest Continental styles. One public beach, Luquillo, is now so crowded on summer days— occasionally, on a beautiful Sunday, even during the quite fictitious "off-seasons" of fall, winter, and spring—that the government recently decided to erect a fine public bathhouse, the first of its kind on the Island.

Countless other examples of the Continental-Insular process of acculturation could be cited—some mentioned earlier. The recent importation of Catholic priests familiar with North American ways of activating religious programs; the spread of consumer cooperatives throughout the Island; the introduction of modern agricultural methods such as crop rotation and fertilization; the growing participation of women in economic and public affairs; the mixture of English and Spanish advertising signs; the electrification of rural areas with accompanying refrigerators, radios, washing machines, and similar devices purchased on the installment plan; the tremendous decline in illiteracy (a sizable number of the parents of grassroots respondents but none of the latter were illiterate); the equally tremendous improvement in sanitation and control of diseases like malaria; the sharpening awareness of time schedules and of the need for punctuality in an age of technology—these are miscellaneous samplings from our subcultural respondents. That they may be of unequal importance or that many, such as literacy, cooperatives, and public health, are not distinctively North American at all but international and intercultural in no way detracts from the central fact that they underscore—namely, the complexity of cultural dynamics even in a Lilliputian country.

ASSIMILATION IN THE CULTURE

We have come far enough in support of the argument that acculturation is a basic phenomenon of Puerto Rican experience to ask now whether this process may be leading in turn to the virtually complete assimilation of certain North American traits and complexes—and thus whether at some points significant differences may no longer prevail between the two cultures at all. The same question could, of course, be raised about Spanish-Puerto Rican assimilation, but again we limit ourselves, not only because we confess that it is simpler to do so, but because interest today centers less in the latter than in the previous question.

Here we return for guidance primarily to our leader respondents. Several refused to admit that, as defined, this process has thus far actually occurred in important ways. The majority held that assimilation has occurred, but again they disagreed as to where and what kind.

The largest affirmative consensus was at the point of economic processes—merchandising, banking, and manufacturing all being selected by one or another to exemplify its accomplishment. Here, however, one respondent recalled a point stressed in Chapter 4: some long-established Puerto Rican businessmen still cling to Spanish-conditioned business methods—often in the face of keen competition by Mainland-trained managers and owners. Agricultural practices, moreover, are considerably farther away from assimilation than are industrial practices.

Others chose the political sphere. Granting failures now and then, two leaders contended that respect for law and judicial order is the primary instance of assimilation from the United States. A third chose to emphasize acceptance of the political principle of human equality. All three reaffirmed that, while the system of law remains partly Spanish, Puerto Rico has gone farthest among Latin American countries in identifying itself with the Continental conception of political authority.

One leader who took the majority view selected journalism, by which we assume he meant the U.S. format of newspapers, styles and standards of reporting, editorial policies, play-up of syndicated features such as comics and columnists, and display advertising. Education was selected only once as the prime example of assimilation.

The most impressive argument offered by the minority against the fact of assimilation in Puerto Rico was by means of analogy with Mainland states that border Mexico, as well as with Louisiana and the Province of Quebec. In New Mexico and Texas, for example, a great deal of acculturation has occurred, yet Spanish-Mexican traits still remain abundant. Similarly, French influences continue to permeate such urban subcultures as New Orleans and Montreal. Surely, then, a country not only surrounded by a vast expanse of ocean but with a longer history than any of these places could scarcely become assimilated in a mere half-century.

True, industrial and technological techniques as well as modern housing, more recreation, better health and education, are being rapidly adopted. These, however, were regarded by one leader as dubious examples of assimilation by one culture of a second because they remain "impersonal"; they are "similar results from similar causes" that could have come from many cultures, North American or otherwise. True, too, assimilation may occur on a surface level—in a style of hat or lipstick, for example, or in the display of foxtails on cycle handlebars. But where personal factors are dominant—such as in the mores of the family—few if any native customs and habits have yielded to assimilation. Nor are they likely to for a very long time. After all, the minority implied, Puerto Rico is not a remote, primitive culture with an obscure tongue all of its own. Its heritage is a great and ancient one. So too is its native language.

THE "NATIVIST REACTION"

Anthropologists have helped us to perceive the "boomerang" effect of culture contacts that are too rapid or too coercive or both. India, South Africa, Norway, Hungary, Poland—the recent history of these and other countries attests to the powerful resistance, both passive and violent, that can be mustered against any imposing culture, however rich and mighty it might be.

The processes we have thus far examined require us to ask whether such resistance is not also a factor in Puerto Rico to be weighed with care. The role of force, negative or positive, is one crucial factor that bears upon the issue. Acculturation and its extreme consequence of assimilation are equally germane. The illegal Nationalist party, with its record of violence on the Continent as well as on the Island, is, of course, the most publicized evidence that resistance is no illusion. The legal and moderate *Independentista* party (a significant quota of its remaining members were reported to be veterans of the armed forces who resented real or imagined discriminatory treatment) is further evidence.

But the total number involved in these groupings is comparatively small. A more controversial issue confronted by our respondents was whether or not a "nativistic reaction" to acculturation vis-à-vis the Mainland is now occurring within the Popular party itself, and therefore within the great majority who support this party and its government. In the past few years, the issue has become a prime topic of conversation among intellectuals. Perhaps the most tangible evidence of the government's sympathies is the establishment of the Institute of Puerto Rican Culture, with its own building, staff, and anthropologically trained director. And one political effect is a contention of the Statehood party that the Popular party is, despite protestations, beginning a slow retreating action from its earlier policies toward one that is potentially more nationalistic than its ideology affirms.

This viewpoint was not the prevailing one on either level of resource persons. In the first place, the question of nativism did not seem to most subcultural respondents to be either urgent or especially meaningful in theoretical terms. To be sure, we have noted how most of them have wanted to see Puerto Rican traditions preserved and appreciated; equally, however, they have wanted Continental history and culture to receive wide recognition and acceptance. And even among intellectuals the nativist reaction, most leaders were sure, is confined principally to a small minority—intellectuals, moreover, who were said to have little influence among the people as a whole and who are governed by romantic and emotional moods more than by logic or political acumen.

In the second place, the point was made that there is nothing really new about the phenomenon of nativism in Puerto Rico—in fact, one expects it of a culture that is "wide open" to prevailing cultural winds and that must accordingly take frequent bearings as it sails forward. Granting the ever-present danger of chauvinism, Puerto Rico ought intermittently to take inventory of itself and to come to terms with what should be preserved as well as discarded. Perhaps a little nativism could compensate, as long as it does not *over*compensate, for a certain amount of cultural inferiority that derives not only from its minute size but from a bitter colonial past.

In the third place, some misunderstanding may have arisen particularly from efforts of the present Governor to place the culture in more balanced perspective. One of his favorite roles in clarifying a problem was said to be that of the "devil's advocate"—to take the affirmative for, say, nativism not because he necessarily believes in the whole case himself but to "smoke out" the negative case. Such a dialectic is fruitful, no doubt. But sometimes it leads to misquotations!

In the fourth place, recent concern by the Popular party with the Puerto Rican heritage may perform a realistic political role. That is, entirely aside from the intrinsic merits of such concern, it may also wean votes away from the *Independentistas* who regard cultural distinctiveness as close to the heart of their party philosophy. Against this strategy, if indeed such has been the case, must, however, be placed a possible loss of votes to the Statehood party, which sees no virtue even in a temperate nativistic movement.

These were the main points in explanation of recent events. Yet just how seriously the whole issue ought to be regarded was not answered quite unequivocally by those most sympathetic with governmental attitudes and actions. Whether the Cabinet itself is of one mind on the issue is a reasonable question. Moreover, while the Institute of Puerto Rican Culture was for the most part endorsed, one Popular leader was skeptical that it could have any lasting influence in the face of present trends toward acculturation if not assimilation of North American attitudes and practices. Indeed, he was fearful that the Institute—already weighted, he said, with government personnel —would perhaps unwittingly encourage the development of an "official culture" and that, if it must function at all, it thus would be safer as a private than a public venture. Several others, however, defended it as not so much a way to glorify the culture of the past as an organized means of adapting the past to creative present and future opportunities through arts, crafts, and many other media.

For these and still other resource persons there seemed to be less worry of emasculating unique cultural qualities than of failing to take adequate advantage of cultural opportunities—above all, Mainland opportunities—that would modify and enrich those qualities. Here we are reminded of the concept of syncretism developed in Chapter 8: Puerto Rico can neither turn back upon itself nor so completely acquiesce in the processes of assimilation as to lose its own cultural flavor. One leader recalled an amusing metaphor in order to clinch this point of view. Assimilation is something like the Angostura bitters in a Manhattan cocktail: you can't quite identify the taste though you guess it's there, dissolved in the other ingredients. A little nativism is more like the cherry: it doesn't claim to be the whole Manhattan but it has a place of its own, a taste of its own, and, most important, it contributes a distinctive quality to the character of the whole. Puerto Rico ought to be the cherry in a Continental-Caribbean cocktail.

The importance of the nativist issue was placed in fresh perspective by a respondent unusually familiar with the United States. Up till almost the close of the nineteenth century, he reminded us, nearly all of its art and thought were faithful replicas of or, at best, slight deviations from those of the Old World, of which it too had been a colony. From the growing pains of the young nation, nevertheless, originality slowly emerged until, as the twentieth century took hold, the works of philosophers, musicians, dramatists, architects, novelists, and other creative Continentals acquired a power and respect of their own that were anything but imitations. In one sense, and of course on a smaller scale, Puerto Rico suffers now from its own creative growing pains. It has had to learn all it could from the two cultures that affect it most. But soon it must launch out, borrowing much but not enslaved by debts to its lenders. In this respect, the so-called nativist reaction is not accurately a regression at all. It could, he said, become a quest— an adventure in cultural discovery.

THE PROBLEM OF CULTURAL CONFLICT

Such a quest is never an easy or simple one. There are always risks, uncertainties, and therefore tensions, bewilderments, and gropings.

Arguments over nativism itself are one natural consequence. More serious is the problem of how deeply, beneath the busy surface, conflict occurs—conflict of such a nature as to split rather than unify the culture.

This problem, too, has been anticipated. Also, since it is psychological as well as strictly cultural, we shall return to it in our discussion of personality.* When, however, the question of conflict was directly raised in the present setting, respondents were not inclined to regard it as one of their paramount anxieties.

On the political plane, several argued that the creation of the Commonwealth has dissolved much of the confusion and worry chronic before that time: no longer are the majority of people split asunder, as they were for decades, over the dilemma of statehood versus independence. As long as that dilemma remained central, the lure of independence, on the one hand, was bound to generate ambivalent feelings of inferiority to the United States at one moment and superiority to it at the next—a common polarity in ailing cultures as well as ailing personalities. The lure of statehood, on the other hand, was bound to generate not only fears that the cultural essence would somehow be lost but likewise gnawing doubts that the objective in any case could really be won. With the dilemma once resolved for most citizens, they were able to turn their attention to education, health, economics, transportation, and other urgent needs.

The conflicts that do remain were considered minor compared with those of, say, India during the British imperialist era or even of today. Rigid caste systems are nonexistent, and racial discrimination is, as we have seen, far less serious than in the United States. Class conflict, while certainly one facet of vertical order, is hardly militant; even peaceful strikes have recently been comparatively few. And while hostility to Spanish entrepreneurs and landlords has by no means disappeared, it too is fading.

What of the real feelings toward *americanos,* thousands of whom have come to Island industries, to government posts, to positions as consultants and teachers, not to mention the many more thousands who spend brief times as tourists and vacationists? Our earlier answer coincides, on the whole, with a fuller answer here. The majority of Puerto Ricans, it was held, do not harbor pronounced feelings of

* See pp. 208-210.

hostility toward this minority group (or indeed to any other) but incline to look upon them in a friendly way.

Nevertheless, ethnocentric tendencies are not unknown to either nationality. Social life in the faculty residences of the University as well as in the nearby residential section of Dos Pinos, where many well-educated American and Puerto Rican families live in close proximity, appears to be typified by more *intra*group than *inter*group fraternizing. Children of the two nationalities, moreover, do not always play together as spontaneously as one might expect—a consequence due partly to language barriers but partly also, no doubt, to the still potent Puerto Rican customs both of parental protectiveness and of the extended family with its interests and gatherings in which visitors might seem rather out of place.

Actually, if one leader is correct, rural people on low socioeconomic strata express greater warmth toward *americanos* than do upper strata —more so than, say, businessmen or lawyers—although the proper amenities are performed in meetings of middle- and upper-strata people from both groups.

This contention would be questioned by another leader of different background. It was his experience that the higher that people of both cultures rise on the class and status ladder, the more mutual understanding and mutual respect they tend to acquire—a contention bolstered by a point previously noted to the effect that top-level Puerto Ricans and Continentals accept each other more comfortably than do those even on the middle levels. At the University of Puerto Rico a reluctance of the permanent staff, itself chiefly middle class, to accept visiting North Americans into its own circles or even to utilize their competencies at all efficiently in professional endeavors was mentioned by several leaders, none North Americans themselves. (One insisted that this failure was not due to "ill will," however; nor is it true only of the university professor.) A subcultural respondent was also sure that, at least in his sugar-cane area, suspicion of *americanos* in middle-class managerial posts is due to remnants of colonialism that persist in their own attitudes and thus in those of their workers.

Two other explanations were offered for residues of ambivalence on the middle level. One: Puerto Ricans on this level are less secure than those of higher class and status in their mastery of English, while, unlike the lower levels, they feel that Mainlanders expect them to speak fluently. Two: a certain amount of unconscious conflict results from superiority feelings on both sides (feelings that could, of course, extend beyond the middle class)—on the *americano's* part, because he may remember that he comes from a more powerful, more developed nation; on the Puerto Rican's, because he may think of himself as belonging to a spiritually more mature and much older culture.

A full analysis of the causes of remaining ethnocentric barriers could hardly be expected from interviewees. What did emerge, from our own observations as well as from theirs, is that some exclusiveness remains a fact. One may observe the frequently meager proportion of Puerto Ricans in such organizations as the College Women's Club and in social affairs sponsored by the officer personnel of military bases on the Island. One may observe that racial segregation has by no means altogether vanished from North American groups, however fast it is said to be diminishing. One may observe the not infrequent occasions on which, when one or two non-Spanish-speaking Continentals are present in a small professional meeting with bilingual Puerto Ricans, Spanish nevertheless is the language used. One may observe the tendency of the Puerto Rican to wait for North Americans to make first overtures toward social or professional association—a hangover, one respondent held, from the first decades of this century when they monopolized most positions of power and prestige. And even if one has not observed discriminatory treatment suffered by migrants in the States, surely it would be surprising if some resentment from such treatment were not transferred back to North Americans in Puerto Rico, too.

Granting, furthermore, that some Continentals may thus become convenient "scapegoats" on whom troubles are falsely blamed, by no means all are innocent. Recent fleecing of numerous Puerto Rican citizens through an imported scheme to "get rich quick"; distortions at the hands of U.S. "experts" who write and speak pontifically about the Island's culture after one or two brief visits—these are but two examples of legitimate reasons for hostility.

And yet the remarkable fact is not so much that conflict continues from year to year as one aspect of the total process; it is rather that so many Puerto Ricans now subordinate this factor. Of course, some disturbances inevitably follow in the wake of accelerating change. How, for example, is the legal structure of the Commonwealth bound to the federal legal structure?—an intricate problem indeed. The tremendous movements of people from rural to urban areas, from lower to higher classes, from unskilled to skilled occupations—not to mention incessant movements overseas with their aftermath of family instability—these, too, generate a variety of problems that were held to border on, even when they do not overtly generate, conflict as such.

The tendency to minimize this problem was reinforced at the grass-roots level. There our respondents seemed much less fearful that historic beliefs and customs would gradually deteriorate from, for example, the incessant pounding of North American wares, habits, and shibboleths on the ears of radio listeners than that their way of life would not become Continentalized rapidly enough. The young graduates of San José High School were perhaps typical: well over half, we were informed, had no desire to remain in that unusually traditional community; they wished to move on to San Juan or New York, to go to college if possible, to rise in the social scale, to earn money in the quantity that Stateside citizens reputedly do. True, they professed devotion to their customs. But when a choice was offered (and to many it was offered in the form of scholarship aid and job opportunities), there seemed to be little hesitation.

The same attitude was paramount in considering what kinds of recent changes met with their approval. Far from opposing the major ones of the past twenty years, respondents in all three subcultures repeatedly endorsed them. Let us list, in no particular order, the changes that they volunteered to mention: better living standards, higher literacy, more and improved roads, public housing, public electric power, many athletic fields, more efficient public administration, widening industrialization, unionization of workers, the eight-hour day, free schoolbooks, rural electrification, the school lunchroom program, decline of the piecework system, more hospitals, the immunization program, legalized birth control and sterilization, proportional-benefit farms, consumer cooperatives, the scholarship program, better relations with the United States, public medical and dental clinics, more socialized religious activities, appointments of Puerto Ricans to key Insular posts (especially the Secretary of Education), increase of savings accounts, the Commonwealth constitution, new school buildings, and greater hopefulness for the future.

This extensive endorsement was not devoid of its own ingredients of conflict. Let us list our informants' replies to the question: "Of what changes, if any, do you most strongly disapprove?" While two respondents could think of none, the remainder selected these examples: low-quality television and radio programs, woman's weakening role in the home, spreading juvenile delinquency, expansion of private schools, growing reliance on government, fear of criticism by officials, rising cost of living, greater moral laxity and divorce, failure to apply scientific principles of criminology in Puerto Rican prisons, decline of old traditions such as kite flying at Easter, decline of home responsibilities by children, rapid mechanization of sugar-cane farming.

It is hardly necessary to add that some of these examples are incompatible in part or whole with some on the previous list. Thus they help to establish that, though most respondents on both levels were inclined to minimize conflict, it still remains a phenomenon of the total process that cannot be ignored.

HOW AMENABLE ARE PUERTO RICANS TO CULTURAL CHANGE?

One of the tendencies discernible in any culture is its internal variability in accepting and supporting change. That is, some phases of a given order tend to be more amenable and pliable than other phases. This phenomenon, we remember, is sometimes termed cultural focus.

Looking at the question in terms of the class and status structure, grassroots respondents were oftenest of the opinion that the lower levels are most amenable for the obvious reason that they have the least to lose and the most to gain by change—an opinion expressed with vigor by a number of those who themselves previously or currently belonged on these levels. No one considered the top level most amenable, although one conceded that it may be, in so far as thereby it is sure of "cashing in." A minority held either that the middle group is readiest to change or that it is at least as ready as the other main groupings. Only one respondent took the view that all class and status levels are about equally amenable, but two others felt that the lower levels are least amenable because too preoccupied with sheer survival to worry about anything else.

Leader respondents had fuller opportunity to examine the question, but they were quite as divided on the matter of levels as were their compatriots. A larger proportion focused upon the middle levels than upon the others—thus far disagreeing with the grassroots majority and impelling us to note that both groups of respondents tended to claim greatest amenability for the respective levels with which they themselves were identified. A minority of leaders did select the lower levels; yet even this minority differed on whether rural or urban people of these levels are the readier to change. Those who insisted upon the greater amenability of the urban lower levels cited the increase of skilled laborers and the radical readjustments that they must make both in home and work in order to fit within the emerging industrial order. Those who chose the lower rural levels supported their case by the eagerness of many underprivileged groups both to migrate and to tackle local problems by cooperative effort. The fact, however, that many low-status people continue to live in the same extremely humble houses after their income rises may be some indication, it was claimed, that they are not nearly as interested as many urban dwellers in ostentatious display.

This claim could hardly be made for the middle levels. A number of respondents who detected the greatest susceptibility to cultural change on those levels also found them to be motivated by inflated ambition for material success, for possessions that assure "conspicuous consumption," and thus for living standards beyond the financial means of many. (The incredible proportion of large, latest-model automobiles, very few fully paid for by their drivers, was one testimonial, lavish social affairs another.)

One leader reminded us of the grim history of middle-class anxieties and instabilities which demagogues exploited so skillfully in countries such as Germany—anxieties and instabilities that he thought could become acute in Puerto Rico also. Already, we recall, enthusiasm of middle groupings for the reform program of the government in power has apparently tapered off. And while no one could say that they have as yet turned overwhelmingly conservative, some would say that these groupings are more so today than they were only a few years back.

Fear of a severe middle-class reaction was not widely shared. Other leaders held that increasing education combined with travel abroad equips the middle levels not only with the greatest readiness of all strata to participate in social reconstruction but the greatest competence to make adjustments to it without the likelihood of such disasters as have elsewhere occurred.

Only two leaders, incidentally, thought that the upper levels are particularly amenable to change, and both qualified their opinions— one by including the middle levels along with the top ones, the other by limiting the top ones to the *nouveaux riches* as contrasted with Spanish-oriented families of high status. One other leader, however, partly agreed with a lone grassroots respondent who had felt it impossible to choose one level more than the other in the vertical structure. It all depends, he said, upon the groups you mean *within* each class or status.

This cautious judgment was well borne out when leaders were asked to select those cultural institutions and occupations that best express the phenomenon of focus. Here consensus was fairly wide: business is the most pliable, hence the readiest to adopt new techniques, and the quickest to promote new products. At the opposite extreme, the most resistant institution, a majority agreed also, is organized religion. Both agreements would be supported by the anthropological postulate (made also by one leader) that "material" changes are easier to make than "immaterial" ones.

Yet deviations were once more revealing. Thus, when speaking of the amenability of business, we were reminded to distinguish between technology, industry, and banking, on the one hand, and retail merchandising, on the other. When the latter is controlled (as much of it hitherto has been) by owners trained in Spanish practices, it is often regarded as one of the most serious blocks to "progressive" economic change in Puerto Rico and one serious reason for above-average prices on staple commodities such as food and clothing. (The establishment of over twenty latest-model supermarkets in less than three years' time, some of them consumer cooperatives, is a major effort to meet this serious problem.)

Similarly, it is essential to distinguish between religious institutions. Most respondents agreed that Protestants are on the whole less resistant to change than Catholics—an understandable consequence of the fact that many of the former have themselves known from first-hand experience what it means to transfer their allegiance from the dominant Church and to effect the considerable emotional and social readjustments involved in such a transfer. One respondent went so far as to contend, however, that both religious bodies are now becoming more amenable to cultural change than the government itself —an opinion related to his insistence that the nativist reaction discussed above has seriously dampened the earlier aggressive mood of political reform. This opinion, it is only fair to add, did not appear to be shared by other resource persons.

Another respondent, though he would disagree with the viewpoint just expressed toward the government in power, disagreed also that religion is the single most resistant institution. Granted that religious dogmas are inflexible, their methods need not be—a fact apparent in the quickening of social initiative by both major sects on the Island today. Rather, he said, the family is the most resistant of all institutions, with agriculture somewhere in between the family at one extreme and industry and the professions at the other.

As for political parties, it is doubtful whether most respondents would agree with still another leader's view that the Nationalists and Independents are the most resistant to cultural change, while the Populars and Republicans are the most open. All four parties, of course, claim that they advocate a good deal of change, though of varying kinds and in varying directions.*

Miscellaneous comments by individual respondents on the question of cultural focus also deserve recording. First, the Puerto Rican *Ateneo* (a long-established, quite exclusive "academy of arts and letters" with strong historical allegiances) was called the single most resistant institution of them all! Second, labor unions are sometimes greater obstacles to cultural change than are managerial groups because, as in the sugar industry, they block mechanization. Third, some public administrators and lawyers are at the focus of cultural process, although this would not apply by any means to all of them. Fourth, it is illogical to generalize about the conservatism of the family as a whole since some members, notably the younger ones and those with a migratory record, may be much more resilient than other family members. Fifth, and here we turn at last to problems of education as a process, the schools are the best example of focus among all institutions of the culture.

* See pp. 326-332 for further discussion.

CHAPTER TEN

EDUCATION'S ROLE IN THE DYNAMICS OF PUERTO RICAN CULTURE

UNFORTUNATELY, the opinion expressed at the close of our preceding chapter—namely, that education is the single best example of cultural amenability to change—was far from a general one. While all informants recognized the crucial role that education plays or at least should play in the processes of the culture, only one leader seemed prepared to concede that it is as yet well synchronized with the transformations occurring elsewhere. Subcultural respondents appeared less dissatisfied with, for example, education's acculturative responsibilities than did those at the national level. Yet more than a few even of the former were ready to point out deficiencies and to suggest ways of strengthening such responsibilities.

Let us take the same concepts of process in the sequence with which we have thus far operated upon the culture at large, and apply them now to education.

INNOVATION

No aspect of either the primary or secondary schools—liberal arts and vocational alike—was singled out to illustrate a cultural innovation. With the exception of the second-unit junior high schools, which were said to have been borrowed from Mexico and elsewhere with but slight variations, the system is Continental.

The only program to which innovation properly applies is, according to the largest obtainable consensus, the Division of Community Education. This program, already touched upon several times, is not devoted to adult education in the conventional sense. Courses in literacy, vocational or agricultural skills, and similar programs of "fundamental education" (such as are now sponsored by a large number of other underdeveloped countries) are provided also in Puerto Rico. The Division, however, is concerned with "helping the people to help themselves" by patiently encouraging them to face their own problems in their own neighborhoods, and then to follow through with their own cooperative actions. Films planned and made by the Division are one of the important motivations: most actors are everyday people, settings are real communities, and film scripts are usually built out of actual experiences. *The Bridge* is a dramatic model—the story of how rural people built a bridge for their children to reach school and homes in safety after heavy rains. These films are shown throughout the Island, often in connection with a group discussion program conducted by some forty specially trained leaders, each of whom may work year in and year out with a single community deep in the mountains, while serving a group of five or six others at the same time.

Many other learning instruments are brought into play besides films. The art work of the Division—its fine lithographs are one instance—has been honored by critics abroad, as have several of its films at international festivals. Creative writing and music are also integral to its plan of operation—so much so that, in the judgment of one informant, some of the most original Insular art now emanates from the Division staff.

No one claimed, of course, that community education in Puerto Rico is completely unique—certainly not in the intervening years since its establishment in 1949. (Hundreds of Point Four and other foreign visitors have seen and borrowed from the program.) But in its neighborhood-centered philosophy, in the persistence with which it "sticks with" a community, in its repudiation of superimposed leadership and indoctrination, as well as in governmental backing both by way of policy and money, this program, we were told, still more accurately meets the cultural criterion of an innovation than any other in the educational field.

The program of general studies at the University was the only other development mentioned as approaching such a criterion. As in the case of community education, influences from the outside were frankly recognized. The rather commonly held notion, however, that the program in Puerto Rico is merely an imitation of the University of Chicago plan was sharply qualified. The requirement of general studies for all undergraduates in three domains of culture—humanities, social science, and natural science—as well as the reading of classics in each of these fields does, to be sure, reflect the Chicago program. Indeed, we shall have occasion to note the resemblance to what we may call the perennialist philosophy of education.* But the influence of Latin American and Spanish members of the faculty, as well as ideas and experiences developed by Puerto Rican educators, were said to modify and transfuse both content and methods of teaching the general studies.

FORCE

Many respondents agreed that the most dramatic example of "force" in the Island's history of education was the early English program—a subject to which we return in Chapter 13. The relevant point now is that this program was a result of still wider North American coercion in the sense that the whole educational policy was determined by commissioners of education appointed by Congress rather than chosen by the people of Puerto Rico through their elected representatives.

This policy, prevailing for the first fifty years of American rule (1898-1948), resulted in the almost universal superimposition of textbooks, ideologies, methods, ceremonials—indeed, the whole paraphernalia of conventional Mainland schools. For many years, apparently, meager opportunity to modify, much less to question or to criticize, was afforded anyone connected with Insular public education.

Whether acquiescent habits on the part of school personnel that were well entrenched during the relatively long period of North American control would help to account for their perpetuation under the present centralized, although now formally autonomous, system of education was a question that we did not help our respondents to pursue. That coercions and pressures of various kinds and degrees from supervisors and similar officials remain conspicuous phenomena of this system was, however, vehemently stressed by several at the grassroots who could speak from direct experience.

ACCULTURATION

To the question, Is education deliberately and consciously concerned to help citizens come to terms with the interactive effects of North

* See pp. 179-180, 410-411.

American and Puerto Rican cultures upon each other? the answer was more negative than positive. Several leader respondents went so far as to volunteer the opinion that Island educators, by and large, thus far reveal minimal awareness of acculturative problems.

The program of the Division of Community Education was singled out for criticism here by several spokesmen, perhaps because it was otherwise so often praised. The fact that no anthropologist thus far has been included on a staff represented by many other competencies was regretted by one respondent. A tendency to underestimate intelligence of adults involved in the excellently motivated community discussion circles (a tendency revealed not by its films but by oversimple, ungraded printed materials that were said to "talk down" to the people) was alleged by another.

Feeble attention to urgent problems of family migration was stressed by still others—a point one informant underscored by recalling the relatively mild difficulties of, say, nineteenth-century Irish immigrants (with their English language and Anglo-Saxon customs) as compared with twentieth-century Puerto Ricans when they land for the first time in a city like New York. Nor should acculturative problems related to migration be confined, another felt, to a few discussions and pamphlets: simple but important matters, such as how to dress on an airplane trip, what *not* to wear if one does not wish to be singled out, should be frankly faced and examined.

Similarly, the transition that thousands of countrymen are undergoing as they move to urban industrial centers is accompanied by problems of cultural readjustment which, it was held, community education should more squarely confront. Thus far, although a start has been made, urban people have not been primarily involved in the Division's efforts—the explanation being that, with so few trained leaders, there is danger of dissipating the effectiveness of a program that cannot reach even rural people to nearly the extent that it should.

This does not mean that problems of acculturation are ignored by the Division. As was pointed out, when a community builds its own road it opens the way to closer contacts with other communities and ultimately with the large cities. When it learns to play new games, to enjoy folk dancing, and to develop perhaps for the first time a sense of its own communal spirit and democratic powers—here again processes of change and readjustment are tacitly at work.

Numerous proposals were made also for other levels of education. Much more attention to cultures besides the Puerto Rican and North American is required if problems of acculturation are to be met with any kind of intelligent awareness—an obvious reason being that most other cultures, too, are now involved in rapid changes due largely to increasing contacts. One concrete suggestion at this point was that new university courses be established that deal with diffusion and acculturation in all Latin American cultures.

Again, a "two-way track" between every local community and its own school would enable each to contribute to the changing patterns of the other. One recommendation was that physical education and recreation provide instruction in swimming, at least for students in schools within a mile or less of the sea. Pure and applied art, moreover, should depart from conventional notions of prettiness and encourage free, creative sharing in community life through many media. (Special courses in industrial design, already proposed by the *Fomento* administration, signalize this need.)

In the training of teachers, it was urged that acculturation become a focal concept of the curriculum rather then be relegated to incidental treatment. Better scientific understanding of the social psychology of *growth,* for example, would enable teachers to serve both children and parents of communities that require patient and informed guidance from those who should be best equipped to offer it.

Additional educational suggestions with acculturative implications will be incorporated under the remaining concepts. One point, meanwhile. When leader respondents were asked whether Puerto Rican education today more greatly helps or hinders acculturation, the great majority by implication refused to adjudge education guilty of a serious "cultural lag" even when they were equally agreed that its role is far less vigorous than it ought to be.* One leader thought that the great difficulty is not so much that education limps behind other cultural processes; it is rather that education is not well integrated with them—that its own processes are piecemeal and planless to such a degree that they work at cross-purposes with economic, political, moral, and other expressions of acculturation.

But a minority were unwilling to be even this charitable. They felt that Insular education, on the whole, retards more than it sparks

* For comparison, see pp. 417-419.

acculturation—that other developments such as the industrial have to wait repeatedly for the schools to catch up. One leader went so far as to assert that, in his judgment, they are more than a quarter-century behind the culture as a whole! In the opinion of another member of this dissenting group, the danger is that the gap will widen further —that radio and television will increasingly but haphazardly replace classrooms as the chief instrument of acculturative processes through education.

On the subcultural level, one teacher among our respondents volunteered to ask twenty of her fellow teachers whether in their opinion Puerto Rican education manifests a serious cultural lag. Of these, seventeen supported the leaders' minority opinion that it emphatically does. All twenty, however, regretted the fact and expressed the belief that it should not and need not be so—that if the schools do not perform a vigorous acculturative role, this is due to a deficient philosophy and program rather than to any inherent or inevitable weakness.

The chief cause of the present lag in education, this respondent held, is the centralized system of authority and control—a system that discourages active participation and encourages passive acceptance of orders all the way from the top of the hierarchy down through echelons of lesser officials to the classroom teacher himself. The deeply entrenched habit of followership that accompanies such a line-staff structure compelled her, as a long-conditioned member of that system, to doubt whether any major improvement in education's role as an Insular agency of acculturation could be effected in less than twenty years.

ASSIMILATION

The prevailing opinion on the issue of whether Puerto Rican education does and should promote assimilation of North American culture patterns was more negative than on the issue of acculturation. Formally, the Mainland educational system has already been adopted. But this is quite a different matter from assimilation, defined in this context as the absorption of both the spirit and substance of that system.

For example, the philosophy of progressivism (the essence of which, according to its greatest exponent, John Dewey, is that good education is continuous, active experiencing of the democratic life[1]) has doubtless influenced American-trained educationists in the Department of

Education and in the College of Education at the University far more than any other. Yet, partly because of limited acquaintance with its principles, partly because of still more limited training and facilities by rank-and-file teachers, but partly also because of complex, often subtle differences between Puerto Rico and the Mainland culture which gave birth to and nourished the theory of progressive education, our evidence would indicate that the average classroom in the average Island school is nothing like a fair demonstration of that theory.

This judgment would not receive unanimous support. One leader held that some assimilation of North American education and of progressivist principles not only has occurred but that it is more than welcome to most Puerto Ricans. Especially is it welcome when they contrast the relative progress of the system here with that of sister countries of the Caribbean—with the attempts of Jamaica, say, to absorb the English educational system, or of Haiti to absorb the French system. Why, indeed, if Puerto Ricans are to work more and more closely with the United States, should their system *not* assimilate the best of both its educational ideas and its current practices? Actually, he argued, many Puerto Ricans have already moved *ahead* of many Americans in one significant respect—in their reverence for learning and the worth of education. Perhaps, by assimilating all that they can first, they can move ahead still faster.

Another minority voice at the national level offered the provocative opinion that the best single instance of assimilation in education is not even its attempts to emulate progressivism; rather it has been by way of the perennialist philosophy of education often associated with the ex-Chancellor of the University of Chicago, Robert M. Hutchins. This philosophy, which is strongly opposed to the progressivist, holds that the key to good education is the discovery and assimilation by all cultures of universal truths and values—the single most fruitful source of which is the great minds of history.[2] The center of this philosophy in Puerto Rican education was said to be (although it has affected other centers) the Division of General Studies at the University—a contention which, we recall, was questioned in discussing innovation.

Issues raised in connection with the two contending philosophies of education (we have, of course, greatly oversimplified their meanings) have contributed to, though they are far from the sole causes of, far-reaching disputes in Puerto Rican education on the policy and administrative level. These disputes are not germane to our present interest. What is germane is the central point made by the same respondent: the most significant educational assimilation that has taken place in Puerto Rico is not actually by way of the United States at all. The fact that the University of Chicago happened to provide the immediate stimulus is quite incidental. It could have been provided just as well by a European seat of learning—better perhaps, since the philosophy of education which lies beneath the concept of general education at the University of Puerto Rico is much more congenial to the total heritage of Western culture than to anything so provincially North American as the progressivist philosophy.

NATIVISM

Since assimilation was regarded by most respondents as a minor educational issue, it is logical to anticipate that any "nativist reaction" against efforts at assimilation would be regarded as equally minor. Not that history and customs were considered irrelevant to the educational program; Chapter 5 has shown that, treated in proper perspective, they are relevant indeed. Any proposal, however, that the schools should discard their Continental-shaped curricula in favor of curricula based as far as possible upon native and national traditions would apparently receive infinitesimal support.

On the contrary, the consensus of all but three at the grassroots favored more rather than less Stateside influence upon Puerto Rican schools. In the language of this chapter, they favored increasing acculturation if not even some assimilation. One of the minority held that the degree of such influence is now about right, the other two expressing much the same opinion as a minority of leaders: the schools still suffer from an overdose of artificially imposed North American methods, courses, and materials. Yet even these dissenters would apparently resist anything like a militant nativist reaction. What they wanted, rather, was a policy that would help Puerto Rico to deal more aggressively with its own needs—to face its limitations along with its strengths and hopes. Such a policy cannot possibly succeed as long as it copies, often slavishly, the ready-made curricula and methods of another culture. Yet it can and should borrow a great deal.

Further light was thrown on the nativist issue by the leader cited above for his contention that the one important instance of assimilation is the general studies program of the University. In his view, the nativist issue has become, despite popular indifference, a critical one. When, however, it is understood in philosophic terms, the apparent conflict between assimilation and nativism as opposing cultural processes could prove to be spurious. Assimilation, rightly understood, leads not to Americanization primarily but rather to Westernization—ultimately, in fact, to the universalization of culture. Nativism, also rightly understood, encourages appreciation of the indigenous qualities of any culture, including Puerto Rico's, that are at the same time concrete expressions of this universalization. Just as each individual citizen is both a unique person and a member of one human species, so education must seek both to express the distinctive traits of any culture and, simultaneously, their "commonality" with every other culture. The task that remains in Puerto Rico, he argued, is to recognize and synthesize these polaristic concepts rather than to treat them as antagonistic.

CONFLICT

Although we have found that cultural conflict was not a chronic worry of our panels, nevertheless, in keeping with their readiness to concede it as a fact, they were ready, also, to recommend educational steps toward its alleviation.

The most fundamental step was the expressed need for research in the social sciences, channeling the resources of the University through the Department of Education into the typical community. Such work should preferably develop as *action research*—that is, it should go farther than so-called pure research by testing out hypotheses in real social situations that could lead, when and if proved, to resolution of conflicts of the kinds we have considered. The desirability of establishing a "center for human relations education," utilizing the experience of similar centers on the Continent, was recommended by one leader as a way to implement such action research. Equally recommended was a high-caliber graduate school of education, with interdisciplinary studies in the behavioral sciences as the core of its curriculum.

One subcultural respondent considered the disputes among high-level educators over philosophy and policy as symptomatic of more pervasive cultural conflict—a condition but not a cause of the latter, he said. In any case, such disputes cannot, in the opinion of a leader, be resolved by merely intellectual discussion. The only practicable way is to effect compromises at the level of policy—to recognize some worth in, for example, both the progressivist and perennialist philosophies of education. A vital program can borrow much from each in method as well as content—perhaps from others too.

Ethnocentric clusterings of *americano* and Puerto Rican cultural groups are an instance, we were told, of a conflict that as yet receives almost no direct attention at any level of the schools. Anthropological concepts and findings, if they were included in the social studies on all levels, would be one way to deal with these clusterings. More attention to Puerto Rican literature in schools with many American children, and to American literature in schools with many Puerto Ricans, would be another.

Problems of cultural conflict should also much more consciously enter into adult education. Confusions and anxieties over the political status of the Island, the meaning of the "commonwealth" concept, and similar questions should be clarified through public lectures presented by the most competent authorities, Continental and Insular alike, as well as through discussion groups, films, and radio and television programs. Adult education, organized in special programs under public school auspices, could deal constructively with other types of conflict—between urban and rural groups, between worker and employer, between the younger and older generation, and ultimately even between ideological and metacultural beliefs.

One leader expressed concern over what he regarded as unhealthy competition—bordering at times on conflict—between various agencies concerned with public welfare. The result, he held, is not only waste of money and effort but a failure to cope with problems that ought to be met by combined resources. Selecting as an example the educational program of the University's Cooperative Institute, on the one hand, and the Division of Community Education, on the other hand, he held that neither one had thus far entered into any joint program despite methods and aims that are equally committed to fostering the democratic way in everyday life.

To what extent did subcultural respondents indicate their own awareness of conflict in the program of their schools? Let us record several examples: well-worn customs of boy-girl relations versus liberalizing tendencies in these relations; vocational training for skilled occupations versus liberal-arts education for upper-class ambitions; a democratic ideology of teacher-pupil participation versus long-established authoritarian routines; public schools versus private ones; finally, a desire on the part of many children to remain in school versus parental poverty or other reasons for withdrawing them. On the last point, consider this subcultural example: out of one recent group of 417 students who started the seventh grade, 54, or roughly 12 per cent, graduated from high school six years later.

One teacher respondent took pains, with the help of colleagues, to prepare a list of strong and weak features of the schools in his municipality—schools with above-average tax resources and therefore with advantages not available to many. The best features were these: good roads on which country children may walk to school (no public busses are provided); a local English supervisor, music teacher, and physical education teacher; a majority of high school teachers with bachelor's degrees; the lunchroom program; and "fairly abundant" learning materials. The features that most needed improvement were these: overcrowded classrooms; double sessions; insufficient books for some classes; meager vocational or craft education in a community that must speedily industrialize if it is to survive; no teacher of art; no elementary school library; a poorly stocked high school library with no librarian in charge; little firsthand study of community problems or resources; no faculty collection of professional books; inefficient provision of audio-visual resources by the Department of Education; and paper-work chores for the superintendent of schools of such magnitude as to prevent him from active leadership. This list is, we believe, revealing not only in suggesting certain implicit sources of conflict, even where they are not explicit, but also in what it leaves out. The observation above that most respondents were not acutely concerned with conflict as a major process is thus far reinforced.

FOCUS

This chapter began with the observation that only one respondent was inclined to regard education today as at the focus of change in Puerto Rico. Yet, when they were asked to suggest how education might become more focused—how, in other words, it might become a great force for cultural development—most respondents here, as at so many other stages of this study, were hopeful and enthusiastic. After all, in a culture whose prevailing mood is change, why shouldn't education serve as such an agency? Indeed, for at least one leader it ought to be *the* agency par excellence. But the question is, how can it?

In answering this question, a preliminary need was to face as frankly as possible some current limitations. The standard curriculum of the elementary and secondary school was adjudged to be much less amenable to problems of change than that of vocational and agricultural schools, or, for that matter, of informal but potent agencies such as television and the newspapers. Again, granting exceptions, most teachers and principals were considered to be ill-equipped as yet to deal with questions of cultural change for at least two reasons: first, because their responsibilities have been too delimited by the sheer burden of providing the three R's for overloaded classrooms; and second, because they lack minimal psychological and other behavioral knowledge that is prerequisite to coping with these issues.

The Department of Education was regarded as further handicapped not only by the magnitude of its job but by day-to-day routines, political considerations, staff insecurities, and limited funds. As for the University, while one opinion was heard to the effect that it is the most amenable of all institutions concerned with cultural change, a contrasting opinion held that in several respects (among them, industrial engineering, applied political science, teacher training, and firsthand experience with the Puerto Rican "market place") it was said in some ways to have recently regressed.

Turning to more positive reactions, consider first these specific proposals from subcultural respondents. (1) Expand the scholarship system by raising taxes so that still more students may remain in school and continue into college. (2) Enforce more strictly the laws of school attendance, especially in rural areas where too many children still are kept at home to do farm work or to carry lunches to their fathers in the fields. (3) Provide teachers in training with principles and practices of democratic human relations. And (4) experiment with programs that break the "lock-step" structure of requirements for students of unequal abilities—in language, say, and science.

Three imaginative recommendations were made on the national level. The first was that a "Division of Community Dynamics" be established by one or more educational agencies for the explicit purpose of analyzing and implementing cultural change. The premise governing this recommendation was that problems and tasks in so gross an area will not be faced effectively as long as they are left to peripheral treatment. Focus upon change must be *conscious* focus, and education is the most logical of all institutions for developing such consciousness. At the same time, one of the most fundamental of all scientific problems facing the Division should be the problem of emotions, of *nonconscious* factors, that operate in every individual and group effort—even the most intelligently organized. The Division should provide continuous experience for teachers, students, and other citizens to deal with concrete economic, health, political, and other problems, beginning at the local level but extending finally to the whole Island and even overseas. Programs of the Division should be approved by a board of directors made up both of educators and leaders, with the aim of maintaining maximum communication between both groups. Finally, the Division should be governed by a policy of participating *in* cultural change rather than merely of learning *about* it.

A second proposal was that two special high schools be established —one in the field of science, the other in art—their objective being to afford promising young people utmost opportunity to become well-trained contributors to the life of the Island. Continental high schools of these types should be carefully studied but not imitated. One of the clearest differences between them and any schools established here should be in an articulate awareness of both science and art as *cultural* processes and goals.

A third proposal was that a junior college be organized as a "community-centered" and experimental institution. Here the "folk high schools" of Denmark were said to provide one important precedent from which much could be learned. New ideas in curriculum organization, in liberal arts as well as vocational and teacher training, in methods of teaching and learning, and in building a cooperative program between community and school—these would all have opportunity to prove or disprove their applicability both to other levels of education and to additional junior colleges that should eventually be established. Whether such a college should be of the four-year or two-year type, whether residential or nonresidential, and other important questions of policy, should be determined by a specially selected board somewhat similar in make-up to the one suggested for the "Division of Community Dynamics." But its members should be committed to the desirability of unhampered experimentation in Puerto Rican education.

RECAPITULATION AND REASSESSMENT

Looking back at this chapter and the preceding one together—the first dealing with certain processes in their bearing upon the whole culture, the second dealing with their bearing directly upon education—how shall we epitomize the total impact of these processes?

The most obvious conclusion was caught in the phrase of one grass-roots informant who has lived in the same subculture for over fifty years: "Things certainly have changed!" A corollary of this conclusion—perhaps a cause of it as well as an effect—is that full agreement on the meaning of the complex elements to which this flux may be reduced is less typical than are ranges of disagreement. Let us, nevertheless, try to distill from our evidence the greater or lesser generalizations that emerge from each of the selected concepts as they bear upon culture and education considered now as one interactive process.

First, almost no dramatic *innovation* appears in Puerto Rican culture as a discernible result of Indian and African diffusion, and very few such innovations have resulted even from the Spanish or earlier North American periods of acculturation. While some originality, however slight, must have occurred if only because no culture ever *merely* duplicates another, the only conspicuous innovations have been viewed as very recent. The political concept of the Free Associated State or Commonwealth was regarded as by far the most original institutional invention in Puerto Rican history—the Division of Community Education being so regarded in the educational field. No recent economic programs were considered as original as these, although all of them have been adapted to Insular conditions in the course of being transplanted from Europe, South America, and the United States. In art, while outstanding creativity still lies in the future, greatest expectations were entertained for the field of painting.

Second, *force* as a cultural process has been regarded as subtle and subterranean much oftener than as overt. Also, it has occurred more by virtue of the absence of alternative choices than by direct coercion, although some superimposition over centuries of Spanish cultural traits and complexes, and now of the North American, has been and continues to be potent in virtually all institutions, including education.

Third, while some of the most important manifestations of *acculturation* (notably, those in the sphere of technological change) flow mainly in one direction, nevertheless many other manifestations, especially when they deeply involve human relations, were found to flow in more than one direction—today most conspicuously between the Continent *and* Puerto Rico. Communication and transportation are the two most ubiquitous means through which holidays, forms of recreation, and hundreds of other Insular habits and customs are now being modified. Education, by and large, was adjudged to be a less important agency of acculturation than it could and should become were it to give deliberate attention to this multidimensional phenomenon.

Fourth, some *assimilation* was perceived in several areas, most prominently in the economic. But this no more engendered the opinion that the unique cultural flavor of Puerto Rico is in danger of being lost than it would be justified in French Canada or the American Southwest. Education, meanwhile, was found to play even a feebler role in effecting assimilation than it does in acculturation—in this case a fact by no means as universally regretted. In the philosophy of education, it was said that Puerto Rico has not actually assimilated progressivism from America, despite the dominant ideological status of that philosophy among Island educationists. Whether perennialism has been more successfully assimilated in a limited sphere than has progressivism, and, if so, whether this is due partly to its classical European origins, was a controversial view.

Fifth, partly no doubt because twentieth-century Puerto Rico was said to have witnessed neither a great deal of overt cultural coercion nor of sweeping assimilation, the reaction termed *nativism* has been far from extreme. True, some pronouncements and activities by the top leadership have been interpreted as encouraging this reaction, but such an intention was also denied. Apparently the issue has not aroused the general population. Nor has it, except meagerly, affected formal education. Even among intellectuals, only certain "romantics" were said to want the pendulum to swing very far in a nativist direction. Actually, the two opposite extremes of assimilation and nativism

were viewed as an "either-or" choice which few citizens wish to ma
and which, on philosophic grounds, may in any case be a fa
dichotomy both for education and for the wider culture.

Sixth, formal establishment of the Commonwealth removed, ·
were told, one of the chief sources of cultural *conflict* that had hithe
driven many thousands of citizens apart. At the same time, tensio
and even hostilities in the form of ethnocentric behavior by both Pue
Rican and North American groups on different status levels are by
means as trivial as is sometimes superficially supposed. Nor shou
racial, class, moral, and other areas of conflict be dismissed light
Educationally, social-science research in these areas, much better teach
training in cultural understanding, and less exclusiveness among pub
service agencies were among the constructive proposals for alleviati
whatever conflicts were conceded to remain.

Seventh and finally, the fluidity of Puerto Rican life was illustrat
by the observation that the *focus* of cultural change is not conce
trated in any one class but is shared by both lower and middle class
and, though markedly less, by the upper class as well. Institutional
business was widely considered the most amenable to change, religi
the least. Education was not commonly regarded as a focal institutio
Nevertheless, our panels wanted it to spark and accelerate cultur
change much more than it does—a requirement demanding adve
turous programs in, for example, cultural dynamics, in seconda
education for science and art, and in community-centered expe
mentation on the junior college level.

In the framework of the educational theory through which v
have been reviewing these qualified consensuses, we must hearti
endorse such a requirement. Our position has been that educatio
rightly interpreted, is a formal and/or informal institution establishe
by every culture to support and promote its pervasive interests. Su
an inclusive function varies from culture to culture. In some, perha
most, cultures education has been regarded primarily as a conservin
reinforcing institution. In others, its role may be conceived much mo
as an agency for deliberate change.

Puerto Rico, as our respondents have thus far revealed it to us,
the latter kind of culture. The relatively gigantic sums pumped in
schools and other programs devoted to education are not spent chief
to habituate citizens to customary roles. Nor are they intended to d

velop worshipful humility toward power figures or inherited mandates. Respect for traditions is far from ignored; the establishment of the Institute of Puerto Rican Culture with a substantial budget is one graphic proof that it is not. But the mood and accent are different in tone—a contention perhaps as well supported by the apparent weakness of the "nativist reaction" as by the vigor of acculturative if not assimilative energies.

Serious problems, to be sure, emerge from the processes now under way. Differences of judgment as to virtually all of these processes are indicative of insufficient understanding on all levels of what they mean and how they are to be utilized to maximum advantage. We select one or two examples reminiscent of our previous examination of the class structure. Assuming with some respondents that the middle strata of the population are now eager for innovation, what does this herald for the future? The warning of one leader that these strata could congeal into conservative if not reactionary forces, as recent European history has proved they are entirely capable of doing, received no explicit support from other leaders. Again, on the questions of force and conflict, there seemed to be no greater sensitivity by either panel to covert manifestations—in class relations, say— than in the earlier discussion. Nor did retarding effects upon the acculturative process that result from segregation and discrimination suffered by migrant Puerto Ricans concern our panels very seriously— the resultant difficulties that migrants experience in learning English, for example, or the exploitative practices of Mainland farms and factories.

Both chapters could properly be criticized by anthropologists for insufficient distinctions in questions as well as answers between those processes that are the direct effect of Continental-Insular contact and those that involve a much wider network of intercultural relations. Thus the point should have been sharpened that the impact of technology upon Puerto Rican life is certainly not a peculiarly North American effect. As it was in parts of South America, such impact could have been derived just as well from industrial countries of Europe—Germany being one. Yet anthropologists would also agree that it is often hazardous to try to separate these impersonal forces from cultural traits involving personal attitudes and habits. Efficiency, for example, though everywhere a characteristic need of technological enterprise, is associated to an unusual degree with North America indeed, they often seem to regard it less as a means to maximu productivity than as a virtue in itself.

But even where acculturative processes and products could not characterized as deriving originally from the United States culture and very few probably could—we must bear in mind that they ha been carried to Puerto Rico during the past fifty years mainly a directly by that culture. To a lesser degree, the reverse process equa applies: however difficult it is to determine which cultural traits a Puerto Rican and which are originally Spanish, the fact remains th the Island style of life is being carried to the Continent by hundre of thousands of migrant citizens. The question of the ultimate sour of these traits in either culture is less germane to our interest th that of their current function in the interrelations of both.

We have dwelt briefly on these matters mainly to exemplify t kind of critical interpretation that education should itself underta if it is to meet the demands rightly placed upon it by our resour panels. Many further illustrations could be offered. One of the mo fundamental is the search for a Puerto Rican philosophy of educ tion. That the acculturative influence of both progressivism and pere nialism in their Continental formulations is substantial, but that neith has been effectively assimilated, seems to us reasonably evident fro the data presented. As we shall consider further, we question, indee whether the philosophy needed for the Island's schools or high learning has thus far reached anything like adequate expression.*

This issue is related to a still wider one: How profound or hc superficial are the changes now taking place in reshaping the tra and complexes of the Island culture? Here the concept of focus is ap it helps us to understand that these changes are probably much mo sweeping in, say, the economic sphere than they are in a sphere su as moral behavior. To the extent that this is true, it suggests to educ tion the need for a *strategy* of process—namely, to focus at first upc those spheres and groups most amenable to innovation, moving fro them slowly and carefully to those less amenable. Such has been, degree, the strategy of the Division of Community Education, thoug whether it has moved aggressively or consciously enough into the mo expectably resistant spheres—family relations, say—is a fair questio

* See pp. 402-415.

The pioneering proposal that a "Division of Community Dynamics" be established to guide educational processes in relation to those of the wider order strikes us as deserving of serious attention. Implicit in the proposal is a belief that we share fully: education in Puerto Rico could be, though it is not as yet, a major agency in measuring both obstacles and amenabilities, and in implementing desirable cultural change by public and scientific means in behalf of indigenous but also democratic ends.

CHAPTER ELEVEN

THE PUERTO RICAN PERSONALITY IN A TRANSFORMING CULTURE

BECAUSE CULTURES do not exist without human personalities, every preceding page has dealt in some way with the problem of this and the following chapter. Nevertheless, the problem of personality now requires more sustained attention for two chief reasons.

In the first place, the culture-and-personality movement has attracted the close interest in recent years of two major disciplines—psychology (including, of course, psychiatry) and anthropology. Although many more questions have been raised than answered, this kind of interdisciplinary effort is demonstrating that problems of human experience can seldom be met effectively by any one specialization.

In the second place, our own resource persons have continually indicated their concern for the nature of the Puerto Rican personality in its cultural milieu. In discussing the national character of their culture, for example, several respondents had difficulty in separating it from the character of the typical human being who lives within and contributes to the whole. This is expectable: actually, culture and personality cannot be separated. Hitherto in this study we have usually tended to view the culture through frameworks of large scope; now we view it from an opposite vantage point. Yet we shall see, over and over, that topics already discussed demand renewed attention when personality becomes the center of concern.

Here we approach the problem by considering whether, in general, a type or mode of Puerto Rican personality can be delineated and whether, in particular, any such characterization would apply to the traditional countryman. Then we return to the family, with special regard now for its influence upon personality formation. After attempting in a preliminary way to characterize our own subcultural panel, we conclude by asking whether the average personality could be described as neurotic.

Chapter 12 continues the discussion by relating the process of personality development to problems of learning and teaching. Thus, as in the case of Chapters 9 and 10, the present pair of chapters are to be regarded as complementary. Our summary and appraisal, presented at the conclusion of both, center in four principal judgments: first, the Puerto Rican personality, no less than the culture at large, is beset by numerous disturbances and negative traits; second, it is typified also by positive, constructive resources tending now to outweigh the negative; third, education shares responsibility for both the first and second judgments, but perhaps more heavily for the first; finally, it could and should play a more potent role in behalf of the second—a role that requires far greater implementation than at present of an activistic and creative theory of cultural learning tempered by the syncretic motif of the national character earlier considered.

IS THERE A PUERTO RICAN PERSONALITY TYPE?

One of the alluring frontiers in the culture-and-personality field deals with the type of personality that distinguishes the members of one culture from those of another. As in most other frontiers of the social sciences, it is not yet possible to find wide agreement either on principles or methods of research. Certainly, if only because we are confined mainly to the relations of personality to cultural process, our own investigation is at best preliminary. Nevertheless, the fact that our informants—especially on the national panel—expressed so many emphatic judgments on the "modal personality" is symptomatic of the concern they feel.

A commentary on the logical acumen of several of these respondents is that they at once recognized the impossibility of delineating such a personality in a way that would do justice to all kinds of people. Thus, when we talk about the "mode" or "type" or "character structure" of the Puerto Rican personality, we must always remember that we are talking about an abstraction, or perhaps about several classes of abstraction. Its usefulness, while thus circumscribed, lies in the degree to which it enables us to symbolize more clearly and thereby to cope

the traditional small home. Similarly, the plot of land around
despite the profusion of native flowers and shrubs, is often tota
neglected. (Many of the decorative plants that one sometimes fin
in the yards of middle- and higher-strata citizens have been recen
imported.)

The characteristic of aesthetic obtuseness was related to a comm
disregard for precise details of almost any kind. Such disregard,
true, could help to support an earlier observation that Puerto Rica
thus far are weaker in science and logic than they are in the humaniti

Also perhaps related is the insensitivity mentioned by various
spondents to the effects of personal conduct upon the comfort or co
venience of other people—loud-playing radios, say, or blinding aut
mobile lights, or littering of streets, washrooms, and other pub
places. For another respondent, such examples of insensitivity to t
surrounding environment were symptoms of a more fundament
trait: an immature sense of social and political responsibility. In
far as his contention is valid, it could be connected with the perso
alismo phenomenon discussed in Chaper 6—that is, with the habit
leaving responsibility to leaders once they are voted into office. Also,
might help to explain a concern still more distressing to one of
peers—namely, a low level of concern and imagination not on
among many business and professional men in improving their servic
to the community but also among many college students who are co
fident of well-paying jobs even after second-best exertions.

Turning to the positive side of the Puerto Rican personality, t
first point to note is that unanimity by no means prevailed with r
gard to all the negative traits singled out for comment. Thus, tw
respondents did not agree that suspiciousness or sensitiveness a
dominant. Two others held that while these traits were once conspic
ous enough, they are either waning or have largely disappeared.

Positively, the most frequently stressed quality was that of hospita
ity. One leader respondent who had grown up in the country spo
of the custom in his simple home of setting aside an extra plate
food for any visitor who might wander by. Charity, generosity (eve
amidst adversity), solidarity, and friendliness were stressed as suppor
ing traits. Another spokesman went so far as to suggest that the ave
age individual is so warm, outreaching, and gay that he should
regarded as more of an extrovert than an introvert—quite an opposi

are just as friendly if you give them half an opportunity; for still others, they are more versatile and flexible than rural citizens but also less self-reliant and less cooperative.

At one other point, however, consensus at the national level was high. The typical personality of individuals considered to be "Spaniards," as distinguished from long-resident Puerto Ricans, was weighted much more on the negative than positive side. Leader respondents thereby tended to support those at the grassroots, many of whom, we recall, resented the "superiority attitudes" of Spanish employers and *hacienda* owners. Here the appraisal was charged with such terms as "tight," "money-grabbing," and "clannish." Several contrasted them with the well-to-do *americano* who, they said, has often contributed to hospitals and other worthy causes, while the typically well-to-do *español* has contributed almost nothing either aesthetically (to the arts, for example) or to the material welfare. On the contrary, his typical plan until recently, these respondents said, has been to live in Puerto Rico for some years, to make as much money as he can, to return to Spain as soon as possible, and then to send a son or nephew back to take his place and so to continue the cycle for another generation.

This description, too, was modified by a minority. Such a picture of the Spanish personality in Puerto Rico was, for them, mainly a stereotype—an emotionalized "rubber stamp." One respondent was sure that Puerto Ricans still identify themselves more with the personality of the *español* than they do with the *americano*. Another suggested that the stereotype is analogous to that of the Jewish "scapegoat" in many countries, as well as to that of the Portuguese among Brazilians. Moreover, from the side of the Spaniard himself, the native Puerto Rican might be regarded partly in the fashion that native North Americans are regarded by Britishers. Both kinds of natives, a spokesman reminded us, were originally colonists and both have hardly behaved as loyal subjects ought to behave. Just as it has been said facetiously that the North Americans and English are a people "divided by a common language," so on occasion Puerto Ricans and Spaniards may likewise be divided.

Yet, despite these intriguing variations on a common theme, the argument was advanced that Puerto Ricans are now gravitating toward an amalgamation of all such variations and nuances in personality type. Rural and urban areas are not moving farther apart but coming closer together. Class divisions, though still wide enough, were held to be narrowing. The Spanish overload is disappearing. North American and Hispanic traits are blending. Thus, as the disinherited begin to receive their long overdue share of the Puerto Rican heritage, and as the Commonwealth thereby becomes more unified in meaning and practice, so will the character of its human members likewise become more unified.

THE JÍBARO AS ARCHETYPE

The problem of modal personality may be analyzed further by considering the case of the *jíbaro* (countryman)—the official symbol, incidentally, of the Popular Democratic party. Fluttering from hundreds of little rooftops, the simple white flag with its straw-hatted silhouette in red is an even more familiar sight in remote mountain *barrios* than in the largest cities.

The flag is significant. The party won majority support in the 1940's primarily through the vote of many thousands of rural people who had never before known the meaning of political power except in the hands of others. The original platform of the party was directed centrally to their interests, and they believed its leaders. In largest part, they have continued to believe.

From the standpoint of this chapter (we continue for the present our concentration on national-level responses), the problem we wish to raise is the extent to which the *jíbaro* could be described not only as the most characteristic Puerto Rican but as, in some sense, the ideal type as well—that is, the type which mirrors the people to themselves in their most admirable psychological light. We shall use the term *archetype* to mean not only the description of an original model (in this case, of personality) but also a model that ought to be approximated. Clearly, some such normative intention is symbolized by the Popular emblem.

It is to be expected that many of the same traits considered under the more general heading of the Puerto Rican modal personality would be reiterated here. Let us list those selected by our respondents to typify the *jíbaro*. Mentioned oftenest again were dignity and hospitality. Also on the positive side were seriousness, folk wisdom, courageousness, brotherliness, firmness of conviction, independence, respect for achievement, love of one's own plot of land, and hard-working habits. On the negative side were suspiciousness, authoritarianism, cupidity, rigidity, reticence, and defeatist attitudes.

Some of these traits were elucidated at length, others were questioned. Thus, while suspiciousness was conceded to be common, it was also said to disappear as rapidly as a *jíbaro* becomes convinced that he can trust an individual or group. Similarly, while it was not denied that he enjoys "putting it over" by sharp dealing and "horse-trading," (so does the traditional New Englander, one leader pointed out), this trait, too, is partially neutralized by his native generosity. Defeatist attitudes were said to be waning in proportion to increasing opportunity, though (as previously noted by grassroots respondents) the feeling has been potent that one cannot accomplish much by one's own hard work, that luck is all-important, and that others are largely to blame for one's own troubles.

The importance of dignity and self-respect was clarified further by two informants. *Jíbaros* and urbanized ex-*jíbaros* will not willingly take abusive or domineering orders. They were said to be quite shocked upon observing for the first time a Continental fellow worker meekly accepting a "bawling out" from some factory "boss." Discipline on the job cannot thus be maintained with the average Puerto Rican worker of rural background. Because he considers himself, however humble, as a *caballero* (gentleman), his way of retaliation is often to say little but then quietly to quit.

We come now to the original question: Can the *jíbaro* be regarded as the Puerto Rican archetype? Answers were skeptical. A few respondents went so far as to contend that the life of the *jíbaro* has, in greatest part, been fraught with so much poverty, ignorance, ill health, and just plain misery that the quicker he disappears, in fact as well as fancy, the better for the Island's welfare. The attempt to glorify his character has been, for still more respondents, an over-emotional romanticizing connected with the "nativist reaction." As one leader asked sardonically, Why does he want to leave if the life of the *jíbaro* is so attractive?

There were other reservations. One was that even the *jíbaro's* most admirable traits cannot be considered as anything like universal to Insular countrymen; at best these traits have applied unevenly to *some* countrymen. A second was that, whether we regret the trend or not, the *jíbaro* is now being rapidly displaced as the culture moves toward industrialization—that, in fact, the migrant is already the more representative type. Thus, while the emblem of the dominant party was politically appropriate to an agricultural country as few as ten years ago, it is fast becoming an obsolete emblem—so obsolete that a Popular leader in search for votes may soon be "shaking his own hand"! As a matter of fact, the whole campaign of the Popular party was said to be directed, in a sense, to the liquidation of the *jíbaro,* and hence of the archetype itself.

A last reservation was that there is comparatively little about countrymen in Puerto Rico that distinguishes them, except superficially, from those in various other cultures—not only from those of Spanish derivation but from English farm people, say, or from the "hillbillies" of the Tennessee mountains. To be sure, the *jíbaro,* like other countrymen, often acquires a noble caste as the tiller of the earth who persists in endless generations of toil despite terrible adversities. But even if he survives in substantial numbers, this is hardly enough to single him out as a unique Puerto Rican type.

These reservations, while impressive, were by no means unanimous. A number of respondents still maintained that among all Insular classes and groups the *jíbaro* comes closest to the ideal personality. True, he is not now usually admired by the growing middle class, but the question remains whether the middle class is not thereby the loser. This is not to say that all the qualities and habits of the *jíbaro* ought to be preserved—certainly not his poverty or the evils that poverty spawns. An archetype, however, may properly stress qualities on the positive side. And these qualities are more often harmonized and strengthened than suppressed or twisted by the anxieties and conflicts that admittedly accompany transition to an urban way of life. Thus transfused, they enrich *all* levels and *all* areas of the culture.

PERSONALITY AND THE FAMILY

Authorities in culture-and-personality research have contended with a good deal of empirical support that the primary cause of personality structure is the family pattern—above all, the habits and attitudes instilled in the earliest years of a child's life. Numerous respondents on both levels agreed with this contention as equally appropriate to Puerto Rico, one leader even referring to familiar Freudian hypotheses in its support.

Once more, however, the judgment was amended. Two were unwilling to say that the family pattern is the primary cause; while granting its great importance, they thought that other causes, such as the ecological, might be at least equally important. Another considered it primary during the era of agrarian life when the family was the center of daily life, but not so any longer—a view challenged by a peer who held that, on the contrary, the family today is more crucial than ever before in that it, more than any other institution, prevents the erosion of desirable personal traits. Two other leaders were unwilling to commit themselves.

Although the role of the Puerto Rican woman in family relations was discussed in Chapter 3, we wish to look a little more carefully at her personality with the hope that this role may be clarified further. Some of the same characteristics emphasized in that connection were reemphasized in this. Typically, she has been greatly attached to her children, indeed too much attached in her habit of prolonged overprotectiveness (though this habit has been questioned). She has been submissive to her husband. She has been preoccupied from early childhood with anticipated marriage—a trait that was alleged to manifest itself in the elaborate way that even little girls like to dress in order to attract little boys. She is coquettish—so much so, one respondent insisted, that he can almost invariably spot a Puerto Rican woman among other Latin Americans by the way she "gives him the eye"! This characteristic was denied by another, who held rather that her direct way of looking is mostly "curiosity," a characteristic no less true of Puerto Rican males.

How does she otherwise compare with the male personality? Several respondents—all males themselves—were inclined to rate her as a more admirable type on such counts as these: she is more self-controlled; she is more adaptable; she is less authoritarian; she is more straightforward; she is more reliable; and, because she much oftener practices the single standard, she is more consistent. Finally, for at least one respondent, she is more intelligent!

Other respondents were less magnanimous. Two could discern no essential differences between Puerto Rican male and female personality types. Another was unwilling to concede that the woman's traits are either worse or better than the man's. Curiously, only one reiterated the point scored earlier—that the average woman's customary role in family life, hence presumably the impact of her personality on both husband and children, are being seriously impaired by the shift to an urban-industrial culture.

PERSONALITY IN THE SUBCULTURES

Thus far in this chapter we have departed from the methodological rule usually followed hitherto. The picture we have drawn is chiefly the result of what we have learned from national-level respondents. The procedure has been deliberate, for we wish now to compare this picture with a composite one that we shall attempt to draw of the twenty grassroots respondents (plus occasional impressions derived from other personalities whom we came to know in the three sub-cultures). How far or in what respects these impressions would be affirmed or denied by Rorschach or other objective personality tests is a question that we invite experts to investigate.

In preparing our subjective appraisal, a master chart was constructed of all negative and positive traits emphasized above. We then checked each item against each grassroots respondent, according to whether he (a) moderately evidenced the trait; (b) evidenced it strongly; (c) tended to negate it; (d) negated it strongly; (e) evidenced it somewhat ambivalently; or (f) revealed no discernible impression one way or the other.

Once more, let us consider the negative side first. While a small majority revealed strong symptoms of defensiveness, only half the group gave any clear evidence of shyness. Aggressiveness toward the self was not observable because of the environment of the interviews, but again about half did reveal the trait in outward attitudes and habits—especially so in authoritarian family relations, in hostility toward Spanish expatriates, and in a bodily attack that occurred during our research when one respondent felt that he had been insulted by a fellow Puerto Rican. Insensitivity to aesthetic and other kinds of outward detail was noticeable in one-quarter of the respondents, while an immature sense of social and political responsibility applied to about one-third. The trait of cupidity was also not observable, but a degree of rigidity seemed applicable to slightly more than half.

This latter quality had, however, its positive side—a noticeable firmness of conviction revealed by three-fourths of the respondents. Self-confidence, seriousness of attitude, and manifestations of "folk wisdom" applied consistently to about the same proportion. *Dignidad* and such closely related qualities as pride and independence also appeared to be strong. Friendliness was pronounced, increasingly so as shyness and defensiveness receded. Hospitality, however, was less spontaneous than might have been expected. Family loyalty and brotherliness were manifested only in a sizable minority, but observations were limited here also. Great respect for education was conspicuous in three-fourths of the respondents.

In view of our interest in personality and the cultural process, what of the cluster of traits identified by the qualities of *being* as compared with those of *becoming?* It was our impression that the two qualities were in considerably greater balance than they are among Mainland personalities, where, we recall, *becoming* is often said to be dominant. At the same time, *becoming* tended to be more noticeable both among younger participants as contrasted with the older and among those in the upper status and class levels as contrasted with those below the middle range. Between rural and urban respondents, however, no differences as to these bipolar qualities were perceptible. Nor did the two latter groups appear to vary in their display of such traits as friendliness or defensiveness. Finally, as to differences between personality by sex, only one of the noted female traits—namely, self-control—seemed to stand out.

Compare now a few explicit judgments offered at the grassroots with regard to the personalities of their fellow Puerto Ricans. Their most interesting judgment concerns the *jíbaro.* A majority supported those on the national level who maintained that the *jíbaro* is no longer, if he ever was, the archetype. Not only is he disappearing, several agreed, but he ought to disappear. But a large minority (one-third in all) maintained that he is still a symbol of the finest personality to be found on the Island. A student respondent put it succinctly: the *jíbaro's* mode of life should be changed, certainly, but not most of his personal qualities. Some of these qualities were reiterated several times. He is generous, hospitable, hard-working, honest, friendly, and respectful—traits which, incidentally, the two most representative *jíbaros* among our respondents heavily stressed.

But a number at the grassroots were even more critical than those on the national level—an interesting reaction in view of the fact that well over half, if they were not *jíbaros* themselves, were either children of *jíbaros* or were closely associated with them in everyday experience.

One respondent, for example, underscored their suspiciousness and independence, his opinions being supported by another who held that they distrust almost all political leaders except the Governor. Cunning and cupidity were also punctuated by recalling a saying to the general effect that "The only one who can beat a *jíbaro* is the devil himself." Also, the quality of *being,* while recognized as dominant, was criticized as inviting too little thought of the future, too much superstitious trust in Providence, too easy a contentment and submissiveness. But excitability and courage were pointed to as partially balancing traits.

Speaking of the Puerto Rican personality as a whole—not the *jíbaro* alone—a number of enlightening supplementations were suggested by subcultural respondents. One, for example, spoke of two principal types rather than of one—in his terms, the ambitious, climbing type (in our terms, *becoming* is here the primary quality) and the stoical, complacent type (in our terms, the quality of *being* is dominant). The Puerto Rican soldier, he said, is noted for his calmness and poise in the face of danger. But, again, the panel heavily stressed negative traits also: cheating by small merchants and vendors, disregard of the rights of others, and ill treatment of public as well as private property.

IS THE AVERAGE PERSONALITY NEUROTIC?

It is not too surprising that more respondents on both levels answered the question of this concluding section in the affirmative than in the negative. Leaders held that neurotic symptoms are proportionally more chronic among migrants than among the population as a whole. Loss of protection by the extended family (though this loss may be partly compensated by relatives abroad), difficulties in readjusting from the rigidities of the patriarchal pattern, linguistic insecurities,* and the real or imagined hostilities generated by a strange environment—all add up to widespread anxieties and conflicts.

One leader spoke of a "collective neurosis" that is the product of "second-class citizenship"—of being indoctrinated, on the one hand, with the North American democratic ideology while, on the other, being denied full rights such as the vote in national elections. "Collective neurosis" can therefore be cured only when and if Puerto

* For further discussion, see pp. 254-256.

Ricans are accorded exactly the same privileges as all other U.S. citizens. These inferiority feelings are intensified when migrants discover, sometimes with almost traumatic shock, that they are discriminated against in the United States because of skin pigmentation, or when their keen sense of pride is offended by discourtesy.

Neurotic propensities were blamed by grassroots respondents chiefly on three factors: lack of education, lack of deep religious feeling, and fear of the future induced by uncertainty that the present industrial program is sufficiently stable. Two leaders supported this last opinion: What will happen, they asked, when the tax moratorium is over and when the government has borrowed to the saturation point? Related to these questions was a concern that too many people go deeply into installment buying at high interest rates—and then worry "day and night" over the next payment. Finally, it was contended that neuroticism is ultimately due, more than to any other factor, to a lack of *raison d'être* on the part of many jobholders—particularly of ex-*jíbaros* who, though they may sometimes enjoy the discipline of an assembly line, have no sense of the relations of their minute routine to any more comprehensive pattern.

Despite the vigor of these judgments, a number of respondents—again on both levels—were unprepared to accept them without reservations. The question of neuroticism, they held, is much too complicated for laymen to answer; it requires trained psychologists and scientific studies. Actually, there is good reason to argue (though we cannot prove it, since no statistics are available) that the rate of mental illness was much higher during the colonial era when frustrations, persecutions, and physiological ailments were all more widespread than they are today. The fact that mental clinics and hospitals are now crowded does not in itself prove anything; perhaps they would have been even more crowded in an earlier time had such services existed. Nor should we forget that the frustration and aggression complex, one of the common causes of neurotic behavior, may be lessening as family life induces a healthier emotional climate during the crucial early years of character formation.

For reasons such as these, three subcultural respondents were convinced that the majority of personalities are not neurotic, while a fourth respondent held that about half of the total could be so classified, the other half not. One leader went so far as to argue that the people of Puerto Rico are more stable emotionally than are the people of more developed countries: they worry less and are surer of help from neighbors or friends in case of illness or other adversities. Moreover, the rapidity of cultural change is taken in stride; the average person is aware of and likes this phenomenon. Even children, he said, are emotionally healthier today as a result of their mothers working, and they are proud that their fathers work for months at a time in the States. Thereby they become more self-reliant and more secure because less dependent than they were before.

Another leader respondent was equally sure that whatever neuroticism does exist will be found, not primarily among the migratory lower classes, but in the middle-class minority because of its exaggerated ambitions, material indulgences, and overindebtedness both to banks and often to personal acquaintances. Still another held that intellectuals and artists in Puerto Rico are the most acute sufferers. Finally, even granting that suicide and divorce rates are abnormally high, the rate of sex offenses was reported to be low. In any case, generalizations concerning mental illness based upon statistics were considered dubious.

We conclude with the same kind of mixed reaction concerning neurotic tendencies that we have come to expect on many issues—a reaction that is perhaps all the more significant by virtue of that fact. For if it is true that the personality type in Puerto Rico tends to be discordant, would not efforts on the part of peers to depict that type possibly reflect comparable symptoms? Granting, meanwhile, that no agreement was attainable as to their ubiquity, how shall education deal with these symptoms? This question, along with others raised by the present chapter, is our next concern.

CHAPTER TWELVE

LEARNING, PERSONALITY, AND THE CULTURAL PROCESS

CULTURE-AND-PERSONALITY theory and research are intensely concerned with the nature of learning—a consequence of the postulate that all personalities are chiefly the product of the cultural conditionings to which they have been subjected. This does not mean that personalities are *merely* such a product: their inherited physiological and neurological equipment provides the foundation upon which their characters are shaped. Nevertheless, the way any culture impresses its patterns upon people and how, in turn, people acquire these patterns is crucially important to the kinds of personalities that emerge. Here then the role of education, defined in the present context as the total process through which any culture transmits and modifies itself through learning, becomes directly concerned with all the questions discussed in the preceding chapter.

Let us frame these questions as follows: How can education cope with the problem of neuroticism (the last one discussed)? What alternative theories of cultural learning are most apropos? How do these apply to the process of enculturation, to audio-visual education, to concrete methods of teaching, and to ways of learning in Puerto Rican schools?

EDUCATION FOR MENTAL HEALTH

A majority of respondents inclined toward the opinion that education on the Island has thus far been unable to cope with the problem of mental health in any effective way. Reasons are by now familiar: inadequately trained personnel and funds, combined with inadequate appreciation of the problem. In the University of Puerto Rico, for example, two part-time psychiatrists were said to provide all available services for a full-time student body of about 13,000. Yet even this is better than on lower levels, where, as we learned previously, "visiting teachers" are supposed to serve as combined truant officers, counselors, and experts in mental health. Actually, their own training is not only very limited but the number of students in their charge is quite overwhelming.

Consider San José. There, we were informed, the single visiting teacher (who has a B.A. with some social work) is responsible for about 1,600 children. Since she does not cover the rural schools in the municipality, the result is that many more than this number have no contact whatever with even partially trained personnel (most teachers in Puerto Rico have taken no course in mental hygiene) unless a case should become so serious as to require hospitalization or other intervention by public health authorities.

It is understandable that criticisms in this area tended to be sharp. One leader was sure that the incidence of neuroticism among teachers themselves is probably higher, due to overwork and underpay, than it is for the whole population. Others felt that education is "drifting along"—some of its policy makers apparently not realizing that the typical young personality is undergoing severe though often hidden strains and stresses as it endeavors to readjust to a culture in flux. And yet, according to one administrator respondent on the grassroots level, the most serious of all problems in his school is that of child behavior.

Several were more charitable. Not only did a few concede that education is already doing "something" in the field; others felt that it is perhaps a good thing if schools help, by default if not by direct intent, to "destabilize" character structure more than to "stabilize" it—their implication being that the older modal personality no longer fits the patterns of today. As one leader reminded us, this process of human readjustment occurs in all cultures undergoing rapid change. Its effects, while painful, are not in long range inevitably bad.

A grassroots respondent, with many years of educational experience both in rural and urban areas, made the arresting observation that teachers today partly compensate for negative home influences upon children's personalities. Feelings of uprootedness and diminishing controls noted in our chapter on the family call, this respondent held, for a type of discipline that might normally be unwarranted. Thus, while authority in the average classroom strikes many observers as strict, it may be justified in part not only by the vast enrollments but also by the sense of security and respect which it provides children otherwise often neglected.

In the field of emotional health, the single most hopeful event discovered in the three subcultures was the plan to establish a "mental-hygiene" clinic in a senior high school. With financial backing from both the local PTA and the Department of Health, and with office space authorized by the Department of Education, the clinic would function as a pilot project with the hope that other schools might follow suit. Psychiatrists and physicians would serve on a part-time basis. Parents would be kept informed of the clinic's services and urged to cooperate in cases involving their children.

One of the more fundamental recommendations was that culture-and-personality theory and practice become a part of all teacher training. Another was for an experiment in the rudiments of psychotherapy for a group of carefully selected teachers—the aim being to test the hypothesis that intensive though brief supervision by professional experts could produce enough competence to enable them to detect and in degree to cope with neurotic behavior, while at the same time restraining them from acting beyond their competence. The argument here, granting that "a little psychiatry could be a dangerous thing," was that teachers make all sorts of snap judgments about behavior problems anyway—and oftener than not without scientific support. If they merely learned when to refer ill children to mental clinics (an action they now very seldom take), the experiment would have justified itself.

All teachers in training should be given opportunity, moreover, to probe their own personalities—a procedure that would require less book learning and more opportunity for close association with instructors skilled in drawing out anxieties and other emotional troubles to which young people on the threshold of careers are rarely immune.

Additionally relevant if partly familiar proposals included the following: the need for basic personality research in Puerto Rico that could be channeled for educational use; the need for parent and family education, with stress upon emotional problems; the need for kinds of learning that excite student interest and support rather than the kind that turns them against education (how far is the high rate of drop-out in the early years—in one rural school visited, from sixty in

the third grade to twenty-five in the sixth—due to such rebellion?);
the need for adjusting aspirations closer to expectations; the need for
more skilled counseling services in schools on all levels; finally, the
need to provide at least one thoroughly trained psychotherapist for
each of the seventy-odd school districts. (The Island, said one leader,
can ill afford *not* to meet this need.) Some of these proposals are
elaborated below.

TWO THEORIES OF LEARNING AND
THEIR IMPLICATIONS

A moot issue among experts in culture-and-personality theory concerns the nature of learning—that is, the meaning of the psychological
processes involved and the manner in which these are conditioned by,
as well as the ways they may condition, the cultural process itself.

Culture-and-personality authorities have tended recently to congre-
gate in one or the other of two great camps. In familiar psychological
terms, the first of these camps is strongly *behavioristic;* that is, it assumes that learning is primarily a process of stimulus-response conditioning—a "stamping in" of presumably desirable features of the
cultural environment and a "stamping out" of presumably undesirable
features, so as to form habits that enable a personality to adjust to the
customs, routines, and practices of that environment. The second camp
is strongly *functionalistic;* that is, it assumes learning to be a total
organic process involving participation on the part of learners who
not only respond to but help in selecting stimuli and interacting with
them so as to reshape as well as to be shaped by the cultural environment. In the former of the two theories, learning to accept and adjust
to the culture is the primary emphasis; it tends to be deterministic. In
the latter, learning to carry on "transactions" *with* the culture, so as to
produce changes both in it and in those who are thereby learning, is
the primary emphasis; it tends to be activistic.

We hasten to warn against too sharp a separation. In both theories,
for example, culture-and-personality authorities share a respect for the
contributions of psychiatric theory as developed by Freud and his followers; and both usually seek to incorporate its findings in different
ways and degrees into their own theories. Neither the behaviorist nor
the functionalist, moreover, denies a measure of validity in the position
of the other; each recognizes that learning may occur to some extent

in ways that the other describes. Nevertheless, after conceding all qualifications (and there are literally hundreds), the fact remains that
both implicitly and explicitly the two approaches lead to different perspectives not only upon the field of culture-and-personality but upon
the consequences that follow for education's role within that field.

Since no one could discuss the heavy tasks confronting Puerto Rican
schools without considering the place that learning and teaching have
in their fulfillment, some of these consequences have been anticipated.
Here, however, we should like to know how far and in what ways one
or the other or both of the two great theories are supported when attention is given to problems of learning in a direct and conscious way.

ENCULTURATION AS A LEARNING PROCESS

One approach to an answer is afforded by the concept of enculturation, defined broadly as the process of learning to live in a culture by
conscious or unconscious conditioning. Some anthropologists make a
rather sharp distinction between the earlier and later years of enculturation. For them, the former—the years of childhood—are devoted
primarily to inculcating the customary rules and habits of a given
culture; the latter—the years of adolescence and beyond—are properly
concerned with more abstract and critical learning, which may include
cultural change itself. Inferentially, the former is primarily behavioristic, the latter functionalistic, in the ways that we have defined these
concepts.

To what extent did our respondents agree with such a division of
labor? A majority on both levels tended to support it, an impressive
minority did not, while several were disposed toward a compromise
position. Those who held that enculturation in the early years should
be limited primarily to the process of conditioning in the skills and
mores of the culture were also the most vehement in their support of
the three-R's type of elementary education. A few held that the first
obligation on this level is not even the impartation of knowledge, but
the teaching and learning of skills as prerequisite to such impartation.
Others held that behavioristic learning is now dominant in the primary
schools and that, facilities being what they are, it must continue to be
dominant. Any attempt to introduce alternative methods is unrealistic,
indeed impossible, as long as classes are overflowing, materials sparse,
and teachers meagerly trained.

A vigorous minority took the position that even in the elementary schools of Puerto Rico enculturation need not be so circumscribed. Granting serious handicaps, nevertheless the functionalistic viewpoint —associated by several spokesmen, incidentally, with "progressive education"—is the more defensible and should be encouraged as soon and as much as possible. For these spokesmen, it is a mistake to wait until the adolescent and postadolescent years to emphasize the solving of social problems, emotional involvement, and other experiences in which students engage individually and cooperatively. As one leader held, such *habits* as critical thinking and democratic sharing must be developed early in life if they are to become engrained in the personality. If they are not, if elementary schools cultivate primarily the habit of passive learning instead, the chances that healthy intellectual skepticism and activistic attitudes will develop on the secondary and university levels are thus far reduced.

All respondents agreed that learning of the skills of communication and computation is important. They parted on the same issue that divides educational theorists as well as teachers and parents in the United States. Two leaders admitted that they were not familiar enough with psychological and philosophical principles to say which methods of learning may be most effective—one reminding us that the progressivist, Dewey, is a controversial thinker in education. Several respondents insisted that a combination of both basic approaches is better than either.

To be sure, progressive education, one maintained, sometimes goes too far in the direction of "license." After all, just as the culture sets limits on the amount of liberty a citizen is entitled to, so the school must set limits to the child's self-expression. This does not mean a three-R's curriculum of the traditional type: those who now press for such a curriculum—and some vocal citizens do—ignore a great deal of recent scientific evidence in behalf of the superiority of modern methods of teaching fundamental skills (arithmetic, say) by relating them to personal and cultural interests and activities. Education can no more afford to turn its back on this evidence than a merchant can afford to restore old-fashioned ways of buying and selling merchandise.

For those who preferred such a moderate position, enculturation in the early period of life is both the absorption of basic cultural beliefs and habits *and* the encouragement of active sharing, problem solving, and critical-mindedness; it is likewise both of these in the later period. At the same time, education may at moments stress the former more strongly than the latter in the child's first years, while in adolescence and beyond the reverse stress may properly be stronger.

AUDIO-VISUAL LEARNING

Enculturation is not a process that occurs only within the school. All respondents who were asked whether in their judgment more learning takes place inside or outside Puerto Rican classrooms agreed, with but one exception (and he was unprepared to generalize), that more learning takes place on the outside. This situation is even truer than it would be if so many children were not constricted by double sessions or if more of them did not withdraw at such an early age. But even if daily sessions and years of attendance were stretched longer, such enculturative influences as family patterns, travel to and from the States, and movies, radio, and television would produce, they felt, a greater total effect than does formal education.

Mention of movies, radio, and television brings us to an issue which has recently aroused perhaps as much discussion in Puerto Rico as it has anywhere. One principle upon which behaviorists as well as functionalists would find common ground is that audio-visual learning is a potent instrument indeed, and we see no reason to suppose that our own informants would challenge this consensus. Nor would they deny that audio-visual learning is already at work almost everywhere on the Island: with over 400,000 radio sets in daily operation (about two and one-half times the number of daily copies published by the largest Insular newspaper), with dozens of movie theaters, and with the number of television sets also promising to pass the newspaper output, it is only too apparent that audio-visual education is already a fact.

And yet, several leaders asked, can it be said that *education* is really taking place? Or is it rather *miseducation*—that is, learning which may have more of a destructive effect upon personality than it does a constructive effect? While one radio station, government owned, was commended especially for its fine musical programs, the percentage of listeners was said to be low. Other stations were judged more severely. But it was television that received by far the most attention.

No respondent expressed the opinion that the bulk of television fare is anything but mediocre—even more so than typical North American fare. One leader went so far as to suggest that many present programs should be eliminated: their total effect is demoralizing to family life, they are saturated with commercialism, and they are often in very bad taste. And, when another leader was asked "to say one word" about commercial television, he literally did: his answer was "Damn!"

The question, then, is not whether television is already becoming significant in the development of Puerto Rican personalities, but rather what must be done to channel its potentialities as an *educative* agency in behalf of such development. Two controversial issues now arise.

The first issue concerns the new noncommercial government station that was in the final planning stage at the time our research was under way and is since in operation. While one respondent expected that this station would force others to raise their standards, and while most respondents were happy that it was to be launched, a forceful dissenting voice on the national level was heard: such an enterprise should be opposed because it could be used, as it is used today in numerous countries, to indoctrinate the electorate in the doctrines of whatever party holds the seat of power. (The reply of its supporters was that careful safeguards have been set up to prevent such an eventuality. Political discussion, for example, is forbidden by law.) In any case, a better solution, he held, is to obtain substantial time for education from commercial stations—a proposal viewed by another respondent as supplementary rather than as opposed to the need for publicly owned and controlled television.

The second issue centers in the educational methods that should be employed regardless of station ownership. A minority were skeptical: television "depersonalizes" the learning process; it too easily becomes a "two-dimensional" device for passive conditioning by stimulus-response, where the student never "talks back." Even this minority, however, admitted a willingness to experiment with the medium provided that it is regarded from the outset as an aid to effective learning rather than as adequate in or of itself.

Suggestions emerged for pilot projects in televised education. Utilizing the experience of a growing number of Continental communities, experiments both in closed and open circuits should be instituted in which fields such as science or mathematics are dramatized with the latest laboratory equipment and the latest techniques of demonstration. In every case, programs should be preceded and followed by classroom learning with "real" teachers and "real" examples drawn from the experience of "real" students. In the phrase of one spokesman, "what happens *after* the set is turned off" is the important thing.

The finest available teachers in Puerto Rico (not to mention filmed presentations by similar teachers from other countries) could thus reach a dozen or a thousand classrooms simultaneously instead of merely one at a time. Less able teachers, meanwhile, would be learning too—learning not only richer content but how to functionalize their own methods more successfully. In addition to professional teachers, experts from many fields could be drawn upon intermittently.

In dollars and cents, one leader argued that the cost of providing at least one life-size screen and television set for each school in Puerto Rico, beginning with the new ones, would amount to less than the salary of a single average teacher in that school for only one year. Yet the increase in learning that he predicted from this investment would pay back in dollars and cents, plus compound interest. By the same kind of reasoning, he was equally sure that "master teachers"—some brought from abroad if necessary and employed especially for television instruction—could be paid ten or fifteen times the salary of regular teachers and still assure a high return on the cost. Finally, the saving alone in scientific equipment for demonstrations could eventually reach "millions."

These suggestions were not offered with any thought of reducing educational expenditures. At the same time, since current research studies predict a rapid increase in enrollments as children remain in school for a longer period of years, the already serious problem of providing anything like enough teachers with minimum preparation is bound to be intensified. Here television, properly safeguarded in the ways suggested, could become a gigantic aid by providing superior instruction to *all* students—the teacher's role being modified accordingly in order to become more of a discussion leader and less of a routine purveyor of textbook information.

That Puerto Rican educators are coming to recognize the potentialities of audio-visual education is already indicated not only by the establishment of public television (under the auspices, incidentally, of the Department of Education), but by an audio-visual center with a trained staff in the University of Puerto Rico and by the operation of sizable film libraries. Also, we recall the pioneering production and wide dissemination of original films by the Division of Community Education. The only sharp criticism of present facilities came from subcultural respondents who spoke of long delays and confusions (due partly to the lack of a central depot) in obtaining films for classroom use, and of difficulties in providing projectors and operators especially for rural areas.

Nevertheless, we conclude that audio-visual learning is widely accepted in principle and to some extent in practice. To build as quickly and efficiently as possible upon the beginnings already made— above all, in television—was regarded as a paramount challenge. For, if one leader is right, television is the single most revolutionary means of mass enculturation that has ever been invented. To make certain that such a means will be at once constructive and democratic was the chief concern of most of our respondents.

LEARNING THROUGH TEACHING

The indispensability of teachers to the learning process, whether or not they are formally so designated, is as universally true of cultures as is the process itself. In Puerto Rico, the importance of the teacher's personal role has been highlighted in the section above by the insistence that television is not to be regarded as a substitute for that role but, at best, as supplemental.

It comes as no surprise to readers of this study that many of our resource persons—particularly those not teachers themselves—were nevertheless skeptical of the success with which the average teacher now performs his tasks. True, they recognized that hundreds of Puerto Rican teachers are devoted to their students and loyal to their obligations. Yet, in terms of our present interest in the relations of personality to learning, the consensus was emphatic that informed sensitivity (for example, to the emotional dimensions of human growth) is far from typical. More pointedly, the charge was made that teaching on all levels, including the university, is still widely regarded as a process of pouring subject matters into the "receptacle" of the learner's mind. Little awareness was said to prevail that learning may also be interpreted as an affair of the whole personality interacting with countless facets of the culture.

For related reasons, respondents were almost equally negative in holding that most teachers discourage self-expression in children—that is, opportunities to develop individual talents, to raise questions, to express personal feelings, or, in the phrase of one respondent, "to fight back" by challenging fellow students or the teacher himself. Verbally, to be sure, all Puerto Rican teachers would no doubt admit that self-expression is a desirable trait; in actual practice, however, it was said to receive slight encouragement. The rather meekly sweet friendliness observed in the classroom behavior of children may well be an effect of habits of disciplined passivity to which family patterns, including "mothering" by teachers, have contributed their share.

It is only fair to note that respondents were far from consistent among themselves as to the criteria of effective teaching. A small majority on the national level held that the University has the largest proportion of good teachers. But only one respondent considered this to mean that they were the most skilled in functionalized methods of give-and-take between themselves and students—methods confined largely to the general studies faculty. In opposition, another respondent proceeded from implicitly behavioristic premises: by contrast with lower levels, professors are the best teachers, not because they are adept in methods of teaching, but because they know and impart the most truth.

But several again disagreed. Granting some good teachers in the higher learning, one leader was sure that Puerto Rico is no different from the United States in that the best teaching, by and large, occurs on the elementary level and dwindles in competence on the secondary and even more on the college levels. This judgment would not be acceptable to many respondents, but several did indict the University for the widespread practice of lecturing, for rote memorizing, for "true-false" and other mechanized examinations, for discouraging critical reactions by students in the classroom, and for a dearth of opportunity to learn by sharing directly in cultural experience.

One respondent thought that possibly a handful of private schools provided the best teaching. Two were confident that, because functionalized methods are consistently practiced by its field staff of "leaders" (they are not formally called teachers), the Division of Community Education heads all other programs. Two others were unable to answer the question: there is, one said, a good deal of "buck-passing"—one level of education trying to blame another for the generally low quality.

Have North American influences been salutary here? While some grassroots respondents wanted still more Continentalized forms of teaching and others were either uncertain or content, a few others joined forces with a large proportion of leader respondents in expressing dissatisfaction on one main count. Teachers trained in the United States, added to the much larger number of teachers trained in turn by these trainers, have tried too often to press imported methods upon students without discerning the good versus bad features of these methods. To cite an example stressed by one respondent, Continental-ized methods are good in their encouragement of creativity but less satisfactory than, say, those of England in developing communication skills.

None of our resource persons would probably deny frequent exceptions to these adverse comments. Student respondents, though they could recall almost no functionalized teaching in their elementary school years, reported that it is occasionally practiced on the secondary level—a practice that they hoped would expand. A number of other grassroots respondents believed that such teaching should be encouraged on that level, though they differed as to its suitability for the elementary school. In at least two schools within the cooperating sub-cultures, teachers were themselves experiencing active learning through study groups, through frequent faculty meetings with a teacher rather than the principal at times presiding, through unit planning sessions, and through degrees of flexibility in the manner of presenting some subjects.

These steps toward functionalistic methods were partly justified by both an administrator and teacher respondent on the ground that arbitrary mandates by authorities result, in the long run, in a "waste of time." The teacher, they said, feels more a part of the enterprise when he has shared in problems and decisions. For this reason, they underscored objections previously cited concerning supervisors and other officials who try to impose their will, sometimes without consulting the respective principal in charge. Such a practice, they held, results only in feelings of discouragement, hostility, and, above all, uncertainty among many teachers as to the extent of their own authority to modify subject matters, to teach in original ways, or to exercise classroom discipline.

What shall be done about these deficiencies? Five proposals stand out. The first is that the summer "activity month" be devoted to abundant experiences for teachers to perceive the differences and similarities between behavioristic and functionalistic approaches to learning, and to discover that competent teaching is measured by ability to handle children as well as by knowledge of subject matters. Workshops conducted by visiting instructors in the University's College of Education have already helped to provide these experiences, particularly by way of demonstrating in their own teaching how functionalized learning works. As presently organized, however, objectives of the "activity month" were criticized as too often circumvented by routine tasks, such as clerical work, rather than utilized as an opportunity for teachers to acquire better understanding of the theory and practice of learning.

The second proposal exemplifies the kind of practice that a number of respondents had in mind—namely, the method of learning often called "group dynamics." According to this method, which is supported by a large body of research, the traditional classroom structure should be completely altered. Instead of the teacher facing rows of students and directing recitations, he arranges seats in one or several circles, with his own seat in the same relative position as those of his students. The aim is to create back-and-forth participation among all members of the circle—the teacher serving as resource person and guide rather than as commander. Numerous techniques are possible by this method that are not characteristic of behavioristic learning—role-playing and "sociometric diagrams" (which chart the interplay among members of the group) being but two examples.

Only one respondent on the national and none on the subcultural panel raised any doubts about group dynamics as a way of learning (although a number were apparently unfamiliar with it). While recognizing its value, there is always the danger, he felt, that if improperly used it could lead to overconformity—not to the usual conformity of pupils with their teacher, but rather of individual members with the will of the group. In the College of Education or elsewhere among institutions of higher learning, the danger could hardly be called ominous, however: the method thus far has been applied even more rarely than on lower levels.

In Puerto Rican high schools, to be sure, one does find a teacher here and there who is trying to practice group dynamics despite such handicaps as oversized classes. More than this, in one of our sub-cultural high schools, the principal has encouraged both faculty meet-ings and various classes to practice these methods. Thus, social-studies classes in this school were organized in subgroups with rotating student chairmen, recorders, and observers of the process itself. Topics were chosen by student-teacher cooperation. Role-playing was used in at least one class to dramatize the problems of local farm workers. At intervals, panels made up of subgroup members presented their find-ings and conclusions before the class as a whole. While the panels we observed lacked spontaneity and generated only lukewarm interest, it should be remembered that this way of teaching and learning was a striking departure from habits to which young Puerto Rican personal-ities have long been conditioned in the lower grades. Most significant, perhaps, was the warm endorsement that the method received from respondents in that community—one teacher pointing out that it en-courages shy students to participate more actively.

Turn now to the third proposal. An experimental training program should be set up independently of the present curriculum of the Col-lege of Education (though with its endorsement), the immediate purpose of which would be to develop a new kind of "teacher-leader" for rural communities. A still longer-range purpose would be to de-velop greater community pride and self-sufficiency, thereby contrib-uting toward the goal of a decentralized society. Educationally as well as economically, the problem today is distressing. Most teachers, we were told repeatedly, regard appointments to rural schools as "a necessary evil"—as an apprenticeship to urban positions which they hope to win as soon as possible. As noted in Chapter 3, they rarely live in the neighborhoods where they teach, preferring to travel back and forth daily even when their schools are many miles from home. The result, of course, is that rural teachers are seldom identified with the community life of students or their parents. The usual type of rural school becomes, in turn, a place where children flock to "learn their lessons" but almost nothing more.

The aim would be to attack this problem by selecting a group of young teachers who show promise of leadership, and who are devoted to service in public education, to life in the Island democracy, and above all to its common people. The training program would last from one to four years, depending on financial and staff resources. It would be built upon a basic philosophy of education appropriate to the culture. And it would require extensive preservice practice in rural communities.

The rural schools themselves would be related in every phase of learning and teaching with their natural and social environments. Higher than average salaries would be paid to the assigned teachers. In many cases, homes would be built for them and their families (a proposal that once received consideration by the legislature). Husband-and-wife teams of teacher-leaders would be encouraged. And the present law providing that new schools may not be built for less than sixty students would be amended to a minimum of twenty-five or thirty students.

The fourth proposal is, in some respects, the most revolutionary of the group. What is needed, another leader held, is a drastic change in the whole approach to teacher education in Puerto Rico. *All* teaching and learning on every level and for every group—not just in rural areas—require that the young man and woman about to embark on a training program be sensitized, first of all, to the life of human beings in the neighborhoods around them. Instead of beginning with lectures, reading assignments, and similar conventional tasks, they should set out to look, listen, examine, and experience—returning to their classrooms mainly for the purpose of sharing impressions, asking and being asked questions, receiving stimulation and guidance from those in charge. As they become more alert, books and lectures should very gradually be utilized as resources through which to clarify and deepen understandings of what they have observed firsthand.

The intent of this unorthodox initiation into professional problems of teaching is, for this leader, to break "bad habits" that have been reinforced by years of memorizing and verbalized learning divorced from the milieu. Concepts would emerge from this experience that are more meaningful than if taught in abstract isolation—the concept of culture-and-personality being itself an example. Functionalized methods would, of course, predominate in the training program.

The last proposal is not so much concerned with specific problems of learning through teaching as with a still more pervasive problem reiterated in the present context by another leader: how to finance a profession of high enough caliber so that *any* proposals of the kind we have outlined can receive implementation. His argument was the all too familiar one that until people are willing to pay adequately for it, teaching will continue to suffer from low standards and low competencies.

Despite the fact that the Commonwealth was said to spend a larger proportion of its total budget on education than any state of the Union, the proposal was that salaries be substantially raised so that above-average teaching personnel may be recruited and retained in the profession. At present, teachers by scores were said to be leaving their jobs to work in shops and offices. (For example, twenty-seven ex-teachers were working near Cañamelar in a single factory.) Of course, some persons of high ability here as elsewhere devote their lives to teaching regardless of financial sacrifice; but too many teachers, we were told, are "clock-watchers" more or less indifferent to their great responsibilities.

In view of these circumstances, as well as of dim prospects for substantial federal aid in the foreseeable future, three steps were suggested for public consideration. One: an average 5 per cent increase in total per capita taxes should be assessed on net incomes, to be earmarked for teachers' salaries only. (Such an increase would still total considerably less than average total per capita income taxes in the United States.) Two: much quicker, more efficient tax collection and assessment methods should be instituted by the Department of the Treasury. (At present, substantial losses were said to occur here.) And three: the educational expense deduction normally allowed corporations by internal revenue rules should be collected as a Puerto Rican tax. Without actions of this kind, this leader held, few problems of teaching for effective learning can hope to be resolved.

BUILDING PUERTO RICAN PERSONALITIES THROUGH CULTURAL LEARNING

We turn the spotlight from the teacher back upon the student. Granting such mountainous hurdles as we have noted, it is well to recall that many citizens have faith in their capacity to overcome them. What, then, can they do to vitalize learning as it shapes their personalities?

Before facing this question directly, certain deviant opinions must be recorded. One was that the trouble with many of the proposals made in the preceding section, as well as those below, is that they overstress educational methodology at the expense of solid knowledge. Another was that education should be concerned with the character development of two main classes of students—those of superior ability, for whom the best liberal arts and scientific training possible should be provided; and those of average or inferior ability, for whom vocational training should be dominant.

Still another opinion differed with a major postulate of culture-and-personality theory itself—namely, that personality is primarily learned. Grassroots respondents who were asked the question split evenly on the issue of whether religious traits, for example, are inherited or acquired, while one held that facility to learn a particular language is innate. One leader held the opinion (on which behavioral scientists themselves differ) that personality types in different cultures genetically inherit different temperamental "make-ups"—the Mediterranean type, say, being much more volatile than the Scandinavian, thereby accounting in part for the modal personality of the Puerto Rican himself.

The less deviant views of respondents on both levels were apparently governed by two premises. The first was that, judging by most of their criticisms and proposals, functionalized learning oftener than behavioristic learning seemed to them conducive to desirable personality development. The second premise was that learning experiences can and should be of such a nature as to maximize positive and minimize negative personality traits. Both premises help us better to understand the grounds for the kinds of learning experiences that were recommended. We draw these experiences into several main clusters.

1. There is need to *develop potentialities in learners for creative expression* through both the arts and vocational training. Limited opportunity for learning through any of the arts has been mentioned before. Here this limitation was pointed up by almost unanimous agreement among both major groups of respondents that children should have more time, more simple materials, and more guidance from trained teachers in music, the graphic arts, and the dramatic arts.

Granting a few partial exceptions, the great majority of school districts in Puerto Rico provide little guidance of this kind—so-called art and music experiences being limited to the brief "activity period," and supervised by the regular teacher whose professional preparation in these fields is usually negligible. Even in Hermosa, where facilities are well above average, a special art teacher was reported to visit the elementary school exactly once per month, a music teacher three times per month. (The large high school had one full-time music teacher and one in commercial art.) No special teachers either of the drama or of the dance are employed by the Department of Education, and no teaching majors in any of the fine arts except, in part, literature, have been provided hitherto by the College of Education.

While two subcultural respondents were skeptical as to the practicality of increased time for learning through the arts, all others agreed that even now drastic improvements should be under way. As one leader intimated, the basic question is: What is important to the growth of personality? Are knowledge and skills the sole desideratum? Or are aesthetic qualities, enhanced through opportunities for children to express themselves freely, emotionally, and imaginatively, equally important?

If the answer lies in the latter alternative, then, it was implied, art is not to be adjudged either a luxury or a fringe activity; it becomes as essential as any other kind of learning. As another respondent held, Puerto Ricans have a "natural bent" for music (including perhaps the dance?). Thus the schools should provide as many types of activity as possible—orchestras, bands, and choral groups were among those mentioned—by which this "bent" could be developed.

In vocational education, creative expression is equally possible. Carpentry, furniture making, architecture, and printing were all exemplified as means. Citing a recent report on the subject, two respondents criticized low standards of training for the printing trade; and though they were chiefly interested in the need for higher skills, their outlook was such as to imply that one incentive could well be the release of creative energies in the applied art of printing itself.

Finally, learning through art should be integrated with learning through other subjects. Again the relevant point was that art is to be regarded less as a "course" than as an inclusive medium through which students find ways to develop their latent interests and imaginations. In this endeavor, all kinds of subject matters have a place. After all, if the culture as a whole is in a creative mood, then art should be its partner—not something apart.

That a number of teachers appreciate the importance of this integrated approach was discernible during our research. Classrooms, for example, differed radically in their use of pictures, models, plants, or color schemes that helped to make the environment of learning affirmative and inviting. Some classrooms were utterly drab; pictures or simple graphic displays that could have helped to visualize and functionalize community problems, say, were at a minimum. Other classrooms reflected the zeal and originality of the presiding teacher. One mathematics classroom in a rural subculture, to recall one instance, was brightened with wood and paper models constructed by students themselves—even to a Christmas tree of geometrical design.

2. There is need to *give students wider opportunities to participate in planning and carrying out learning experiences.* Ways of interfusing art through various subject matters, the point just made, are one proposal that could open up such opportunities. Others include school cooperatives, 4-H Clubs, Future Homemakers, and Girl and Boy Scouts.

At the same time, the more conventional view that enculturation in the early years is predominantly a matter of habituation to custom and skills received reinforcement in the present context. A number of subcultural respondents, especially parents, were doubtful whether children in the elementary school are sufficiently developed to share with teachers in the planning of units of study. Administrative respondents were divided on the question, while one who favored the attempt "in principle" questioned whether it would be possible in practice as long as curricula are so fully prescribed and controlled "from above."

For the secondary and college levels, teacher-pupil planning received concerted support. Thus, all three student respondents favored the idea, though none had experienced such planning except meagerly. Parent reactions, too, were mainly favorable. Initial steps toward integrating courses with student participation were also reported (Spanish and social studies, most commonly; physics and mathematics occasionally), though apparently the number of such ventures remains as relatively rare in the secondary schools as in the higher learning.

Another means of participation—elected student councils—has made comparably slow headway. The two largest senior high schools involved in our study had no interclass councils whatever (though the smallest did have one). Individual classes, some of them beginning in upper grades of the elementary school, were also said to choose their officers and plan their own commencement exercises, among other duties. Moreover, one of the elementary schools we visited had student committees elected by three classrooms to "observe how the children behave." Class discussions, sometimes under a student chairman, were at times conducted by these committees. The hypothesis, however, that even very young students can begin to learn the trait of responsibility by abundant experience in helping to formulate and implement school programs—curricular and extra-curricular alike—has as yet scarcely reached the stage of experimental testing.

3. There is need to *deal more extensively with controversial issues* in the classroom. The same criticism that has often been raised against Mainland teachers—that large numbers are either afraid or forbidden, even assuming they are equipped, to handle such issues—was also made against Island teachers.

A little ironically, few problems were raised in this study toward which greater verbal unanimity prevailed as to the right solution. Only one subcultural respondent stood in opposition to the inclusion of controversial issues under any circumstances, while two others confined their doubts to the elementary school. Whether or not all respondents would go as far as one parent respondent in urging that even the philosophy and practice of communism—a test case—should be studied impartially and thoroughly with due regard for possible strengths as well as weaknesses, the general attitude was, on the whole, in favor of wide academic freedom.*

Endorsement of this attitude by the test of action was, unfortunately, much less conspicuous. Among our respondents, one high school social-studies teacher admitted that communism was never discussed in her classes, while a second said that it was discussed only to an insignificant extent. Other controversial issues, such as race relations, juvenile delinquency, and the political status of Puerto Rico, fared somewhat better. Yet the extent of attention to such issues, even on the secondary level, appeared to be sparse.

The problem of *how* any such issues should be studied was also a matter of concern. Should all sides merely be presented, leaving the matter there? Or should effort be made by members of the class to reach conclusions or consensuses with due regard for differing opinions? Grassroots respondents who faced these questions directly—

* For further discussion, see pp. 296-298, 341-343.

and not all did—were again divided. Several, for example, held that teachers should limit study of controversial issues to impartial treatments and leave their own convictions outside the classroom. Puerto Ricans, one said, are too emotional to try to attain conclusions in any dispassionate way.

The lack of a clear educational policy on this important question was perhaps best exemplified by the reactions of eight veteran social-studies teachers interviewed by one of our respondents. Of these, five said they sometimes discussed controversial issues, one said never, and two said, in effect, "We try not to." Only one of the eight said he tried deliberately to help students reach consensuses.

On the national level, one leader favored the attempt to reach consensuses provided that teachers are trained to conduct the process fairly. Another leader was fearful of the common practice of imposing particular viewpoints upon students—an example being the issue of nativism versus assimilation. What is needed, he said, is uncoerced opportunity to weigh every strength and weakness of the contenders in such a dispute. Full exposure to all relevant evidence from as reliable authorities as possible, and full discussion of that evidence without pressure by the teacher to accept his own choices, should be the standard practice. A third leader added the need to cultivate the habit of "delayed" rather than "flash" reactions: give students plenty of time to think out controversial problems so that they can learn to be less impulsive when they assume responsibilities as citizens and parents.

One administrator respondent on the grassroots level strongly seconded this general point of view even for the elementary years. Since, he argued, the average child hears about social and other controversies in any case, the school's responsibility is to afford rational conditions for them to be considered and resolved.

4. There is need to *construct more and better library facilities* in all public schools of the Island. As long as students have access to few books, magazines, newspapers, and similar materials of learning, it becomes impossible to analyze controversial issues, for example, according to the norms stated above. In all fairness, however, the fact that school libraries are poorly developed thus far may not be as much due to lack of official recognition of their paramount importance to good education as it is to such emergency requirements as buildings,

teachers, textbooks, and shoes for every child.

Nor should it be forgotten that Island high schools do have libraries of very uneven quality, occasionally with a full-time librarian, though much oftener managed by a teacher with no special training. Even more indicative of public concern with the problem are the pioneering "bookmobiles"—several of which travel into remote rural areas with collections both in Spanish and English for children and adults.

Perhaps partly for these reasons, only a few respondents, all of them directly connected with the schools, urged more attention to the library problem. Frequently criticized was the "red tape" in obtaining either books on loan or for purchase through the Department of Education without such long delays (six or more months were said to be common) as often to make them useless to particular units of study by the time they arrive. Librarians are not authorized to order books themselves.

School libraries observed in the subcultures appeared to be pathetically short of current periodicals and pamphlet material, as well as reference books. None subscribed to a single newspaper in English —some to one or two in Spanish. (*Semana* and *Escuela* were often the only observable sources of news about current affairs.) Government publications, such as those of the Departments of Agriculture, Health, and Economic Development, appeared to be sparse. Many volumes in the largest high school library were reputed to be obsolete; indeed, some teachers were said to find no occasion to use or visit this library for semesters at a time. Even more serious was a program already under way to dispense entirely with school-wide libraries on the elementary level, substituting for them collections of books in each classroom under the teacher's control—collections which, so far as we observed, were limited to handfuls and which sometimes included badly printed comics on dubious themes.

How can the problem best be attacked? One leader urged that trained librarians be added to school faculties in every municipality. Students and teachers need guidance in how to use the library facilities they do have available, another leader insisted. A few PTA's were said to be taking responsibility for building library shelves and beginning collections as a contribution to their children's welfare. A few other PTA's allocate part of their membership dues for the purchase of new books. One was considering a project to obtain books from alumni of the school, their names to be inscribed in gift copies.

Unfortunately, no spokesman on either level offered additional suggestions. One respondent at the grassroots took the position that the community need not involve itself in the library problem, since additional books were really not essential!

5. There is need to *broaden adult education* as a service of the public schools. As all subcultural respondents explicitly agreed, learning is a lifelong process. To paraphrase one, every adult should aim to be like the physician who performs with maximum efficiency only so long as he keeps up in his field.

Would adults react favorably to public school opportunities for learning of the kinds thus far considered in this section? Would they favor courses in arts and crafts where creative expression is the central goal? Would they like to participate in planning their own projects? Would they enroll for courses in controversial issues—in local and international political or economic problems, say? Would they draw upon school libraries more fully if resources were richer than they normally are?

Directly or indirectly, the answer was predominantly "yes." Only two respondents were doubtful whether many adults would attend such courses—especially if problems were limited to the local community. (It is "not important enough.") The majority were confident that, just as thousands of adults now take courses for secondary diplomas as well as in English, vocational training, and other fields, while other thousands share in the program of the Division of Community Education, so they would respond to functional ways of learning that would widen their experience and stimulate the positive qualities of their personalities.

These kinds of education would have far-reaching retroactive effects upon personality development on the lower levels. As in the case of family education, the argument was underscored that better education of adults means better education of children as well. One leader reminded us of a principle now firmly established among psychologists: learning not only starts at birth, but the first five or six years of a child's growth are crucial to his lifelong character. Thus the kind of learning to which he is exposed before he ever attends school depends primarily upon the learning to which, in turn, his parents have already been exposed.

6. There is need to *intensify the use of community resources*. In order to meet this need, which applies to all levels of education including the adult, two further ideas merit our attention.

One idea was that a group of elementary schools, both rural and urban, should develop a pilot project in the growing of vegetable gardens. Though fairly common some years ago, they are now almost nonexistent. The purpose of the gardens would not be vocational, nor would it be to augment the food supply of the noon lunch program, although both benefits might incidentally result. The major purpose would be to permeate the curriculum with environmental experiences—to dramatize elementary science, say, by learning and applying simple botanical laws and processes, as well as the chemistry of soil and nutrition. Arithmetic, Spanish, English, and art could also be included: children who engaged in the project could learn to measure, weigh, and count in connection with their "work experience"; they could learn to read, write, and discuss such problems as fertilization and cultivation; and they could draw, paint, sing, and dramatize some of their activities.

The leader most enthusiastic about this project urged friendly competition between participating schools, with prizes to be offered by firms or civic groups for the finest gardens. He was sure, too, that resource experts, such as horticulturists from experimental stations of the Department of Agriculture, could be utilized. And PTA's might become so much involved that parents would be learning at the same time as their children. Another leader, though he did not propose this project, was confident that the kind of functionalized learning which it exemplifies will produce more subject-matter knowledge than learning of more customary types. This is a hypothesis that requires checking by means of control groups, with extensive preplanning. One teacher respondent was rather skeptical; she was afraid that children would destroy the plants.

Actually, schools already differ widely in the extent to which the plots of land around them are made useful or attractive. In the town of Cañamelar, children help to plant and care for shrubs and flowers that abound outside its elementary and secondary schools. But certain other schools in the three subcultures lacked any evidence of interest in how their immediate surroundings might affect the attitudes and feelings of learners. Nor were playgrounds with special equipment for games and exercise anywhere observable. In at least two subcultural schools (one in a Hermosa neighborhood with a record of juvenile delinquency), children were not permitted to play on the premises after class hours.

The other intriguing idea, to which several respondents contributed, was that children be given opportunity to study their milieu by taking frequent trips both in their own vicinities and at greater distances. This is not a new idea: student respondents recalled a few trips in their elementary years—a few more in their high school years. Teacher respondents also spoke of occasional class visits to various institutions, such as *Fomento*. One had hiked with his class to a dairy farm and to a nearby beach.

But it was apparent that these events were anything but commonplace. Expense has been one serious handicap; for trips of some distance, parents are expected to pay as much as $2 for a single child—a prohibitive cost for some. (No budget for trips is provided by the Department of Education, though occasionally funds are granted by municipalities.) Large classes are another handicap; it is difficult for a single teacher to supervise so many children. Still others are the lack of public school busses. A rural teacher respondent recalled that, because on one occasion a child had been lost temporarily and several slightly hurt when they fell off a truck, nearly all parents in his school refused permission for further trips.

Most serious was a meager awareness noted among many teachers and administrators of the potentialities for learning that well-planned trips are able to provide. Few subcultural classes on any level were reported to have left their classrooms for excursions even into their own neighborhoods. Thus, in the Cañamelar sugar subculture, though high school groups occasionally ventured forth, one teacher respondent of long local residence could recall only a single elementary class that had ever visited a *central* (grinding mill). Two or three operated only a few kilometers away.

The same leader who proposed a school garden experiment was the most vigorous in urging an Island-wide program to permit all children eventually to learn through well-organized, well-supervised trips. Expenses should be met, not by parents at all, but by a special budget in the Department of Education of, say, $50,000 for the first year, with a small special staff both to plan events with teachers and students and to give in-service training to those in charge. Stores and factories; the legislature when in session; the various colleges; consumer and producer cooperatives; newspapers and broadcasting stations; the water-power authority; rural and urban housing projects; homes of the poor and rich; pineapple and other plantations; courts and police stations; projects of the Institute of Puerto Rican culture; labor unions and business associations; beach and mountain areas; and specific communities for intensive study over a period of weeks or even months—these are among the resources that such a venture could make possible.

7. Finally, there is need to *develop better ways of evaluating the process and products of learning* itself. One of the difficulties posed by the suggestions in this chapter lies precisely here: How far and in what ways can it be determined that learning *is* actually better when it is thus made more functionalistic and less behavioristic—or, for that matter, when the opposite occurs?

The only answer offered was that systematic evaluation is greatly needed in Puerto Rican education. As in the modest garden project, few if any proposals made by our respondents could be regarded as more than hypotheses that deserve to be tested out (many initially on a small scale) in order to determine whether or not they are successful in practice.

Half a dozen suggestions, however, were offered for better evaluation of present learnings. Cumulative records should accompany students through all stages of advancement—records that include not only grades and health but evidence of personality development, strengths and weaknesses in skills or other accomplishments, and general information from teachers and counselors that would be useful to employers or college officers. Especially would it be desirable for junior high schools to provide more substantial evaluation and guidance so that intelligent direction could be given students entering senior high schools. One grassroots respondent also urged stricter rules of selectivity; he opposed "mass promotions."

In schools where students are grouped according to alleged abilities, careful attention should be paid to the effects on morale among those with high as well as median and low I.Q.'s that could result from invidious comparisons. Opportunities should also be given for students of superior intelligence to progress more rapidly than the average and to be evaluated accordingly. For students who show weaknesses, more frequent check-ups are required along with better planned and more abundant remedial work. Lastly, techniques of evaluation on both the public school and college level should be developed that are as objective, automatic, and comprehensive as possible. At the same time, all teachers should take into consideration such qualitative learnings as growth in originality, cooperation, and participation.

CULTURE, PERSONALITY, AND LEARNING: ACTUALITIES AND POTENTIALITIES

The themes of this and the preceding chapter are integral with each other and they prepare for the next. They have been concerned with a single main question: How may we most effectively characterize the personality type as it develops through learning and as, in turn, it shares in the processes by which the culture is transmitted and remolded?

The answer is far from simple, not only because the Puerto Rican personality is itself intricate, but because the kinds of learning that occur are sometimes in conflict in theory and practice. Both negative and positive traits, for example, were found to be conspicuous. Similarly, both behavioristic and functionalistic approaches to learning (these terms broadly meaning the two chief, though overlapping, viewpoints now prevalent in culture-and-personality theory) were supported in varying ways by our respondents.

Nevertheless, granting that negative traits are by no means trivial, they were found to be increasingly outweighed by positive traits. To this consensus on both levels, our profile of the personality of subcultural respondents largely subscribes. For example, while defensiveness and its cluster of related traits would seem to be much more typical than not, even more conspicuously typical is a readiness to be genuinely friendly once any sign is given that friendliness will be reciprocated. On the whole, the average Puerto Rican strongly respects himself as a personality, and he expects others—including North Americans and Spaniards—to respect him just as much.

At the same time, our evidence shows many disparities—not only by way of differing stresses upon various traits, but also by way of emotional disturbances with a pronounced neurotic tinge. To recall an important instance, the extent of more or less suppressed aggressiveness may be fairly acute when placed beside the bipolar phenomenon of considerable frustration. Also, the qualities symbolized by *being* and *becoming,* because they express differing though potentially complementary patterns of behavior, inevitably tend to generate tensions in these patterns. It is not too much to assume, indeed, that every one of the processes inherent in the evolution of modern Puerto Rico —from innovation through conflict and the "nativist reaction" to the foci of cultural change—are reflected overtly or covertly in its modal personality as well.

On the whole, and conceding that full agreement among our respondents was rare, recommendations for the building of unified, constructive personalities tended oftener toward functionalistic forms of learning than toward behavioristic forms. This is a way of saying that, however limited the acquaintance of respondents with the technicalities of educational psychology, education for most of them should be concerned with maximum ways to share critically and actively in the order, process, and goals of the culture, rather than merely to hear or read about them or to absorb them passively in the form of skills and facts. In behalf of this objective, our panels pressed for greater attention to mental health; to widened audio-visual learning (especially television); and to improved professional training through such means as richer utilization of the "activity month," practice with group dynamics, a pilot project for rural teacher-leaders, direct immersion in community problems, and substantially increased remuneration. In terms of the student, personality development would improve more rapidly if much greater attention were paid to the following: creative expression through the arts, study of controversial issues, improvement of library facilities, vitalization and expansion of adult education, experience with a wide range of community resources, and more systematic evaluation of the methods and fruits of learning itself.

Our own reaction to many of these proposals is enthusiastic. However much the criticisms and judgments that we have elicited concerning culture-and-personality are open to debate, Puerto Rican education could, we believe, share importantly in a magnificent enterprise— the enterprise of building a modal personality increasingly strong in the cluster of characteristics that are now most admired, increasingly weak in those that are not, yet increasingly different from either cluster. The fact that respondents often disagreed in their efforts to delineate that personality, or that they were sometimes at odds in their educational suggestions, is not surprising. Indeed, considering that they, too, are personalities shaped by a highly mobile culture, unanimity would have been much more surprising.

Further questions could, however, be raised not only about such disagreements but about the limited consensuses as well. Possibly something of the same unsubstantiated optimism detected in our chapter on history is detectable in the conspicuous opinion that positive personality traits are now increasingly, even rapidly, overshadowing the almost dominant negative traits of earlier generations. Again, it could have been argued (though it was not) that the middle-stratum personality (for reasons anticipated by Chapter 4) tends to be more ambivalent than that of other classes: his aspirations, for one thing, may be further from his expectations than in the case of either lower or upper strata. More, too, could have been said on the question of the *jíbaro* as archetype; we incline to agree with the comment that there is more than a touch of romanticism in this view, though we also respect the nice distinction of a student respondent who, we remember, contended that the *jíbaro's* mode of existence is much harder to defend than his personality. Nor can we overlook a number of errors of scientific fact—for example, that given religious traits are genetically inherited.

The question will also occur to critical readers as to whether the bias of our panels toward functionalistic learning may not have been induced partly by the questions asked. For our part, though many on our panels may have genuinely favored this kind of learning, we incline to agree with such readers. The fact that the new government-owned television station forbids free discussion of political controversy is one of numerous symptoms that this kind of learning is by no means unqualifiedly approved. Also, the discussion of enculturation showed that any consensus in favor of functionalistic as against behavioristic learning was far from clear-cut.

Such eclecticism may not be entirely unfortunate. We recognize that each psychological position borrows something important from the other. Moreover, in terms of Puerto Rican education, perhaps each *should* borrow from the other. To take an instance, we are impressed by the observation of the grassroots educator who defended the need for firm classroom discipline as a partial compensation for its absence from homes demoralized by the new industrialization.

This is not to contend that behavioristic learning, as defined, affords the only psychological basis for that kind of discipline. Rather, we suggest the need for a new theory of *socialized* discipline that develops with a maturing sense of mutual responsibility to achieve agreed-upon tasks and objectives of the emerging culture.[1] Here the wide utilization of group dynamics is especially apropos; it enables even very young children to develop interactive rather than passive habits of learning.[2]

The needed conception of learning is not entirely clarified. But if the genius of the Puerto Rican culture today centers in its syncretic potentialities, then perhaps it has opportunity to develop such a syncretism in the area of personality-and-learning as well as in other areas. In this endeavor, the functionalistic approach, with its stress upon the many processes encompassed by the term *becoming,* continues to be fundamental. But it should be supplemented by a deeper sense of *being*—of emotional as well as rational identification with the whole culture which begins in the human relations of children as they play and work together.

CHAPTER THIRTEEN

LANGUAGE AS A CULTURAL PROCESS IN PUERTO RICO

No PROCESS is more universal to cultures of all ranges of development than language. Indeed, some anthropologists and philosophers have sought to prove that the "symbolic system" is *the* differential feature of culture—the feature which marks it off from all other forms of either animal or human association.

In Puerto Rico, unlike cultures where the native tongue may be taken entirely for granted, the problem of language learning has been called both chronic and acute. Its causes have protruded from many preceding pages. For over a half-century, the question of how best to cope with the difficulties that result from trying to modify if not to transform monolingual habits established by more than four previous centuries of uninterrupted practice and transmission has plagued political as well as educational policies. Also, it has without much question contributed to sociopsychological maladjustments both on the Island and the Continent—maladjustments which, though as yet largely unmeasured, may be much more injurious to mental and social health than is evident on the surface.

In view of need for careful analysis and interpretation of the language problem in the setting of culture, one can only express astonishment at the total absence of both from the Steward study of Puerto Rican culture. An occasional remark on the place of English in the schools or of Spanish as a symbol of nationality can scarcely be termed either analysis or interpretation.

This chapter tries to close a segment of the gap by placing the problem in the context of the preceding pair of chapters—that is, in terms of learning as a central cultural process of personality development. At the outset, however, it may be well to recall a little history, after which we turn to our respondents' reactions both to the educational problem as such and to the still wider issue of "symbolic disturbances."

Our own assessment, while appreciative of the advances made thus far, will be negative on two chief related scores: the first, that the language program is vulnerable in its deficient grasp and application of functionalistic learning; the second, that it has not yet been perceived in adequate cultural-philosophic perspective. Steps toward a policy that could correct these weaknesses are finally suggested.

ENGLISH VERSUS SPANISH: A SIXTY-YEAR DEBATE[1]

The concepts of cultural process that most graphically help us to understand the language problem in Puerto Rico are those of force and of conflict. Beginning in 1900 with the appointment of the first Commissioner of Education (North American, of course), Insular policies regarding the respective places of English and Spanish in the total program have until recently been contradictory, chaotic, arbitrary, and determined more often by the political biases or educational "intuitions" of those who happened to be in positions of authority than based upon any reasoned-out theory or scientific evidence concerning the teaching and learning of a second language.

The zigzags of fifty years are staggering. The first policy required that the elementary schools of villages and towns be taught in the vernacular, English being a separate discipline under a special teacher (often North American), but embracing all other subjects on the high school level. Before it had hardly been put into effect, this policy was radically changed by another Commissioner: from 1905 and continuing for over ten years thereafter, English became the official language of all public schools. In order to effect the change-over as rapidly as possible, Puerto Rican teachers augmented the U.S. supply by in-service training. Thus by 1912, 98 per cent of all elementary children from the first grade were officially reported to be taught wholly in English. Of course the vernacular remained their language outside the classroom.

Although this policy continued until 1916, public opposition was widely voiced on the ground that children were not learning other subjects. There was a general clamor for use of Spanish in the schools. In response to this demand, the school year 1913-14 made the first step toward restoring Spanish as the medium of instruction: it was to be used, rather than English, in teaching nature study in the first four grades. In the first grade, sanitation and hygiene were also to be taught in Spanish. As a further innovation, reading in Spanish was to be started in the first grade. During this period, party politics and a strong nationalist feeling swept the Island and became involved with the language issue. One's politics, it was claimed, determined one's stand on the language question, and much confusion and emotionalism resulted.

Up to this point, changes in policy had come about through prejudice or personal opinion, rather than from scientific evidence. The first attempts to test the validity of any policy objectively were made in 1916; they proved the weaknesses of the all-English policy. The result was a middle-of-the-road policy, which remained in force from 1916-34. The first four grades were taught in Spanish, with English as a special subject; the fifth grade was transitional by combining both; while the next three grades and high school were entirely in English, except for Spanish as a special subject.

This policy was continued with little change, despite critical evaluations and recommendations made by the International Institute of Teachers College, Columbia University, in 1925. Its findings indicated that most public schools were failing to produce anything like a bilingual people—indeed, that the great majority of children (more than 80 per cent) were dropping out of school without having learned either language well enough to read or write according to minimum standards. Also, they had substandard attainment in other subjects that require command of at least one language. It was recommended that English be excluded until the fourth grade, and that Spanish be used as the medium of instruction until the seventh grade. The Department of Education, however, continued to ignore these recommendations.

In the thirties, after several years of study of the problem, the first Commissioner of Puerto Rican background once more changed the policy. Beginning in 1934, Spanish became the language of all grades of the elementary school. English became only a special subject, while remaining the official language of high school instruction. This change of policy in the elementary school incurred the displeasure of the American-appointed Governor, who preferred a policy of enforced English for all grades.

In 1937 President Franklin D. Roosevelt appointed as Commissioner another Puerto Rican, with many years of experience on the Continent. The prime importance of the language issue is illustrated by the fact that in his letter of appointment the President made no reference whatever to other educational problems. He did, however, make three revealing statements: (1) "It is an indispensable part of the American policy that the coming generation of American citizens in Puerto Rico grow up with complete facility in the English tongue. It is the language of our Nation." (2) But "it is obvious that they [Puerto Ricans] always will and should retain facility in the tongue of their inherited culture, Spanish." (3) Therefore it is necessary "that the American citizens of Puerto Rico should profit from their unique geographical situation and the unique historical circumstance which has brought to them the blessings of American citizenship by becoming bilingual."[2]

It would be hard to find any more succinct formulation of the whole language issue. In a sense, indeed, the three sentences read separately could almost be taken as epitomizing three different policies, each of which still has its coterie of advocates. The letter did not, however, raise the heated question of the language to be used as the principal medium of instruction.

But President Roosevelt's appointee, although he had accepted with the understanding that he would place heavy emphasis upon English, and although he tried valiantly to do so by returning part of the way to the policy of teaching other subjects in that language, nevertheless had restored by 1942 much of the policy of his predecessor. Once again, the vernacular became the first language of the elementary school, with English a special subject. To be sure, English remained the principal language of the secondary school, but even here the trend was now toward Spanish—in vocational subjects, for example. And once again, pressures from Washington were brought to bear, resignations were offered and accepted, and general confusion prevailed.

Late in the decade the Senate refused to confirm President Harry S. Truman's appointee, because of doubts about the latter's attitude toward English. It was only in 1949, after the first elected Governor took office with power to choose the new Commissioner, that the appointment took effect.

ASPECTS OF THE PRESENT POLICY

The policy prevailing from 1949 has been based primarily on a theory of linguistics. Far more than any previous policy, it attempts to approach the problem of a second language from a logical viewpoint and with a set of carefully formulated postulates that can be implemented in terms of precise methods and concrete materials. Before the policy was adopted, some preliminary tryouts were held; but so far as we could learn, few teachers were consulted as to their own wishes.

The historical record sketched above reveals that, in the last decade or more before 1949, the pendulum once again was swinging toward the vernacular as the primary language of instruction. The pendulum has swung even further since. English is required as a separate subject from the first grade through the last year of high school, but at no time is it the language of instruction for any other subject and at no time is the length of study per day increased beyond a single class period. Thus, in the respect that even in high school the first language is now Spanish (some private schools are an exception, of course), the predominant policy of nearly fifty years has now been rescinded.

The trend has also extended to the University. While many required books are still in English (as, indeed, some are in the high schools also), Spanish is the printed as well as oral means of instruction in many college-level courses. North American professors may teach in English, for after twelve years of public school instruction students are formally expected to know both languages. Typically, however, fluency in the second language is much too limited to permit anything like the level of spoken or written discourse that is taken for granted in like courses of college caliber in the United States.

The extent to which the systematic program of English study in the primary and secondary schools shares responsibility for this limitation is thus far undetermined. Certainly many variables enter into so intricate a problem. Nevertheless, since it is this program which now officially prevails in Puerto Rico, further attention to its principles and methods is appropriate.

These principles and methods are identified chiefly with one leader in the field of linguistics, Dr. Charles C. Fries of the University of Michigan, who has worked directly with Puerto Rican linguists. The new series of textbooks and teachers' guides, prepared by the Department of Education and entitled the "Fries American English Series," is said to be pioneering in its application of "scientific" principles to the teaching of English as a secondary language in the public schools, and the only series that covers so many consecutive years of the child's life in school.

It is relevant to note that Fries acknowledges the influence, among others, of the late Edward Sapir, a notable North American anthropologist who specialized in linguistics, to whom he gives primary credit for inception of the theory. In one major respect, the postulates of structural linguistics have much in common with what is now often termed "field theory" in both the physical and behavioral sciences. According to this theory, the relations among the parts of any natural event or experience are just as crucial to the whole as are the parts themselves—indeed, the relations, in a fundamental sense, determine the meaning of these parts. In the same way, the term "structure" connotes the organic relations of language. Therefore, as against the older grammatical system of building an understanding and facility out of separate elements, such as alphabets, lists of separate words, and verb forms (in philosophic terms, this method reflects mechanistic or atomistic theory), the system of structural linguistics stresses *patterns* of sounds, words, and sentences—patterns that affect meanings because of the way letters and words relate to one another and to the specific cultures within which they function.

Another basic characteristic of structural linguistics, especially as it is applied to learning a second language, is the so-called oral approach. Just as a small child normally learns his native tongue through listening and speaking, and only later learns to read and write, so the best results will accrue when stress is placed upon mastery of a "sound system"—that is, listening and speaking. Fries and his disciples do not mean that the other two processes are to be given meager consideration. What they do mean is that, especially in the first stage, the sequence of learning is listening and speaking, followed by reading and writing.

The necessity of automatic habits in the new language is thus established by listening to the teacher, imitating and constantly repeating the patterns that the teacher provides through the guide book, then by reading and writing these patterns or related ones. Each unit thus typically includes all four steps, although reading and writing do not begin until the third grade. Even if desired facility is limited to reading a second language, the oral approach is recommended as the most effective means to that end.

There is much more to the system than a summary can suggest. For example, Fries insists that each language and cultural situation require somewhat different techniques and materials. Again, stress is placed upon contrasts in sound that produce contrasts in meaning (e.g., "leave" and "live") in words, sentences, and finally whole paragraphs. Much attention is paid to contrasting intonations and inflections. Even more significant to us, the new textbooks and guides try to implement the principle that a language must be learned in the context of meanings provided by the culture to which it is indigenous —in this case, the United States primarily.

Thus, the claim of the directors of the Puerto Rican English program that it is ground-breaking seems, from the viewpoint of a layman in linguistics, to be justified. The question of how successful the new system appears to citizens who are involved either directly or indirectly in its operation is our next concern.

CRITICISMS AND PROPOSALS TO MEET THE LANGUAGE PROBLEM

Respondents, with a single exception, agreed that English is a necessary skill which all people in Puerto Rico should master as well as possible. The lone dissenter held that English is necessary only for those who would come into direct contact with North American life— the business classes, for example. But even he later corrected himself by agreeing that English should be taught one period per day as a separate subject beginning with the fourth grade, his reason being that increasing migration now makes the second language useful for many on the lower as well as higher strata.

Most respondents on both levels, moreover, endorsed the ultimate objective of complete bilingualism—an objective that they conceded would be difficult to attain, but one important enough to justify the magnitude of the task. Nor was their reason exclusively the Island's relations with the Continent: English, some said, is becoming the foremost international language and thus the best means of communication with other parts of the world as well.

Is genuine bilingualism likely to result eventually from the present system? The prevalent answer was "no." One period a day for twelve school years cannot possibly, no matter how excellently the time is used, result in parallel fluency even in reading or writing, much less in the more difficult oral and aural skills. Ample, continuous practice in English outside of school is a minimum additional need.

Authorities responsible for the present program would not be likely to deny this evaluation. The kind of facility they aim to achieve is not to be measured by comparable facility in Spanish, but rather by norms established for a *second* language. Simplicity in discourse, stressing the most common patterns of English, is a major rule of the system. Also, it is recognized that the average student's "receptive" capacity (to read and hear) will outrun his "productive" capacity (to write and speak) in English.

On the adult level, where many thousands—largely in rural areas —complete the free English course each year, even less fluency is to be expected. The aim of this course is limited both in the amount of time consumed (seventy-two hours of instruction) and in the resulting skills. Courses are designed largely for migrant workers and for special groups, such as policemen, although a full elementary and secondary program is also available to adults. Teachers, recruited from the public schools by paying them extra compensation, have had experience in English whenever possible. The principles of structural linguistics are utilized in the program, though not as strictly as on lower levels. The government television station also offers regular instruction.

But even the modest norms of second-language facility for high school and college graduates cannot be achieved, many informants held, as long as tremendous handicaps remain. Inadequately trained teachers—the most frequently considered of these handicaps—is chronic in the elementary schools where language habits are most readily formed. Considerably less than half of all primary school teachers, we were informed, have more than a two-year normal school training in all subjects; some have as little as six weeks of training beyond high school; and only about 1 per cent of those assigned to teach elementary English have a B.A. degree in that field. On the secondary level, the situation is better but far from satisfactory: only about half of the teachers of English in senior high schools have majored in their specialization, and only about one-fourth have done so in junior high schools. On the elementary level, a substantial number (the percentage is undetermined) cannot communicate in English except to a meager extent. And when teachers do speak, as of course they must in every lesson built on the "oral approach," their accents even on the secondary level are frequently heavy—so heavy in some instances that Mainland visitors to their classrooms have difficulty in comprehending the English presumably being taught.

These handicaps, too, are readily admitted by experts in the program, as others would be admitted that were listed earlier. Limited resource materials, such as North American magazines, newspapers, pictures, books, and pamphlets; huge classes and double sessions; early drop-outs and poorly enforced attendance rules—these are only the more glaring of the factors that retard progress.

But controversy looms when we push further. What, for example, of the system taken on its merits? To judge by our informants, little familiarity prevails as to the basic principles of that system; yet critical judgments were profuse indeed. On the grassroots level, nearly all respondents were eager to see changes. Most serious were the opinions that, on the average, students dislike the English period much more than they like it (this was heard even in two subcultural high schools with North American language teachers) and that almost no attempt is made to practice outside the required class period except in special programs or in occasional "English clubs." Yet the recommendation that more time be provided for English instruction was reiterated oftener than any other: double the present period to one hundred minutes in high schools, double the present time in single-session elementary schools, and as rapidly as possible eliminate half-day sessions so that the same double time may prevail in every school.

Other grassroots recommendations were equally vigorous. Modify the routine of "choral practice," so central to the "oral approach," in order thereby to reduce both the fatigue and boredom of which both teachers and students frequently complain. Provide opportunity to integrate English with learning of other subjects. Utilize phonograph recordings and tapes in order to improve intonations and pronunciations. Build language units around problems of meaningful interest in the lives of students. Reevaluate the present system by consulting random samples of students, parents, principals, and teachers. Give teachers more leeway from the prescribed lessons of the guides and textbooks. Provide more abundant reading material, especially for rural communities where magazines and newspapers in the English language may be almost nonexistent. Increase the use of Mainland educational films, both by integrating them with English instruction and by incorporating them in science, social studies, and PTA programs. Set up an experiment in matched elementary classes, one group of which would utilize a plenitude of illustrative resources, the other not, and measure the rate of improvement in each. Where a textbook is written in English (e.g., tenth-grade world history), why not *discuss* in English too? Lastly, bring more U.S. teachers to Puerto Rico on an exchange basis.

Perhaps the most unexpected reaction on the subcultural level was the relatively strong (though still minority) preference for the earlier system of required English for all subjects. Next to the recommendation that the amount of time be doubled for English instruction, this preference received the most concerted support among both younger and older respondents—notably from those most deficient in English themselves. Among the group who favored this recommendation, two would like English to become the first language. (But another grassroots spokesman, not in this group, was sure that Spanish would "always" remain the first language of Puerto Rico—a conviction explicitly shared by more than one leader as well.)

Every respondent who could converse only in the vernacular hoped that his children would not follow his example; indeed, he wanted them to become as proficient in English as in Spanish. The only reservation any respondent was willing to concede was that, for some citizens, it seems more important to assure facility in boys than in girls—the implication presumably being that boys are more likely to venture forth to make their fortunes in the United States.

A wide range of reactions would suggest that the problem continues to be worrisome on the national level also. Yet, unlike the grassroots level, no leader respondent favored return to the earlier system of all-English public schools, at least without alterations. Several spoke of their own great difficulty as students under that system, of their dislike of the superimposition, and of the resentment that it caused.

One leader did assert that, even with the real difficulties of an all-English policy, it enabled the Puerto Rican people to learn the language much more successfully than they do today—a task which, moreover, many welcomed. But even he was prepared to admit that Congress had been negligent in failing to underwrite the very program that it had expected its colony to foster. Although some North American teachers were sent to Puerto Rico, they rarely reached the rural areas, with the result that the major burden still fell upon native teachers of very meager fluency. If, he argued, Congress had been as generous to Puerto Rico as it was to the Philippine Islands in providing many hundreds of Continental teachers, the language situation today would not only be much less serious than it is, but the whole level of education would be higher because the rate of drop-out would have decreased. For this same leader, the primary solution then is essentially the same: convince Congress that its responsibility is to provide a large corps of well-trained Continental teachers. Pay salaries high enough to get them, and then teach English to all Puerto Rican students with thoroughness and competence.

Whether this gigantic task should be accomplished through a curriculum once more extensively or primarily in English, and what would happen to displaced Island teachers of English, were questions that remained unclarified. The chief contention was, however, very clear: English for this leader is still by far the most crucial of educational issues on the Island today. More than this, it is the key to wider and deeper issues already noted—especially the issue of whether a "nativist reaction" shall be allowed to develop or (as he, of course, preferred) acculturation and assimilation of the North American culture shall be accelerated. The political trend which for several years has gradually moved in the former of these directions is perfectly exemplified, so this respondent held, by the shrinkage of English to a separate subject taught one period per day, with a mere handful of U.S. teachers left in the public schools.

But several others pointed out that if many Puerto Ricans learned English yesterday better than most Puerto Ricans learn it today, this effect was by no means due merely to the presence of Continental teachers. Smaller classroom enrollments, all-day sessions, generally higher standards, relatively better salaries, and still other variables prevent a fair comparison between the earlier all-English system and the present one.

Moreover, another argued, the proposal that many hundreds of Mainland teachers be brought to the Island is fraught with difficulties. Most disturbing is the unemployment it could cause among the regular Puerto Rican teachers. Also, a relatively high salary scale for competent North American teachers (and this is inescapable if they are to be attracted in sufficient numbers) would raise cries of unfair discrimination.

A more feasible solution, some leaders said, lies in sending many Puerto Rican teachers on scholarships to the United States to study and live in typical communities for as much as a full year. Through this experience they could practice English constantly, improve their accent, and familiarize themselves with the cultural patterns to which the U.S. language is indigenous. This proposal has already been initiated: nearly 150 teachers, in addition to some promising high school graduates without teaching experience, were sent to the States in one recent year and the annual number will be increased. The ultimate goal, indeed, is to provide such an opportunity for all teachers of English in both elementary and secondary schools.

Also in effect is a small program whereby Puerto Rican teachers fill temporary posts in Continental schools, by exchanging with North American teachers of English who come to Insular schools. This plan has the advantage of creating no serious imbalance either in personnel or salaries: guest teachers continue to receive their regular salaries, while Puerto Rican teachers receive a modest bonus in order to meet the higher standards of living to which North American teachers are accustomed. In the slight degree that the plan has been put into effect, criticisms have been raised to the effect that some Continental teachers have not successfully adjusted to Island school routines, while Puerto Rican teachers in the States have frequently been assigned courses in Spanish which, of course, reduce opportunities to improve their English.

Still another step already taken in a few instances is the assignment of Continental wives of Army personnel and businessmen to part-time or full-time English-teaching positions. The difficulty here has been twofold: a frequent lack of professional training and a relatively low rate of compensation. Nevertheless, the plan has apparently worked with enough success so that one spokesman was eager to see it promoted more zealously.

In largest part, then, leaders were agreed that in coping with the dual language issue a good deal more can and should be done. (No leader, however, went so far explicitly as the small minority at the grassroots who hoped English would become the first language of the Island, although implicitly a few may have that hope in mind.) Methodologically, some of the same proposals made in the sub-cultures were reinforced. The suggestion that English be integrated at least partly with other subjects was heavily stressed—one spokesman being careful to insist that such integration should not be attempted until students had learned the rudiments of the second language. Another opposed integration in learning mathematics while favoring it for both history and geography.

Two leaders came close to defending the *status quo*. English, they said, is now taught better than most other subjects in the public school. It is better constructed for use in large classes than the earlier system. It is based upon the best available knowledge of linguistics. And students enrolling in the University (at least in one division) were said to continue to improve in English year by year. In fact, about one-fifth of these enrollees compare well in fluency with entering students in Continental liberal-arts colleges, while another fifth compare favorably with North American students from the sixth to ninth grades.*

One of the two leaders was critical on other grounds, however. Like all courses in Puerto Rican schools, English, he said, is regarded as a self-contained subject and taught with little concern for the mainstreams of cultural experience or the interests of young learners. Actually the problem of two languages cannot be solved by structural linguistics or by any other system, no matter how defensible it may be on scientific grounds. The basic problem, rather, is one of an adequate philosophy and psychology of general education—one that will encourage active expression in *every* field—in the arts as well as science, in Spanish as well as English. As a grassroots respondent also emphasized, we must not forget that it is not merely English that

* The validity of these figures was questioned by two experts in English instruction with whom we conferred.

is not now being well learned. The vernacular is not either!

Remaining suggestions were provocative, too. First, give more in-service training to teachers of English through workshops, the "activity month," and in other ways. Second, give more attention to the emotional factors in communication: language is a way to convey meanings, and meanings are at least as much an affair of feeling as they are of thought. Third, bring in more North American teachers by paying them bonuses from Commonwealth funds even if this does generate resentment; the job to be done must come first. Fourth, offer various high school courses in both languages—for example, physics —and permit students to choose. Fifth, teach Spanish better; then English, too, will be learned better.

And finally, reexamine the aims of the entire English program. Why is it important? For whom and for what is it important? Fresh answers to these questions may, we were told, reveal that the present program needs not only modification in content and method, but greater flexibility in application to different types of students in terms of varying objectives.

SYMBOLIC DISTURBANCES

If the proposal just made, to reappraise the present over-all program, is to be done successfully and conscientiously, it must be brought back to the character of Puerto Rican culture.

Consider the difficult question of whether or not the present culture suffers in any severe way from "symbolic disturbances" comparable to those of others in extraordinary flux. Anthropologists mean by such disturbances that habitual media of communication and expression have become inadequate to the task of expressing and communicating typical cultural experiences. New cultural processes require new symbols. But often these symbols are, for a time at least, unavailable. Conflict and distortion result from the fact that old symbolic systems are retained and applied to events, beliefs, institutions, and attitudes for which they were never intended.

In clarifying this question with leader respondents, the example was given of North American Indian tribes which suffer so acutely from such conflicts and distortions that they are sometimes said to be "sick." The point was also emphasized that "symbolic systems" include much more than spoken or written language: art and religion, especially, are expressed nonverbally perhaps oftener than verbally. Language in the ordinary sense is, nevertheless, by far the most common of all symbolic systems.

Perhaps the closest anticipation thus far of the presence of symbolic disturbances in Puerto Rico has been our analysis of explicit and implicit beliefs concerning democracy, religion, morality, and science. All four of these great spheres of belief revealed varying degrees and kinds of incompatibility between what were called their ideological and configurational levels of expression. No one would contend that such incompatibility is traceable merely to confusions generated by the problem of two languages. Puerto Ricans fluent only in Spanish may suffer just as acutely from disparities between, for example, the symbolic codes or rituals of the Catholic Church and their Hispanic-influenced moral conduct as do bilingual citizens. Still, it would be surprising if the added difficulties of a foreign tongue did not widen these disparities.

To punctuate the point, consider the example of democracy—a political institution first associated in the minds of many Puerto Ricans with the United States. The language through which democracy is accordingly described is much more directly identified with that country than with either Hispanic cultures or the colonial era in Puerto Rico under Spanish rule. Thus, since political conceptions are necessarily also verbalized, some confusion in these conceptions would quite plausibly result from the attempt to fit Spanish and Puerto Rican symbolic customs into North American symbolic molds. Perhaps even the habitually simultaneous display of two nonverbal symbols—the Puerto Rican and U.S. flags—could aggravate these confusions.

To what extent did our leader respondents express concern along this general line? The fact that almost exactly half were ready to say that symbolic disturbances are chronic in the culture, the other half that they are not, was itself another of many symptoms of ambivalence that, perhaps inadvertently, lend further credence to this very fact.

Those, moreover, who disagreed did not do so without reservations. While the upper social strata were said by one respondent to be less disturbed symbolically than the lower strata—the former command both languages—this contention was contradicted by the argument of a second that the least disturbance is found in the lower strata precisely because they command only one. A third contention was that both arguments are wrong—that the widest symbolic confusion pervades the middle levels where, because fluency is expected and yet limited, communication is thereby oftenest distorted and guesswork most frequent.

One leader felt, however, that all forms of symbolic expression in Puerto Rico, in art as well as everyday language, have been too circumscribed and uncreative to generate acute disturbance. In language, facility in both Spanish and English is normally within a narrow range —an effect due in part to the attempt to teach two languages only half efficiently instead of either one well. For another leader, while symbolic disturbances have been decreasing rapidly in the last fifteen years as Puerto Ricans have begun to rediscover their own identity, one cannot generalize for the culture as a whole. Actually, such disturbances as remain may have therapeutic value: they challenge the culture to find more appropriate modes of self-expression—in literature, for instance—and thus to discard obsolescent modes.

Probably the keenest observation by any respondent on the problem of symbolic disturbances turned for direct support to Ernst Cassirer, the famous German philosopher of "symbolic forms."[3] One of Cassirer's principal theses is that symbols must not be confused with the realities they symbolize—that symbols have no objective force or existence of their own but are simply tools that man has fashioned for explaining and controlling his environment.

Puerto Ricans, this respondent held, are now in the process of grasping the import of so far-reaching a distinction. As elsewhere, they have moved only part way toward a rational, scientific symbolism. Emotion rather than intellect continues to rule many men here as it does in, say, the United States, and emotional symbols in the hands of the wrong people are always dangerous. Nevertheless, to recall the language of Chapter 7, the people are slowly learning how to use symbols scientifically, operationally, rather than to regard them as possessed of some external and esoteric power able to determine their lives.

A NEEDED LANGUAGE POLICY

In a sense, this chapter has continued the discussion of our two preceding ones. But instead of dealing with the whole vast area of culture, personality, and learning, it concentrates on a single large field—or rather battlefield—within that area. We now review and recommend.

At the present time, following half a century of acrimonious dispute, resentment, and bewilderment during which the Island wavered from one arbitrary program to another, a plausible policy concerning the place of English in a traditionally Spanish-speaking country may at last crystallize. Rudiments of such a policy include the following, all presently in effect: (1) Spanish is the first language of instruction in all public schools (in private ones, English may be first); (2) twelve years of English are required, with instruction offered daily; (3) all public schools, and to a considerable extent both the University and adult programs, base such instruction on a system called structural linguistics, two important features of which are the "field" or patterned nature of language and the "oral" as against the "grammatical" approach; and (4) the purpose is to learn English as a second language, not to replace or to equal Spanish as the principal medium of communication.

Respondents, characteristically, were both skeptical and hopeful. Teachers by hundreds who themselves can barely speak English, much less teach it skillfully; a dearth of resource materials combined with bulging classrooms; negative reactions by both teachers and students toward the constant "choral practice"; lack of correlation with other subject matters and student interests; too few Continental teachers; and, perhaps most disturbing of all, symbolic confusions which, though by no means entirely due to the bilingual problem, are aggravated by it—these were among the most skeptical reactions.

The recommendations which we ourselves most strongly endorse were these: double the daily time devoted to English instruction; strengthen teacher training through workshops and other means; reduce program rigidity and routinized practice by devoting proportionally more time to simple communication directly related to children's experience; utilize English in other courses and, on the high school and college level, offer some work such as science and social studies chiefly in English; utilize more abundantly such audio-visual tools as films and phonograph records; evaluate methods and results much more carefully; increase both the number of Continental teachers permanently in Puerto Rico and the number of Island teachers temporarily in the United States. We dispute the minority who favored a return to all-English instruction, and also those who thought it less important for girls than for boys to become bilingual.

What further steps are needed toward the formulation of a satisfactory policy? In our judgment, the present system of structural linguistics, though sound and commendable in many respects, provides too narrow an educational basis on which to construct an effective second-language program. Granting that conditions in Puerto Rico under which to test that system are far from ideal, yet even in the writings of Fries[4] most frequently cited one finds almost no explicit evidence of the influence of such potent social philosophies of language as Korzybski's, Cassirer's, and George Herbert Mead's, or of such functionalistic social psychologies as Kurt Lewin's and Gardner Murphy's[5]—all of which reach much further toward a modern theory of culture-and-language in general and of learning in particular than does a "science of linguistics."

Were the present circumscribed framework broadened to include this kind of theory, Puerto Rican educators would surely realize how vulnerable the present program is both in its appreciation and its application of functionalistic learning. The present almost total isolation of English instruction from the rest of the curriculum would be recognized for what it is—a perpetuation (except for its important emphasis on "patterns") of chiefly behavioristic principles and practices of learning, and of accompanying attitudes toward enculturation that are largely deterministic rather than activistic. Thus, though we agree that the time devoted to English should be substantially increased, we cannot agree that mere quantitative expansion is the important need: much more important is another need stressed by some respondents, namely, *to integrate English with many kinds of learning*—emotional and intellectual—and to do so, not merely through courses and texts (which, however excellent in other ways, include relatively little from the Puerto Rican cultural environment), but above all in the extracurricular and other meaningful experiences of children.

The use of modern tools such as films and film strips, tapes and phonograph recordings, under increased supervision is a related imperative. Where oral learning is the primary technique, and yet where the teacher's accent often violently distorts pronunciation (to mention only one deficiency), we should suppose that this kind of venture would have been launched on an Island-wide scale long before now. Nor is the factor of cost a convincing objection: hundreds of thousands of dollars in less than one decade have been spent in publishing the Fries textbook series, with little ongoing effort to test effectiveness in careful experimental ways—through control groups, for example. We applaud the vocabulary studies and current plans for such evaluation, but we also urge immediate pilot projects where the *principal* instruments of learning are audio-visual tools.

And yet all such processes, however imperative, are subsidiary to the broader question of a philosophy of education in which language is regarded as a cultural key. Here the problem of symbolism comes once more to the fore. We support wholeheartedly the leader who insisted that the question is not merely one of better English teaching, but of the whole conception of general education. But it is even more: it is a matter that embraces the reshaping of the Puerto Rican national character itself. That the syncretic ideal described by many respondents—complete bilingualism—will perhaps never be perfectly achieved is less significant than the fact that it appears to be so widely shared.

Still more urgent is the need for a philosophy of symbolism that can reduce, not compound, the disturbances that must accompany the struggles to approximate this difficult ideal. Such a philosophy cannot be concerned merely with maximum bilingual facility (though this is desirable, of course); its main concern, rather, is *clarity of meaning, of cultural self-identity*—the chief implicit motivation, we believe, to that kind of facility. The need, pointed out by another leader, to understand the ubiquitous role of symbols themselves—above all, to distinguish with Cassirer between operational-scientific and other fundamental forms—exemplifies the magnitude of the task involved.

But it is equally the need to recognize that just as all symbolic systems are inextricable from socioeconomic, political, religious, and other dimensions of given cultures, so the prolonged disputes in Puerto Rico over Spanish versus English are equally inextricable. All this is another way of saying that the issues of this chapter, too, interweave with many other issues. Indeed, they lead straight to the third of our major categories of interpretation: the problem of cultural goals.

PART IV

THE PROBLEM OF CULTURAL GOALS
IN PUERTO RICO

INTRODUCTION TO PART IV

THE SUPREME purpose of education in Puerto Rico is to provide opportunity for every child to develop his fullest potentialities so that he may live as satisfying and creative a life as he is capable of living.

This paraphrased statement of one of our most influential respondents is the theme of this part—the problem of cultural and therefore educational goals. But the questions that it generates are anything but simple; they require us to enter a field which anthropologists themselves have begun to explore systematically only within the past few years. A second look at the statement will indicate the magnitude of the problem: What, after all, is meant by a "satisfying and creative life"? And what are the child's "potentialities" which should be developed to the fullest extent so that such a life becomes an actual and not merely wished-for experience?

As we begin to dwell upon these questions, we come to see that we are really asking: What kind of culture ought to develop in Puerto Rico so that it can approximate those norms or standards of the "good life" to which its people may now be in the throes of clarifying and accepting as their fundamental goals? Where, in short, do they want to go, and why do they want to go there?

Clearly, the problem is far from new to this study. On the contrary, we can regard it as an opportunity to crystallize many topics and issues already touched upon. For the fact is that every culture is permeated with its own conscious or subconscious beliefs about its deepest aspirations, hopes, purposes, ideals. In other words, every culture possesses more or less consistent patterns of *value*—a crucial term that shall now be defined (borrowing from an influential anthropological viewpoint) as any implicit or explicit conception of what any individual or group considers to be desirable, and which thereby influences the means and ends through which the desirable may be actively attained.

This definition itself points to many issues familiar to us. Let us illustrate. The phrase "implicit or explicit" recalls Chapters 6 and 7. It should be reiterated that Puerto Rico is typical of all cultures in the respect that its ideological beliefs are by no means always consistent with those on deeper levels—that is, in our present context, with values that are less often verbalized as official doctrines of state, church, or school than they are inferred by the way people ordinarily behave and by how they symbolize such behavior. These implicit values we have previously included under the wider categories of the configurational and metacultural. They usually lie, as it were, beneath the surface of the culture, and yet they are of paramount importance to its entire way of life—to its order and processes as much as to its goals.

Take as another illustration the discussion of progress in Chapter 5. The question of whether progress can be regarded as a legitimate event in the temporal sequence of cultural order in Puerto Rico is also a question of values—that is, of the criteria by which one decides whether or not historical development has been or is continuing in a *preferred* direction. Other aspects of cultural order, such as national character, the family, and the class structure, are equally pregnant with valuational implications.

Our definition above included the proviso that values affect the ends and means of action. In terms closer to our present interest, we take this proviso to suggest two important points: one, that values are fundamental to (though not always synonymous with) cultural goals; and two, that cultural goals are both influenced by and help to influence cultural processes themselves. This is a way of saying that the ends and means of a culture always sooner or later affect each other—a commonplace of culture theory constantly exemplified throughout the preceding part, where we were concerned with delineating the cultural processes—the means—of Insular development. One need only scan Chapters 9 through 13 to perceive how cultural goals are inherently at work in every aspect of the cultural dynamics of Puerto Rico.

As we approached the final stages of our study of cultural process, the problem of values was even more persistent. Thus, all through our effort to delineate the modal personality, judgments of value were being made whenever "positive" traits were compared with "negative" ones. Similarly, we found that learning as a cultural process was governed by standards of what learning should be in terms of the norms of culture-and-personality.

As a matter of fact, all education as an enterprise of culture is guided by norms—however diffused or confused, satisfactory or unsatisfactory, these may prove to be. More strictly, education is normative in the sense that it is created in some form by every culture as a way to transmit and sometimes to improve that body of beliefs and practices considered most desirable to those in a position of sufficient power to implement and enforce their mandates. By the same token, it is a way to prevent the establishment of beliefs and practices considered undesirable. The intense concern that the Puerto Rican people manifest toward their educational program attests to their implicit if not always explicit acceptance of these principles.

We propose to deal with the problem of goals for Puerto Rican culture-and-education in four perspectives. First, we wish to inquire about some of the most widely held values and how they compare with those of other cultures. Second, we return to the problem of religion and look at it more carefully than before in terms of cultural values. Third, we are interested in the valuational problems of young people today. And fourth, we should like to know whether and, if so, how profoundly Puerto Rico is already dedicated to any great overarching cultural goal such as human freedom. The role of education is central to each of these inquiries. For—the axiom deserves repeating—all education culturally conceived is governed by values.

CHAPTER FOURTEEN

WHAT ARE THE VALUES OF PUERTO RICAN CULTURE?

IT HAS BEEN said that every personality is like all other personalities in various respects, like some other personalities in further respects, and like no other personalities in still further respects. This generalization is not only true of the typical Puerto Rican citizen; it is also true of the values of his culture. We may assume, in other words, that certain values in Puerto Rico are entirely similar to human values everywhere in the world; others are similar to the values only of certain parts of the world; and some are unique to the Island alone.

Not that it is an easy matter to demarcate one group of values from the other two. Especially is it difficult to determine those that could be called unique. As one respondent contended, Puerto Rican values may be different from those of remote cultures, but they are hardly different from those of the Greater Antilles. Another went even further: they are really no different from Europe's or North America's. Nevertheless, as in the case of cultural innovations considered in Part III, degrees if not kinds of distinctiveness of value would seem plausible if for no other reason than that Puerto Rico as a culture is itself, as we have seen, in some ways distinctive.

Let us consider first those values that were selected as among the most conspicuous. Then we turn to the likenesses and unlikenesses of such values to those of other cultures. In conclusion, we ask our respondents, as is our regular practice, what bearing the problem has upon education—in this case, the problem of what kind of goals and purposes should govern Insular schools. Our own plea will be for more conscious attention to the development of cultural goals that harmonize with the conspicuous values, yet that are sensitive both to similarities and differences between Puerto Rican values and those of other countries, and that are attained by the most critical possible investigation rather than by exaggerated behavioristic forms of enculturation.

THE CONSPICUOUS VALUES

Recalling our working definition of value as, in part, a more or less articulate conception of whatever is considered by an individual or group to be desirable, it is logical that many respondents first selected for reemphasis some of the personal and social qualities that they admire most—qualities that they would like to see preserved and strengthened. The reader may wish to compare them with positive traits of the modal personality depicted earlier.

These values include, first of all, the familiar cluster denoted by such terms as friendliness, outreachingness, kindness, sharing, hospitality, brotherliness, and gregariousness. Others that were underscored include devotion to the family, personal pride, honesty in government, racial egalitarianism, respect for learning, loyalty to the homeland without fanatical nationalism (the value called non-nationalism), an accent upon *being* rather than *becoming,* and love of the Spanish language.

Our references in previous pages to the arts and sciences also lead naturally to the question of aesthetic values as compared with the more prosaic kind associated with technological goals. A majority of leaders were prepared to argue that Puerto Ricans tend to place more worth upon the "heart" than upon the "hand"—two going so far as to detect an "innate" feeling for musical values.

A minority could accept no such contention. For one respondent, aesthetic and scientific values are about equally developed. For others, it is fallacious to suppose that because typical citizens may attach insufficient regard to, say, mechanical efficiency, therefore they have higher regard for aesthetic accomplishment; the truth is that they are weak on both scores. Although women of all classes are usually neat and attractively dressed, the drabness of typical boxlike Puerto Rican homes (compared with those on the same economic level in a country like Costa Rica) was mentioned as an everyday illustration of the low degree of aesthetic sensitivity. Moreover, such sensitivity may now be weakening still further as many families become preoccupied with material possessions and as they begin to give more attention to job skills and outside interests. Thus one respondent was sure that country people take less trouble today than they did a quarter-century ago to landscape their yards, to exchange plants with their neighbors, and in other ways to make their homes attractive.

What of the values of cooperation and competition? Variations of judgment here were wider still. The national-level group was divided almost equally as to whether Puerto Ricans prize one more than the other, while the subcultural group leaned only slightly toward the opinion that competition and independence are admired above co-operation and interdependence. Two grassroots respondents were unsure as to which of the two sets of values are the stronger, while one leader held that (as in the case of aesthetic and scientific values) neither set is well developed. Indifference to both is more character-istic, he said, than commitment to either.

Nor was clear consensus attainable on the question of whether regard for and practice of cooperation is now growing more rapidly than competition. One *jíbaro* respondent, though not without op-position, was sure that the former value is receding—that the tradition of the *junta* so widely practiced under the pseudo-feudal system of harvesting and owner-worker relations is no longer a lively one. This opinion was shared by a leader who held that, though the feudal type of cooperation was far from admirable in all respects, it at least encouraged a kind of solidarity and mutuality that are now being de-stroyed by the habits of self-interested individualism that accompany jockeying for higher status and material aggrandizement. The view hitherto expressed that people used to be more independent than they are today was therefore denied by this respondent: the opposite, he held, is closer to the truth.

Nevertheless, even he shared a widespread opinion on both levels that the cooperative movement, while by no means as well developed as in Scandinavian countries, develops the values in practice for which it stands in theory. As was pointed out by more than one respondent, this movement is not merely an economic device; it rests upon a "philosophy of life," centering in democratic human relations. Courses in the University conducted by the Cooperative Institute attempt to develop this outlook as well as to deal with technical questions of production and consumption. The dozens of small and large grocery stores scattered throughout the Island, as well as other cooperative programs encouraged by the government, already attest to their practical importance. Even the ambitious middle class was said to be acquiring more and more cooperative attitudes and habits. By recent count, 75,000 Islanders belong to the League of Cooperatives.

Curiously, another leader expressed mild concern that the values of cooperation may on occasion now even be *over*stressed—that individuals need to learn how to compete more vigorously with one another by developing, say, higher standards of skill and efficiency. Indeed, he saw no reason why both sets of values should not be complementary rather than antagonistic. Though a Catholic himself, he accordingly urged greater regard for such "Protestant virtues" as thrift and hard work. Children, especially of the middle and upper classes, should learn to assume more household chores, to make spending money by delivering papers and other after-school jobs, and to develop the attitude that doing housework or earning a living by wearing overalls is not a disgrace. As he epitomized his point, too many clerks have cleaning maids rather than money in the bank! At the same time, he was careful to distinguish between the value of wholesome self-assertiveness and the kind of competition that produces such negative values as cupidity and anarchy. In the words of a peer, many Puerto Ricans still have trouble in working well together because everyone wants to "run the group"—one noticeable effect of which in meetings is the chronic habit of several members talking to one another at the same time.

Meanwhile, the value of cooperation was examined still further. One subcultural spokesman maintained that it remains much stronger among countrymen than among city dwellers. Also, one leader insisted that different institutions manifest the value in different degrees —that while Puerto Ricans are genuinely cooperative in their religious practices (charity might be an instance), they are much less so in their economic behavior. Another leader was sure that, granting limitations, many persons can and do quickly learn cooperation when they are convinced of a tangible result—as in the many recent instances when rural communities have solved such problems as providing running water or building a group of houses through collective effort. Others, on the grassroots panel, recalled the promptness with which the average individual, no matter where he lives, will come to the rescue when, say, a stranger's car is stalled. Similarly, if a Puerto Rican becomes hungry in some great foreign city, the first thing he was said to do is to "look for another Puerto Rican."

Let us record a few more conspicuous values noted by resource persons. Leaders selected such values as property, health, belonging-ness, and status. Grassroots spokesmen were asked whether, to obtain the good life for themselves, it would be more desirable to satisfy all of their desires to the utmost or, on the contrary, to restrain their desires to the utmost. Equal minorities chose one or the other of the two extremes—one respondent holding that restraint produces too much suffering; another insisting, on the contrary, that it is the secret to a long life; still another denying that "cohabitation," particularly, is ever a good in itself, indeed that it is bad because it increases the population! But more than twice as many refused to side either way. Rather, they held that the good life is attainable only when expression and restraint of desires are kept in careful balance.

Or consider their reactions to the connected question of whether or not happiness is most likely to result from concentrating upon one of the following three values: contemplation, pleasure, or action. Only a single respondent felt that pleasure offers the best assurance, two ruling out pleasure entirely. Two others held that a life of contemplation affords the greatest happiness in the long run (one respondent, a zealous Catholic teacher in a public school, sometimes encourages girl students to become nuns), while three favored an equal weighting of all three values. The remaining majority were sure that a life of action is to be preferred, one arguing that it keeps us from thinking of "bad things," several others contending that pleasure and contemplation can be incorporated with action itself. Only one explicitly insisted that action must in turn be governed by "ideals."

Another question sought subcultural judgments as to why Puerto Ricans hold the values they do—whether because of their biological make-ups primarily, or their minds primarily, or their culture primarily. No one held that the biological is the basic source of values, but two did hold that body, mind, and culture each contributes about equally, while another thought that mind and culture, but not body, do so. Five were sure that mind (which some respondents may have conceived in a spiritual or idealistic sense) is the most important factor—one student respondent reminding us in good Aristotelian fashion that a body without mind is still not a man. Another respondent pointed out, however, that a brilliant mind can sometimes produce more evil than good.

The rest, again a substantial majority, agreed that the culture is the primary source of human values; hence body and mind are secondary factors. In the words of one panelist: "Culture makes the man."

THE PROBLEM OF RELATIVE AND UNIVERSAL VALUES

The interesting contention just noted, that the values of Puerto Ricans are the products of their culture much more than of physiological or psychological conditions, leads us to a problem that has disturbed many philosophers and anthropologists: If culture is the chief cause of values, must we not conclude that values vary radically from culture to culture? If so, however, must we not then further conclude that what Puerto Ricans may consider to be desirable for them is not necessarily desirable for people on other parts of the earth? In technical terms, we are confronted here, of course, with the venerable issue of "relativism" versus "universalism"—the former doctrine holding that all values are relative and unique to particular cultures, the latter holding that some values are cross-cultural and perhaps as ubiquitous as mankind itself.

The first clue to an answer is that Puerto Ricans, according to many respondents, are relativistic in the sense that they are exceptionally tolerant of attitudes and practices different from their own. Despite the volatility attributed to their modal personalities, they were said to abhor violence of a mass variety; hence they would much rather acculturate and even assimilate foreign values and accompanying practices than militantly resist them. Compared with several other Latin American countries, such as Cuba again, it is even possible to say that this "elasticity of accommodation" becomes a value distinctive in several ways—in a lack of chauvinistic quarrelsomeness; in the centuries-old evolutionary rather than revolutionary approach to cultural goals; in the friendly curiosity with which people listen to while seldom challenging outsiders; in a "purposeful patience"; in respect for the democratic voting process as a slow but sure way of achieving such goals; in the comparative success with which migrants accommodate themselves to a new cultural environment; and in the high regard attached to cultural change.

Tolerance as a value is itself, of course, a product of culture. As one leader reminded us, the conquering Spaniards were so overpowering that there was little choice but to accept their values as well as possible and then to hope for the best. The Negro slave population required further adjustments to racial variations and customs, as did the influx of cultural stocks—including Protestants—from Europe, South America, and, above all, North America. Even the Catholic Church was said to contribute, if rather paradoxically, to the conciliatory attitudes of Puerto Ricans: as in several other cultures (the Italian is one) the very absolutism of the Church produces, as it were, a reflex in the form of a kind of "tongue in cheek" tolerance because, as the same respondent put it, no one can hope to take its dogmatic mandates literally. The double standard of traditional morality is perhaps thereby further explained; certainly, according to earlier evidence, a large proportion of citizens are not intolerant of those who depart from the Church credo of marital fidelity.

In the course of this study we have come to expect dissent from some quarter even toward judgments receiving heavy support. Such is the case here. A minority of leader respondents were sure that Puerto Ricans tend, on the whole, to be more intolerant than tolerant toward people with values markedly different from their own. One held that this is due primarily to lack of sophistication—that appreciation of cultural differences requires more acquaintance with the way people of other lands feel and think than most Islanders are able to command. Another disagreed even with this contention; while he, too, felt that people are rather intolerant, the uneducated classes are less so than the educated, particularly University personnel (though the latter may appear to be tolerant enough in superficial manners).

Two others thought all such views to be wrong. It is impossible to say that Puerto Ricans are either markedly tolerant or intolerant, for the reason that most are simply indifferent to the whole question. More specifically, one leader doubted whether more than fifty thousand of his fellow citizens have ever given a serious thought to the culture and values of a country like India. Another held that if the average Puerto Rican thinks of the Chinese people at all, it is only to regard them in a passing moment as exotically different from himself.

These contradictory opinions were tested in a small way with the help of grassroots respondents. Contrary to the minority view on the national level, not a single one of these respondents dissented from the position that in education it is just as important to develop respect for unlikenesses among people (including children in classrooms) as for likenesses. Indeed, as a student respondent reminded us, the world will remain an "armed camp" until its various cultures can learn to respect one another's values. Many thought, too, that learners should come to understand and appreciate such diverse marital customs as polygamy—to recognize that while monogamy is the approved standard of Western cultures, it is not universally so. The same open-mindedness should be developed even toward an impartial study of communism, as long as it produces no violent actions. (Here, two respondents disagreed, however—one holding that it should not be studied at all, the other that it might be dangerous to do so since some might be persuaded.) Similarly, respect for religious differences should be encouraged. Missionaries should never "force" their faith upon people of different creeds but should use "reason" to persuade them. Non-Christians should "discuss" the Bible and "think out" their choices. (One devoted Catholic feared that she was inconsistent in this view since Catholicism is, by definition, the "one, true faith" and hence beyond dispute.)

In supporting the right to learn about values hostile to Puerto Rico's, several respondents reminded us that such a right does not necessarily mean approval. Yet several seemed ready to take the risk that impartial comparison might result in acceptance of new values. As one pointed out, democracy means among other things the privilege even of criticizing and questioning the rights provided by democracy itself.

This demonstration of tolerance should not lead us to infer that Puerto Ricans, as mirrored in our informants, are necessarily more relativist than they are universalist in their attitudes. One reason, indeed, why the majority of respondents on both levels were so conciliatory may be traceable to their conviction that their own values are, after all, at least as similar to as they are different from the values of other cultures.

Consider the reply of grassroots respondents to the question in effect of whether most Puerto Ricans aspire to life goals fairly similar to those of other cultures or, on the contrary, to dissimilar goals. Over twice as many replied positively to the first alternative as to the second.

While a few insisted that the Island's natural and cultural environment compels its people to want things different from those of other people, the majority thought otherwise. All cultures on earth, some argued, aspire to attain such goals as adequate nourishment, shelter, recreation, happy marriage, education, health, "well-being," and "liberty." Moreover, since "all people are created equal," they have broadly equal goals even when their methods of obtaining them differ.

One subcultural respondent who had served in the Korean war poignantly supported his belief in the "commonality" of human values. When he first went to that country, he was sure its people belonged to a "lower race." But in common with many an American soldier, he soon changed his mind. The goals of Koreans, he found, were largely the same as his own—their thirst for education being but one example. And speaking of North American and Puerto Rican boys, another grassroots respondent who has lived in both countries thought that, underneath the surface, they are "just alike."

This prevailing view was bolstered on the national level. Not only, as we have seen, did a majority of leader respondents hold that Puerto Ricans incline to be tolerant of values dissimilar from themselves even when quite aware that real differences exist; they also held with subcultural collaborators that their own values are ultimately more like than unlike those of other cultures. While reiterating some of the same aspirations mentioned above, leaders added several: Puerto Ricans closely resemble human beings everywhere in their appreciation of the aesthetic and in their "creative urge," in their quest for "peace of mind" and security, in the wish to develop their potentialities without too many complications or curtailments of self-expression, and in their desire to "understand life."

Despite deviations, then, we infer the acceptance, along with a relativist orientation, of a strong orientation toward cultural universalism. Nor are the two necessarily incompatible. As influential theorists have contended, the alleged conflict between universalism and relativism can be effectively resolved not by an "either-or" but by a "both-and" approach to the issue.

Hence, while one leader frankly regarded himself as a "cosmopolite" (that is, a citizen of the world with primary concern for universal values), and while three others preferred to be called "pluralists" (thereby favoring a wide diversity rather than any kind of uniformity of cultural values), even these few respondents did not entirely rule out a fusion of both goals. The remainder were emphatic in their preference for the frequently used metaphor of "orchestration"—a term suggesting that just as a symphony orchestra is made up of many instruments that yet manage to produce a harmonious whole, so the values of the Puerto Rican culture are both distinct from and common to the values of humanity.

This dominant viewpoint was elaborated in various ways. One leader spoke of the need for a cultural system of "checks and balances" that would provide for the values both of pluralism and cosmopolitanism. A good culture, he said, must always be flavored with both local and world-wide values. Another thought that the present Commonwealth aims to provide exactly this combination, as symbolized by the terms "free" and "associated." Still another cited the Spanish philosopher Unamuno in support of the position that it is necessary always to start with the values of one's own culture, but then to move outward until finally the whole world is embraced by a single conception.

Further, we were reminded that the issue of relativism and universalism reduces finally to metacultural assumptions, even if only a few Puerto Ricans are as yet aware of this fact. For example, the conclusions reached in our discussion of the "nativist reaction" closely parallel the conclusions reached here: most citizens, in our present terminology, do not favor a process of withdrawal into native or national self-sufficiency any more than they favor unadulterated cultural relativism or pluralism. At the same time and for comparable reasons, neither do they support a process and program that would lead to cultural assimilation any more than they support unqualified universalism or cosmopolitanism. What they do seek is a reconciliation between these alternative goals.

It follows, if one national-level informant is right, that the acrimonious disputes which have plagued Insular leadership concerning educational policy are due much less to fundamental differences over the issues involved in universalism and pluralism (less accurately termed by another leader, incidentally, as "occidentalism" and "localism") than to power struggles and conflicts of personality. Whether, however, other issues of a fundamental nature may still be involved in these disputes,* this informant did not choose to say.

What now of pluralistic differences of value within the culture

* See pp. 410-414, 428-431, 439-440.

itself? A small majority accepted the findings of the Steward study that such differences are detectable—particularly between interior and coastal areas. It was reiterated, for example, that the values of the traditional extended family seem more durable in a coffee subculture like San José than elsewhere on the Island. Also, the point was made that African-rooted values are strongest on the coast: because *hacienda* owners could not persuade *jíbaros* in sufficient numbers to leave the interior in order to become sugar-cane workers (mosquitoes and heat were the reasons cited), the result was that Negro slaves became concentrated in south coast communities such as Cañamelar and in north coast communities such as Loíza. In the latter, the people were said to be the least integrated of any in Puerto Rico.

But this pluralistic viewpoint toward even so small and compact a culture was not supported without its own amendments. Several leaders familiar with the Steward research were unconvinced that it has proved any hypotheses as to a variety of subcultural values. One held that the belaboring of such differences is motivated more by "romantic" than scientific attitudes—that the traffic, for example, between sugar and coffee areas by seasonal workers helps to reduce valuational distinctions to the infinitesimal. Another maintained that Steward and his collaborators have made their case with regard to genuine ecological differences among subcultures, but he denied that these have produced significant distinctions of values. Still another contended that the greatest disparities of value are actually to be found between urban and rural subcultures—the former becoming increasingly competitive and individualistic, the latter retaining older values associated with the authoritarian family and semifeudal paternalism. One further respondent took the view that if important valuational differences can be discovered at all, they do not lie in the Insular subcultures but in the several class and status levels that cut across these subcultures.

We may accent the predominant answer to the central question of this section with the help of one more leader. The case for cultural relativism in Puerto Rico is strong, he contended; we must therefore learn to appreciate the values of people as they are, and not to judge them (as tourists so often do) by imported standards. At the same time, we must come to see that Puerto Ricans in what they want from life are much more like than unlike human beings everywhere—a fact continually commented upon by rural citizens of his acquaintance and reinforced by the experience of thousands of migrants (Puerto Ricans, incidentally, being among the most traveled people in the world). The great task is to make sure that the Continental, above all, benefits from the values of the Islander at the same time that the latter benefits from his. Each has much in common *with* the other; but each likewise has something richly distinctive to offer *to* the other. To "orchestrate" both is the heart of the problem.

THE ROLE OF VALUES IN PUERTO RICAN EDUCATION

When, however, respondents were asked to appraise the effectiveness with which schools deal with such problems of value, their answers were far from enthusiastic—indeed, they were probably quite comparable to the kind of answer one would receive in the United States from frank critics of its own educational system. One leader was even sure that, judging by the experience of his son's professional training, Continental colleges are even more derelict in their conscious regard for the norms that do and should govern their programs.

Yet for Puerto Rico, too, the over-all judgment was more negative than positive. Exaggerated concern for grades and other artificial goals was again censured—if anything, it was said to be still more damaging than in Mainland schools. Equally disavowed was the inflation by educational programs of North American standards of material success (although, in the judgment of two informants, these standards continue to be admired less in Puerto Rico than in the United States).

It was also contended that the middle- and even upper-status goals inculcated in university students often suppress or disrupt the entire framework of valuational attitudes acquired during their own predominantly rural, lower-status childhood and adolescence. Whether such a result, if true, would help to explain the neurotic tendencies already discussed, one leader was sure that the painful conflict in values from which many young teachers suffer produces by contagion a similar conflict in children—especially children in the rural areas to which these teachers often return.

What can be done? Numerous respondents—those on the national level most emphatically—recommended systematic attention to the whole matter of cultural-educational goals. At the same time, several were careful to distinguish between the kind of attention that would indoctrinate a particular set of "short term" values and the kind that would encourage young people to develop broad, permanent choices and commitments by thoughtful discussion and reflection. It is essential, they said, to develop questioning rather than acquiescent attitudes toward cultural purposes—to analyze such values as cooperation and competition with scrupulous care. One leader, particularly, was fearful that over-conscious attention to values might lead to preaching conformity—for him, the worst "disvalue" in education. Far more important, he held, is the encouragement of nonconformity and heresy. Education should be one institution where it is not required to "toe the line."

Others, though not necessarily disagreeing, urged that Puerto Rican leaders try to reach more consensus than they now have about educational, economic, and social goals, and to encourage rank-and-file citizens to think out issues of value that leaders have trouble in resolving. Patience must be the watchword here, for the democratic way of learning is slow. The program of the Division of Community Education was cited again as an example of the proper method, but not without the reservation that the Division should exert more aggressive effort in the sphere of political decision and action. The problem is how to "broaden the base"—to excite ordinary people about direct participation in public affairs that involve, as they inevitably do, the normative directions of Insular life.

Since, moreover, a "vacuum" often exists between values in words and in experience, why not afford young people more practice with such a prized Puerto Rican value as hospitality? Why not extend invitations to Point Four students to visit many more schools and homes than they normally do? Why not give the same privilege to, say, children in the Army and Navy schools which are virtually self-segregated now? Again, why not see by firsthand contact how political values are expressed in legislative action? The lament of one respondent that his daughter, while attending a private school five minutes from the Commonwealth Capitol, never once entered it under the guidance of a social-studies teacher could be dispelled easily enough with a little effort and imagination. The criticism hitherto made that Puerto Rican education is much too "bookish" was thus reaffirmed.

Cooperation is another value calling for further dramatization.

The University of Puerto Rico, unlike a number of North American universities, has no student consumer cooperative—and this, ironically, despite its pioneering Cooperative Institute where training in the field is regularly offered.

But in the public schools, consumer cooperation in practice as well as theory is already far ahead of most Mainland schools. Three full-time persons in the Department of Education (one accountant and two supervisors) promote the development of consumer and credit cooperatives as well as study groups among school children. A few teachers also take in-service courses in the Cooperative Institute, and one summer workshop has already been held, with a second contemplated. School cooperatives, which are run on formal Rochdale principles by the children themselves, sell school supplies, candy, and other small items. Each member wears an emblem and pays twenty-five cents in annual dues, for which he receives an annual dividend of one or two cents that is usually turned over to some worthy school project. On occasion, groups make trips to nearby consumer-owned stores and other projects.

Unfortunately, the percentage of schools with functioning cooperative groups has thus far been minute—due, it was held, to the rapid turnover of teachers with some knowledge of the field, to a dearth of teachers interested enough to serve as advisers, and (at least in one of our subcultural high schools) to possible objections from local businessmen. Thus in 1957, "juvenile cooperatives" totaled only about thirty, most of these being in second-unit schools. Prospects for a marked increase are nevertheless good. Newly developed units of study on consumer and credit cooperatives, to run from one week to one month and to be required on the eighth grade and senior high school levels, were being planned at the time of our research.

Other types of cooperation need to be developed, too. Games and similar forms of recreation that teach children the satisfactions derived from well-planned play were said to be much less developed in Puerto Rico than in the United States. Social affairs such as dances should be held in school gymnasiums or halls wherever possible rather than in hired outside quarters, as is now the rule. Ways of strengthening cooperation between home and classroom—stronger PTA's would be one example—were considered as desirable as they are thus far negligible. Underlying some of these suggestions was a comprehensive one to the effect that more attention be given to universalities in the values of the culture and less to their relative uniquenesses.

Opportunity for meaningful experience in such common values as cooperation was elucidated further by the proposal for an additional experiment. A selected number of second-unit schools should become two-year, post-high school teacher-training centers. This experiment (it should depart just as radically from the standard curriculum of the College of Education as the experimental program for rural teachers hitherto outlined) could train about ten teachers a year in each of, say, fifty such centers. The selected second-unit schools would become laboratories in "on-the-job" school-community experience. One of the unique features of the experiment could be a conscious concern for the goals of rural life—goals that could, in turn, shape the program through which they might be realized. In order for any such goal-centered plan to succeed, however, the first necessity would be, in the opinion of its advocate, to "de-Rio Piedrasize" the whole proposal. By this he meant that the values now governing the program of the College of Education (located in Rio Piedras) must be largely exorcised. At the same time, the closest possible cooperation between the University and the Department of Education is essential to the success of any such experiment—cooperation which has often been meager in recent years.

Is it possible to agree upon some of the values that should be stressed in ventures of this kind? One respondent thought that they are symbolized most graphically by the desirable traits of the *jíbaro*. Others chose values for reemphasis that apply equally well to all Puerto Ricans, urban as well as rural: the desirability of doing any job thoroughly and systematically; of "excellence for its own sake"; of learning as a lifelong ideal; of a balance between industrial and agricultural goals; of an equal balance between the achievements of Island and world history; of the complexity and fallibility of all value commitments; of curiosity and inquisitiveness; of tolerance, open-mindedness, and creativity; and of technological efficiency that can lead eventually, in turn, to greater leisure and thereby to richer aesthetic expression.

One other reaction by a leader respondent is not so much an addition to as a reiteration of various points discussed in this section. In his opinion, no more important or challenging obligation confronts any human being, whether a Puerto Rican or anyone else, than to be as clear as possible about the goals of his life and then to struggle with all his power to achieve them. Here is the key to the greatness of a scientist like Pasteur: the test of a person's maturity of character is his capacity to "keep at it" until proved wrong. Here likewise is a supreme value of education itself.

In a sense, most grassroots respondents would apparently agree with this inspiring commandment. For when they were asked whether the main purpose of education is to help people to make a living, on the one hand, or to develop strong character, on the other hand, only two decided that making a living should take precedence, five that the two values are reciprocal or at least equally important, and one that the home's main responsibility is building character while the school's is making a living. The remainder—over half—were firm in their opinion that character is education's paramount concern. In this opinion they were also reflecting a metacultural judgment implicit in much of our study: the values of *being* are at least as prized as the values of *becoming*. For the latter, after all, are only the instruments by which the intrinsic goals of Puerto Rican life may be expressed, shared, and richly enjoyed.

We summarize and assess the main findings of this chapter with the aid of another useful anthropological concept—*value orientation*. This may be redefined as a broad, organized conception of desirable (as well as undesirable) human relations that influences the way any people behave toward themselves, other people, and nature. Every culture possesses some kind of value orientation, just as every culture possesses some kind of configuration. The two concepts, indeed, are intimately fused.

The value orientation of the Puerto Rican culture, as we have examined it up to this point, is anything but a simple, coherent whole. Its own chief consistencies perhaps lie, first, in the extent to which, also like other cultures, its values are both different from and common with values elsewhere; and, second, in the striking degree to which it parallels the discrepancies noted in other phases of this study. Yet dominant attitudes often stand out sufficiently to enable us to affirm that at least some important values are not only conceded to be culturally induced but are preferred by many members of the culture to alternative values.

Among them are the following: values inherent in the positive traits of the Puerto Rican modal personality; aesthetic appreciation and expression more than technical or scientific skills; cooperation about equally with competition; a life of moderation more than of either indulgence or restraint; a life of action more than of pleasure or contemplation; a high degree of tolerance for different kinds of value; at the same time, a conviction that the values of foreign peoples have much in common with those of Puerto Rico, just as the plural values of its subcultures have much in common; hence, that the culture is disposed to be both relativist and universalist at the same time.

There is, nevertheless, acute dissatisfaction with the extent to which education is sensitizing learners to the problem. If anything, typical policies and programs are, according to our data, either diverting many children and adults away from the value orientation or are distorting some of its most prized qualities. True, deliberate efforts are now beginning to clarify, strengthen, and improve these qualities. But by far the largest tasks remain.

For our part, none strikes us as more fundamental than the task of developing commitment to goals and correlative values, not by super-imposition, but by encouragement of untrammeled "nonconformity and heresy." Exactly as in the case of cultural configuration, even the most cherished features of the value orientation should receive search-ing criticism, for only in this way is it possible to construct democratic consensuses that assure an informed public loyalty in times of strain and possible crisis.*

Cooperation is an apt instance. No value is easier to accept in words; few seem harder for the Puerto Rican people, conditioned as they are by the Hispanic kind of "inner-directed" tradition, to accept it with an informed allegiance. The fact that the cooperative movement is represented in the Governor's Cabinet by a full-time director, and that efforts are under way to increase student understanding of the movement both in theory and practice, strikes us as farsighted as well as statesmanlike. But we would urge that weaknesses as well as strengths of the movement be ruthlessly analyzed, that comparisons with other economic philosophies such as private enterprise be given

* For further discussion, see pp. 412-414, 430-431, 440-441.

extended consideration in general education (not just in economics courses, say), that the Cooperative Institute dovetail more closely with other service programs than it has thus far, and that the personnel of the Department of Education devoted to school cooperatives be at least tripled.

The problem of relative and universal values, once it is translated into everyday educational terms, is no less practical in its implications. Here cooperation could be utilized to demonstrate the transcultural character of values: the gigantic growth of the movement on the Scandinavian peninsula, in England, in parts of the United States, and in many other parts of the world is in itself a dramatic and revealing story not only of an economic movement but of common interests and common goals among disparate cultures.

The high degree to which citizens appear to be tolerant of cultures holding different values from theirs is equally provocative. And yet, as must be observed at a later point,* there appears to be too much complacency toward either differences or similarities of value between Puerto Rico and other countries—a problem that can be met educationally only as and if fuller, more exciting attention is paid to ways of life that depart radically from those most familiar to students on the Island.

* See pp. 310-312.

CHAPTER FIFTEEN

PUERTO RICO AND RELIGIOUS VALUES

No OVERVIEW of any culture would be complete without attention to the place occupied by religion and hence to the values central to religious experience.

And yet, recalling the preceding chapter, it is interesting to note how rarely respondents mentioned religion in enunciating the conspicuous values of Puerto Rico, in weighing the case for or against cultural universalism and relativism, or in considering education's valuational role. Almost the only exception was the occasional use of "Christian" as an adjective before such desirable qualities as dignity and cooperation.

It is impossible to be sure of the reasons for this relative lack of spontaneous association. One reason may have been a not uncommon propensity to compartmentalize—that is, to regard the everyday, mundane struggle for human goals as something quite apart from spiritual preoccupations. Another reason may have been foreseen by our discussion of religion in Chapter 6: there we found that Puerto Rican culture maintains a religious ideology separated rather markedly from its deeper configurational beliefs and habits. In the degree that respondents tended to identify religion with the ideological—that is, with the ecclesiastical superstructure—they would be unlikely to stress the importance of religious values. For, as we have found, formalized religion for the great Catholic majority has been of singularly minor import. Moreover, as one leader argued, poor church attendance is some indication of low interest, just as it is in other organized groups —PTA's, for instance.

Nevertheless, when distinctions were made between the institutional, ritualistic level and the underlying configurational level of religious life, judgments were modified. Most citizens, we were often assured, *are* strongly religious after all. Not only do they believe in God and immortality, but they wholeheartedly accept such mandates of Christian doctrine as human brotherhood.

The aim here is partly to retest this earlier consensus but, still more relevantly, to weigh the significance of religious values in relation to cultural and educational goals. On both scores, our findings will be affirmative in the sense that the importance of religion as an essential quality of the Puerto Rican ethos is undoubtedly great. But new complications appear: there are pronounced differences between the two panels as to what constitutes religious values—differences ranging all the way from Protestant and Catholic orthodoxy to completely nontheistic humanism. We ourselves, while respecting fully the right of anyone to his own religious faith, join forces both philosophically and educationally with those who prefer the latter approach.

The pivotal question, however, is whether or not a religious dynamic can be provided for public education that would be entirely harmonious with the doctrine of separation between church and state. The solution is, we think, to infuse learning and teaching with the qualities of creative adventure in behalf of the highest goals of mankind —goals which the Puerto Rican people increasingly and rightfully share.

WHAT IS MEANT BY RELIGIOUS VALUES?

Nowhere in our study does a more striking differentiation emerge between the national and subcultural levels than in answers to this question. Among grassroots respondents, only two (both of them urban) made their first choice from among what may be called "nonsupernatural" or "nontheistic" values—that is, religious values that do not necessarily require theological tenets or dogmas of Christianity to support them. The first respondent, though a regular churchgoing Catholic, chose the Golden Rule as the single most important religious value for the reason that it provides a "brake" upon impulsive behavior. The second, also a Catholic, though with less steady habits of attendance, thought that the "humane spirit" of consideration for others should be placed first. All other grassroots respondents, Protestant as well as Catholic, chose one or more of four values, each of which would be correctly regarded as supernatural and theistic, and therefore grounded in Christian theology: faith in a Supreme Being, faith in an afterlife, faith in prayer, and faith in the sacraments. The fact that neither of the remaining two respondents would be likely to deny these values means, then, that the subcultural panel was unanimous in accepting a conception of religion not only harmonious with the Island's Hispanic heritage—indeed, with the whole heritage of theistic Christianity—but that helps also to explain the attitudes that we shall find toward the issue of religious education itself.

True, one subcultural respondent, though still regarding himself a Catholic, was not only skeptical of the priesthood but went so far as to deny both the "doctrine of damnation" and the supremacy of his own religion. (Each religion is true for its believers, he said; the Koran is therefore just as true for the Mohammedan as the Bible for the Christian.) Even he, however, not only claimed to accept certain theological axioms of Catholicism but encouraged his children to take religious instruction. Another, calling himself a "liberal Catholic," confessed some doubt as to Christ's divinity.

The remainder were more orthodox. A religiously sophisticated Protestant held that religious values must meet four tests: knowledge of God, daily reading of the Bible (especially the New Testament), understanding of the philosophy of Christianity, and service to mankind. Another Protestant was active with her large family in a sect that stresses the sinfulness of such worldly pleasures as dancing, smoking, drinking, and card playing. (Her use of lipstick was confessedly against church rules.) Others—both Protestants and Catholics—spoke of "fear of the Supreme Being" and of "trust of God and His laws." (One was confident that God would reward him for practicing the high Puerto Rican value, hospitality.) Still others emphasized prayer—two saying that every member in their families prayed each night, another that "everyone prays hard" when a hurricane threatens. No grassroots respondent, interestingly, selected salvation before other theistic values.

But turn now to the national group. The first radical contrast with their subcultural collaborators is at once apparent from the fact that approximately two-thirds could not be classified as theists or strict supernaturalists at all. Just what term, however, they might prefer to characterize their outlook was volunteered by only two leaders: both called themselves scientific humanists, that is, persons whose religious values are centered entirely in "this-worldly" human struggles and human aspirations.

Of others in the majority, five spoke of "something more" in the universe that defies human comprehension. As one phrased it, a man would be a "very limited fellow" not to recognize this fact. Two leaders spoke of the sense of "mystery" that pervades life and nature—a mystery so profound that man in his humility can never expect to "pierce the vale." Truly, the world "passeth understanding." One went further: there is a "guiding force" in the universe that makes it purposeful—a position partly congenial to a peer but qualified in the respect that the universal "purpose" has no control over any man's personal affairs. No "anthropomorphic God" keeps track of our destinies by means of some glorified "IBM machine."

The remaining members of the national-level majority were unprepared to make even this much of a concession to what may be defined as a religious philosophy bordering on idealism or deism. For them, religion is apparently best expressed in "naturalistic" rather than "*super*naturalistic" symbols—in other words, symbols that convey a faith in man's natural, scientifically ascertainable powers to master his own life. To avoid confusion, one leader thought it best therefore to separate strictly "religious" from "spiritual" values—the former implying for him a theistic doctrine, the latter his own strongly naturalistic outlook.

However such terms are defined, the predominant orientation on the national panel led in turn to the selection of values that are consistently nontheological. Most are familiar to us as conspicuous Puerto Rican values: self-realization, creativity, curiosity, cooperation, nonacquisitiveness, brotherhood, service, equality, charity, peace and security, respect for truth, and concern for the ethics of one's personal actions.

For the sake of accuracy, let us record that several of this majority were unsure of the degree to which their own nontheistic—or perhaps humanistic—outlook would be suitable for all Puerto Ricans. The usefulness of the Church, one implied, lies in its ritualizing of values that would otherwise be difficult for the average man to comprehend. Also, it becomes an "anchor" in the face of daily stresses and strains. Some kind of "supernatural sanction" may be necessary for many people, another conceded, but not for himself: unfortunately the masses of people do not possess the capacity to formulate their values in rational terms; or at least they are so preoccupied with the struggle for survival that they have no time to attempt such a formulation.

What of the leaders' minority position on the issue of religious values? All of this group (one a Protestant) presupposed, of course, a theistic position. Belief in a Supreme Being was therefore inherent in their position and, though none spoke explicitly of prayer, two also reaffirmed their faith in an afterlife.

Yet even they could be contrasted with the conventional orientation of the subcultural majority in the quality of argument with which they defended religion and its values within that orientation. One leader offered a poetic formulation that could be interpreted in either theistic or nontheistic terms: religious values are those of an ideal world of the future—"polestars" that serve as guides to the ship of humanity on the ocean of its present life. Another offered Toynbee's *An Historian's Approach to Religion*[1] in support of his own clearly theistic faith. The Western world, he contended, is returning to this kind of religion because man needs to accept a transcendental power and to identify himself with that power. Indeed, all leading religions of the world—Oriental as well as Occidental—were said to accept much the same ultimate beliefs.

Still another in the minority group of leaders defined religion as a search for the meaning of life and of man's final destination—a way both to achieve good on earth and to prepare for immortality. But such a view was drastically modified by one of his peers: while belief in a Supreme Being—a "Great Cause"— is essential to his own faith, belief in immortality is not. In fact, this respondent approached the majority's views in the respect that one becomes religious, he said, whenever one develops fervent loyalty to some larger whole than oneself—whether that whole be a God, a state, or humanity.

Here we return to the viewpoint as enunciated perhaps quite representatively by one spokesman for the majority of leaders. There is in Puerto Rico, he said, a readiness to respond to such a larger whole —"something deeper" than merely material advancement—and to feel a part of the human adventure which the culture now undergoes. It is not so much the "construction of a facility," such as a bridge in a remote mountain *barrio* that is valuable in itself, as it is the almost intuitive sense of mutual effort and achievement that accompanies and results from the construction. Granting that one may get a "spiritual lift" by going to church, this is not the important thing. Unfortunately, the values of some Christian sects are even more life-denying than they are life-affirming. Nor, he was sure, is salvation in supernatural terms any more crucial to most Puerto Ricans than it is to him: by being absorbed in the struggle to create the richest possible life for and with present and future generations, they sense with him that they share "eternal life" *now*.

IS "OPERATION SERENITY" A RELIGIOUS VALUE?

The term "Operation Serenity," which some readers may feel has already been partially epitomized in the preceding paragraph, was coined by the present Governor as a kind of encapsulation of the goals of the culture. Frequently it is discussed in comparison with "Operation Bootstrap," which, we recall, symbolizes the process of economic development discussed in Part III.

While subcultural respondents did not answer the question directly, about an equal proportion of (though not in all cases the same) national-level respondents who preferred a nontheistic orientation with regard to religious values also decided that Operation Serenity does symbolize some or all of these values. A minority found it difficult to regard the concept in religious terms, but here the question again became partly a matter of definition. Thus one of this group, after reiterating his distinction between "religious" and "spiritual" values, conceded that Operation Serenity partakes at least of the latter sort. A second held that "moral" values apply best to the idea; a third thought it should be interpreted in terms of "psychological" values; while a fourth distinguished between its motivations and effects—a distinction, however, that remained ambiguous.

Only two leader respondents—both of them articulate theists— were unwilling to credit Operation Serenity with any kind of meaning that could be associated with religious or closely allied values. For one of these leaders, it is "nothing new"; indeed, it continues to stress material goals. For the other, it is deficient not only because it contains no implication of concern for the afterlife; its attempt to "slow down" the pace of industrialization, by stressing the ends rather than the means of life, is largely superfluous: the Puerto Rican people are habitually slow in any case!

It is, however, with some astonishment that we find two respondents in the majority group also criticizing Operation Serenity. Though conceding that it is inherently religious—indeed, it may be motivated by a certain "mystic quality" that derives from the long tradition of Spanish theism and may even point toward a "new Christianism"— nevertheless it was regarded with doubt. To ask a *jíbaro* to dedicate himself to the "serene life" before he can afford even one square meal a day sounds a little premature. Nor, he said, does the ostentation with which the elite of Puerto Rican officialdom repeatedly hold elaborate receptions at public expense and engage uniformed chauffeurs seem quite expressive of the spirit of the concept.

Moreover, as one expressed it, there is nothing wrong with the desirability of material possessions—refrigerators, say—when these are utilized to reduce drudgery or to make life healthier. To disparage the United States for its preoccupation with labor-saving gadgets is not quite fair either. A trace of European snobbery toward "Yankee materialism" is detectable in those who ridicule North Americans for their alleged "coarseness"—an attitude that may be reflected likewise in a supercilious opinion of progressive education by comparison with European classicism. In short, before we scoff at North American standards, let us not forget two facts: the first, that many Continentals do *not* overprize crass material success—indeed, their novelists and essayists are increasingly self-critical of precisely this value; the second, that the United States has eliminated extreme poverty at least partly because it has aimed so zealously at technological achievement.

Meanwhile, defenders sought to capture the meaning of Operation Serenity in more specific ways. Though Puerto Rico, to paraphrase one leader, is not as much obsessed by the passion for gadgets as certain other cultures, still "it is not running away from them" with quite enough speed. This does not mean that the concept is a negative value in the sense that it tries merely to discourage that sort of "passion." On the contrary, while emphasizing that money is not everything, its real interest is in the meaning of what makes life deeply worth while—the kind of life that was variously characterized in this context as modest, comfortable, free from poverty, respectful of the rights of human beings, dedicated, patient, tolerant, and aesthetically creative.

Operation Serenity, furthermore, transcends as an ideal all particular types of economic system—socialist and capitalist alike. Its primary intention, another spokesman held, is to place efficiency at the service of understanding. Also, since it encompasses every important human value, it includes a place for religious worship regardless of the form in which expressed. Above all, it seeks to establish "fortresses in life" strong enough to withstand blind pressures and destructive human conflicts.

Such an ideal is not then, for its proponents, a kind of "Operation Nostalgia" that seeks to restore the simple virtues of a romanticized past. Nor is it in the least premature, as some of its critics hold. Actually, according to one leader, Operation Serenity and Operation Bootstrap need to share a partnership—that is, to become a single "active equilibrium" of ends *and* means. Thereby the processes of culture such as factories can themselves, when well organized, come to possess intrinsic as well as merely instrumental worth. They can help to provide good labor conditions, schools for the children of working mothers, pleasant homes and recreation for all of their personnel.

THE ISSUE OF RELIGION IN THE SCHOOLS

Although subcultural respondents did not face explicitly the question of whether Operation Serenity is in certain ways a religious goal, they did reveal sympathy with several of the same religious or spiritual values stressed on the national level in relation to that concept. More specifically in terms of education, it is noteworthy that some of these respondents, too, were concerned lest Puerto Rico become unduly enamored of North American standards of ambition and success.

This does not mean that education should not encourage confidence in the capacity of people to improve their life rather than to be satisfied with their humble lot. Nearly all grassroots spokesmen reiterated confidence in what we earlier termed an activistic orientation—including those whose personal history has been one of tragic hardship, of unemployment and even hunger, of loss of farms after hurricanes and loss of tiny businesses. One student respondent said that he would hold himself responsible if he failed in his goal of becoming an engineer. Several parent respondents, too, wanted their children to go farther than they had gone in school.

But education for contentment—for serenity, if you please—is not to be dismissed either. Indeed, for a minority, it is to be cherished even more than the alternative of healthy discontentment. Education, they maintained, should help young people *not* to reach for the unattainable, but to appreciate the qualities of human life that industrialization and economic competition threaten to dissipate.

The problem becomes more controversial when religious education is interpreted in a conventional frame of reference. Puerto Rico's constitution requires, as does the federal Constitution, the separation of church and state. The teaching of religion as a formal doctrine or sectarian creed is thereby excluded by law from public, though not of course from private, schools. Is it, however, excluded in fact? And is it, in any case, a *desirable* exclusion?

The first of these two questions, as far as the evidence of this study permits, must be answered in the negative. While religious instruction is not offered as a formal exercise, one or more schools in our cooperating subcultures expected children to recite a theistic prayer before each noontime lunch or during the "snack period" held in midmorning or midafternoon. Large framed pictures of the Virgin Mary and other sacred figures hung on the walls of many classrooms—one spokesman defending the display because they are "works of art." One elementary classroom contained a large illustrated chart depicting, among other events, Christ's crucifixion and resurrection. During our visit the chart was not only utilized by the teacher to familiarize his students with the significance of Holy Week but was singled out for special approbation by the superintendent of schools.

To be sure, unlike hundreds of public schools in the United States, none of those visited in Puerto Rico began the day's routine with prayer or Bible reading. But like many of the former, nearly all of the latter prepared papier-mâché models of the Nativity or other religious scenes for the Christmas season. One student respondent indicated that certain of his teachers "helped" children to accept Christian beliefs during the daily program. And one parent respondent told of a teacher awarding church medals to students in her classroom.

Answers to the second question above, as to the desirability of including or not including religious instruction in the public schools, were both negative and positive. But respondents on neither panel were always consistent in their personal reactions. One leader was in favor of teaching faith in a Supreme Being and immortality. He was confident that such teaching would help to reduce juvenile delinquency—drug addiction near a large urban high school being cited as an instance. Yet, because he also favored academic freedom to the point of studying "all sides" even of such questions as religion, he frankly confessed that he was becoming entangled in the "meshes" of his own frankly "liberal" point of view. Another leader of theist faith who favored the separation of church and state would oppose prayers in public schools: it would make them seem like churches! Yet he favored reading of the Bible.

Or consider the views of two grassroots public school teachers. Both insisted that all children should be taught to believe in the existence of God, one asserting not only that each school day should begin with prayer but that no nonbelieving teacher should receive appointment. At the same time, both were perfectly willing to have the case for atheism studied by children along with the case for Christian theism, on the ground, apparently, that young citizens ought to have the right freely to reach religious commitments of their own. In support of such a right, one of the two informants recalled President Eisenhower's famous plea at Dartmouth College against the burning of controversial books. The other drew an analogy with political education: all religions, like all parties, should be studied impartially, the teacher revealing his own preference only at the close of such study.

Nevertheless, considering the complexity of the underlying questions involved in religious education (one need only scan Continental literature on the subject to see *how* complex), both panels of respondents tried to attain over-all consistency in one important respect: the principal viewpoints summarized in the preceding section concerning religious values, in general, usually continued to prevail in their respective answers to the issue of religious education, in particular.

Thus, on the one hand, a majority of subcultural respondents, at least by implication, adjudged the present educational policy to be undesirable. They favored either outright indoctrination of the Catholic faith in the public schools or, much more commonly, the teaching of those principles of theism acceptable to virtually all Christian sects. On the other hand, a majority of national-level respondents were willing to support religious education only if it meant nonindoctrination of *any* theistic faith. A minority of leaders—all of them theists, of course—disagreed with this position, supporting rather the subcultural consensus. Yet at various points a few on the latter level tended to agree (despite their own theistic predilections) with the national-level majority.

Let us analyze these several alternatives. Though the view that theistic teaching should be sponsored by the public schools took several forms, one grassroots respondent was unequivocal: Why, even granting difficulties in the way of policy, shouldn't all schools teach children to believe in Christianity? After all, it's the one religion that the people know. And several of his peers would require prayer—the Lord's Prayer being specifically mentioned.

On both levels, a number of Catholic respondents (though not without objections from at least one fellow Catholic) favored "released time" as a solution to the problem—the plan now operating in various Mainland cities, including New York. The present plan in Puerto Rico permits children to receive instruction in their churches only outside the hours of class. (At least two hundred were said to be taking such instruction in the town of San José during our research, their zealous Catholic teachers being—quite legally, of course—employees of the public schools.) Under released time, children would be assigned a weekly period during the school day itself, though also beyond school boundaries. But this proposal was rejected by a grassroots Protestant on four distinct grounds: first, that the schedule is already overcrowded; second, that one church (the Catholic) would try to dominate the program; third, that children would be split into self-consciously disparate groups; and fourth, that the teaching of religion should be the rightful task of home and church alone.

Yet this same respondent, like many others in the subcultures, also endorsed a form of "nonsectarian" religious education. Indeed, he considered it imperative to inculcate the Christian creed in every Puerto Rican classroom. This means, in his view, to teach that "God is present in everything." It also means—and several of his peers agreed with him—that the great miracles of Christian doctrine such as the Virgin Birth should be taught in the public school as true. For another subcultural peer, a Catholic, it means to teach three main principles of faith: the divinity of Christ, immortality of the soul, and the supremacy of God. (Yet, on second thought, this latter respondent distinguished between the "literal" truth of these principles as they are accepted by average devotees and a "symbolical" interpretation by sophisticated Christians. In support of the latter view, he cited Barnett's *The Universe and Dr. Einstein*.[2])

Learned arguments for religious education in a clear-cut theistic sense were offered on the national level. The postulate of many Christian theologians that democracy is a moral concept, hence that it is based upon moral laws which presuppose a divine Lawgiver, was advanced by one leader to support the view that democratic education must, in turn, be based on religious faith. (But that this respondent also approached inconsistency may be conjectured by his parallel contention that public education should not, after all, directly teach students to believe in God.)

A second leader in the minority group took the position that, while no child should be forced to learn a particular religious doctrine (he would perhaps agree with an associate's suggestion that "freethinkers" be excused from religious classes), every child should have opportunity to learn the creed of his parents' choice. To be denied such opportunity is, in fact, undemocratic since democracy assures freedom to worship according to one's faith. This objective could be accomplished in either of two ways: (a) by amending the constitution of Puerto Rico to permit the teaching of religion in the public schools; or (b) by earmarking certain funds from the Commonwealth treasury to support parochial schools. He did not indicate whether the second proposal would equally require a change in the Commonwealth constitution, nor did he appear concerned over questions of federal constitutionality that would arise from either proposal. What he did insist upon was the right of children to attend schools that provide religious training without additional tuition. Rather than the present system (this requires a parent to support public schools through taxation even while paying again to have his children in private religious schools), the proposed policy would emulate that of countries like Holland and Belgium where state financial support is rendered to both systems. Nor, he argued, can the issue be resolved by efforts of the public schools to teach "moral and spiritual values" divorced from theology: basic religious values *are* theological.

Among the majority of leaders holding a nontheistic conception of religious or spiritual values, it is necessary to distinguish between two approaches to the educational issue. The first approach would limit the school's responsibility entirely to humanistic and naturalistic values—to what one spokesman called "a feeling for life," another "Christ without the Gospel," still another a "practical religion" of service and neighborliness which, he thought, could be especially effective in the agricultural curricula of second-unit schools. Two leaders conveyed the conviction that their own involvement in the struggle to provide vital education for the people is itself a religious experience. And one other leader, whose views tended toward what was termed earlier a deistic-idealistic philosophy of religion, recommended courses that would bring out the purposeful nature of the universe of which man is part—study which would, however, avoid the Christian catechism or any notion of "religion as a doctrine."

The second of the two approaches would deal with religious education as a controversial issue somewhat in the manner considered by Chapter 12 on learning as a cultural process. One leader who also leans toward an idealistic point of view favored full discussion of unorthodox views such as his own—indeed, he felt that Puerto Rico would be more tolerant of them than would some sections of the United States, where they would be considered "odd." But he also protested against any attempt at their indoctrination. Moreover, he was sure that such a "rational" conception of religion is too profound for high-school students; it should be confined to the higher learning.

Another leader—incidentally, a theist—would go still further. Beginning as far down as the elementary schools, he would have children come to understand the tremendous role that the major religions—the Judaic-Christian heritage is, of course, one—have played in the evolution of all great cultures. Neglect of this role is, in his judgment, a serious defect of American schools. The purpose of such study would not be to persuade young Puerto Ricans of the supremacy of any one faith but rather, granting many difficulties in the way of effective teaching, to help them come to grips with religion in terms of their own lives—above all, to help them face squarely the age-old question of the origin and destiny of man.

The study of religion as a controversial issue was endorsed also in the subcultures, though not without reservations. One teacher respondent would, if students asked him, reply that he believed in God, but he would also have to say that His existence has not as yet been proved. Indeed, the value of tolerance, discussed in the preceding chapter, was here reconfirmed in two further ways—first, by the will-ingness of a Protestant informant to discuss with people of other faiths such problems as religion and social service, and to do so in the public schools (he had, in fact, already joined in such activity); and, second, by a consensus among a substantial ratio to permit arguments for atheism to be fairly studied along with arguments against it.

At the same time, two respondents insisted that while an atheist teacher should have the right to reveal his preference, he should not have the same right as a theist to "explain" it to his students. Another was also restrictive: the atheist case should be "stated," but the teacher should try in every possible way to convince his students that it is as false a doctrine as Christianity is true. (Atheists, he said, often repent in their last hours.) And one of his peers, while allowing atheist ideas to be fairly considered in the higher learning (after all, "Puerto Rico is a democratic country"), would prohibit them in the lower schools.

Tied to these proposals was a strong recommendation, again by both groups of informants and by theists equally with nontheists, that courses be established in "comparative religion." Though differing as to the best age level (limited attention already is paid to the subject in the University), arguments in favor were enthusiastic. Grassroots as well as national-level respondents spoke of the values to be gained from the teachings of Lao-tse, Confucius, and Buddha, as well as of Jesus. One insisted that the history of religions is just as important as political history. Impartial, well-trained teachers in the field; scien-tific study of "primitive" as well as "civilized" religions; their histori-cal role in relation to the power forces operating in every culture—these were mentioned as invaluable. Only one respondent on each level opposed the study of comparative religion at all, in both cases mainly on the ground that qualified "nonchurch" teachers would be too hard to find. One other was skeptical of its effectiveness unless it were taught in terms of the struggles and hopes of the human race rather than as "just another course."

The concern of this last spokesman was apparently close to the thinking of a fellow leader: Puerto Rican education should become mature enough so that fundamental issues of religion and its values can be treated just as critically and vitally as others about which people disagree. One of the greatest weaknesses from which a program of education can suffer—on this Island like anywhere else—is the pro-

hibition of *any* questions of importance to human life. Such a prohibition is not only one cause of anxiety but a barrier to the kind of
"dynamic serenity" which, however paradoxical, is a religious goal.
It is a goal, moreover, pervaded with a sense of wonder about life.
Indeed, for students to come to realize, not so much through direct
teaching as through the cultivation of subtle attitudes, that the world
is filled with mystery is essential to good education.

DIRECTIONS FOR RELIGIOUS EDUCATION
IN PUERTO RICO

We conclude that the issue of religious values in Puerto Rico and of
the school's responsibility to them is anything but clarified. Indeed,
the fact that the Island-wide parent-teacher organization was reported
by two respondents to be split asunder by this very issue is not as
surprising as it might have been if respondents in our study were
themselves united on the "cause and cure" of the problem.

But they were not united. In the first place, they diverged in their
conceptions of religion and its values into two main groups—theist
and nontheist (with a third smaller group that might be called deist
or idealist). In the second place, their recommendations as to what
public education should do about religious values also diverged,
though far from exactly or consistently, in roughly the same alternative directions that governed their conceptions of religion itself.

These conflicting recommendations include a policy to provide released time, tax support of parochial as well as public schools, indoctrination of the Catholic religion, nonsectarian indoctrination of the
Christian creed, the teaching and practicing of nontheistic "moral and
spiritual values" (symbolized for some by Operation Serenity), the
study of religion and its values as a controversial topic, and comparative courses in the religions of mankind.

Our earlier evidence revealing a rather wide gap between ideological and configurational religious beliefs is, in general, also reinforced.
Most Puerto Ricans, it appears, are much less concerned to practice
religion institutionally than they are to embrace it as an integral
quality of their cultural experience. Perhaps for this reason, the frequency with which even theistic symbols permeate their public schools
does not seem, in their eyes, a violation of their own constitution.

For our part, we must regretfully disapprove of every such violation. The Secretary of Education is respectfully urged to direct the removal of all theistic symbols (pictures and charts, for example) and to acquaint public school teachers with the necessity of obeying the constitution by avoiding all other forms of theistic indoctrination, overt or covert. Nor can we agree with those who favor a program of released time; the view of one respondent that this "solution" to the problem separates children into different sectarian groups is just as impressive as the argument in Chapter 4 that private schools tend to become a divisive force. Released time is, indeed, one of many signs in several countries of renewed pressures from organized religious groups—signs which, though applauded by one leader respondent, seem to us regressive, just as the argument of another leader that most people are not rational enough to do without supernatural sanctions is equally regressive.

We do, however, endorse two of the important proposals suggested by other resource persons. First, we share the attitude of those who find the religious spirit of Puerto Rico to be expressed, not predominantly in supernatural or sectarian forms, but in conspicuous "life-affirming" values. Education, regarded as a major cultural force, has every right to permeate its entire program with concern for these values.

Thus we support respondents who regarded Operation Serenity as, at heart, a religious goal. Indeed, it could become one of the most brilliant contributions of the present leadership to an original and vital philosophy of education. Its explicit concern with ends as well as means (granting the necessity of Operation Bootstrap, too), and the motivation it provides toward the development of intrinsically prized personal and social values, contrast sharply with the relative indifference of many political and educational leaders on the Continent toward such imperatives.

The point made by one or two respondents that the values symbolized by Operation Serenity are termed "spiritual" more properly than "religious" deserves further consideration. Our own grassroots panel obviously incorporated theistic Christian beliefs in their own religious faith, and no doubt most Puerto Ricans (no less than most people in Europe and America) normally do likewise. At the same time, when we look at the great religions of history, we find that theistic and supernatural tenets are by no means central to all of them;

hence, if we are to find some common denominator of *all* religious experience among the cultures of the world, we shall certainly have to look further than Christian theism. Moreover, even in Puerto Rico considerable evidence has been presented to show that secular aspects of the Christian heritage are already influential, perhaps more so than the theological. For these reasons, then, we disfavor a separation of "spiritual" from "religious" values in the school program. But it is also necessary to distinguish clearly between a program of religious education that would seek to indoctrinate either or both kinds of values and a program that would not.

Here we are led to the second main proposal. In accordance with the functionalistic type of learning urged in Part III, the need is for a program that will acquaint students directly with as many types of religious belief and practice as possible, but will do it with the same critical, exploratory methods of investigation that are urged in the study of any other controversial issue. Every possible safeguard should be provided against the imposition of a teacher's own religious biases. More than this, as some grassroots respondents insisted, the case for, say, atheism and deism should be presented with the same fairness and thoroughness as for various forms of theism.

We agree fully that such an approach would not be easy to implement, whether in courses on comparative religion or in pilot projects dealing with religious life in Puerto Rico itself. Certainly in the latter case, we would urge careful in-service training of all participating teachers, with a cautious beginning in a few secondary schools where the project could be tested before deciding whether to extend it to the whole system. Puerto Rico affords a promising laboratory for such an educational adventure: the value of tolerance, we have found, is exceptionally high so that, given careful advance planning, the prospects of success are probably greater than they would be in many parts of the United States.

Whether the result of an experiment of this sort[3] would eventually mean a greater or lesser devotion to one or more of the present organized religions, or whether instead it would encourage widening allegiance to nonsectarian and perhaps humanistic religious values, cannot be determined in advance. Democratic education, when it is completely honest, always leaves the door open to alternative choices and courses of action. Indeed, to allow room for such choices is the only logical reply to those sectarians who contend that the separation of church and state leads to indoctrination of an exclusively secular outlook.

Our own hope, however, is that doctrinaire attitudes and religious ethnocentrism could be superseded by broader understanding of the tremendous role that religious values play in the life of cultures. To come to appreciate, as several of our leaders now appreciate, that the very core of these values lies in the active dedication of any person to a larger, more meaningful whole than he himself—this, we hold, is the first goal of religious education in the Puerto Rican public schools, and the chief reason why it could become a central force in the renascence of the culture.

CHAPTER SIXTEEN

VALUE PROBLEMS OF PUERTO RICAN YOUTH

OF MANY that might be chosen from a large field, we consider here but three controversial questions, the first very general, the other two more specific but at opposite poles, as it were: What are the over-all norms of Puerto Rican adolescents? What are the values bearing upon sex experience? And what appraisal does the younger generation place upon its relations, and those of the culture as a whole, to the world situation? Educational aspects will in this case be taken up in connection with each question.

Perhaps because our evidence is derived more from older people than from the younger generation itself, answers to these questions are almost never unified. To be sure, three grassroots respondents were below voting age; four others were still in their twenties. Nevertheless, the median age of respondents on the combined panels was close to the mid-forties.

The picture they will draw of Puerto Rican youth is far from a completely happy one. Conformity, complacency, and instability are among the negative characteristics heavily stressed. But positive values are not overlooked, and on at least two scores educational agreements prove to be wide: first, on the need for sex education; and, second, on the need for international-mindedness. We commend both agreements, but hope for a program that can further arouse Puerto Rican youth to its grave responsibilities in the decades ahead.

THE NORMS OF ADOLESCENTS

One of the most intriguing of recent theses argued by students of contemporary mores is that teen-agers and young adults, at least in the United States, are directed more by the wish to win the approval of others from their own age, class, and status group than of, say, older prestige groups. Puerto Rico, in the judgment of most national-level informants (to whom this question was confined), reveals much the same phenomenon.

Two factors that motivate the young Islander toward conformity with peers were held to apply much less to his Mainland cousin. One is the abnormal pressure to acculturate and assimilate patterns of belief and practice that are not indigenous—a pressure that tends to stimulate an unhealthy because artificial effort to accept the norms of comparable groups in the imposing culture. (Teen-age styles of dress would be an obvious example.) The other factor is an urge to revolt from the authoritarian family pattern. This process, in turn, often generates emotional conflict not only between parents and their maturing offspring but within the latter themselves.

And yet respondents seemed rather undisturbed. One thought that there are already signs of a reaction against such conformity in favor of closer relations with parents. Others argued that, though there may be more awareness of the phenomenon, there is really nothing new about adolescent zeal to win approval of peers even at the cost of parental opposition—that their own youthful experience had been similar and, indeed, both a healthy and natural one.

This judgment was challenged by two fellow leaders. Disagreeing with the majority, the trouble is, they implied, that the younger generation has not revolted *enough*. The average parent remains such an imposing figure of authority that his approval frequently still counts the most. Moreover, the young Puerto Rican is likely to be less fully developed emotionally or socially than *americanos* of equal age (though not necessarily less than young Europeans) precisely because he has been protected too much. His sense of humor, for example, is often more juvenile, as, indeed, are many of his emotional reactions.

The attempt to formalize children's behavior at an early age, to garb them on social occasions as "miniature adults," and to expect them to behave in all the "proper" ways ordained by their elders was held to prevent them from growing as normally as they otherwise would. They tend to skip, as it were, the awkward but necessary process of teen-age development—one effect of which is that they frequently reveal themselves even when well beyond adolescence to be a good deal less mature and self-reliant than external appearance might deceive one into supposing. That this hypothesis could apply to the typical woman who, up to the age of marriage, has relatively seldom known emotional involvement with young men would seem also to follow from our earlier portrayal of her cultural role.

Aside from the question of parental overprotection, there were other adverse value judgments. Members of the younger generation, three respondents agreed, are increasingly self-centered, pleasure-seeking, and disrespectful of the wishes of their parents, both of whom, in turn, are often too busy with their jobs to disturb themselves very much. Also, North American notions of success have rapidly superseded more traditional life goals. One respondent—with vigorous disapproval—even applied Veblen's famous ironic standard of "conspicuous consumption" to Puerto Rican young people, particularly to those of the middle and upper classes.

Several, however, distinguished between the level of aspirations of Continental and Puerto Rican youth. While two respondents thought them closely comparable—indeed, the latter, too, may seem "exhibitionistic" about their prospects of success—a larger number thought them to be less ambitious than the former. As one put it, they believe more firmly than North Americans that "men work to live rather than live to work" (a distinction which a fellow panelist considered, by the way, unfair to the young Continental). Though seldom idle by choice, the average Puerto Rican youth nevertheless thinks in "smaller terms," another held, partly because (unlike young North Americans still affected by the "Horatio Alger myth") he has much less reason to think in grandiose terms.

Perhaps, one leader argued, this is just as well. To become a slave to ambition aggravates frustration and neurotic tendencies by generating hopes that can rarely be fulfilled in a country of such minute size and scarce natural resources. In one sense, the realization of this limitation is also an asset to the teaching profession: many teachers, appreciating that their best assurance of security lies in this field, prefer to remain in it rather than to gamble with some more lucrative but more precarious opportunity. Thereby the problem of turnover, while still great enough, is reduced.

Returning to adolescent values, the negative tone of the comments thus far must now be qualified. Not only were two respondents unsure as to how to appraise young Puerto Ricans; a few others were inclined toward a favorable judgment. One felt them to be a fairly well-balanced generation—more so than his own had been. Another spelled out this feeling: young people on the Island are becoming slowly but increasingly democratic both in family and political relations; they are learning the value of social sports and recreation; they are developing aesthetic appreciation; and they are improving in economic efficiency as they acquire better health and better education than were possible for preceding generations. To this optimistic evaluation still another leader added his opinion that, in the long run, the average youth places the enduring values of his culture ahead of such transitory ones as merely economic gain.

One realistic educational proposal emerged from the discussion of adolescent norms. Replying to questions asked of a number of colleagues by one of our teacher informants, the consensus among them was overwhelmingly in favor of more thorough vocational guidance on the junior and senior high school levels than students now normally receive. Often the goals of these students were said to be shockingly out of line either with their capabilities or their opportunities. As is perhaps equally true in the United States, one consequence is that too large a proportion of secondary youth who pursue a general precollege liberal-arts program never attend college. Yet parents, unfortunately, often insist upon this program on the assumption that a vocational diploma carries less prestige—another of many symptoms that middle-class goals are indeed a potent magnet.

VALUES OF SEX: THE EDUCATIONAL TASK

As in cultures everywhere, adolescence in Puerto Rico is a time of intense concern with sex drives and hence with the acute moral problems that frequently accompany the desire for relationship between young men and women. In earlier chapters—notably, 3 and 6—we have offered a brief description of the patterns of sex conduct that currently prevail. Here we wish to recapitulate briefly, but more pointedly to ask our informants what they consider education's task to be in dealing with these patterns.

Despite their rather critical judgment of other youthful values, national-level informants approached a consensus that current adolescent attitudes toward sex are, on the whole, healthier than formerly. True, the public schools have done little to cope with the double standard or for that matter any other problem of sex; nevertheless, especially among better-educated groups, parents were said to discuss these problems more openly with their children than has been traditional. More of the attitude also prevails that sex relations are not just a necessary evil but may express rich value in and of themselves.

To be sure, the traditional virginity cult with its multiplicity of rituals remains very strong. (It is firmly accepted, one leader estimated, by at least 75 per cent of all inhabitants.) Even here, nevertheless, subtle changes were said to be discernible. Though far less free than in the United States, young women often have slightly wider opportunity than earlier to become well acquainted with young men before marriage—a trend approvingly attributed to acculturative processes. Hand-holding and other overt manifestations of affection during "dates" were also adjudged an improvement over the more furtive practices of even a few years back. Finally, despite the problems created by the changing social status of the Puerto Rican woman, the point was reconfirmed that her growing sense of democratic rights is beginning to create more wholesome sex attitudes on her part as well as on that of her mate.

Subcultural evaluations, while less detailed than those above, were in some respects more conservative. Not only did birth-control clinics and the widespread practice of sterilization meet slightly greater opposition; it was apparent that time-worn values concerning sex experience remained more influential. One parent respondent, for example, hesitated to discuss problems of sex in the interests of this study because, he said, his priest would disapprove. And he was especially worried over erotic stimulations provided by dancing and movies.

Another, also a Catholic, thought that the mother alone should speak to her daughters about sex matters and then only "within limits"—a rule which the father should follow also for his sons. And yet compare the views of a third parent (himself an active Protestant): he considered moderate premarital "petting" to be a normal and not immoral expression of youthful ardor; he regarded sex relations in the married state as an act of great beauty and good; he refused to condemn divorce (though he thought it solves few problems); he approved of sterilization; and he adjudged the use of contraceptives to be neither right nor wrong in and of itself.

On the issue of sex education in a formal sense, the majority of subcultural respondents somewhat surprisingly gravitated toward the preceding spokesman's liberal orientation. One of the Catholic parents cited above held that prudery is really no excuse for ignoring the issue. Another Protestant made the point that, since youngsters learn about sex anyway, the school is the best place to teach them. Only one respondent opposed the subject entirely; only one other was unsure. The remainder endorsed it—a consensus that received not quite unanimous backing on the national level as well.

What should sex education include? The answers were debatable. One teacher respondent said that he already dealt with the matter in a high school course; what he really meant was that he had occasionally discussed prostitution on the Island, along with problems of overpopulation. Again, although no study of animal reproduction—even in "birds and bees"—was said to be provided at the elementary level, the physiology of mating and birth is treated in the junior high school. Also, a student respondent reported that he had attended a lecture on "boy-girl relations," which, however, proved to be confined to etiquette! This student had never seen a film on human reproduction, nor had he ever participated in any class session on problems of birth control. (A class of juniors and seniors in the University also testified that none had ever heard a discussion on sex in the public schools. Nor would they, after becoming teachers, ever expect to discuss it.)

A brief secondary unit dealing with the population problem in Puerto Rico does, to be sure, mention birth control as one possible solution. Moreover, some attention in home-economics classes limited to girls is paid to such phenomena as the cycle of menstruation; aspects of sex were reported to be considered in the University high school with somewhat greater frankness than is typical; and some sessions on birth control and family size, sponsored by outside organizations, have been held for parents in the public schools. Beyond these boundaries, sex education remains more in the nature of hesitant proposals than of actual teaching and learning.

What are some of these proposals? One of the most frequently stressed by both panels of respondents was that the physiology of reproduction be taught at an early age—the fourth or fifth grade was suggested by several—rather than delayed until the high school level. While a small minority supported the delay (children, one feared, would use the "language of the street" rather than scientific terms), another minority favored initiation into the subject as early as the first or second grade. In this connection, one teacher recalled the Continental practice in some modern elementary schools of keeping pairs of animals (guinea pigs are popular) within the classroom itself. Another respondent, who wished to provide knowledge of menstruation for twelve-year-old girls, thought the best tactic would be to discuss the proposal first with the local Mothers' Club.

For the senior high school, a substantial proportion urged direct and frank attention to the pros and cons of birth control, including techniques. Several Catholics, however, were willing that only the nonartificial "rhythm method" be explained. Another respondent suggested that the sexes might be segregated during sex instruction. Still others remained dubious as to whether birth control should be explicitly treated by the high school at all.

Two leaders went further in their opposition. One, though supporting the government birth-control program (the lower classes, he said, should have the same right to plan their families as the upper classes), opposed sex education in the public school for three impressive reasons: it irritates the Catholic Church; it makes sex more alluring ("something like studying narcotics"); and such education should, in any case, occur in the home. (Yet he also doubted that the average parent is competent to handle the question!) The second leader, though he seemed willing that sex education be opened to adults under public auspices, agreed that with this one exception the home is the proper place—his own objection to the schools being based mainly on fear that teachers might be "unscrupulous" in conducting the study.

This same spokesman was also the only one to voice outright opposition to birth-control clinics. They tend to increase immorality, he said, and thus the kind of irresponsible conduct exemplified by the high rate of illegitimacy. The poor, he argued rather curiously, should have no more right to exploit methods of birth control than do the prosperous classes. The widespread notion, moreover, that large families are somehow wrong is itself morally wrong. Many families of very meager income have succeeded in raising eight or more children to their credit and satisfaction—an achievement which, apparently, young parents might well emulate.

It is hardly necessary to emphasize that this point of view received scant approval from either group of respondents, two of whom, incidentally, have pioneered in the Society for Planned Parenthood (a privately financed agency whose director, it was reported, is himself a Catholic). Several, on the contrary, insisted that Puerto Rico's dense population is the chief reason why sex education is now desperately needed.

But the question remains partially unanswered: What *kind* of education? Respondents differed as to whether and when ethical as well as objective topics such as physiology should be introduced. While one thought that the ethics of sex relations should be considered in the elementary school, and physiological aspects on the secondary level (his point was that the damage would be done by waiting too long), another recommended the opposite sequence.

Just what might be meant by "ethical" in this context was not clear either. For some, inculcation of the Christian values of chastity and fidelity was surely implied. For others, honest examination of issues such as the double standard and premarital conduct was equally implied. One respondent held that the main tasks for education are first to "cut away the mystery" from normal sexual behavior; second, to reduce the sense of guilt that often accompanies even slight transgressions from the conventional code (one subcultural informant still believed that, physiologically, masturbation is very injurious); and, third, to help young people recognize that even the most successful marriages are fraught with variables that can be met only with patient understanding—understanding toward the development of which the schools, after all, ought to have great responsibility.

To accomplish these and other goals, several respondents pressed again for functionalized learnings. To require a course or unit in the subject, and then to expect children to learn in the same passive way that most of them still learn other subject matters, is not a defensible approach. Rather, questions of sex ought never to be "forced" but answered naturally whenever children (always in mixed groups) spontaneously raise them—beginning in the nursery school, if questions should first arise there, and growing in complexity not by grades or ages so much as with varying rates of maturation.

The fact that, already in Puerto Rico, hundreds of married teachers continue with their professional duties during pregnancy far beyond the time when they would be required to resign or go on leave from many Continental schools is one wholesome practice that could well be extended to other attitudes and practices. Again, Insular problems of overpopulation should enable the skillful teacher to accommodate questions on birth control in the same open way that he accommodates questions on migration. In order to create this atmosphere of learning, lectures or recitations on sex would have to be much less common than flexible discussions in which students felt both respected and free to communicate their worries. Ultimately, we were reminded, problems raised by the values of sex embrace the whole circumference of human life and love. Yet, however difficult, the teacher's goal should be to help young people come to terms with them just as un-restrainedly as problems on a more immediate plane.

Finally, careful selection and preparation of teachers qualified to deal with these problems were considered of paramount importance. Above all, the need to cultivate a balanced perspective was held to be essential to any success that may result from ventures in sex education —a perspective that appreciates how the issues involved are rarely settled either by the hallowed mandates of ecclesiastic institutions or by the inflated estimates that behavioral scientists sometimes place upon the role of sex in cultural experience.

YOUTH AND THE WORLD SITUATION

From the delicate intimacy of sex values we turn now to the op-posite extreme—to the grossly public nature of Puerto Rico's relations with the world situation. In an age such as ours the problem of how far young people do and should urgently concern themselves with the values and disvalues of that situation would seem more crucial than in earlier ages of national self-sufficiency.

The evidence presented in Chapter 14 revealed that, while most citizens are tolerant enough of values both like and unlike those of their own culture, they are not greatly concerned about those of other cultures. Does this generalization equally apply to Puerto Rican youth?

The answer once more was "yes" and "no". Though one leader respondent remained uncertain, the rest were rather at odds. Several maintained that young people, especially veterans, are not only sensi-tive to the values of classes and statuses other than their own but are increasingly world-minded. Hundreds have traveled to remote lands.

Movies, television, and radio have brought the Island into close contact with other ways of life. Also, the very fact of its geographic position has intensified awareness of the large land masses upon which the people are dependent. Nor have the Great Depression of the 1930's which caused tragic suffering in Puerto Rico, and later the submarine blockade of World War II which briefly cut off food supplies, been lost upon the younger generation.

Indeed, according to some spokesmen, the average young adult may not only acquire more knowledge of world geography than his average Mainland counterpart; he is probably less provincial than many in the U. S. South or Midwest. And he may be better informed than even young Easterners partly because he has less to distract him and partly because, being isolated, he feels more need to keep in touch with the outside world. Again, the continuing quest for the political rationale of a "free associated state" has generated concern among at least some young citizens as to Puerto Rico's goals in the network of international relations.

Other respondents were less sanguine. Absorption in immediate excitements typical of youth far outweighs, they felt, any alternative interest. Not only were class as well as national provincialism said to be common; the growing prosperity enjoyed since the early 1940's encourages complacency. True, the Puerto Rican government pays annual official homage to the United Nations. But young people here appear in these respects to be much more like than different from those in the United States, where, according to many recent observations, complacency has reached epidemic scope.

Let us test such conflicting responses more concretely by introducing one additional concept of cultural process—namely, crisis—which we shall define for our purpose as any emergency created by the deprivation or dislocation of previously accepted conditions of cultural order, process, and/or goals. When leaders were asked whether they regarded the world today to be in a state of crisis, a large majority agreed that it is. Though three reminded us that all periods of history are fraught with crises of one kind or another (Puerto Rico, one said, has been going through them for at least a century and a half), the consensus was that the present world period is abnormally severe.

Reasons offered are well-known but important ones: greatly altered forces of technological production, dread of atomic conflict and "fallout" radiation, the endless series of small or large international and civil wars (in Hungary and Venezuela, say), and the growing articulation of millions of people especially among so-called inferior races of the earth. As one spokesman expressed it, World War II never really ended; the result is that today we are involved in a three-way conflict between totalitarianism, democracy, and the vast underdeveloped areas that are really neither one.

And what is the reaction of Island citizens in general and of youth in particular to this grim picture? Some insecurity, largely psychological, was said to prevail among young men unable to make definite plans for the future because of the expectation of compulsory military service—a reaction that may affect the morale of their families as well. Also, Puerto Rico is vulnerable to atomic attack because of the strategic importance of its military bases and international airport. Finally, feelings of insecurity (but also, for many, of security) have accompanied achievement of the Commonwealth status—a complicated and novel political relationship far from easy to grasp or to explain.

Yet, granting these modifying factors, the degree of disturbance over world instabilities was held by some to be slight. The fact that, having no federal vote, Puerto Rico is without direct voice in U. S. foreign policy is one contributing factor; indeed, it may encourage some young people still to hold (thereby echoing the familiar *jíbaro* belief) that one can do little but accept "whatever comes." Also, concentration upon internal problems of the Island (the standard of living, first of all) usually precedes interest in less immediate problems—a reaction normal to all cultures unless, as in the recent case of Israel, they confront some catastrophic threat.

Of course, it was argued, a few individuals, and not always those of the younger generation, are beset by "sleepless nights" over the world crisis. But even they, oftener than not, "pull the bedclothes over their heads" rather than face frightening realities. The bulk of the population, meanwhile, is not frightened at all. There is even little worry that another depression might strike. For, as one expressed it, the average citizen—youth perhaps most?—has come to believe that somehow he will be taken care of by the rich and powerful Uncle Sam.

Consider, then, a hypothetical situation. Suppose that Puerto Rico were to find itself confronted with a major crisis of its own—a crisis induced by cyclonic forces loose in the world, yet no less severe because the people of the Island were not themselves responsible. Suppose as a result that prosperity were quickly to cease, jobs to vanish, schools and clinics to close, hunger and fear to spread through every city and every rural *barrio*. How would the people react if in the midst of this dreadful situation a leader of ostensible sincerity and great persuasiveness were to promise, on one condition, to provide food, schools, hospitals, and jobs for every able citizen? That condition would, of course, be the crucial test: to yield basic democratic rights (although no clever leader would put the choice in such obtuse terms) in exchange for the restoration of security.

The answer, again mainly on the national level, was disturbing but realistic. A sizable proportion admitted that contingency. Granting with two respondents that only "a very clever demagogue" could thus persuade the majority of people, the fact still remains, others conceded, that the roots of family, community, and political democracy have had too little time to grow deep into the Island soil—less than two decades, actually, while a full quarter-century is still required for "consolidation." And it must always be remembered that a demagogue is chiefly interested not in "how to strengthen" but rather in "how tender are" the democratic roots. The *personalismo* tradition considered in Chapter 6 is also a dangerous factor. So, too, is the record of Latin American struggles, many of them failures, to achieve democracy. One spokesman went so far as to assert that, though the Puerto Rican people might have mildly resisted (mainly because of three preceding decades of North American influence), they were sufficiently desperate so that in 1930 they could well have yielded to a Trujillo type of dictator.

But, we were reminded, even countries with long records of democratic experience are by no means free from similar dangers. According to one spokesman, demagogues at times have virtually taken over parts of the United States itself—in Louisiana perhaps most recently. According to another leader, even President Franklin D. Roosevelt played the demagogue's role sufficiently to win vast powers; and the point is that another leader with less admirable values might have equally succeeded.

Consistently, however, with the hopeful spirit earlier described, the likelihood that democracy in Puerto Rico could be "sold out" in a crisis was by no means supported without impressive counterarguments. One respondent, recalling its national character, insisted that the roots of democracy are already firmer in Puerto Rico than they are in the United States. Another distinguished between, on the one hand, the strong democratic governments that people sometimes support in times of emergency and, on the other, demagogic governments. Many, moreover, are already conscious of the meaning of dictatorship (they have watched several at painfully close range—the Dominican Republic and Cuba being mentioned) and they could detect the difference between a dictatorial and nondictatorial type of demagogue, even assuming that they could be attracted by one of the latter type.

Certain personality traits of the *jíbaro* would also come into play in any real crisis—above all, his independence and suspiciousness—traits which, though regarded as more negative than positive by some respondents, could have here a value that was considered positive indeed. Actually, despite the dazzling popularity of the present Governor, he could not himself, we were told, successfully persuade a majority of people to act against what they considered their simple rights—for example, to cut consumption of their beloved coffee in order to profit by high market prices. Nor could he convince them to back a program for Insular independence: they know too well that the resulting tax and tariff burden would be shattering.

The fact that Communists in Puerto Rico have never gained a foothold even during the depths of the depression was cited as still further proof of a long-conditioned wariness toward "pie in the sky" and similar political bonanzas. The labor movement, too, has helped to develop political astuteness, as have repeated efforts of the Popular party to deepen public consciousness of the meaning of democracy. A few leaders, indeed, were confident that the people would simply ridicule any dictatorial attempt to win them over. Another thought that, though the Island still remains more vulnerable to demagogic lures than, say, England, Norway, or the northeastern United States, it is already less vulnerable (unless we except areas under the British flag, such as Trinidad and Jamaica) than any country "south of the U.S. border."

One further question. With the world in crisis, with the little Island's own democratic future far from impregnable, how would the people respond to a proposal that Puerto Rico become part of a world government—a government in which all member states would relinquish important elements of sovereignty in favor of enforceable international authority?

On the grassroots level, of those respondents who answered the question, twice as many favored as opposed such a goal. Two were unsure. On the national level, support was even stronger. While one leader preferred to confine Puerto Rico's future international relations chiefly to North America, and while a few others doubted that a world government can be formed in the near future, nevertheless most panelists hoped that it would come as soon as possible. One respondent was sure that, however great the obstacles, this goal must be attained if only because new forms of communication have already broken through all national barriers. True, a colleague was skeptical as to the workability of an international army. And another warned that too much focusing upon the goal of world government could serve as an "escape" from the realities of Puerto Rico's present situation—an escape which, he said, some intellectuals have recently encouraged. Nevertheless, to paraphrase still another, international controls over evils such as the opium traffic mean that national sovereignty is rapidly becoming, as it were, "a self-liquidating concept." Thus, even now, some of the political debate over Insular status seems rather "dated"—particularly the issue of permanent relations with the United States.

We are readier now to consider, in the light of the world crisis and of Puerto Rico's unavoidable involvement, how education may assist young people who soon must, after all, shoulder the preponderant burden. One social scientist among our respondents was particularly incensed, not only at the growth of specialized training for competition in the market, where values are rarely examined at all, but at the professorial practice among his colleagues of referring glibly to the importance of values in all human life and then of dismissing them from patient criticism or appraisal. There is also pressing need, he said, for more qualitative, philosophic analyses and evaluations of the world's cultures and less merely quantitative descriptions of, say, the height of their mountains or the prolificity of their populations.

A second far-reaching suggestion was that young people be helped to develop more awareness toward conflicting issues of value underlying the policies of the University administration and those of the Department of Education. They are issues that, as we have noted elsewhere, focus partly in alternative assessments of the struggle to clarify Puerto Rico's future in relation to planetary norms.

A third suggestion reiterated the great potential importance of the Point Four program. If world-mindedness is to develop among young people, there is urgent need to make that program a "two-way street" —in other words, to enable them to work and study in other parts of the world at the same time that citizens from India and dozens of countries work and study here. Guided tours to Europe, Mexico, and elsewhere under University auspices help to widen vistas; yet they are of meager influence compared with plans that should be provided for young people to live for prolonged periods in cultures distant from their own. At the same time, opportunity to acquaint high school and college students with Point Four visitors should be widened. One leader, particularly, urged that all such visitors spend at least one day per month in the public schools, and that classes anticipate their coming both by study of their homelands and by carefully prepared questions that would help to cross cultural boundaries.

Within the curriculum, concentrated attention upon world cultures and world geography (to which, one said, there used to be more attention than there is today) is imperative. Instead of sporadic UN meetings and discussions, problems of the United Nations should occupy a much more prominent place in the social studies on all levels. Special attention should be given to the goal of "universal culture" and of a world government in which Puerto Rico would share full membership—always in relation to a "mature historical consciousness" rather than as a remote end separated from the difficult problem of political and economic means.

How to motivate young people to a genuine zest about world problems and world goals is, of course, the "sixty-four dollar question." Establishing contacts with young people of other cultures through personal correspondence is one rewarding method. (Even on the adult level such correspondence has been successfully carried on for a period of years between a few Puerto Rican and Haitian communities that were ravaged by hurricanes.)

The likelihood that motivation can be achieved merely by adding more courses on world affairs seemed dubious to one respondent. At the same time, another was sure that education must tackle the problem of how to develop stronger reading habits—one of the most essential means to international understanding. As is now beginning to occur on the Continent, television could be used here to stimulate interest in important works by authors of many lands—works that stretch youthful imaginations and awaken them both to dangers and promises of the world that, for worse or better, they too will help to shape.

Prospects of the future may be gauged to some extent by appraising youthful values in the present. The evidence of this chapter has shown them to be, much like those of young Continentals, strongly conformist in their value orientation. Yet they tend to differ from the latter both in the culturally provoked intensity with which many young people try to achieve this orientation and in a contrary resistance to it by many others who still remain dominated by the patriarchal structure of authority. Perhaps something of the same cultural conditions would help to account for conflicting appraisals of youthful ambition—some respondents regretting that it is already too zealously materialistic and self-centered, others either regretting that it is not strong enough or applauding its constrictions.

Youthful attitudes toward values of sex, though only gradually changing, seemed to many resource persons to be moving in a liberal and, for them, commendable direction. Similarly, while disagreeing as to age levels, content, and methodology, they widely endorsed the need for sex education—a field which at present is largely taboo.

As to how young people tend to look upon the world situation with its value conflicts and allegiances, judgments differed again more sharply. Some respondents held that world-mindedness is rapidly increasing, others that the younger generation is infected with complacency toward problems of the outside world. But as to how they, along with older citizens, react to the world crisis that was conceded by most leader respondents to be of alarming scope, consensus leaned far toward the side of relative indifference. This evaluation might help to account, in turn, for an equally strong consensus that the Puerto Rican people could quite conceivably succumb to a demagogic leader who would emasculate their own democracy. Offsetting such a tragic consequence are, however, several factors—among them a long-engrained habit of political wariness, and a growing sophistication that now concedes the need even for world government.

Concerted attention to the place of values both in social science and in educational policies, expansion of opportunities to work and study in other cultures, and enrichment of the curriculum by, for example, intensive study of the United Nations—here, we were told, are some of the steps that must be taken today if the youth of Puerto Rico are to meet the obligations confronting them tomorrow.

We find no quarrel either with these or the other steps most strongly recommended. We only urge that they be expressed much more concertedly, and that they be *acted upon* with vigor and courage. With regard to sex education, particularly, our impression is that the majority of the people may be well ahead of official educational and political policy—that is, more amenable to forthright projects that deal both with scientific and moral aspects of the problem than has been generally assumed. The same inference could be drawn regarding the crisis in world affairs: it is quite possible, though only careful experimental ventures could prove or disprove the contention, that Puerto Rican students, despite their alleged complacency, are potentially readier than many to serve as models for students of other democratic nations in developing a national and international democratic outlook that could permeate their habits of thought and emotion —and thus become eventually indigenous to the implicit culture itself. Certainly such an outlook is fundamental to any goal-centered education adequate for our day. Certainly, too, it becomes imperative as a safeguard against demagogic lures. To achieve this objective functionalized learnings (e.g., the informal but constant utilization of Point Four visitors) are as indispensable as they are to any single aspect of the total program.

CHAPTER SEVENTEEN

FREEDOM AS THE GOAL OF PUERTO RICAN CULTURE

LOOKING BACK over our analysis and synthesis of the varieties of value that intrigue the Puerto Rican people—young and old, rich and poor, urban and rural—the question at last arises whether any one supreme value could be chosen and delineated that might succeed in fusing most or all others into a crowning, universal goal. In the judgment of some eminent students of the human quest, freedom is that goal. Might it be equally central to the Puerto Rican culture?

If so, then we must ask: Precisely what does this ancient and noble concept mean to the people of our microcosmic Island? How deeply are they committed to its maximum achievement? Are they clear as to the political goals and commensurate institutions most likely to assure that achievement? Are they fearful, for example, that their present form of government will, with all its welfare services, eventually weaken individual responsibility and soften the fiber of personality? Or, on the contrary, are they confident that an era of freedom will emerge from the transformations now in process—an era in behalf of which education should become the first and most important agency?

These seemingly rhetorical questions are by no means as simple to dispose of as might at first appear. Readers of previous chapters may, to be sure, predict the direction of the answers: with many qualifications, we have found over and over that the mood of the culture is hopeful and congenial to democratic values. Yet, as is true of all ideals, and as the following sections demonstrate, it is one thing to glorify freedom in the abstract and quite another to practice it in the arena of political, educational, and other kinds of everyday experience.

We shall find our panels not unmindful of such disparities. Indeed,

they so readily admit them that one can only admire their critical out-
spokenness—an essential ingredient of freedom itself. All in all, our
own estimate here is much more favorable than not: freedom *is* becoming a meaningful goal of the Puerto Rican culture. Education's
role—with no exception, *its single greatest role*—is to make it still
more meaningful, in act as well as word.

WHITHER PUERTO RICO?

Before examining the meaning of freedom as such, it is well to
inquire further as to whether the culture is engaged in creating values
that may be related to this magnetic goal—values which, at least for
Puerto Rico, are comparatively new; values, moreover, which become
embodied in political policies and conduct and thereby help to set
the directions and aims of the culture as a whole.

On the specific point of new values, only one respondent on the
national level was unable to point to any; for him, the single new fact
is a greater consciousness of old values. One other spokesman chose
to emphasize a negative value: a fresh acquisitiveness which, he felt,
goes far beyond the middle ground of healthy competition. The remainder mentioned the following positive examples which, though
of course not new in any universal sense, were adjudged to be relatively so in Puerto Rico: industrial capacity and skill (these were the
most frequently selected); education, inventiveness, and creativeness;
adaptability, especially to Continental values such as punctuality and
financial reliability; a mutual concern and respect among people of *all*
classes and regions; expanding self-confidence; democracy, with its
cluster of values such as peaceful discussion and responsible government; finally, the Commonwealth conception with its related cluster
—a conception which, it may be remembered, was widely regarded
as the outstanding instance of cultural innovation.

But do "new" values such as these provide enough awareness of
Puerto Rican goals? The clearest answer was much more negative than
positive. While more sense of direction prevails than perhaps twenty
years ago, and while agreement exists on immediate courses of action
(*Fomento* was cited here), it is hardly true, many leaders felt, that
far-reaching objectives have as yet been clarified or received popular
endorsement. The upper classes, for example, may be articulate about
what they think they want, but oftener than not they are superficial

and in conflict with what other classes think *they* want.

Nor, several respondents maintained, can it be proved that the dominant political regime has thus far convinced most followers as to the Island's ultimate goal—above all, as to whether, regarded as a permanent solution, the Commonwealth is "the best of all possible statuses." Only a few were sure that the bulk of people are already persuaded that it is.

Moreover, while most of our own spokesmen on both panels regarded the Commonwealth as by far the most expedient device viewed as a short-range goal (some venturing to suggest a future boundary of twenty to thirty years), they differed on the thorny question of any long-range goal. About half on the national panel were prepared to support the Commonwealth as a permanent arrangement. The remainder on this panel were roughly divided between the goal of eventual statehood, on the one hand, and a "wait and see" attitude, on the other hand. Only one leader supported independence, with another admitting that some unforeseen crisis could lead to the latter goal.

The uncertain leaders were unwilling to commit themselves because, they felt, all present formulations may prove inadequate to future contingencies. As one expressed it, the need is to exercise as much political flexibility as possible, meanwhile confronting each problem of relations with the United States in a pragmatic way so as to allow maximum room for accommodation to changing circumstances. For, as another suggested, new operating concepts are now emerging in the world that may relegate all current solutions of problems in international relations, including Puerto Rico's, to the "political museum."

On the subcultural panel, nevertheless, an impressive majority already favored statehood as the ultimate objective. The minority were again about equally divided—one group hoping that the Commonwealth would be permanent, the others either supporting independence or preferring a noncommittal attitude.

These striking divergences of judgment on such an important issue compel us to conclude that no clear-cut answer now prevails, at least in the sphere of politics, as to "whither Puerto Rico?" In order further to clarify the significance of this sphere, let us return to a question at its core: How far is there agreement concerning fundamental values such as freedom itself? For all political systems are channels to the fruition or destruction of these values.

THE EMERGENCE OF FREEDOM

What, then, does freedom mean to our respondents? One leader at once reminded us how difficult it is to distinguish typically verbalized freedom from the kind to which people may aspire on the more obscure plane of their cultural configuration. No one contended that the people of this Island have fully attained the goal of freedom. Yet the goal itself is no less important because of that fact. Rather it becomes, as it were, a normative measuring stick by which to decide in what ways Puerto Rico falls far short, in what ways it now begins to meet the test in cultural behavior rather than merely by the shining symbols of its ideology.

On both levels, respondents indicated that they had come to fairly articulate terms with the meaning of freedom. At the same time they helped to demonstrate its boundless scope by viewing it in a number of perspectives. We epitomize the most frequently emphasized of these perspectives: freedom implies the right of every individual to pursue his own interests, to develop his own potentialities, without jeopardizing or destroying the same right for other individuals. Every human being is thereby enjoined to limit his freedom as well as to attain it, for the unbridled pursuit of individual interests always conflicts sooner or later with that of one or more of his fellows. Thus freedom is possible only in a society of law that ordains the limits of each individual's pursuit at the same time that it protects his privileges.

More specifically, how does one manifest this right? Several respondents, again on both levels, selected various principles reminiscent of, if not always explicit in, the Bill of Rights—especially the privilege of thinking, speaking, deciding, and voting without fear of intimidation or retaliation. One leader reiterated here the right of dissent, incidentally commending both leading Puerto Rican newspapers for publishing letters by political extremists. Likewise, the U. S. Supreme Court was praised for several of its recent civil liberties decisions.

Emphasized, too, were such privileges as doing the kind of work one wants to do (correlatively, not being forced to do the kind one doesn't want to do), with enough reward so that one never has to go hungry or suffer from debt; the protection of one's privacy against intruders; obedience to the mandates of one's conscience; and the selection of one's own friends as well as a place to live. One grassroots respondent sought to characterize freedom as peace of mind and heart, while one leader suggested that the supreme test comes when a man would rather starve than relinquish his freedom.

In a somewhat different though not contradictory vein, others sought the essence of freedom in knowledge and experimentation. One spokesman placed understanding of himself as the first test. A second made the point negatively: freedom is the elimination of superstition and ignorance. A third focused upon creativity. A fourth stressed calculated risk-taking. A fifth, revealing something of the scientific spirit examined in Chapter 7, held that man becomes free only when he can engage in careful planning, consider alternatives according to his aims, and then execute the plan of his choice. The right of an individual to think and choose for himself was, indeed, a common thread running through several definitions.

One respondent provided a connecting link between the several views above and still another perspective. Freedom, he said, is the knowledge of how people may live well with one another. The approach seems again intellectual, but now it is also explicitly social. Whereas the emphasis thus far has appeared to reflect more than a little of the classical individualism of eighteenth- and nineteenth-century democracy (which assumed that social freedom will result from laissez-faire freedom), the emphasis now is the more recent one of the relations and mutual responsibilities among individuals and groups. As another leader put it, freedom is as much a matter of institutions as of individuals: unless both achieve it, neither one does. Still another found freedom to center, not in a lack of regulations, but rather in participation—in people criticizing, changing, and making "rules of the game" together.

One spokesman, citing the English philosopher T. H. Green as authority, rejected the traditional negativism inherent in freedom as "absence of restraint" by the state over the individual; instead he focused upon the positive harmonizing of conflicts among many individuals and among many groups. With a peer, he accordingly viewed the goal also in pluralistic terms: since there are numerous freedoms—in religion, philosophy, politics, and economics, among others—the great goal of freedom is that of achieving the most work-able partnership possible among all of them. It is not therefore to be equated either with individual or political independence. Rather, it is both a relative and universal value at the same time—relative to each person, group, or nation, as the case may be, yet inclusive of them all.

Is it possible to discover any goal that could be placed still higher—a goal to which Puerto Ricans might aspire even beyond freedom itself? Significantly or not, no one chose any religious value in the theistic sense. Indeed, the only explicitly religious comments during our discussions of freedom were volunteered by three respondents at the grassroots level, the first of whom held that free men must be guided by the written or unwritten laws of God as well as those of government; the second, that love—the highest Christian virtue—is the way to the value of freedom; and the third, that organized re-ligion constricts that value.

On the same level, two others were unsure of freedom's place in the hierarchy of values, and one held that for her at least it is not the most important human goal. Freedom, she said, could be "taken for granted"; far more precious is the aim of a happy and fruitful mar-riage—an aim which, incidentally, another woman respondent would in turn evaluate by such ingredients of freedom as self-expression for each member of the family.

On the national level, since all but two respondents likewise re-garded freedom as the highest human goal, there would probably be wide acceptance of one leader's vigorous assertion that freedom is the basic test of all human progress. Of the two dissenters, one in-sisted that respect for personality should be placed at the apex of all values. The other, while at first regarding freedom as only a means to the end of happiness, also tacitly agreed with a collaborator who considered it not so much distinct from as the active embodiment of happiness. Indeed, they implied, when we think carefully of the intent of "life, liberty, and the pursuit of happiness," freedom becomes integral with the highest of all values: the enjoyment of life to the utmost.

How fully, now, are the people of Puerto Rico deeply dedicated, in one or more of these manifestations, to the goal of freedom? Several leaders were sure that it is an increasingly meaningful goal—more so, probably, than elsewhere in Latin America and certainly more so than in, say, the Gold Coast cultures of Africa. True, it remains rather a provincial ideal: corroborating one point in our preceding chapter, Insular devotion to freedom, like devotion to other values, is hardly of planetary scope. It would be less provincial, one held, if Puerto Rico were directly involved in shaping U. S. foreign policy.

And there were further reservations. Doubt was expressed whether freedom as yet has unqualified commitment in the minds and hearts of Puerto Ricans, too many of whom suffer still from value conflicts. One leader, distinguishing between an "interior" freedom of spirit and attitudes, on the one hand, and an "exterior" freedom of democratic political organization, on the other hand, was sure he had known but a few genuinely free persons in his life—persons who, by the same token, are free from the ravages of guilt. The former quality, which he said is primary but which is far from prevalent as yet, requires freedom from prejudice and from domination by others. The latter requires both enormous courage and much less fear than now prevails in government circles—fear of reprisals among petty bureaucrats, say, and constant fear among its leaders of violence from fanatical enemies of the regime.

Even more fundamental was the contention that Puerto Rico, like the United States, continues to suffer from the exaggerated influence of classical philosophies of freedom conceived in terms of individual rights—philosophies therefore deficient in their regard for modern conceptions of group relationships and duties. One direct result is a lack of social discipline and responsibility that manifests itself in economic, educational, as well as other kinds of anarchic behavior.

Nevertheless, granting such deficiencies, both levels of respondents were strongly disposed toward a consensus that freedom as defined in theory is increasing in practice as well. At the grassroots, all but a few were positive that more experiential freedom exists in the culture today than, say, twenty years ago. Following various criteria noted above, they supported their judgment with definite examples: there is, they said, greater freedom to speak, to choose one's work, to join labor unions, to vote as one pleases, to participate, to move about, and to print dissenting ideas. One informant chose to mention the diminution of ill treatment at the hands of police and similar officials. And a *jíbaro* respondent understandably regarded the vast difference in hours of labor as, for him, the single most important instance of growth toward freedom: when he was fifteen, he worked twelve hours per day, from six in the morning till six at night; now at forty he works eight hours.

Of the remainder, one respondent was not sure whether freedom has recently increased. A second agreed that political freedom is greater than, say, in 1930; yet in other ways—in the changing status of women and in the indebtedness caused chiefly by installment buying—he was still not convinced. A third held that, while more freedom prevails than half a century ago, it has not notably improved within the last twenty years. And a fourth respondent could not find that she herself had gained in freedom, though she did concede the gain for many others.

All national-level respondents either directly or inferentially supported the dominant viewpoint on the grassroots level. Freedom on the Island has, they thought, markedly increased. Particularly lauded was the public right to criticize, to make decisions, and to effect social or other kinds of change. Perhaps the greatest shortcoming, two government leaders felt, still lies in the relative weakness of dissenting pressure groups: before freedom can really claim maturity, the culture must provide more vigilant ways by which minorities may serve as "countervailing forces" to the prestige and power vested in the present government by the vast majority.

POLITICAL PARTIES IN THE STRUGGLE FOR FREEDOM

The preceding comment leads us back to the political arena. Utilizing the several perspectives on freedom, and bearing in mind the differences prevailing as to both actual and desirable political directions, let us ask our resource groups to make their own appraisal of the three main parties.

Stateside readers may be astonished to learn that, in the judgment of an impressive ratio of respondents, differences between these parties both in their commitment to freedom as delineated above (not, be it noted, in a sloganizing sense) and in their policies within the Island itself appear to be minor. As to their policies toward Puerto Rico's external relations (meaning primarily, of course, relations with the United States), differences are more pronounced. Even here, however, sufficient overlappings occur so that it is more difficult to think of the major alignments in separate political domains than in a kind of spectrum. No extreme "right" or "left" is discernible—unless one includes the minute group of illegal Nationalists or the equally minute Communist group. The Popular, Statehood, and Independence parties all cluster somewhere toward the center of the spectrum—or rather a little to the left of center as compared with the recent orientation of the two great U. S. parties.

Take, to begin with, the weakest of the three: the *Partido Independentista Puertorriqueño* or PIP (the Puerto Rican Independence party). Not only do many *Independentistas* support the "mixed economy" and "welfare state" policies of the *Populares;* they were said to be inclined toward still more vigorous policies of social reform and thus, in the judgment of at least one informant, to function as a political spearhead in somewhat the way that the small Socialist party of the United States has functioned there. For example, they have favored further drastic steps against the sugar corporations: they would turn more of the large *haciendas* into public holdings for the benefit of the small farmer or the *agregado* (propertyless rural worker).

In the interests of precision it is only fair to point out that the PIP is hardly a unified party. If one leader respondent is correct, there are actually two kinds of *Independentistas*—those who are much more emotionally than logically opposed to the *Populares* for having forsaken the cause of independence, and those who see the problem as chiefly one of political dynamics—that is, of how best to achieve the goal of maximum freedom. The latter group, though they continue to differ on the issue of formal separation from the United States, tend more than the former to agree with the internal program of the Popular party. Yet even they are unlikely to deny that some forms of association must be continued with the United States; to do otherwise would compel them to support an isolationism quite incompatible with contemporary political realities. Their main concern, another leader held, is to preserve the identity, to prevent the assimilation, of Puerto Rican culture and its indigenous values—a concern which, although shared likewise by the rival parties, was said to be least intent among statehood supporters and somewhat less intense (though, as we have seen, far from ephemeral) among many *Populares.*

These fairly tolerant attitudes toward the Independence party were not unanimous. Though two grassroots respondents who supported

the Popular party as an interim measure hoped for eventual independence (only one respondent on this level, a veteran, was an outright *Independentista*), another was hostile to the PIP because, he
held, it is supported by too many who remain Nationalists at heart.
Two leader respondents questioned whether the party would ever
effect the internal reforms it advocates were it to achieve power, while
a third considered it merely a waning "splinter group" of disgruntled
individuals. It also lacks, he felt, a well-formulated political philosophy.

Of the three parties, the second largest—the *Partido Estadista
Republicano* or PER (Statehood Republican party)—received the
harshest criticisms in the present context of discussion. Bearing in
mind that several respondents were themselves influential *Populares,*
the point was reiterated several times that the Statehood party is "less
sincere" in its proposals than either rival party—indeed, that statehood
itself, although earnestly desired by some members of the PER, is also
used as a vote-getting strategy for the purpose of restoring power to
the top socioeconomic class. Though the official platform on internal
policy is remarkably similar at various points to that of the Popular
party, nevertheless it was termed a "money party" that would do little
if anything to carry forward the liberal reforms it, too, advocates "on
paper." Its leaders, some politically inconspicuous, were said to have
formed a coalition of industrial power and wealth that repudiates at
heart much of the political philosophy now in operation.

But precisely in what ways the Statehood party actually opposes that
philosophy recalls the spectrumlike character of Puerto Rican politics.
Certainly on the ideological level the description offered by certain
respondents would suggest a matter of degree rather than of kind.
The PER policy, we were informed, is frankly skeptical toward what
it regards as an alarming tendency toward governmental paternalism
and collectivism of a socialist-democratic type. Therefore it wishes to
limit state activities more than does the Popular party and to encourage
greater effort and responsibility on the part of individuals. Yet, simultaneously, it recognizes the need for government both to engage in
many undertakings and to prevent "vested interests" from blocking
the pursuit of happiness to which the state is admittedly one important
though never more than one means. In this general formulation, the
Statehood party was said even today to reflect the spirit of the New
Deal period to a greater degree than it does the conservative orienta-

tion of the U.S. Republican regime, to which it claims affinity. Indeed, the New Deal was specifically lauded by one PER spokesman for having prevented "revolution" in the 1930's.

On external policy, to be sure, *Estadistas* are in sharper disagreement with both *Independentistas* and *Populares* than they are on internal policy. Yet even here we note overlappings. One informant contended, for example, that in matters of external policy the Statehood party is closer to the Popular party than is either of these to the Independence party; both of the former at least agree on the need for strong, permanent ties with the United States. The latter, on the other hand, is closer to the Popular party in its internal policies. Yet here again the lines are far from tightly drawn: not only, as we have seen, does the Statehood party also endorse considerable portions of the Popular program within the Island itself; the Independence party, or at least the moderate section of it, in turn endorses degrees of cooperation with the United States.

Meanwhile, the most distinctive goal of the Statehood party, symbolized by its title, remains a matter of dispute. As noted in the first section of this chapter, our own respondents were far from agreed on the ultimate desirability of full membership in the federal Union. Again, as noted in our chapter on vertical order, the recent increase in the vote for this party—centering as it does in the middle levels—could be interpreted more as a protest vote against higher taxes and similar measures adopted by the Popular regime than as a clear-cut vote for statehood. Actually, the latter question was regarded as "largely academic"; even if a plebiscite were to support such a step (as one grassroots respondent was sure that it would), the U.S. Congress would refuse in the foreseeable future to consider the proposal seriously. And such a refusal, insisted a peer, would have at least two causes: one, race prejudice of the Southern bloc in both the House and Senate; two, and related to the first cause, the comparatively large number of representatives to whom Puerto Rico would then be entitled in the House. This consequence would follow from the fact that only twenty-two states of the Union have a larger population.

By far the largest political organization is, of course, the third alignment: the *Partido Popular Democrático* or PPD (Popular Democratic party). Its policy and program, since it has been in operation for about twenty years, permeate the life of the culture. Indeed, for one of its ardent though nonpolitical advocates, the PPD is neither primarily an expedient device to solve the problem of association with the United States, nor is it a mere substitute for either colonialism or independence. Rather, it is a new though still incomplete concept of human relations and human goals both within and without the Island.

Take first the matter of external policy. On one issue, agreement with the Popular position among our respondents was, though not unanimous, exceptionally wide: independence is impossible even were it thought desirable. For economic reasons, if for no other, the tariffs that would result on such exports as rum and coffee would be ruinous. But on the alternative issue of Commonwealth status versus full-fledged membership in the federal Union, our panels, we recall, were much less harmonious.

The most significant addition to previous comments is the differences of opinion revealed among *Populares* themselves. The present structure was defended on the ground that it provides more "states' rights" than are enjoyed by any one of the forty-nine states: since it pays no federal taxes, it saves about $130 million annually for its own development—an impressive sum by comparison with a recent reduction of less than $1 million in federal appropriations. Also, the point was made that the lack of a direct voice in foreign policy is, like the question of statehood, a "little academic": in an age of global war, Puerto Rico would once more be swept into the maelstrom quite as inevitably as any Continental state that does have the privilege of a federal vote. Finally, it was contended that, since the people by their vote for the PPD have also tacitly endorsed the Free Associated State, no plebiscite is called for.

But arguments by *Populares* in behalf of eventual statehood were impressive, too. One leader put the matter in terms of the crisis of our age, especially the revolution in technology—an inevitable consequence of which is ever closer relations in time and space with the United States. The five and one-half hours, for example, that now elapse in flying between San Juan and New York will shortly be reduced to three and perhaps, before many years, to the incredible time of a single hour. Television—bad and good alike—will be "piped in" perhaps as soon as jet planes are on regular schedule. And *The New York Times* (already flown in daily) will quite possibly be radiophotoed to the Island to be sold on the streets at the same moment as *El Mundo*.

What is the point of these dramatic expectations? Granting that statehood is unthinkable *now,* they are warning signals of a possible *fait accompli* to come—that is, of an encompassment by the Continent that may be accomplished, this leader argued, less by advance planning, democratic decision making, and fervent commitments to freedom than by the irony of giant forces unleashed through man's own genius. The political consequence may be the necessity of finally deciding whether or not to pay what it costs to join the federal Union.

Moreover, what was termed by a colleague as a unilateral transfer of funds from the U.S. Treasury to Puerto Rico (for housing development, say) cannot and should not, he felt, continue indefinitely. For reasons of pride alone the people of the Island will wish, as their income rises, to pay for federal services according to "value received." But when the time arrives that reimbursements are balanced against these services, will they not also wish to take the next logical step—namely, to obtain exactly the same status as other U.S. citizens?

It is even possible, we were told, that many rank-and-file members of the PPD are themselves sympathetic to statehood. The term "opportunism" was introduced by one subcultural respondent here to suggest that lower echelons of the party membership often manifest apparent enthusiasm for a permanent "free associated state," not because they are "sold" on it, but because they know that this is the approved official policy—an "enthusiasm" that would not be inconsistent with one trait of the modal personality. More charitable was an additional opinion: the real trouble simply is that the whole issue of statehood versus Commonwealth has not been clarified in the average citizen's mind.

This lack of clarification was alleged to extend even to the language problem. Granting the need of far better mastery of English, it is not necessarily true, one leader held, that Spanish would have to be relinquished as the first language in order to win serious attention as a candidate for statehood. Even now, Puerto Rico is closer to bilingualism than any other Spanish-speaking country—an asset that Congress might recognize as a useful bridge between North and South American relations. Nor should a precedent be forgotten: the addition of New Mexico to the federal Union occurred when Spanish was still the mother tongue.

Turn now to internal Popular policy. This was frankly characterized by one leader of the party as "democratic centralism"—a policy that entrusts the government with considerably more authority by vote of the people than is true of any American state. Indeed, the New Deal philosophy of the 1930's remains, he said, still more frankly condoned than by either of its rivals, especially the Statehood party. The Hispanic tradition of strong government was also cited here—a tradition which, though it can lead to the evils of a Franco dictatorship, can also lead in the opposite direction toward a productive because empowered arm of the majority's will.

Nor should it be forgotten that the Popular party emerged partly out of the now defunct but once influential Puerto Rican Socialist party. Although far from orthodox in many of its proposals (indeed, according to another spokesman, it was less inclined toward socialism than the Popular party itself), nevertheless the Socialist party did help to clarify and establish political directions. That it largely failed to implement its own "New Dealish" program was due less to the workability of its proposals, one informant held, than to its feeble leadership.

Let us recapitulate briefly in terms of the goal of freedom. Recognizing that the concept is often perverted to ulterior ends (Trujillo, too, advocates "freedom"), it is only fair to conclude on the basis of our evidence that no such perversion should be attributed to the major Puerto Rican parties. Not only are all three remarkably nondoctrinaire; they are committed to aspects of freedom as a meaningful goal of democratic life and human destiny.

This does not mean that, after all, no significant political differences exist between the parties. On the contrary, both panels of respondents recognized such differences. Yet if a final informant is correct, these operate less in terms of overt policy than in terms of a covert struggle for social and economic power. Thus, even assuming that all three parties are committed to the goal of freedom, he was sure that the varying consequences of political success by one party as against another could still become substantial.

DOES THE WELFARE STATE IN PUERTO RICO EXPAND OR CONSTRICT FREEDOM?

But there is need for greater specificity. How, particularly, do people of the Island react to the indictment so often made elsewhere in the world that the trend toward governmental responsibility for the general welfare vitiates freedom despite sincere intentions?

The predominant answer on both levels was to deny the indictment. At the same time, no one explicitly supported either pure "capitalism" or pure "socialism" but rather a mixture of both. Only one respondent in the subcultures considered the welfare trend a dangerous one, and even she favored the public housing program. On the national level, about one-fourth of the group were critical at one or another point. (One leader pointed out that since the people knew very little freedom before, its increment under the welfare state may still be relatively small.) Yet not a single respondent opposed the principle of substantial governmental intervention in behalf of the common interest.

On the contrary, the majority would endorse more rather than less such intervention. Thus individual spokesmen, again on both levels, advocated public ownership of all utilities (the telephone company should follow the already "nationalized" telegraph and power systems) as well as expansion of the present system of proportional benefit farming through government ownership of land. At least two grassroots respondents would eliminate all of the remaining large private plantations—sugar, above all. And on neither level did any spokesman oppose the hot lunch or free shoes program in the schools; rather, especially among those who knew the program best, support was enthusiastic.

Whether or not private medical practitioners have been instrumental in preventing any Island-wide program of "socialized medicine," the fact is that, despite a broad and progressive program of public health services, the welfare state of Puerto Rico in this respect is much less advanced than, say, Chile or New Zealand. Yet, in Cañamelar, where one-half the total municipal budget was reported to be earmarked for public medical, dental, and hospital services (and where, incidentally, organized labor not only owns two drugstores but fills prescriptions for its members without charge, as well as for nonmembers at lower than average cost), no local respondent was opposed in principle to the program operating in that municipality. The only complaint heard was that services are inadequate. One physician was serving a population of 14,000, while the public dentist may have been somewhat distracted during his extractions by his second profession of lawyer! Additional physicians and dentists, who would charge fees only to those able to afford them, were urged by one spokesman.

While no one, then, resorted to oft-repeated arguments of Stateside conservatives (for example, that the welfare state "coddles" individuals), there were, nevertheless, misgivings. One leader, though not a member of either minority party, detected symptoms of "parasitism" in the expanding welfare program. Pointing to San José as one instance, hundreds of its citizens, he alleged, had obtained food and other relief from public sources after a recent hurricane, whether or not they had suffered from its ravages. Indeed, when (as in that case) "means tests" are not efficiently administered, or when social services are not regulated democratically at the local level, too many people still abuse their privileges.

It was also this leader's opinion that the public welfare program, as measured by current resources, has expanded about to its limit. Granting that still more services are needed—in, say, the field of health—his argument was that the welfare state to be successful must rest upon a sound economy, not the economy upon a welfare state. Chile was cited as a country that has already gone too far; thus over a third of its retired people were said to live upon state pensions.

Another leader pointed to the British Labor party of the early 1950's as a lesson in what the *Populares* must try to avoid. Under its leadership the welfare state of England had so outreached itself, he claimed, that no longer did it stir enthusiasm or galvanize public loyalty. Such an eventuality could happen in Puerto Rico, too, unless the habit of "letting the government do the job" is corrected in time by such programs as community education.

And there was further skepticism. The Planning Board was considered (in zoning regulations, say) to be too "paternalistic." Also, the government was accused of controlling some propagandistic media that would better be left to private enterprise, printing being singled out. (Half of all printing plants in Puerto Rico were said to be government-owned, as against less than 1 per cent in the United States.)

Related to these problems was the more purely political one of the present system of elections. One grassroots respondent recommended primaries as a way to reduce party control of candidates, and thereby of the welfare program. Another spoke of the *"compadre* government" in the Cañamelar municipality, a strategy by which Popular party members of extended families were accused of controlling key political committees in each of the six *barrios*. Finally, a leader respondent urged that elections for municipal offices, especially for that of mayor, should alternate with gubernatorial elections—the argument being, of course, that under the present system the latter invariably sweep the former into office.

These forthright doubts should not mislead us. Thus, the leader just cited did not contend that the welfare state in Puerto Rico should be repudiated. While insisting that the goal of freedom must be fought for "in every waking hour," while fearing that many citizens are becoming careless about this imperative, he was careful not to argue that a "leveling down" of the population has resulted from recent trends. On the contrary, there has been, if anything, a "leveling up" toward a middle-class society—a goal which for him is much to be desired.

This kind of judgment, regardless of expression, was far more typical than not. In the subcultures, informant after informant insisted not only that increasing state controls are not necessarily inimical to personal freedom but that—as in the case of traffic regulations—they frequently increase it. To paraphrase one, the fact that there are "more papers to fill out" is not proof of less freedom. One of the few who supported independence was of similar mind: if and when the Island achieves that goal, it should continue its welfare program. The labor movement, too, was cited as an instance of how group authority may widen the worker's freedom by protecting his rights.

Nor should the expanding cooperative program be overlooked. Though not a public welfare service, it does recognize the principle that individual freedom is not attainable in our kind of world without the active partnership of many individuals. For at least one leader, indeed, Puerto Rico should aim for a goal close to that of Finland, where about 50 per cent of the economy was said to be controlled by the cooperative movement.

A further theoretical issue is apropos here. How would our respondents on the national level react to the argument of the great Spanish social philosopher Ortega y Gasset?[1] This argument (likewise greatly oversimplified, of course) is that the modern age of collectivization threatens to become an age of mediocrity—the mediocrity of the mass man.

Answers were largely harmonious with others in this section. Three-fourths of the national panel opposed Ortega's point of view. The other fourth endorsed him in particular respects, but still retained belief that the welfare state in Puerto Rico helps more than harms the cause of freedom. Only one respondent might be charged with inconsistency: while asserting, on the one hand, that freedom for the few is indefensible (for him, a "Christian society" is even more desirable than a "socialist" one), yet he cited the archexponent of "rugged individualism," Herbert Spencer, to support his doubts of too much aid for the many.

Others of the minority agreed with Ortega that "massification" generates real dangers. One cited the aristocratic poet T. S. Eliot in support of his fears. Another held that one of Ortega's indictments is highly pertinent to the Puerto Rican culture, namely, the current tendency to accept services and carry through jobs in a haphazard way. Even more disturbing, perhaps, was a concern that imaginative leadership is not encouraged enough—that the welfare state oftener rewards meek acceptance of the average man's norms than it does creative deviations.

The more pronounced reaction was, nevertheless, hostile. Though often discussed by Puerto Rican intellectuals, the views of Ortega are not, it was held, really influential. Indeed, his philosophy, saturated as it is with upper-class biases and contempt for the lower classes, was belittled as the apologia of a waning bourgeois era. Moreover, one spokesman argued, the allegation that the old social order produced better leaders than the present order is simply to deny historical fact —certainly so in the case of Puerto Rico.

Rather, the consensus was that under the democratic welfare state mediocrity is lessening rather than increasing. Granting that any kind of bigness—whether in corporations, unions, churches, or public services—invites such dangers as conformity, they were held to be fewer today than, say, thirty years ago.

Moreover, several leaders finally reminded us, collectivization does not in and of itself support Ortega's diagnoses. The cooperative movement as it has developed in Scandinavian countries was cited again as one nongovernmental form that does not. In any case, the crucial question is: To what means and ends are the people committed, by and for whom any sort of collectivization, including the welfare state, is justified at all? A culture that gradually learns to integrate freedom with public planning—and Puerto Rico is now learning to be that kind of culture—may also learn to provide greater opportunities for personal originality, for brilliant leadership, than was ever thought possible before.

EDUCATION TOWARD FREEDOM

As a normative enterprise education in Puerto Rico is already a formal adjunct of the practical efforts to move closer to the goal of freedom. Where does it still fall short? And where may it be strengthened?

Let us deal with the former question first, bearing in mind that both questions were answered mainly by the national panel. Previous responses to allied questions would lead us to expect dissatisfaction with, for example, the considerable gap between freedom in words and freedom in behavior.

Thus, some respondents thought that education on the Island remains unclear as to its objectives except in the form of clichés. One blamed this confusion largely on continued conflict over the English policy. Another recalled the need to place the goal of freedom in its historical setting, not through a regressive nativism, but by appreciating that the future depends upon mature understanding of the cultural past. Still others revealed possible conflicts in national-level thinking: while three spokesmen were sure that freedom as an end (the intrinsic enjoyment of self-expression, say) is more important to Insular education than freedom as a means, two others were sure that the opposite is true (such as an overstress on teaching methodology or on "superficial skills" such as driving a car).

As to practice with freedom, the strongest castigation was directed against the majority of teachers for lacking rational and emotional commitment to *either* ends or means. Unfortunately, one leader claimed, they are less concerned with education as a potential force in behalf of freedom than they are with such personal problems as family, salary, and retirement rights. Also, the Teachers Association of Puerto Rico, according to a peer, encourages such attitudes: dominated as it has been by a philosophy reminiscent of old-line craft unionism, its frequently constrictive policies make even more difficult any awakening of teachers to a sense of the vast creative opportunities that await their initiative.

Freedom is not, furthermore, especially meaningful within most Puerto Rican classrooms. Many teachers, it was held, not only appear afraid to discuss questions that touch upon the government, but many students in turn are afraid to disclose disagreement with their teachers on any question at all.

Several comments were less caustic. The University was credited with encouraging awareness of freedom. "Strong arm" discipline has also waned, two leaders were sure, at least by comparison with their own youthful years in school. (Another, incidentally, regretted this trend: children today have too much license, and corporal punishment —the firm application of which he felt had contributed much to the development of his own children's character—should again be author-ized by the Department of Instruction.)

Then, too, let us credit education for providing some students with facts about political parties as well as with formal understanding of the nature of democratic institutions. Nor is it a trivial accomplishment to learn what freedoms are guaranteed by the young constitution. In respects such as this, we were told, the schools already perform well.

But what can they do further? We may group the answers to our second question around three principal imperatives.

1. Provide more opportunities to *come to grips with the meaning of freedom*. The kind of opportunity respondents had in mind rein-forces previous comments on the need to implement the democratic ideology through functional ways of learning.

Although one leader underscored the need for self-expression through art, perhaps the single most important value stressed in the present context was *participation*—a value central to the modern philosophy of freedom noted above. Just as that philosophy differs from individualism in emphasizing social relations and duties, so a modern philosophy of education should likewise differ by developing group experience and group responsibility. Education in Puerto Rico, no less than in the United States, must learn more clearly than it has the distinction between freedom as pure self-interest and freedom as deliberative harmony of varying interests.

What does this distinction suggest for school practice? For one thing, since the same principle applies to all democratic institutions, freedom within the classroom should be synchronized with the struggle for freedom outside. Thus the learner should share *in* those institutions

—labor unions and farm cooperatives, say. (The Future Farmers of America and similar student groups active in Puerto Rico could be regarded as a step in this direction.)

For another thing, teachers as well as students should learn how to experience the meaning of participation. To vitalize this need, one leader proposed frequent seminars where, over extended periods free from distraction (the "activity month" might thus be utilized), teachers would come to grips with basic problems in education and culture. Opportunities for informed lay citizens and experts in various fields to meet at intervals with regular members of these seminars would further enrich their significance. Above all, teachers should discover that participation is a matter not only of *consent* but of *dissent* as well.

Another original suggestion was for a "thinking and planning board" to be established as a "staff arm" of the Secretary of Education. As against the necessary but more pedestrian tasks performed by other divisions of the Department, this board would deliberately concern itself with far-reaching issues and proposals. Fundamental to its task would be the problem of educational norms, and therefore of the goal of freedom as it affects the curriculum, administration, and all other phases of school life. The board should consist of a trio of outstanding, imaginative persons, all full time—one, a social scientist; two, a philosopher of culture and education; and three, an expert thoroughly familiar with practical aspects of Insular education. Its directives would be as broad as the fields represented: to prepare policy papers, to promote cutting-edge experiments based on these papers, and to work closely with all other divisions of the Department. Augmenting the board would be a representative advisory commission of lay citizens to serve as a liaison between it and the general public.

2. Provide more opportunities to *share in the development of the democratic welfare state*. The basic assumption here, as one respondent saw it, is that education rightly understood is a major ally of this kind of state. Hence students and teachers should be directly and indirectly involved at every stage in designing, analyzing, and affecting the latter's numerous functions. At the same time, effective education can, by teaching people how to utilize their own capacities, reduce some welfare functions.

Another saw the task to be chiefly one of constructing experimental models in the schools—models that could be tested out by economic, social, and other public agencies, including education itself. Small children could begin with fairly simple ideas (planning of school gardens is one that has been mentioned), thus acquiring early the habit of improving their environments. Model-making would of course increase in complexity all the way up to the university level. Responsibility, too, would increase: as young people developed pride in their own contribution to the shaping of public services, they would be far less likely later to regard them as something to exploit to their personal advantage.

One of the most audacious of all proposals stemmed from a vision of Puerto Rico as a planned "garden island." A master plan was already said to be in blueprint form which would connect all communities by helicopter in less than an hour, thereby enabling decentralization of population and industry to a still greater extent than already possible through the network of public electric power lines and highways. The effort to spread *Fomento* factories throughout the Island, rather than to concentrate them in the San Juan area, is one preliminary step toward the future goal. Yet the problem of how precisely to maintain a practical balance between metropolitan and rural centers—how to develop what was called "decentralization without scatterization"—remains complex.

For education, meanwhile, the opportunity is clear. Citing Lewis Mumford's *The Culture of Cities*[2] as a resource, one leader urged that problems of Insular planning be brought directly into the schools. Let students share in planning their own work. Let them learn all they can of the thirty-three local planning boards (how many know about them now?), as well as of the impressive operations of the central body. Let them face such stirring questions as how to prevent the evils of the "megalopolis" (the monsterlike city), and how to develop Insular solidarity along with the kind of subcultural differentiations noted by the Steward team.

Here is still another invitation to establish pilot projects. Schools in different regions of the Island should develop experiments in community planning suited to their own conditions. (The sugar workers' union in Cañamelar is one of a hundred laboratories waiting to be used.) Then, as they succeed, the effects of such experiments could "cross-fertilize" with those of other regions.

3. Provide more opportunities to *vitalize education's role in the*

sphere of politics. The wide support earlier noted in favor of teaching controversial questions is reiterated now in a more dramatic way— namely, in favor of bringing the most heated problems of politics into the Island's classrooms.

Subcultural recommendations that these problems be treated "objectively" were bolstered on the national level. In order that teachers become proficient in handling such emotion-charged issues as independence, statehood, and Commonwealth status, one leader proposed another pilot project in the handling of controversy: how to avoid political indoctrination (a practice held by some to be more common in the early days of the Popular regime than it is today), while yet permitting enthusiastic arguments for and against conflicting points of view.

What principles should guide such a project? One relevant suggestion was that discussion leaders learn to avoid the fallacy that the "whole truth" is the franchise of any one party—a fallacy reminiscent of the Western movie with its "hero" on one side and its "villain" on the other. The need rather is to develop the "art of disagreeing" without generating enmity—perhaps, too, the "art of tolerance" which enables one to recognize that one's opponent may possibly be right.

Nor, we were informed, should the practical importance of these "arts" be overlooked. An ever-present danger to democracy is the shock of disillusionment that follows from discovering that the actual values of some political movement are at odds with those officially professed. When citizens are well informed, such disillusionment is much less likely to occur.

To widen their experience, should teachers and professors themselves actively engage in politics? No respondent denied their right as citizens to vote and to express opinions. But to do so in any "professional" capacity was questioned by several spokesmen.

The issue is confused, however. A recent law prohibits elementary and secondary teachers (who are defined as employees of the government) from political campaigning. Yet the law does not apply, we were told, to members of the University faculty (who are not technically so defined), nor does it prevent teachers from being elected to political office (three of our subcultural respondents, we recall, were officers of municipal assemblies) if they are "finger candidates"—that is, chosen and elected without active effort of their own.

Nor were respondents agreed that the law is justified. One in particular felt that the quality of political officials would be improved if teachers as well as professors oftener ran for office, perhaps going on leave from their classroom duties during campaigns. Two others argued that the effort to divide educational from political institutions is in any case false: openly or not, they are always profoundly related. Certainly no teacher or professor should exploit his position; demagogues, as one expressed it, are as despicable in education as they are in politics. Nevertheless, both teachers and students should become directly and conscientiously involved in political problems of the community—indeed, to do so would be one important way to implement the principles of functional learning with hardheaded experience.

But there was also disagreement as to the place political matters should occupy *within* schools and colleges. One grassroots respondent recommended that only the "aspirations," not the programs, of parties be included in curricula; the issues, he felt, are too explosive. A leader was convinced that any kind of political activity would be a divisive force. Others distinguished sharply between lower and higher levels. One favored discussion but not direct participation by students in the lower schools. Another argued that, while elementary and secondary schools should enculturate a framework of allegiance to the Commonwealth (thereby exposing children to indoctrination which he elsewhere abhorred), higher education should not become a party to any one political ideology but invite critical inspection of all alternatives. Still others urged organization of student debating societies and political clubs. (One of the latter now exists in the College of Social Sciences of the University.) Also, mock elections should be conducted during election years and active "political campaigns" should be encouraged among rival slates of student-council candidates—a practice reported to be already under way at Inter-American University, San Germán.

All this, however, was considered insufficient by the overwhelming majority of leaders. A rule established years ago by the administration of the University of Puerto Rico prohibiting candidates from speaking at political rallies on the campus should, they argued, now be rescinded. Despite a record of violence in the mid-twenties, a student strike in the thirties, and another strike in 1947 (protesting, it was said, the banning of a Nationalist party rally in the campus auditorium), the time has come when such a prohibition can no longer be reconciled, if it ever could, with the professed value of academic freedom.

Nor is the rule enforceable, one respondent held. It cannot and does not prevent leaders of the government from speaking on the campus in their official roles. Yet how difficult it is to draw a line between speeches that are political and those that are not! Even lectures by a visiting social scientist on the status of the Commonwealth are bound to be interpreted by some critics in bitter political terms. A more logical policy, then, is to invite all legally constituted parties to express their views freely in classrooms and general meetings under conditions of fair discussion and equality of treatment.

One last point. It will be recalled that the technological revolution has been viewed by one respondent as an omen that the Island's political fate may be decided for it by the sheer power of that revolution. For him this does not mean the acceptance of cultural "determinism." Indeed, the present type of Commonwealth program may successfully continue for some years. Yet it cannot be assumed that such a program offers any permanent solution. Rather, he contended, the need is to look forward *now* and to appreciate that one of the most crucial of all educational tasks is to face "head on" the major political options— options which, in turn, point directly at conflicting issues of Puerto Rico's status in the future.

FATALISM OR RENEWAL?

The preceding paragraph brings us to the climax of this chapter and of this entire part. In the light of Puerto Rico's insecurities, its burden of unsolved problems, are its people realistic, after all, to sustain the note of buoyant hope in the goal of freedom that has illuminated so many of our pages?

Answers are possible in terms of two opposite extremes which we shall call "fatalism" and "renewal." The first symbolizes the attitude not only that cultural patterns of the past have determined the character of a given culture but that its future character is somehow *pre*determined. The second term symbolizes a kind of cultural rejuvenation—an awakening after a long slumber, as it were, to face the issues of life with virile power and "great expectations."

That a fatalistic attitude has hitherto permeated the cultural configuration is not only anticipated by previous discussion (most directly, in Chapter 7) but is bolstered here. Philosophically, the Arabic culture with its strongly fatalistic world view was said to have penetrated Latin America by way of the Mediterranean peoples. Practically, the title of Tugwell's book on Puerto Rico—*Stricken Land*—suggests feelings of despair and defeat which, until recently, have been far more typical than not.

Although one informant refused to dignify the fatalistic attitude with any term except "ignorance," several others held that it is still prevalent on the metacultural level, even among educated groups. It was considered less so, however, in the upper as compared with lower levels of the population (it is "almost nonexistent" among the leadership) and similarly less in the urban as compared with rural areas. Also, fatalism was said to be rapidly receding—birth control being specifically mentioned as one of many reasons, the growth of co-operatives another. Today, one leader contended, a fatalistic *jíbaro* would not go unchallenged in a rural community discussion group—indeed, the notion that one is just "a drifting leaf in the wind" is decreasingly acceptable. Others were sure that Puerto Rico retains less of this philosophy than, say, Africa, India, or China.

Yet, one leader feared, were the Island to fall victim to dictatorship, the seeds of fatalism could germinate again. The question thus arises whether the idea of renewal applies to the culture in more profound ways. On a short-term basis, no dissent was heard. But beyond this, several respondents were chary—one reminding us of the rapidity of political and economic change by comparison with psychological change. Renewal, another said, certainly does *not* mean another "building boom."

Nevertheless, most respondents held the idea to be justified. One spoke of the difference in Puerto Rican poetry: while as recently as the 1930's, Luis Pales Matos, for example, expressed a mood of boredom, emptiness, and pessimism in much of his work, today the poetic mood is oftener in a major than a minor key. Again, whether or not most citizens could subscribe wholly to the spirit of the following dictum taught to his son by another respondent, it is probably congenial to many: "Difficult things we do right away; impossible things take a little longer." Albert Schweitzer's philosophy of "reverence for life" was also mentioned as reflecting more and more of the Puerto Rican spirit.

What, finally, of education's part in enhancing this confident mood? It is impossible, two said, for education here or anywhere else to contribute in any far-reaching way to cultural renewal as long as it remains so largely an authoritarian system—Germany being perhaps the best (or, more precisely, the worst) example of what happens in a crisis situation under that kind of system. Nor can renewal guided by the goal of freedom become, as it should, the touchstone of a philosophy of education until learning and life form an active partnership. Indeed, if the schools have not thus markedly contributed, the blame lies not so much with them as with the culture which provides them with whatever vitality they have.

Yet several spokesmen were insistent that the schools do, of course, make *some* contribution. Partly through them, faith in human equality —the twin goal of freedom—is becoming meaningful. The scholarship program is giving hope to thousands of young people who could not otherwise break the chains of family poverty. The optimistic philosophy of educational progressivism, based on North American pragmatism with its belief in man's intelligent capacity to master his own destiny, has exerted at least minor influence upon Puerto Rican schools—an influence directly counter to fatalistic attitudes. And the notion that the happy life is one of maximum self-fulfillment is by no means, even now, without educational relevance.

Still, by far the greatest opportunity is yet to be grasped. For one leader this means first of all that renewal is impossible without hard, sustained work (a virtue in behalf of which progressive education was not adjudged a sufficient advocate). Just as no one, he insisted, can become a first-rate artist without "sweating blood," so no culture can renew itself until this lesson is carried into practice. The Italian Renaissance, after all, took a good two hundred years of prodigious labor before its creative age reached peak florescence.

By contrast, however, with earlier creative ages the unique challenge of our own was viewed in terms of its *democratic* promise— a challenge, above all, to public education. Musical expression, to take one instance, should not be limited to the few of superior ability; nor should physical training be confined to those with athletic prowess. Moreover, just as economic renewal, though indispensable, should be synthesized with philosophy and art, so vocational and liberal education should equally be synthesized. For, granting the need to provide special opportunities for gifted students and potential leaders, every citizen, we were told, should be able to participate as a unified social being in the renewal of his culture.

THE GOAL OF FREEDOM: SUMMARY AND EVALUATION

New values—that is, comparatively new to Puerto Rico—are now emerging. By far the most important is freedom itself. Self-realization, with due regard for the interests of other selves; the several major rights embodied in the Puerto Rican constitution; the privilege of choice, participation, and experimental planning; the deliberative harmonizing of group interests—these were among the features of freedom emphasized by various panel members.

They are features which, though far from achieved, are accepted increasingly as future norms as well as in present practice. Also, according to our evidence, they are thus accepted by all three major political parties. Indeed, the current platforms of the *Independentistas, Estadistas,* and *Populares* were found to be more alike than unlike, both in their liberal socioeconomic policies for the Island itself and in their belief that some form of continued relations with other countries—notably, of course, the United States—are essential. This is not at all to say that no significant differences prevail among the parties, nor that respondents were agreed on the best solution to the problem of ultimate status. Political independence, to be sure, was favored by a small fraction only. But statehood as one ultimate alternative and the "free associated state" as the other each received impressive support. Nevertheless, especially on current policies, the three parties give the impression of a political spectrum with variations of degree oftener than kind.

This judgment is exemplified by the welfare state in Puerto Rico. Despite occasional skepticism, both panels tended to support the growth of governmental and other forms of collective services as an aid rather than a hindrance to personal as well as social freedom. By the same token, strong opposition was revealed toward the aristocratic social philosophy of Ortega y Gasset.

But there was no opposition to the conviction that Insular education should now take swift advantage of the culture's growing commitment to the goal of freedom. Granting present weaknesses, four important ways were suggested in which the schools could now take hold. These were, first, to come to grips with the *meaning* of freedom in practice as well as theory; second, to share directly as well as indirectly in improving the welfare state; third, to make education an active collaborator in political experience; and fourth, to share, as the fatalistic mood recedes, in cultural renewal.

Our own numerous critical reactions to previous issues have prepared the ground for the issue of freedom. In general, we entertain no serious doubts that our panels are justified in their key contention: growth toward the goal of freedom in Puerto Rico is not only a fact but one that has the genuine, often articulate support of the great body of citizens.

Let us be content, then, to reinforce several of the comments and recommendations already made. The triangular issue of ultimate status is, we think, likely to be less disturbing as time goes on than the issue of enforceable world order—an order to which, of course, Puerto Rico should belong. For this reason, we underscore a plea made in the preceding chapter for realistic and prolonged attention by the schools to the even more complex and wider problem of what kind of international relations can enhance freedom for people everywhere on earth.

This does not mean that the programs and policies of the Island's political parties should be sidestepped. More rather than less attention to them is essential—attention that includes not only the right to study all parties impartially and thoroughly, but to hold political meetings on University premises; not only the right of teachers and professors to become concerned politically, but to run for office (with due respect, at the same time, for high standards of academic conduct); not only the right to discuss political issues in classrooms and forums, but to reach uncoerced consensuses that might fairly resolve specific issues.*

Whether the exercise of these rights would lead eventually to greater or lesser public support for one as against another party remains to be seen. It might even lead in time to a political movement unlike any of those now most influential. Nevertheless, for reasons discussed especially in Chapter 4, we venture the prediction that the Republican party, at least in its internal policies, would especially suffer from searching educational analysis of its motivations. That is, while we do not question the fairly liberal orientation of some of its

* For further analysis of the consensus principle, see pp. 426-431, 440-441.

spokesmen, we are impressed by a revealing point made by one informant: behind their common devotion to the means and ends of freedom, the two principal parties—the Republican and Popular—differ in their premises as to the proper locus of socioeconomic power. There seems little doubt that, were the former to win office, greater concentration of that kind of power in the hands of private industrial alliances would tend to increase; simultaneously, the trend toward its dispersion (a principal aim of the latter party) would tend to decrease. By the same token, the expansion of the democratic welfare state would be checked by a Republican regime in perhaps somewhat the same ratio that it has been encouraged by the Popular regime.

We do not, of course, deny (nor, we remember, do most respondents deny) that the welfare state carries its own burden of dangers to freedom. But the way to deal with these dangers is not, we think, to turn back to older, largely outmoded political arrangements based implicitly upon historic notions of individual (and competitive) rights. It is, rather, to move forward to the social and cooperative conception of freedom stressed by several spokesmen. Such a conception, which the schools are obligated to clarify in the mind of every citizen, calls especially for *democratic planning for democratic goals*—planning which avoids paternalism and parasitism by involving, at every stage, the largest possible share of the people. To suggest that the schools serve as major aids to such activity strikes us as one of the most exciting of all suggestions encountered in this study.

At the same time, freedom is, after all, an individual as well as collective value, and the stress placed upon self-expression as one important—if not the single most important—element of freedom is paramount. In Puerto Rico, where we have found personal *dignidad* and allied values to be high, the recommendation is therefore completely apropos to provide abundant opportunity for children to manifest their own individual qualities in their own distinctive ways. Teachers and classrooms that place conformity first suppress if they do not permanently multilate these distinctive ways. Of course obstacles to self-expression stand in the way. But the measure of Puerto Rico's educational advancement is well determined by the extent to which it moves ever closer, however painfully and slowly, toward the norm of *personal* as well as *social* freedom.

PART V

CULTURE AND EDUCATION IN PUERTO
RICO: A COMPARATIVE EVALUATION

INTRODUCTION TO PART V

THE PURPOSE of our concluding part is threefold: first, to compare our research findings and interpretations with others; second, to draw together some of the most significant of these findings in order to see them in broad relationship; and third, to point ahead by suggesting next steps for Puerto Rican schools.

The immediate problem is one of selection of sources for comparison. Clearly it is impracticable to survey all of them. We have therefore decided upon several delimitations. One is to confine ourselves only to those studies having a central bearing upon culture and education as we have considered these terms. Accordingly we do not attempt to encompass tangential fields of research such as biology, economics, or geography as such.

Another delimitation is to consider only evidence that has been obtained through research methodologies. Thus we do not include highly personalized contributions or other impressionistic works. Although often these contribute much to cultural understanding, it would be difficult for purposes of comparative evaluation to determine with any assurance which of such studies are less or more true to the realities of Puerto Rican life than the opinions and other personal beliefs of our own respondents.

Finally, we have decided to exclude research studies published before 1950. The date is a little arbitrary, but it may be justified by the fact that more material directly relevant to our interest has appeared in the present decade than in any previous ones. In a few cases, the data included in these studies were gathered in the half-decade preceding 1950.

In the following chapter we review social-science studies. For our purpose the most useful is the Steward work. Next in usefulness is a group of recent contributions (likewise developed by the Social Science Research Center of the University) in which aspects of cultural order—family and class, most notably—are examined by a number of experts. Several of these studies were still in manuscript at the time we examined them; therefore what we report may in some instances be modified in their published versions. A few studies not sponsored by the Center are also considered briefly.

Chapter 19 deals principally with educational research, although some of it, while conducted by educators, falls primarily within the field of social science also. We conclude the chapter with an evaluative "balance sheet": this serves not only to point up some of the strengths and weaknesses in the content of our study but to highlight the evidence reviewed. It should be noted that no attempt is made to evaluate our research methodology. This task is left for the Appendix, I.

Chapter 20 returns to the need for "action research." Therefore we ask how and where education may implement our findings and appraisals. This discussion is selective and critical in terms of our own philosophy of education. We do not always agree with the majority of our respondents; in some instances we deviate from almost all of them. Yet for the most part this concluding chapter builds directly upon what we have learned from our investigation. And the proposals put forth are, we believe, in accord with the national character of the Puerto Rican culture.

CHAPTER EIGHTEEN

COMPARISONS WITH OTHER EVIDENCE: SOCIAL SCIENCE

"THE PEOPLE OF PUERTO RICO"[1]

LET US BEGIN with comments upon the so-called coffee subculture (or, more strictly, subcultures) of San José, as interpreted by Steward and his team of anthropologists. In the several intervening years between Eric Wolf's extensive field work and our own more limited venture, one would hardly expect to find glaring changes. It was, nevertheless, possible to observe that the population continues to flow from this rural area and toward more industrialized communities. Also, to reduce the migration of coffee pickers and other agricultural workers, wages have risen somewhat and, simultaneously, the traditional *junta* of voluntary cooperative labor teams has apparently declined further.

The percentage of children in school has increased along with such learning resources as textbooks. Activities of the local Catholic Church have likewise increased, the three local priests now making fairly frequent visits to chapels in the rural *barrios*. Yet perhaps the single most visible symbol of change in the past decade is the sprouting of television aerials from many San José housetops (some no better than those of the San Juan slums)—thirty being counted from the high school balcony alone.

In numerous ways, our own observations and discussions with San José respondents were substantiated by *The People of Puerto Rico*. We select the following examples somewhat at random: the rather crude methods of coffee processing; the prevalence of small farms specializing in mixed crops (especially tobacco), along with a few large "semifeudal" *haciendas;* the high incidence of poverty in both town and country; the gradual fading of some traditions; the common use of child labor by parents; misunderstanding if not hostility between customary personal ways of the *jíbaro* and impersonal ways of the bureaucrat; the lack of coordination between agencies staffed by these bureaucrats; the "nonfunctional" superimposition of North American standards and practices upon lower-class school children by middle-class teachers; a widespread conviction that education offers the best assurance of upward mobility; and considerable conflict (especially in middle-class values) as such mobility develops tensions between older and newer patterns of the culture.

At a number of points, the Steward work focuses upon important aspects of the San José subculture that could have enriched our own presentation. One is the agricultural class structure, which Wolf divides into landless workers, peasantry (owners of small plots), middle farmers (owners of small farms), and *hacienda* owners (of large farms). The significance of this structure may be sharpened by noting that in one of the San José *barrios,* nine *haciendas* were reported to embrace 50 per cent of all the coffee land, with 250 small farms embracing the other 50 per cent. Also, the fact that the government has provided small plots for many *agregados* in San José and elsewhere is an innovation not noted in our overview of the cultural process.

Another revealing aspect is the lengthy recreational character of religious holidays. We did call attention to them, but not sufficiently. Something like forty days per year are set aside, according to Wolf, "to institutionalize leisure." This is culturally significant for several reasons—among them, the somewhat different value traditionally attached to work in Puerto Rico as compared with the United States. It is a difference, however, which we have found declining and which of course varies among the subcultures of both countries.

Related to this phenomenon is the important role played by household saints. If, as Wolf contends, the "saint cult" is the most dominant form of religious expression in rural San José, then it is unfortunate that so little opportunity arose to discuss this culture complex with our respondents.

In a few interesting respects, our findings are either not supported by or tend to qualify the preceding work. Thus hostility to the "Spaniard" as stereotype was expressed still more bitterly and sharply by several of our respondents. On the other hand, Wolf notes the hostility of the native Spanish expatriate to stereotyped Puerto Ricans —for example, that they "don't like to work."

Again, the portrayal of the San José woman as without "any rights to assert herself directly in her own behalf until she is beyond the childbearing period"[2] would be too strong a statement for many of our respondents to accept. To be sure, one of the most traditional rural subcultures is being described here. Nevertheless, the picture is already being modified along with the patriarchal structure of the family as a whole.

Nor would Wolf's description of the town cultural order be quite acceptable at every point. The use of terms like "wealthy" and "newly rich" to describe even the top-level "upper class" of San José is misleading in the respect that, so far as our own evidence reveals, one could hardly include most of them in this category by Insular standards, though they might be so regarded within the municipality.

It is likely, too, that the preceding work errs in differentiating as sharply as it does between the town and rural workers—the former being described as "urban and sophisticated," the latter as rustic and provincial. That rural-urban lines are gradually being dissolved has been frequently stressed in our study—a contention which, to a considerable degree, is borne out in the subjective comparisons of our town and country respondents. Likewise, the racial prejudice noted by Wolf among San José *jíbaros* was not confirmed by our evidence; on the contrary, they revealed less prejudice than did urban respondents. Finally, this statement would be emphatically denied not only by the evidence hitherto presented but, as we shall see, by that of our next chapter: "Most members of this [middle] class . . . want independence in the future."[3] Rather, we have found that most want either statehood or the Commonwealth as a permanent arrangement.

We turn now to Cañamelar. As noted in Chapter 9, changes in this sugar-cane subculture have been so rapid in the near-decade elapsing between the field work of Sidney Mintz and ours that, even though our residence in the region was far less prolonged, it seems safe to say that his description of at least the pattern of mechanization is already out of date. Thus in about the four years preceding our study, all of the following operations were reported to us as virtually mechanized in full for the first time: planting, cultivating, weed-killing, irrigation, loading, and hauling. Also, we recall that the only remaining major operation performed by hand—cutting—is now more and more threatened by experimentation with machines.

Migration is another respect in which the cultural process appears to have accelerated. Whereas Mintz stresses the almost insuperable difficulty of escaping from the toils of the subcultural economy, today thousands of workers fly to the Continent during the dead summer and fall season; many others eventually send for their families and remain there permanently. This increased mobility may have been aided by the improved wages and other benefits provided by the local union: in contrast to the weak condition described by Mintz, organized labor in Cañamelar is now relatively strong and solidly inclusive of the bulk of the working population. (At the time of our interviews, the local union leader proved to be a much more dominating figure in the community than was apparently true in 1948 and 1949.)

Another factor that may help to account for greater migration is the diminishing role of company stores. Though they still exist, they do not, according to our informants, hold such life-and-death power over the workers by extensions of credit as they did only a few years ago. Workers now trade more frequently in the town stores, which, in turn, offer keen competition to those operating at the *colonias*.

While it would be possible to contend that, in the last decade, changes in Cañamelar have been more rapid than in San José, nevertheless the over-all picture provided by the Steward work seems to us equally true to cultural realities. A few of the many ways in which that picture strengthens or enriches our impressions deserve recording: the phenomenon of a "seasonal culture" which, in turn, centers in the "class culture" of a "rural proletariat"; the huge absentee-owned *colonias*, each consisting of thousands of acres, which have totally replaced the nineteenth-century *haciendas* (the latter resembled in various productive methods and human relations the *haciendas* still remaining in San José); the widespread intermingling of Negroid and Caucasoid stocks; the poverty and insecurity of the great majority; the progressive shortening of the harvest season; the high percentage and continued acceptance of consensual marraiges; the hierarchical structure of impersonal authority provided by the *colonia* managers and their subordinates; the system of intraclass ritual kinship centering in the *compadre* tradition; and the complete absence of a traditional upper class in the town.

But, as in the case of San José, certain elements of our own study are not supported by or tend to conflict with the Steward evidence. For example, though our field work was conducted during the busiest season, some unemployment still prevailed—a possible further consequence of increasing automation. Again, while the feeling of suspicion if not hostility by workers toward managers, and vice versa, was quite apparent in our visits to the harvest fields, yet we must recall that one of our young respondents, himself an *agregado*, spoke with real affection of a *mayordomo* who was honored as a *compadre* in his family and often helped the sick by driving them to the hospital or in other ways. In the interpersonal sphere, the contention of the Steward report that Cañamelar husbands treat wives in a more equalitarian fashion than in San José was not indicated by our evidence, though opportunities for firsthand observation were much less frequent than verbal reports from our respondents.

The place of the town in the total life of the subculture is also regarded by the Steward work as more limited than we would suppose from our observations. That it is the headquarters of the powerful labor union and the center of health and other community services, that it contains the only senior high school in the municipality, that it is the political trunk line to the state capital, and that retail trade is shifting away from the *colonias* to its own stores—all add up to a somewhat higher appraisal of the town's importance by our respondents.

The role of magic is revealed in both sets of findings, though not without another variation between them. Whereas the earlier study claims that the "only areas in which superstitious practices appear actively to obtain are those having to do with love and hate,"[4] it will be recalled from Chapter 7 above that both *santiguadora* practices and spiritualist séances remain fairly common.

One of the distinctive features of the Cañamelar report is its systematic discussion of "values and value changes." While excusing itself, rather oddly, for dealing so briefly with contradictions in values "because they were not clearly manifested in people's behavior,"[5] yet any recognition of the problem at all is a welcome aid. For example, some of the positive traits of the Puerto Rican personality stressed by our respondents are reiterated, though none of the negative ones. Mintz also makes the point that value conflicts are likely to be induced particularly by the struggle between traditional group identity and increasing emphasis on individual performance with its drive for upward mobility. Our own evidence, however, indicates many other sources of conflict in Puerto Rican values—one of them for the opposite reason, namely, the shift from agrarian individualism to industrialism with its accompanying socializations. Although most Cañamelar citizens have already been forced to undergo the shift economically, one might conjecture that one of the sources of their value conflicts is that such socializations are still too recent to be amenable psychologically—that is, infused into their personality patterns. At any rate, we have shown in Part IV that the value problem is a good deal more complex than we might be led to assume by the paucity of treatment not only by this section of the Steward study but by the entire volume.

Still, it is hardly appropriate to play up deficiencies and omissions; anthropological research, partly because it is so young a science, is almost always vulnerable to criticism. Rather, let us turn to the primary question: To what extent does *The People of Puerto Rico* tend in general to strengthen or weaken our interpretation?

Perhaps the most important negative comment is that we paid too little attention to subcultural differences. Though we cannot speak with any authority of the other subcultures studied by the Steward team, even our brief comments on San José and Cañamelar above should be sufficient to demonstrate that these two, at any rate, are by no means identical. The class structure, for example, is different between the two communities. So, too, is the impact of industrialism as a force for change. And even in values one notes such distinctions as the stronger Catholicism of San José and the stronger intraclass loyalties of Cañamelar.

Our interpretation is not thereby vitiated, however. In the first place, as the Steward work itself repeatedly stresses, Puerto Rico has many cultural characteristics that are common to the whole; our concern is primarily with these. In the second place, we have not ignored differences: the range of disagreements among our respondents both within and between the two panels amply testifies to the pluralism and, in Steward's terms, "multilinear evolution" of even so small a culture—a range that we may now partly attribute to subcultural differences. The latter could, indeed, be recalled in many specific ways —in the zealous Catholicism and enthusiasm for Spain of one of our San José teacher respondents, for example, or in the equally zealous pro-unionism of a Cañamelar peer. As we shall see in the next chapter, differences extend also to our third subculture—Hermosa—though we cannot compare these directly with the Steward work.

But, in the third place, similarities between subcultures should not be minimized either. Particularly when we throw the spotlight back upon education, we note many resemblances in the Steward work between the brief treatments of this institution in San José and Cañamelar—the middle-class character of the teaching staff, say, or the high value placed upon education as a means to upward mobility. Indeed, education is an especially clear lens through which to focus upon the total culture, because it is much more centralized and hence more uniform at least in formal practice than in a country such as the United States. What is true of education, moreover, is true of certain other spheres—health services being one example. As both the Steward volume and our respondents sometimes imply, the growth of the welfare state tends to diminish dissimilarities and to encourage common structures, programs, and goals.

One further question: To what extent, if any, does the *theoretical* framework of the Steward data reinforce our study? In certain respects, we question whether it does—particularly in the cursory attention it usually pays to such dimensions as the metacultural. Also, its ecological approach offers a causal explanation of cultural effects which would no doubt appear to most culture theorists from whom we have learned as simplistic—a probable reason why aspects of the culture that do not comfortably suit that explanation are often casually treated.

The constraints of the ecological approach might help to account for the relatively sparse attention paid by the Steward team to potentialities for controlled change toward democratically agreed-upon goals—potentialities which are crucial to the educational-cultural philosophy through which we have sought to interpret Puerto Rican life. Steward's primary hypothesis is that pluralistic environmental-technological patterns largely determine the character of all other cultural phenomena, education itself being one, and the resulting work offers brilliant proof of the operational fruitfulness of this hypothesis. We do not, however, find adequate recognition or analysis of what, to us, is at once the essence and the pivotal problem of the culture today: its as yet uncrystallized, largely unreleased, but enormously creative and energetic mood.

THE FAMILY

Several careful research studies have been made in this core area of the Puerto Rican cultural order. The Steward study itself devotes considerable attention to the family; but rather than compare further those findings with ours, it is helpful to note how one of the research assistants in that study, the Puerto Rican anthropologist E. Seda Bonilla, interprets them in the light of an independent investigation[6] that included analysis of another sugar-cane community.

Seda holds, as do many of our own respondents, that the father usually occupies a place of strong authority governed by the norm of *hombre de respeto* (respected man)—a position that exacts obedience both from his children and, to some extent, his wife. The latter, in turn, is expected to be a hard worker, caring for the children and household and working in the fields when necessary. While her social life is largely restricted to her own home, the father is free to move about the community and to practice the double standard. Female virginity before marriage is a categorical imperative, while even in marriage undue erotic activity on the wife's part is looked upon with suspicion. Female unfaithfulness after marriage is a major catastrophe that may result in harm, possibly even death, to suitor or wife or both. Courts as well as public opinion were said to be often lenient of such *crimen pasional* (crimes of passion).

The symbolism of romantic love is apparently more common in some subcultures than others, but the chaperonage of unmarried girls is habitual to them all. Consensual marriages are also frequent, though religious ceremonies are often desired when enough money is available. Childbearing solidifies and legitimizes consensual marriages in the eyes of most of the community. Differentiation of the role of children by sex also begins early—boys and girls tending to play separately and to perform different kinds of tasks. Boys are encouraged to be *muy machos* (very virile and masculine), but the sexuality of girls is protected and concealed.

Seda's over-all picture is much more elaborate than we have indicated. To be sure, he does not stress the distinction noted in the Steward study that husband-wife relations are more equalitarian in Cañamelar than in, say, San José, nor does he support in any emphatic way the contention of some of our respondents that within the home a rather "matriarchal" pattern prevails. Yet on the whole his picture confirms our own. And it supports our assertion that the family pattern, including courtship and sex relations, closely resembles the dominant pattern in Latin America.

Several Center studies deal with the crucial problem of overpopulation— their data being derived from lower urban and rural classes since these have the largest families. The first,[7] by Paul K. Hatt, enriches our own evidence in several interesting ways. He found, for example, that a substantially larger percentage of women approved of their working outside the home than did men—46 and 28, respectively—and that these percentages rose with the amount of education. Also, women wanted fewer children than did men, and fewer of them were willing to accept consensual marriages. Urban folk, on the average, preferred fewer children than rural folk, and so too did those with more education. Birth control was favored by young couples more than by older ones. Perhaps the most challenging conclusion of this study is that "there is scarcely a variable related to either the values of low fertility or their spread which does not show a significant correlation with the educational level"[8]—a conclusion that points up such responsibilities for the schools as we have indicated in earlier chapters.

Hatt's investigation is the precursor of two further works. One, by J. Mayone Stycos, usually supports our view of the family, though not without amendments.[9] His own sample indicates that the drop in consensual marriages is not as great as our information suggested. He also tends to emphasize more than our respondents the relative meagerness of change in the family structure.

Stycos joins with Reuben Hill and Kurt Back in another, more extensive investigation[10] that helps us further. Fathers, for example, were found to be more "progressive" in their attitudes than mothers. Thus, while both tended to be fatalistic, the belief that one must accept one's lot was even stronger in the latter than in the former. At the same time, the "patriarchal" pattern was indicated by the restrictions of social life imposed upon wives. Men were also more satisfied with their marriages than women.

One-third of the sample of women entered marriage almost totally uninformed about sex relations, while two-thirds of the men had experienced sex relations before marriage. A majority of wives likewise expressed some or much embarrassment in telling their children about sex or in being examined by a physician, while substantial majorities were embarrassed to talk about sex with their husbands. Fifty-three per cent, indeed, said they never did so, and 47 per cent never discussed birth control.

The need for sex education, so strongly endorsed by many of our respondents, receives vigorous support from the Hill-Stycos-Back work. Knowledge of contraceptives, the authors point out, is usually learned too late to be useful. Only about 5 per cent of the childbearing mothers were served by the many available clinics, due to such factors as fear, ignorance, inadequate publicity, and sometimes indifferent staff members. Yet 40 per cent of all families have had some experience with birth control—sterilization of women being the commonest means.

The four most frequently mentioned explanations of high fertility in Puerto Rico were said to be (1) the value of large families among agricultural people; (2) the desire of males to prove their masculinity; (3) ignorance of birth control; and (4) the Catholic Church. All four have been disproved, these authorities contend, as major causal factors. The core of the problem centers in the weak motivation for small families, despite this professed ideal. To strengthen motivation, a formal and informal educational plan is essential, in which the Division of Community Education as well as the public schools should take active part. Also, the public birth-control clinics could be made much more successful by fairly simple alterations of practice. Fear of opposition to birth control is largely illusory; the great majority would respond to an effective and vigorous program that could include many of the suggestions made by our own respondents.

Another family study,[11] by David Landy, reinforces many of the points already made. In addition, it emphasizes perhaps more strongly than others the "matriarchal" pattern of child-rearing practices in a sugar-cane community. Obedient and humble children, highly dependent, are the norm. Punishment for infraction of rules is severe but erratic, and demonstrations of affection are less common than one might have anticipated from the picture of, say, Cañamelar or from some comments by our informants.

One other family study, in some ways the most pioneering of all, has provided important background for those already cited. Lydia J. Roberts and Rosa L. Stefani surveyed the *Patterns of Living in Puerto Rican Families*[12] across vertical and horizontal lines. Though the title is rather misleading in the anthropological sense of "patterns" as configurations (this would require examination of the implicit culture, which the authors avoid), nevertheless the work is a mine of useful information. Its decade-old statistics on living arrangements, diet, income, education, and many other objective aspects now require modification. But the over-all description continues, in many respects, to provide an objective framework for the picture we have tried to draw.

A final comment should be offered on a brief but revealing study[13] by Reuben Hill on courtship patterns. Limiting his sample to University students, who might be expected to hold less traditional attitudes than the average, he nevertheless supports our own findings on this subject. While the Mainland belief in freedom to select one's mate is widely accepted, opportunities to practice such selection were found to be much more restricted in Puerto Rico. Dating of any kind is considerably less frequent and woman students have about half as many dating experiences as men. "Going steady," moreover, is much commoner than "open field" dating, with the result that neither men nor woman have as much opportunity to get acquainted with persons of the opposite sex as do Continental young people. Indeed, Hill estimates that the Puerto Rican student rarely knows as many as two persons well enough to consider as a marriage partner.

The practice of chaperonage, stressed by our respondents, was also found to be widespread. Approximately three-fourths of the women and one-fourth of the men in the sample had never experienced unchaperoned dates. Only 18 per cent of the men limited their dating entirely to the latter type, and then the total average number of dates per male student in this group was less than nine. The desire to protect the young woman's "reputation"—itself integral to the virginity cult—was indicated as the principal reason for continuance of this Hispanic-influenced custom.

THE CLASS STRUCTURE

Melvin M. Tumin's elaborate work on stratification and social mobility,[14] so far as it could be made available to us in unfinished form, extends well beyond our own interpretations. Yet in general it tends to bolster them at least as fully as do the studies thus far reviewed. We first note a few points of explicit support.

Basing his study on extensive interviews that also cut both horizontally and vertically, he found that most citizens now tend to classify themselves, at least verbally, in terms of three main strata— high, middle, and low—rather than merely in terms of "rich" and "poor." The middle class may be, therefore, the increasingly important and relatively new fact of vertical order in Puerto Rico. The development of this order is accompanied by various tensions that were less pronounced in earlier periods—for example, the social impulses leading to marked inequalities in wealth and comfort as against the traditional value of human equality; the tendency to exercise authority rather forcefully as against ideological commitment to democratic processes; the focusing upon instrumental values, such as economic development and material success, at some cost to the intrinsic values of family and religion; finally, the shift to impersonal relationships, symbolized by contracts of the market place as against the older personal relationships of individual status.

Tumin, a sociologist, has found further that upward mobility is accelerating. More specifically, fathers are less different from their fathers than they are from their children with respect, say, to the amount of education and income. Thus, in general, Puerto Rico may be regarded as an "open" class society.

Considerable optimism, moreover, prevails with regard to temporal order. Not only was the future hopefully anticipated by the great majority of the sample, but the present was considered to be better than the past. Increased governmental services were seen as an important contributor to this "benign trend," along with better jobs and more education. The minority who adjudged the present to be worse than the past attributed it to such factors as allegedly increasing vice and disrespect.

Correlations of color and class position are high. For example, the percentage of those who were classified as Negro or *trigueño* increased with decreasing education and income. Though high regard was expressed for people of all colors, opportunity for people of dark skin pigmentation was also admitted to be less than for those who are light.

The percentage of Catholics in the sample was about 78. Significantly, Tumin also found, however, that neither religious nor family patterns have changed as much as, say, education or occupation—the latter being more largely matters of public policy than the former. (This observation would be quite in accord with the concept of focus mentioned in Chapters 9 and 10.)

At the same time, traditional familial values were said to be weakening as the values of wealth, luxury, and education strengthen. The flow of population to urban areas could also help to account for this shift in values in so far as both educational and occupational opportunities are greater than in rural areas. And yet, that the influence of the latter upon value orientations remains strong might be inferred from the fact that 78 per cent of the sample were born either in the country or in small towns of the Island. Only twenty-nine of the thousand respondents were born in San Juan.

One other point of support for our own picture derives from Tumin's evidence that a substantial majority of those in the upper stratum rated themselves as middle class. This same stratum, incidentally, felt itself to be most "depreciated" by members of other strata. Yet that it is "looked up to" by the lower strata was also confirmed by his evidence. We shall omit additional confirming data except to anticipate our "Sociological Survey" in the next chapter: there the figures we give on our three subcultures are, with minor exceptions, broadly supported by the Tumin data available to us.

The important question does remain as to some of the ways in which his study throws additional light upon our own. Of particular interest is his discovery (anticipated by Hatt) that education is a more significant differentiator or indicator of class position than any other major factor, such as residence, income, or occupation. In nontechnical language, this means that a person's place in the vertical order of Puerto Rican culture is more likely to be indicated by the number of years of schooling he has received than by where he lives, how much money he makes, or what he does for a living. In this respect, at least, Tumin's findings are at variance with those of the Steward work. The latter, we recall, proceeds from the hypothesis that Insular ecological patterns are the most constant indicators of class as well as various other cultural characteristics. It is also at variance with one leader respondent's contention that several factors, none of them primary, determine class position.

In this framework, Tumin draws numerous relevant inferences, only a few of which we are able to note here. One of the most enlightening is that a "leap" occurs between groups with four years of education or less and those with more than four years. For example, children of parents in the former groups received an average of less than six years of education; while children of parents with only one to four additional years received more than nine years of education— over 50 per cent again as much as children of the lower group. A less impressive ratio of increase occurred above the five- to eight-year level: children of parents who had attended high school received over ten years of education, and those who had gone to college received over twelve years. The amount of education that an average parent expected to provide for his children also sharply increased when his own education rose above four years. A quotation here from a preliminary report (with Arnold S. Feldman) is too provocative to omit:

The new values appear to become effectively institutionalized once the fourth grade of school is passed. The traditional society, with its self perpetuating cycle of illiteracy, landless poverty, and low levels of hope and aspiration, seems to be broken open at this juncture, and there emerge new citizens, prepared for the new world in terms both of attitudes and skills, and ready to move on to new life paths. . . .

. . . . [If] this critical level is the point at which the new emerges from the old, it can become the focus of two very different kinds of development. On the one hand, it may become the central point of attention of efforts to bring all members of the society beyond that point, and thus provide for . . . mass mobility . . . in an open society. On the other hand, this four year level may become a line of increasingly rigid demarcation between a relatively well-to-do middle class and an impoverished industrial and agricultural laboring class. . . .

. . . . [It] would appear to be the greater part of wisdom . . . to think in terms of the ways in which . . . relatively small increments of education and income make relatively large differences in the intelligence and ambition with which new values are pursued, once a minimum level has been reached.[15]

Tumin also points out that fathers of least education are the least perceptive of the way that education can provide opportunities for social mobility. Thus 87 per cent of the illiterate group held that knowing merely how to read and write is primary in making one's way ahead; 75 per cent so held of the group with one to four years of schooling; 55 per cent of those with five to eight years; 18 per cent with nine to twelve years; and none of those having thirteen or more years. In general, the more education a person has, the more efficacious it appears to him as a way of advancement.

Yet, according to Tumin's interpretation, self-perception of class position is relatively weaker among all strata—not merely among the least educated—than our own respondents led us to conclude. Indeed, there was a strong tendency throughout his sample to identify with the lower or middle stratum and to make little reference to the upper stratum. Again, even among middle and upper groups, the average subject was inclined to overestimate his own sense of worth when measured by such tangible criteria as economic rewards. Thus the prestige on which he prides himself, or the importance he attaches to his work or voice in community affairs, is often incommensurate with his income, occupation, or even educational level.

In a sense, Tumin is implying that there is too little correlation between a value such as *dignidad* and the material satisfactions that are necessary to give dignity functional meaning. Accordingly, the kind of class consciousness that develops from a sense of one's total involvement with others of like condition is not yet maturely developed. This conclusion might be exemplified from our own study by the attitudes of teachers: the prestige values that they attach to their position are sharply at odds with their economic rewards. Yet, at least partly because affiliation with organized labor would seem to them a downgrading of professional prestige, most of them oppose the kind of concerted strength that union affiliation might be able to provide.

Nevertheless, the very high regard for values of personal worth is not, Tumin thinks, to be lightly dismissed either. Freedom is one of these values. The problem, he feels, is to open the door to its more complete expression by—among other ways—reducing present inequalities, enlisting a wider range of talent in political decision making, and soliciting disagreement and criticism. All of these suggestions are supported by various respondents of our own.

The only other research work[16] to which we can refer in this section is by Thomas C. Cochran, an economic historian. Dealing principally with cultural and business patterns of the Puerto Rican entrepreneur, Cochran adds to our own incidental data on these patterns. Many top-level businessmen, according to his evidence (derived from a study of seventy leaders), maintain their enterprises on the basis of family and friendship rather than on the kind of impersonal contractual arrangements that are more characteristic in the United States. Smaller commercial firms are still less Continentalized in technological and related processes than the larger ones, but in both types (as we, too, noted in discussing personality traits) there is likely to be paternalistic regard for the worker's pride and similar cherished values.

One of Cochran's principal theses is that, though business and industrial practices are changing, cultural patterns serve as a brake upon them. In general, the business elite of Puerto Rico is "individual-istic" in ways that are rather distinct from those of North America. Citing a number of scholars in support, he finds, for example, that its typical representatives tend to trust their own emotions and values and to depend upon face-to-face relations after the manner of the Spaniard. Thus they also tend to resist the kind of mergers and collective operations that a technological society increasingly demands. The impact of Mainland ideas and techniques has been greatest in heavy industry and banking, least in rural retailing, with wholesaling and light industry somewhere between.

In certain respects, this study deviates from our own. For example, it notes less intermingling with *americano* businessmen either socially or professionally than our informants indicated. Again, we remember that some of the latter (not without opposition) were inclined to regard cooperation as more of a primary value than Cochran indicates, though, to be sure, they were more concerned with the average citizen than with the upper class alone. Nor was there agreement on the Puerto Rican's amenability to technological innovation or habits of efficiency: a number of our respondents considered him quite amenable, though again they were not thinking so exclusively of the business elite.

Our panels did heavily stress, as does Cochran, that the upper stratum of vertical order is more Spanish in its cultural orientation than any of the strata below, that it has relatively meager political influence, and that its resistance to some forms of acculturation and other processes could retard the rate of industrial progress.

PERSONALITY AND OTHER RESEARCH STUDIES

Research in personality has not yet reached the stage in Puerto Rico where much evidence can be offered for or against our interpretation.

Carlos Albizu, a clinical psychologist, has administered Rorschach and other projective tests to cross-sectional groups of subjects with fascinating results. Thus in a lower-class study[17] he found a strong inclination toward fear, shyness, hostility, and distrust. Rigidity rather than spontaneity in emotional expression was dominant, as were pessimistic and fatalistic attitudes. Imagination and the capacity to empathize were weak.

Albizu's findings are supported, he contends, by behavioral patterns. The range of experience of these lower-class subjects is extremely circumscribed, with relatively few contacts and organized activities. Moreover, external manifestations of hospitality and out-reachingness conceal inferiority feelings and underevaluations of self, so that it is difficult to establish friendly relationships that are informal and warm—a difficulty that may be at least partly attributed to patriarchal family patterns of the kind described by Landy, above, with their corollary of overdependency during the formative period of early childhood. At the same time, in Albizu's judgment, the present government with its democratic social philosophy is developing a sense of self-realization as an achievable ideal, so that it is reasonable to expect that the basic personality structure is already in process of being modified.

One other work on personality,[18] by Kathleen L. Wolf, a psychiatric social worker, pioneers in the field of "ethnopsychiatry." It utilizes a number of Freudian or neo-Freudian concepts, but its field operations were chiefly anthropological, deriving data from both San José and Cañamelar. The study supports the Steward thesis of significant differences between these subcultures, but goes further in its differentiations of the town middle-class and deeply rural patterns of the coffee subculture, with varying consequences for personality traits. We select a few of the most germane observations.

According to Mrs. Wolf, women in rural San José are forced to suppress their aggressive impulses because of the dominant male role in the family, although they find some release of their hostilities through such channels as gossip and psychosomatic ailments. Children, moreover, are frustrated by factors that include unsatisfying feeding routines, sibling rivalry, and overprotection, particularly of the girl child. The authoritarianism of the father is induced primarily by the ecological pattern, which requires him to supervise strictly the meager resources of farm and family.

The middle-class town pattern of San José differs from that of the country due, perhaps more than any other factor, to the greater autonomy that women exercise by virtue of their income-producing roles. Although nominally the husband remains the dominant figure, actually he may suffer from considerable conflict between this traditional norm and his acceptance of the higher socioeconomic status that his wife makes possible. Conflict is still further intensified by differences between the rather relaxed standards of work performance of the traditional middle class and the more energetic ones exacted by economic and governmental routines under Continental influence.

Middle-class children of the town, in turn, are victims of conflict for several other reasons, such as uncertainty about the professed authority of the father; differences between customary Puerto Rican practices in child training and those recommended by North American-trained pediatricians; further differences between the practices of grandmothers or rural-enculturated maids (either of whom may assume much of the responsibility for the children's care) and those of the mothers themselves. Also, unlike the rural area, lack of participation in family chores and obligations may be followed by the sudden thrust of adult responsibilities with minimum preparation for them.

Cañamelar personalities tend to differ from either of the other types mainly because of the collective nature of its ecology. For example, aggression toward individuals may be released through group feeling and action against the sugar corporations and through the ritualistic excitements of the Pentecostal sect. The greater equalitarianism of husband-wife relations and wider opportunities for socialization also result in less frustration for the woman than in rural San José. Children, too, are less constricted by a narrow home environment, and suppressed hostility to the father may be reduced since he is less dominating—a consequence of his weaker economic status.

Even the common practice of sending children to live with relatives or ritual kin such as *compadres* is perhaps less injurious to the child's sense of security and identification than it would be in less socialized communities.

In the light of particular research studies cited above, a number of Mrs. Wolf's rather categorical assertions would require qualification or even rejection. (The Seda and Landy studies, for example, would apparently question some of her effort to draw subcultural distinctions as to child-rearing patterns; the Hill-Stycos-Back study contends that both the desire to limit family size and female ignorance of sex are greater than she indicates for the rural subcultures.) Nevertheless, both she and Albizu strengthen our interpretation of personality in at least two respects: first, in stressing chronic frustration and conflict; and second, in underscoring some of the same negative traits. Her explanation of middle-class instabilities partly induced by the woman's less dependent role could also help to explain the critical attitude which a number of our male respondents, themselves middle class, manifested toward this alteration in traditional family relations.

It is noteworthy that neither her study nor Albizu's places as much weight upon positive traits as do our respondents, though both recognize that the present evolution of Puerto Rican culture may lead to a greater balance. Mrs. Wolf implies that the subculture affected most by industrialization—Cañamelar—is already somewhat healthier than the others studied in terms of personality development: children, for example, were said to be more outreaching. Our own efforts to make friends with school children did not confirm this observation: in all three subcultures, many responded to our overtures with little shyness, quick warmth, and a readiness for fun.

One brief study in political science[19] may be mentioned that compares methodologically with those reviewed thus far. Peter Bachrach has shown from a sampling of University students that 40 per cent of the latter rejected their fathers' political preference preceding the 1956 election. More of this large minority favored the *Independentistas* than the *Estadistas,* and more men than women students disfavored their fathers' preference. Students of lower income inclined toward the *Populares,* those with higher income toward the *Estadistas*—a fact in general accord with our own data. Less in accord is the possible psychological significance indicated in the difference between students and their fathers: Bachrach suggests that this may mean a weakening of the *personalismo* tradition with its autocratic overtones, at least among more educated groups. In our terms, it may also mean that, more rapidly than we were led to suppose by some informants, the gap between ideological and implicit attitudes related to the working of democracy is narrowing.

Very little research has been done in the cultural dimensions of religion. Tumin and Feldman briefly studied a mass phenomenon in 1953 when great crowds visited a rural Puerto Rican district expecting the appearance of the Virgin Saint.[20] A sample of the crowds was interviewed; only a small percentage expressed skepticism. Many had attended with the hope of a cure for physical ailments. The investigation strengthens our own in this regard: scientific thinking has by no means penetrated the life of the culture in any consistent or thorough way. Likewise, it reaffirms our findings in the respect that supernatural religion is not for most citizens a pervasive preoccupation. Reaction to the expected "miracle" was transitory and confined largely to an immediate expectation that illnesses or infirmities would be dispelled.

Under the restrictions we have placed upon our selection of other research studies, this completes our review of the field of social science. It is worth repeating that no claim to completeness is made. At the same time, those considered are sufficiently important and representative of recent works to provide us with some basis on which to form a comparative evaluation of our own findings and interpretations. Before rounding out this evaluation, let us turn to studies still more directly concerned with education.

CHAPTER NINETEEN

COMPARISONS WITH OTHER EVIDENCE: EDUCATION

THIS CHAPTER is concerned with some of the evidence thus far available from educational studies that strengthen or weaken our interpretation, but here we also include data that we ourselves have gathered by means of questionnaires. As indicated in the description of our methodology (Appendix, I), these data have severe limitations. Nevertheless, they are sufficiently useful to warrant inclusion because they help, though they do no more than that, to provide our anthropological data with further perspective.

The results of two questionnaires are reported—first, a brief sociological survey of the cooperating subcultures conducted by social-studies teachers in each of the three; and second, some reactions to educational issues by the superintendents of schools in the three subcultures. We then turn to a few additional studies of Puerto Rican education, and conclude by striking a balance sheet of deficits and assets as to our total findings.

THE SOCIOLOGICAL SURVEY

Originally, this survey was planned to help us determine more clearly whether we were justified in assuming that the urban subculture of Hermosa can be regarded as primarily middle class. It was decided, however, to administer the questionnaire (Appendix, III*) also in the two rural subcultures with the hope that useful comparisons with the urban subculture would emerge. The survey further provides a kind of bridge between the social-science evidence just reviewed and the more strictly educational evidence hereafter to be considered.

Beginning then with education, a marked difference prevails be-

* See pp. 451-453.

tween our rural and urban communities as to the amount of schooling obtained by male adults in our sample. In San José, 8.5 per cent (all percentages are approximate) were high school graduates; in Cañamelar they constituted 5.6 per cent; in Hermosa, 33.5 per cent so reported. Again, whereas 20.7 per cent of male adults in the Hermosa findings had graduated from college, only about 2 per cent had done so in San José and Cañamelar.

Correlations between educational and other factors such as family size could undoubtedly be proved high. Thus the number of children per family in Cañamelar was reported to be 5.3 as against 2.3 for Hermosa. (San José figures were not comparably reported here.) Again, the average monthly income of male family heads in Cañamelar was $82, while in Hermosa it was $296, about three and one-half times as much. Or take mechanical devices: 47.5 per cent of the Hermosa families owned a car, as against 17 per cent in San José and 6 per cent in Cañamelar; 85.5 per cent (almost exactly twice as many) owned television sets in the urban as in the two rural areas; 63 per cent owned automatic washers in Hermosa, as compared with only 17 per cent in San José and 6 per cent in Cañamelar. The percentage of radios was remarkably high in both rural subcultures (86 per cent), but virtually 100 per cent in the city.

Reading habits were also revealing. Twice as many families took *El Mundo* (80 per cent) in the city as in the country, and the number of magazines subscribed to, although low, was much higher in the city. As for baseball, movies, races, and cockfights, Hermosa families in every case were more active in these forms of recreation than those in San José and Cañamelar. In all three communities, however, children watched television, if one was accessible, well over an hour a day on an average—Cañamelar being the highest with 3.5 hours.

But the most striking difference was in terms of occupation. In Cañamelar, 33 per cent of the adult males in our sample were classified as laborers (a percentage still lower than would be expected from the Steward research). The remainder were almost entirely skilled workers, none of them holding positions above lower-middle status unless in the possible case of a single merchant. In San José, 26 per cent were classified as laborers, 22 per cent as farmers (at least some of whom were probably nonowners), and 19.5 per cent as merchants (at least some of whom were doubtless lower-class owners of tiny stores).

Only three professionals were included in both samples: two teachers and one lawyer. But in Hermosa white-collar occupations such as those of clerks and secretaries were far commoner than any other kind: 27 per cent. The remainder were skilled workers, merchants, and professionals (the latter, such as engineers, constituting about 10 per cent).

With regard to home ownership, the percentage was much higher in the country than in the city: 91 per cent in San José, 88 per cent in Cañamelar, and 48.5 per cent in Hermosa. But this in no way suggests higher quality in the former communities; on the contrary, the average rural home is extremely small and inexpensive. Some indication of the difference here can be seen in the fact that the average Hermosa home in the sample contained 4.5 rooms, while the average Cañamelar home contained 3.2 (and undoubtedly smaller) rooms.

In a number of interesting respects, differences did not break along urban-rural lines. The San José sample reported the largest percentage of Catholics: 82 per cent. Cañamelar and Hermosa were almost even: 70.5 per cent for the former and 71.5 per cent for the latter. These two subcultures were also very close in the respective percentage of Protestants: 21 per cent and 22.5 per cent, as against only 9 per cent for San José. In all three subcultures, women were more faithful attendants at church than men.

Politically, Hermosa reported 73 per cent, Cañamelar 79 per cent, and San José 67 per cent who had voted the Popular ticket in the last election. The latter was proportionately higher in its *Estadista* vote, 28 per cent, as compared with 12 per cent in Hermosa and 9 per cent in Cañamelar. In all three, the *Independentista* vote was minute: about 6 per cent in Cañamelar, 2 per cent in San José, and 3 per cent in Hermosa.

Finally, a few miscellaneous comparisons. Seventy-four per cent of our San José families contained members who had worked in the States, as compared with 94 per cent in Cañamelar but only 31 per cent in Hermosa—an obvious consequence of the seasonal problem in the two rural areas. The number of children in school per family also revealed that Cañamelar and Hermosa were closely alike with 1.7 and 1.8 respectively, as compared with 2.3 for San José. In all three, women were primarily housewives: 70 per cent in Hermosa, 69 per cent in San José, and 73.5 per cent in Cañamelar. As for the frequent purchase of lottery tickets, San José was highest with 91 per cent, Cañamelar was lowest with 26 per cent, and Hermosa averaged 59.5 per cent.

Returning to the middle-class character of our urban subculture, we may benefit by comparing it briefly with the study of upper-class San Juan families included in the Steward work.[1] Educationally, 50 per cent of the adult males in the latter study had finished college, over twice as many as in our Hermosa sample. The average number of children per family was somewhat higher than for Hermosa but lower than for the rural subcultures. In terms of income, the information provided (not always entirely comparable) would indicate that monthly earnings averaged at least two to three times higher than in the Hermosa community. Nearly all families owned at least one car and over 40 per cent owned two or more cars. The amount of reading materials was also much higher—over 75 per cent of the upper-class families subscribing to four or more U.S. publications, for example, as compared with less than one per family in the Hermosa sample. No comparable data were available for other forms of recreation, but occupations were again indicative of a marked difference: nearly half of the upper class were reported as professional, the other half as engaged in finance, commerce, or agriculture, with a large number obtaining income from more than one occupation. Religiously, the proportion of Catholics was also consistently higher than in Hermosa. (Women again were the most active participants.) Politically, the proportion of statehood supporters was over three times higher. Independence supporters were about the same in both Hermosa and the upper-class group: 3 per cent.

What inferences may be drawn from these comparisons? A number of hypotheses could be suggested for further research—for example, that more cultural similarities prevail between Cañamelar and Hermosa than between the latter and San José, a phenomenon which, if true, could probably be explained by the fact that San José remains more of a traditional rural community than does Cañamelar with its "factories-in-the-field" economy.

We are most concerned, however, with the question of whether or not our urban community possesses the characteristics of a middle-class subculture. The answer depends upon our criteria of what constitutes a middle class and therefore upon a number of value judgments. If we follow such criteria as those of C. Wright Mills in *White Collar*[2] for the Continental middle class, there would seem to be little doubt that our choice is defensible. Or if we follow Tumin in his correlations of education with class and status in Puerto Rico, we are again apparently justified. The Hermosa community is markedly "higher" than either San José or Cañamelar in educational achievement, income, possession of automatic devices, abundance of reading materials, and occupational stability and status. On the other hand, it is markedly "lower" in all of these respects than the Puerto Rican upper class (with the doubtful exception of occupational stability). Politically and religiously, moreover, Hermosa reveals middle-class characteristics consistent with previous generalizations. Thus it gives fairly strong minority support to the Statehood party, but by no means as much as does the upper class. And it is represented by a much larger minority of Protestants than is the upper class.

In terms of family size, the Hermosa profile corroborates earlier findings to the effect that fewer children are born to the better-educated classes, although the fact that the typical upper-class family apparently has more children than the middle class might be accounted for both by the more devout Catholicism of the former and by its financial capacity to support more children. The birth rate of the upper class, however, is also declining, according to the Steward study.

In additional respects, our sociological survey reinforces the validity of our anthropological evidence—for instance, as to the size of families of our respondents noted in Chapter 4. Moreover, differences and similarities between the two rural subcultures reviewed in our preceding chapter on the basis of the Steward work are reconfirmed in at least two respects: San José is more strongly Catholic but less strongly Popular than Cañamelar.

But the Steward portraits are also supplemented by our findings. According to our criteria, Cañamelar is lower in the vertical order of Puerto Rican culture than San José in the following quite decisive ways: it has fewer high school or college graduates, more children per family but a smaller proportion in school, fewer mechanical devices, more laborers, and less home ownership. Finally, it has more members of families who have worked in the States.

As for distinctions between the rural and urban subcultures as represented by our respondents, we venture but one generalization: the higher level of education, occupation, and other factors revealed by the sociological profile of Hermosa supports our impression that the urban panel tended as a whole to be somewhat more sophisticated and liberal in its attitudes toward a variety of issues—sex education being one—than the panels in either San José or Cañamelar. Even so, similarities of attitude and belief between all three subcultural panels outweighed differences more than they do in the Steward study— partly, no doubt, because the majority of our respondents had achieved above-average education with accompanying upward mobility; partly, also, because we were not primarily interested in retesting the Steward hypothesis of subcultural differences.

In only one conspicuous respect does our sociological outline seem to conflict with the judgment of most of our respondents—namely, their concern over the large proportion of women who have changed their principal occupation from housewife to outside wage earner. If this outline is reliable, less than one-third have changed thus far, a percentage which, incidentally, varies but little from that of Roberts and Stefani[3] despite the fact that their data were gathered over ten years earlier than ours. But a more exact analysis might modify this surprising observation.

THE SUPERINTENDENTS' QUESTIONNAIRE

Because no superintendent of schools was represented among our grassroots respondents, a brief questionnaire (Appendix, IV*) was submitted to the top school officials of San José, Cañamelar, and Hermosa. The purpose was twofold: to benefit by their experienced judgments and to provide a further basis for determining how far our own findings could be considered representative of expert educational beliefs and attitudes. We group the answers in the usual sequence.

1. *Cultural order.* The superintendents agreed unanimously that parents would respond to opportunities in adult education dealing with issues important to their own lives, and that home economics for boys should be encouraged. They were dissatisfied with present offerings in vocational education for high schools and they opposed labor-type teachers' unions. Also, they held that Puerto Rican history and traditions are not adequately treated in the curriculum, that new

* See pp. 454-456.

materials are needed, and that high school students are quite capable of dealing with such fundamental problems of temporal order as prediction and progress.

They disagreed among themselves as to the adequacy of parent participation in school affairs, of student preparation for family life, of understanding of scientific method, and of sensitivity among teachers to class values other than their own. Nor could they agree on the question of whether primary emphasis should be placed in the curriculum on the past, present, or future.

2. *Cultural process.* Unanimity prevailed on the following needs: more educational decentralization and local autonomy; more and better teachers in the arts; more and stronger student councils; the holding of student social affairs on school property; higher taxes earmarked for education; more opportunities for self-expression in classrooms; and more attention to problems of cultural change. Indeed, they agreed that a serious gap exists between the program of the schools and that of other institutions, and that the schools can play some part in creating cultural patterns. Finally, all three favored the teaching of controversial issues—communism and political status, say—but they differed as to the proper age level.

They disagreed further on the following: whether or not the present English-language program is, on the whole, successful; what should be done to improve recreation through the schools; the desirability of interracial dancing in high school; the adequacy with which schools utilize community resources; the adequacy of service by the Department of Education in supplying materials; whether or not teachers are sensitive to the emotional dimensions of learning; the adequacy of mental-hygiene training for teachers; the level on which the best teaching occurs; whether or not the most learning takes place inside or outside the school; the adequacy of television programs; and the effectiveness with which the three R's are now taught.

3. *Cultural goals.* Our trio of collaborators unanimously favored greater participation in political affairs by students and teachers, and the organization of juvenile cooperatives. They agreed that students and teachers are not sufficiently concerned with international relations; and while they wished to see sex education in the schools, they again differed among themselves as to age level and method.

They differed, too, on the issue of whether or how to introduce religion into the curriculum; of the adequacy of teacher discipline; of whether the development of character is a more important goal of education than making a living; and of whether teachers are helping students to become conscious of the goals of the culture.

Do these various reactions strengthen our findings? Certainly they do so in the respect that widespread differences on educational issues apparently prevail in strictly professional as well as partly lay circles of the citizenry. More precisely, the three superintendents disagreed in 55 per cent of their answers, as compared with 45 per cent in which they were unanimous. Their disagreements, moreover, permeated all three categories of questions.

A glance at their mutual agreements will reveal that they strengthen certain predominant reactions of our own panels. On perhaps only one issue do they seem more unified than the latter—namely, in their belief that teachers and students should be active in political affairs. Their mutual disagreements, however, would indicate a tendency to be less critical of specific policies and practices than are many of our respondents. This is especially true when we compare their views with those of our national-level panel.

OTHER EDUCATIONAL STUDIES

Among doctoral projects or dissertations in education that were made available to us, Ramón Mellado's is easily the most relevant for our purposes.[4] He attempted to determine whether Puerto Ricans tend to be "conservative" or "liberal" on political, socioeconomic, religious, and authoritarian-versus-experimental attitudes. In all four he found them to be generally middle-of-the-road, with some inclination toward the liberal side. By his criteria, they were, however, less liberal in their religious and political attitudes than in their socioeconomic and authoritarian-versus-experimental attitudes. Moreover, they differed rather sharply according to groups—seniors in the College of Education being most liberal, laymen of the older generation being most conservative, with teachers and others being somewhere between.

Mellado's findings offer qualified support for our own. In the light of our findings we question whether there has been anything like a "radical change" away from "dogmatism and authoritarianism" toward "experimentalism and democracy." But we do detect a gradual trend in that direction, and our evidence also agrees that usually the experimental viewpoint increases in clarity with the level of education. Moreover, if progress is defined as historical development in a liberal direction, then Mellado's study supports many of our respondents who, with him, see Puerto Rico moving toward increasing socialization as well as political and religious freedom.

These conclusions are supported in a different way by Rosa L. Stefani's study[5] of the values held by urban working-class mothers in their child-rearing practices. Nearly three-fourths of her sample were found to be more democratic than either authoritarian or anarchistic in behavior, as measured by such criteria as participation and responsibility. The degree of democratic behavior also tended to increase in public housing as compared with slum areas.

Stefani's results are more optimistic than our own in the respect that, especially in the urban and rural lower classes, the family pattern was adjudged by a number of our respondents to be still largely authoritarian (though, to be sure, the father was held to be more responsible than the mother) and rather unstable in structure. Nevertheless, her findings support ours in three respects: first, there is a trend, however sporadic, toward democracy in family behavior; second, there is need for much wider family education for parents; and third, there is need to give children more encouragement in developmental tasks that lead to growth of democratic values.

One other educational study,[6] by Ramón Ramírez López, deals directly with values in culture and education, though again in a different way. From a rough sample of adults in various walks of Puerto Rican life, he found that they ranked their own values, from greater to lesser importance, in the following order: (1) theoretical (e.g., knowledge and truth); (2) religious (e.g., belief in a deity); (3) social (e.g., friendliness); (4) aesthetic (e.g., appreciation of beauty); (5) political (e.g., power); and (6) economic (e.g., usefulness). The first three types of value ranked more closely together than the last three.

A more carefully validated sample was taken by Ramírez López from teachers and university students. Although the ranking was not quite the same either in these subgroups or between them and the one above (aesthetic values, for example, tended to be placed still lower by teachers than by the wider population sample), nevertheless, for the sample as a whole, theoretical, religious, and social values ranked higher than political, economic, or aesthetic values.

These findings support our own less firmly than those of Mellado or Stefani. Thus the majority of leaders were wrong, if Ramírez López is right, in holding that aesthetic values are more prized than intellectual or theoretical values. Again, a majority of our subcultural respondents were not representative, according to his evidence, when they placed a life of action (associated with economic and political values) above a life of contemplation (associated with theoretical values). Where our findings are sharply divided, however, his own may help to resolve the disagreement: the issue of whether Puerto Ricans are more cooperative than competitive, or vice versa, would tend to be answered, according to his evidence, in favor of the former alternative. Again, whether or not young people are concerned with values inherent in the great political and economic issues of our time would be answered more negatively than affirmatively, at least by comparison with their interest in other values.

On a few important points, nevertheless, Ramírez López also bolsters our findings, such as the view of several respondents that young people may be somewhat less ambitious for economic success than their Continental counterparts. Still more interesting is the agreement that women tend to rank theistic religious values higher than do men—a fact also reported by Mellado and noted in our own evidence. Lastly, the tremendous variation that we have noted in individual reactions to issues of value is supported by the Ramírez López study.

Other doctoral research studies are likewise helpful in endorsing recommendations echoing those of various respondents. Oscar E. Porrata urges an administrative policy that would increase democratization and decentralization.[7] Aida A. de Vergne proposes a practical plan for sustained supervision of beginning teachers especially in rural areas.[8] Herminia Vasquez recommends reorganization of the secondary program under College of Education leadership.[9] Marion Garcia de Ramírez finds pressing need for more effective guidance of the undergraduate teacher-in-training.[10] José A. Cáceres proposes that courses in the social foundations of education be reorganized to give closer attention to research studies of the Steward type, with laboratory experience in problems of rural life.[11]

Cecelia G. Dávila endorses a vigorous program of community education for people in the rural areas who are being resettled in housing developments.[12] Such a program, she finds, would require much more coordination than now prevails among the many agencies now involved in one or another aspect of this movement. Dávila's statistical data also help to validate our less precise findings: for example, 32.8 of the *agregados* in her sample were consensually married, their average annual income being about $500.

A partial survey of research activities conducted by the Department of Education, some of them promoted by the office of the Superior Council (governing board of the University), discloses a few additional studies of interest to our own. Perhaps the most revealing one was designed with the cooperation of the Department of Health: using control groups, the hypothesis has apparently been proved that scholastic attainment rises when social workers and psychologists work systematically to improve mental health in both teachers and students.

For unaccountable reasons, none of our respondents chose to cite the so-called Morovis Plan as an educational innovation. Under this plan, students in towns too small to support regular high schools work independently with study guides and intermittent help from laymen and visiting teachers. Tests by the Department have shown that its graduates do as well in the University as those from regular high schools.

Other experimental projects have been attempted by the Department in the past, we were informed, but apparently discarded in largest part when criticism arose before sustained effort had been exerted to test their workability. Research thus far conducted in the schools has been mainly in the form of statistics and scholastic or related tests. One Division of the Department—Community Education —has been an exception, however.

The Division maintains an "analysis unit," the most significant achievements of which, in terms of our interest, have been two scientifically controlled surveys of the attitudes of citizens toward community problems.[13] Guided by research specialists from the University of Michigan, these studies provide a wealth of data that underscore not only some of our own findings but a number of other studies treated in this and the preceding chapter. They may serve as a partial recapitulation, while also revealing certain deviations.

The first study was concerned with rural life. A "composite" countryman, for example, is a laborer with an income of about $500 per year, a third-grade education, and three to four children. He has a radio, but otherwise his recreation consists mainly of social visiting. His wife's recreation is even more circumscribed, for she mixes little with others outside the home.

Four out of five countrymen indicated that they would like to remain where they now live (a point at variance from some of our evidence), but younger people are moving more and more to urban communities. Half the rural population find it difficult to reach a good road or a town (another point of variance), though very few families are isolated from others. Social contacts tend to increase with the amount of education, but 60 per cent still do not read books or government publications.

How do rural people look upon their local communities? Inadequate roads, lack of water, and lack of electricity were most emphasized as problems—with lack of schools, poor economic conditions, and limited health facilities next in order. Interestingly, poverty was not stressed as a problem for which any local solution could be considered feasible (an echo of fatalistic attitudes?), and facilities for recreation were rarely regarded as an important need.

Of special significance for our educational findings and recommendations was the discovery by the Division's research team that only 40 per cent of the sample could recall any local community efforts whatsoever to deal with their problems. Moreover, 50 per cent thought that the government should provide solutions, while only 17 per cent held that the local community should itself take some action. The commonest barriers to action were considered by the subjects to be poverty, lack of schooling, and lack of prestige. In general, the less education achieved by rural people, the less confidence they appeared to have—a clear anticipation of Tumin's findings. Yet 64 per cent were sure that community meetings would be helpful and useful.

The importance of education is also indicated by the fact that it was more frequently mentioned as a criterion of leadership than either political connections or financial status. Indeed, the latter ran a poor third—a ranking reminiscent of the value study by Ramírez López and to some extent of our own. Dependence on leadership was, nevertheless, heavy*—one of the problems sharpened by the Division's research being that of building new leaders from the resources of the local community instead of depending upon those with already established power or prestige.

The second study covered many of the same problems in the urban area of San Juan. The sample was drawn from slum, middle-class, and upper-class families. Seventy-seven per cent earned less than $3,000 per year, and 36 per cent less than $1,000. Only 7 per cent earned more than $6,000. The average total of education was 7.6 years. Approximately 42 per cent had lived in their present homes five years or less, and about the same percentage hoped to move again soon. The commonest reason for moving to San Juan was, of course, the expectation of improved economic conditions. Sixty-five per cent of the middle-class sample and 48 per cent of the upper-class sample had come from the country or small towns—only a slightly smaller percentage than the slum dwellers (67 per cent).

Although 45 per cent reported that they read a newspaper every day, 50 per cent said they never read books or magazines—only 10 per cent less than the rural sample. But 56 per cent listened to the radio daily.

The problem most often perceived by urbanites was the poor condition of streets, with unsanitary conditions next in seriousness. As in the rural area, the largest proportion thought that the government should assume responsibility for solving such problems. Consistently with earlier findings that we have noted, the upper class was the least emphatic on this point but, a little surprisingly, the middle class was somewhat more emphatic than the lower class.

Two differences appear here between the rural and urban lower class. One was the greater precision with which the latter specified the kind of governmental action required to cope with a problem; there appeared to be more familiarity, for example, with the different agencies. The other was a still weaker feeling that neighborhood groups alone could cope with local problems—a consequence attributed

* More than this, the authoritarian pattern noted in family and other relations is impressively reinforced by evidence that 84 per cent of the rural sample was "somewhat authoritarian" as compared with 46 per cent of the adult population (only partially rural, of course) in the United States.[14]

to weaker ties and less communal solidarity.

Forty-four per cent in the urban study said they had not participated in the solution of community problems (a close parallel to the rural sample). Concerning problems which they themselves had pointed out, 55 per cent said nothing has been tried to solve them. The largest proportion who had done anything consisted of 12 per cent who had signed some petition to the government.

Analysis of attitudes toward leadership did not completely parallel the rural study. What did emerge is striking: 73 per cent indicated that they would prefer a moderately autocratic leader; 16 per cent preferred a democratic leader.

Thus, despite a higher average education and income of the urban sample, the central conclusion reached by the rural study would seem, in general, to apply as well to urban life: the educational task is difficult and long-range. While there are small nuclei of participation-minded citizens in almost every community, the ability to work together as well as group spirit are thus far underdeveloped. Participation as a value remains more potential than actual, but "the task cannot be taken out of the people's hands. . . ."

A concluding word should be said about the two surveys of Puerto Rican education conducted in 1925 and 1948-49 by Teachers College, Columbia University.[15] Though prolonged analysis of the latter, especially, might be fruitful in the light of our study, it is only possible to point out that a substantial ratio of its criticisms and recommendations accord with those we have presented from our respondent panels.

The "Achilles heel" of this kind of survey is, of course, insufficient opportunity to understand the culture of Puerto Rico, especially as it differs from that of the United States. Thus it tends to perpetuate one of the weaknesses stressed by our respondents—namely, the superimposition of Continental, especially progressivist, educational theory and practice with too little concern for the actual complexity of acculturation and other cultural phenomena. In such respects, severe criticisms of the survey that were reported to us are by no means unjustified.

At the same time it must be recalled that, despite inconsistencies and disagreements, our own panels, too, were often strongly progressivist—their qualified endorsement of functionalistic forms of learning being a case in point. Though the 1948-49 survey bogs down in "pedagese," and though it evades issues of great importance to the future of the Island (such as political, religious, and sex education), nevertheless much of the material is as deserving of attention today as it was at the time of publication.

THE EVIDENCE: BALANCE SHEET

The deficits and assets revealed by our comparative review of recent evidence from the social sciences and education are both substantial. This study has many weaknesses of omission as well as of commission. At the same time, its findings are often corroborated by other findings. In addition, it ventures into territories that have not to date been explored by experts of any sort, so that it cannot always be comparatively judged. Still more important, we must remember that no claim has been made that our interpretation is an "objective" one. It is based upon both a philosophy and a methodology that attempt to break new ground and are therefore controversial. Moreover, the resource panels from which it has drawn have been limited in number of personnel.

1. *Deficits.* Let us begin with some typical deficits of cultural evidence. Our comparison in Chapter 18 of the Steward and other findings with our own indicates that we and our respondents have not included or not emphasized many important details—the saint cult being a fair instance. A consequence is underplaying of subcultural differences in favor of similarities—an instance here (confirmed by some though not all research on the Puerto Rican family) being the varying patterns of relationship between spouses. Also, we could have paid more attention than we did to differences between all three subcultures, on the one hand, and the national level, on the other. Of course differences were frequently noted (religious values being a conspicuous case). Still, we perhaps did not generalize enough except to note the more "theoretical" way in which the national panel often reacted to our questions.

And then there are countless observations of the culture to which neither our study nor any of those cited pays attention at all. To illustrate at random: the women of light skin observed carrying umbrellas to shield themselves from the sun; the rather adolescent forms of amusement sometimes noted at adult parties (a phenomenon perhaps related to the pattern of female maturation); and the local newsreels continually playing up middle-class manifestations of conspicuous consumption. (The number of cocktails consumed before cameras is prodigious indeed.)

In other cases we have presented cultural data that fail to stand up under more careful scrutiny. Thus the rate of increase of working women and the rate of decrease of consensual marriages are both apparently lower than we had been led to believe. In still further cases, sharp divisions of judgment among our respondents are partially or largely resolved by other research studies. Instances here are these: whether Puerto Ricans tend to be cooperative or independent in their actions was answered more firmly in terms of the latter alternative; and whether personality traits may be regarded thus far as more "negative" than "positive" tended to be weighted on the former side.

In some areas where considerable research evidence is available, we have not effectively placed our own beside it for comparison. We are thinking here especially of technological data, health investigations, and historical studies. Such evidence has by no means been ignored. But the constrictions we have set upon our choice of studies did not permit us to include them to the extent that an exhaustive work should.

The lack of adequate historical comparisons is glaring. Although we are concerned mainly with the current life of Puerto Rico, our treatment of its past is sketchy at best. But we should also point out that even had we compared this treatment with that of several historians, we might still have had great difficulty in determining how correct we were: historians in Puerto Rico at least as much as elsewhere differ among themselves as to the "true" interpretation—a difference emanating partly from the emotion-tinged "nativist" issue. For that matter, more "objective" social scientists differ too: compare, for instance, Mrs. Wolf's interpretations of family patterns with those of the Hill-Stycos-Back study.

Perhaps the most serious deficit in our cultural evidence is our inability either to substantiate or not to substantiate in any conclusive scientific way a sizable proportion of all our findings. The trouble here is a dearth of research in many of the areas with which we were concerned. Take this example: there is need for more precise knowledge of the multiple process of acculturation—particularly as to the impact upon Puerto Rico of habits, attitudes, and artifacts that could be designated as North American by comparison with those that are more accurately termed Western European or otherwise transcultural. In lesser degree the same question arises as to the acculturative impact upon the United States by Puerto Rico: To what extent is this impact Hispanic and Latin American rather than distinctively Puerto Rican? As anthropologists well know, the problem is intricate. Our own treatment of acculturation because it tended to blur such distinctions did not, we fear in retrospect, contribute much to its resolution.

With some exceptions, the further on we moved, the less research evidence was available. Thus most of the studies cited in Chapter 18 fall within the category of cultural order; only a very few fall primarily within the process category; and only one or two (and these of narrow scope) fall within that of goals. This lack is perhaps no one's fault: time and resources for such endeavors have been limited; and in some cases (as when we were probing the configurational level of culture), standard research methodologies scarcely apply. Nevertheless, the fact remains that much of what we have to offer must be judged on other grounds than by comparative research.

One partial exception not thus far noted has been the question of "universal" and "relative" values. Our own respondents, we recall, inclined toward a universal orientation—that is, likenesses between Puerto Rican values and those of other cultures tended to be emphasized more than unlikenesses. Here it is possible to compare this preference with research studies abroad. To be sure, the latter do not consider Puerto Rican values as such, but they do inquire into the difficult question of the extent to which human values are cross-cultural rather than unique to individual cultures.

As indicated in our companion work, "either-or" answers to this question are bound to oversimplify. Values are *both* relative and universal. To be sure, some evidence is available on each side of the argument. Thus the contention that certain values have world-wide acceptance is partially supported by one study showing that social restraint and progress in action (which Puerto Ricans also tend to favor) are ranked higher by both Eastern and Western cultures than such values as withdrawal and self-sufficiency.[16] The strong belief of our subcultural panel that cultural factors are more important than either biological or psychological factors in determining character is equally endorsed by cross-cultural research.[17] Moreover, similarities of value at least between Puerto Rican and other Latin American cultures could be inferred from various works by anthropologists. One is of special interest to educators—a study of Mexican students in the United States that may apply at numerous points just as well to Puerto Rican students.[18]

But the relativist position is likewise strongly supported by research in the valuational field. Thus the contention of a majority of our panels that Puerto Rican values are more similar than dissimilar to values in other cultures is somewhat weakened. For example, we may remember that a majority of grassroots respondents were inclined to approve a life of action above one of contemplation or enjoyment. But there is inferential evidence that, at least in the United States, the three values are considered to be of fairly equal worth. Again, the value of tolerance of cultural diversity, also favored by our findings, is a preference closer to Eastern than to Western cultures.[19]

It is not, of course, only the issue of universal versus relative values that our study leaves unresolved within the larger areas of Puerto Rican goals. Precisely because this area lies largely invisible beneath the surface of every culture—that is, on the implicit and metacultural level—we can claim little here by way of unqualified certainty. Indeed, some of the disagreements and contradictions reported in these pages (not only about values but about many other matters) may result from our inability to probe far enough rather than from chronic conflicts in the metacultural beliefs of Puerto Ricans themselves. At the same time, we should not wish to belabor this admission: "individual differences" among respondents are significant too—in fact we have found them to constitute the "flesh and blood" of this study.

Turning for a moment to deficits of educational evidence, the principal weakness in our findings is that many of them, too, have been neither proved nor disproved up to this time. Research evidence is simply unavailable, and such evidence as is available is circumscribed.

One interesting divergence between our study and those by Puerto Rican educators is revealed by Ramírez López. Contrary to the prevailing judgment of our leader panel, his research disclosed that aesthetic values are ranked low. And contrary to most of our grassroots panel, a life of action (at least in the economic and political sense) is considered less desirable than a life of intellectual pursuit (at least in the contemplative sense). It is impossible, however, to determine degrees of difference between the respective findings, since the value concepts used by Ramírez López, Mellado, and others are not necessarily identical in meaning with our own.

2. *Assets.* We begin again with cultural evidence. In a number of respects our study supplements the major results provided by other research. Examples on the institutional level are our descriptions of changes in the subcultures—especially Cañamelar, where mechanization and labor organization both have developed considerably since the Steward team's field work.

Our sociological surveys, moreover, place the subcultures of Cañamelar and San José in relationships that are not apparent from the Steward study. Also, by adding to these the middle-class urban subculture of Hermosa, we are not only able to deal with a rapidly expanding level and area that the larger study subordinates; we are able to draw comparisons that the latter did not attempt. And it is worth recalling here that, in a number of cultural effects, Hermosa is more similar to Cañamelar than to San José despite the fact that both of the latter are rural communities. Still more important is our greater preoccupation with the common characteristics of all three subcultures—characteristics which, in the judgment of some respondents, are much greater than the Steward study has led us to believe; characteristics, too, which seem now to be strengthening with the growth of the welfare state and the welding of all parts of Insular life into more and more of a unity.

But perhaps the most important addition to all the studies cited in this part is our attempt to explore areas that hitherto have received slight attention from experts in research. It is our hope, for example, that some contribution has been made toward understanding of the middle-class culture. True, a few members of our panels belonged to the lower levels, a few to the highest. Many others claimed to know those levels either from intimate past experience or from close observation. Nevertheless, besides our inclusion of Hermosa, the fact is that a majority of our respondents on both levels were themselves of lower- or upper-middle status. Such a clustering may constitute another deficit. But in so far as the middle strata are probably the fastest growing groups in Puerto Rico, in so far too as many look toward the future in terms of the values of those groups, our study may be considered not only descriptive of the present situation but prognosticative of future trends as well.

There are other ways in which this work tries to explore new fields.

We refer not only to the interpretations provided by the several concepts of cultural process (nativism versus assimilation, say) or to
those embraced by cultural goals (the hopes of youth, for example,
or the issues generated by religious values); we refer especially to the
metacultural dimension. True, our findings and appraisals here are,
at best, tentative. Yet the evidence has at least revealed that it is far
too important to ignore. For it provides some indication of how leaders and grassroots citizens feel and think about the past, the present,
and the future of their country.

Of course many—perhaps all—Puerto Rican readers of this study
will insist that particular beliefs of one or another respondent are
false or wrong or both. Even so, that a respondent believes as he does,
or at least that he has done his best in the face of many limitations
(such as time) to express what he believes, cannot be dismissed simply
because someone else happens to believe in a different way.

Especially is this true when we remember that several of our leader
respondents are shapers of national policy. Whether or not their beliefs are confirmed by available research, nevertheless how they view
and judge the culture has vast significance for what happens to themselves and the more than two million others whom they represent.
And of course they must act while waiting for such confirmation: to
wait for conclusive proof that they are right in all their judgments and
decisions would permit no action at all. Every society proceeds from
limited knowledge, though few act on even the amount available to
them.

Nor are only leaders important here. In a country aiming to be
democratic, grassroots citizens are, in the long run, still more important. However little or much spokesmen such as those in our three
subcultures may turn out to be correct or incorrect, any democratic
leader tries to respect their attitudes and conduct, and to act in their
behalf. For this reason, too, what we have learned from them deserves
critical attention.

To admit, however, that our evidence is thus far qualified is not to
say that it is therefore false. On the contrary, much of it, including
some in conflict with other research, might eventually prove to be
sound. Indeed, considering the fairly high proportion of evidence in
our study that does withstand research comparisons, we are not un-
reasonable in our expectation that some or much of the remainder

could withstand them too. Such an expectation is defensible on both logical and scientific grounds.

Recall a few of these comparisons. Data provided by our sociological survey are on the whole harmonious with similar data available from the Tumin work, from the "analysis unit" of the Division of Community Education, and from other sources. Of course there are minor variations, but in terms of our qualitative interests these are hardly serious.

Similarly, areas where the greatest research has already been accomplished do not reveal glaring discrepancies with our own research. Family and class studies are the best examples. Certainly our treatment is far less encompassing than theirs. But, notwithstanding interesting variations, our respondents have seldom deviated in their major consensuses even when we have failed to evoke as refined or qualified answers to our questions as both they and we could wish.

Assets of educational evidence, though perhaps less satisfactory than our cultural evidence, are also impressive. Indeed, in two respects our study may throw light upon this important area in a way that other studies have not. First, our flexible and prolonged interviews encouraged more detailed meanings than questionnaire or similar conventional techniques permit. Second, it was possible to explore controversial areas of educational belief that, hitherto, have been largely ignored.

The severe criticisms raised by our respondents against present school policies and practices would also appear oftener than not to be justified by our review of comparative evidence. The lack of class consciousness, the limited reading done by a large percentage of adults, and the confusions in educational philosophy indicated by the superintendents' questionnaire—these are only samples of distressing weaknesses.

And yet, on the whole, the over-all evidence reinforces many recommendations made by our respondents—recommendations that we bring together in our next and final chapter. Above all, they support our core contention that, with all its handicaps, education on this Island is both actually and potentially a primary cultural force. The people profoundly believe in it, and, as Tumin shows, the more learning they have, the greater their belief. Let us turn then to the tasks that lie ahead for Puerto Rican schools.

CHAPTER TWENTY

NEXT STEPS FOR PUERTO RICAN EDUCATION

LOOKING BACK upon our entire study, a final question remains. In terms of the balance sheet just struck, as well as out of the welter of attitudes, practices, conflicting judgments, and recommendations concerning Puerto Rican education, *what now?*

We meet this question in four steps: first, by restating the most concrete proposals for educational experiments and projects made by our panels of respondents; second, by reviewing and supplementing with our own evaluations some of the most crucial educational needs and problems; third, by epitomizing the kind of philosophy of education we believe to be required by Puerto Rico in its age of reconstruction; and fourth, by returning to our respondents for a final look ahead.

SOME PROPOSALS FOR EDUCATIONAL EXPERIMENTS AND PROJECTS

As preparation of this study was nearing completion, the following letter (condensed from the original) was sent to Governor Luis Muñoz Marín:

When we first discussed the research study of Puerto Rican culture-and-education to which you contributed, you asked me to send you a list of experimental projects in education which have been proposed by both leader and grassroots participants. I take pleasure in meeting your request herewith.

It should be noted that the following list of proposals is by no means exhaustive of those included in Parts I-IV. Also, they are grouped in three categories: (a) those that could be implemented with least difficulty as to

394

expense, personnel, and planning; (b) those that would require somewhat more preparation, but are within the range of practicability in the immediate future; (c) and those that involve the greatest investment of money, new personnel, and extensive planning.

All three categories of proposals were made by one or more of the thirty-six respondents, though I have in a few cases slightly elaborated them. The statements below usually do not convey anything like a full appreciation of the original, imaginative contributions of the several respondents. I hope, nevertheless, that you will agree that the proposals are deserving of serious attention.

Group (a)

1. *School garden project:* to test the hypothesis that children will learn more content, develop better social relations, and improve in their behavior characteristics if they engage in the work experience of planning, growing, and caring for vegetable gardens integrated with their regular school subjects.

2. *Family education* for (a) high school seniors and (b) parents. Both projects would try to prove that young adults and parents in separate or combined courses will respond to opportunities to study problems of family life and readjustment, and that their understanding of these problems will measurably increase.

3. *Foundations of education for teachers in training*: utilizing control groups, an experimental course integrating the behavioral sciences (psychology, sociology, anthropology, etc.) with the history and philosophy of education would test the hypothesis that students will acquire more knowledge and interest in these foundational areas than under the present departmentalized structure.

4. *Science education:* to test the hypothesis that children can acquire more knowledge of scientific method and principles than they do in the present Community Problems courses, by means of reorganized units with in-service training for teachers.

5. *History education:* two experimental courses on the high school or college level to demonstrate whether or not greater knowledge and interest in Puerto Rican history are developed when (a) study of the past is integrated with present and future problems, and (b) firsthand acquaintance with historical resources of the Island is provided through field experience.

6. *Acculturation by comparison:* an experimental course in the acculturative processes occurring in Latin American cultures, compared with the Puerto Rican culture, to be tested on the high school and/or college level.

7. *Group dynamics:* to test the hypothesis that students on the elementary, secondary, and/or college level will acquire greater interest in and knowledge of a given subject by utilizing the techniques of group dynamics under the direction of especially trained instructor-leaders.

8. *Democratic planning and participation:* an experiment with control groups to prove or disprove that elementary students can effectively participate in planning and directing classroom activities, with consequent improvement in learning and attitudes. (This experiment is also applicable to higher levels.)

9. *Point Four visitors:* to set up a project in a selected number of schools in which Point Four visitors would be utilized as resource persons in the study of foreign cultures, with careful preplanning of such utilization, to test the hypothesis that knowledge and attitudes in international relations are thereby measurably improved.

10. *Public school cooperatives:* an experiment to integrate juvenile cooperatives with school learning in arithmetic, Community Problems, and other courses, based on assumptions similar to the garden experiment above.

11. *Seminars for teachers in problems of freedom:* to be conducted during "activity month," selected groups of teachers to participate in intensive seminars on basic issues of freedom in education and culture.

12. *Political controversy:* a special training project for teachers in the art of handling controversy, to test the hypothesis that conflicting political issues can be handled dispassionately and fruitfully in the average classroom.

13. *Political forums in the University:* a proposal that the present rule, prohibiting political candidates from speaking on the campus, be rescinded in favor of carefully planned forums under conditions of fair discussion and equality of treatment.

Group (b)

14. *Library project:* a pilot study in one or several high schools to be provided with a special collection of books and other library materials, to test the hypothesis that learning will measurably increase in quality and quantity.

15. *Interschool visitation project:* to provide opportunities for children in various types of private schools to visit and participate in the activities of public schools, and vice versa, with the objective of proving or disproving that ethnocentric biases and class as well as racial conflicts will thereby diminish.

16. *English education:* two experimental courses on the elementary

level to demonstrate (a) that improvement in English facility will or will not occur more rapidly when tapes, phonograph records, and films are utilized as the principal instrument of learning; and (b) that such improvement will or will not occur more rapidly when units are developed which center in the interests and problems of children in their own environments.

17. *Learning through trips:* an experiment in a selected group of schools to test the hypothesis that students will learn more content and develop stronger interest in their learning if certain courses are planned with frequent trips to relevant institutions, communities, etc., with careful integration between formal subject matters and visitations.

18. *Arts and crafts education:* to test the hypothesis that learning of skills and contents in academic and/or vocational subjects will increase in quantity and quality if continuous opportunities are provided for creativity through one or more of the arts (music, graphic, dramatic, dance), with expert guidance and preplanning.

19. *Problems of cultural transition for adults:* an experiment on the adult level to assist adults in coping with problems arising from mobility—rural to urban, Insular to Continental—which would prove or disprove that they are responsive to such an opportunity and that their readiness to readjust is improved.

20. *University consumer cooperative:* to establish a student cooperative in the University, operated on the same Rochdale principles that govern public school cooperatives, integrating the project with the work of the Cooperative Institute in the University, to test the hypothesis that cooperative principles will be vitalized by direct experience.

21. *Religious education:* experimental courses in (a) comparative religion and (b) nonsectarian examination of the role of religion (secular as well as ecclesiastic) in modern culture, to be tried out on the secondary and university levels.

22. *Vocational guidance:* to test the hypothesis that a carefully planned project in vocational guidance in selected junior and senior high schools will result in vocational choices more accurately geared to abilities than is at present typical.

23. *Sex education:* pilot projects on elementary, secondary, and adult levels, adjusted to levels of maturation, with specially trained teachers to deal with reproduction and other physiological topics, birth control, and ethical problems in the relation of the sexes.

24. *Studies of cultural value:* on the university level, concentrated inter-

pretations especially in the social sciences of the role of values in the modern world; on the lower levels, pilot courses in the United Nations with special regard for conflicting international norms.

25. *Modelmaking for the welfare state:* practice in designing models in economic, political, health, and other projects in order to bring the schools into close relationship with other cultural experiments under way in the welfare state of Puerto Rico.

26. *Social planning through the schools:* pilot projects developed in relation to local and national planning boards, to enlist education directly in the rebuilding of Puerto Rico as a "garden island."

Group (c)

27. *Nursery schools:* a project involving the establishment of one or several nursery schools supervised and financed by the Department of Education for preschool-age children, with specially trained personnel, the project to be so designed as to test several hypotheses—e.g., adjustment of parents, adjustment of children, comparisons between groups of first-grade children who have and have not attended nursery schools.

28. *Playgrounds:* a project in selected communities to provide supervised play for children in out-of-school hours and week ends, to test the hypothesis that juvenile delinquency and similar problems will be reduced in such communities.

29. *Vocational and liberal-arts high schools:* to establish an experimental curriculum in selected high schools which will aim to synthesize liberal-arts with vocational education, particularly in communities where industrial reconstruction is occurring and the need for skilled employees is increasing, with tested comparisons between graduates of these schools and of standard schools as to knowledge and other qualities.

30. *Experimental private schools:* to establish one or more private elementary and/or secondary schools with the cooperation of the Department of Education, their curricula and methodology to be deliberately experimental for the purpose of testing ideas in education which, if successful, could be extended to public schools.

31. *Center for human relations education:* to be established under the auspices of the College of Education and/or Department of Education, to be concerned with projects involving the development of more humane and democratic relations through education for racial, class, urban-rural, and other groups.

32. *Division of community dynamics:* to be established in either the University or Department of Education, to be concerned with pure

and applied research in problems of cultural change with special regard for education's role therein.

33. *Psychotherapy for teachers:* an experiment under the direction of psychiatrists to test the hypothesis that carefully selected teachers can acquire, with special training, basic skills and knowledge in the field of psychotherapy with the objective of utilizing these competencies in classroom experience.

34. *Television education:* pilot projects in "closed" or "open" circuit television, designed to prove or disprove that students of different age levels can learn more effectively in science, language, mathematics, and other subjects if demonstrations are presented through television programs carefully integrated with classroom teaching.

35. *Rural retraining program for teacher-leaders:* a project for carefully selected teachers who will become community leaders in rural areas, with their schools reorganized to serve as centers of community life, one of the hypotheses to be tested being that a community school will help to slow the rate of migration from rural to urban areas.

36. *Second-unit schools as teacher-training centers:* an experiment to utilize a selected number of second-unit schools as laboratories in "on-the-ground" rural training centers for two years beyond high school.

37. *Thinking and planning board:* to be established as a "staff arm" of the Secretary of Education, its purpose being to focus upon far-reaching issues and proposals; its membership to consist of a social scientist, a philosopher of culture and education, and an expert on the Insular educational system; to be augmented by an advisory commission of lay citizens to serve as a liaison between it and the general public.

38. *Experimental junior college:* a two-year or four-year junior college beginning with the present eleventh high school year or after high school graduation, where many experimental ideas, including some of those listed above, could be tested on a small scale before determining their Island-wide applicability.

NEEDS AND PROBLEMS IN EDUCATION: A REVIEW

The partial summary of proposals in the preceding section testifies to the wide scope of needs and problems confronting education in Puerto Rico today. They embrace almost every phase and level. Running through many of them, however, is a common thread—a consensus, implicit if not always explicit, of the need for *experimentation,* for imaginative ventures in schools, colleges, and adult programs that could attune the educational system to the spirit of renewal that is elsewhere so radiant and zestful.

The extenuating circumstances that have prevented widespread experimentation thus far have been noted many times in this book. No one denies that a country faced with a high rate of illiteracy, with double sessions, with insufficient school buildings or such requisites as books, with poorly trained, underpaid, and overworked teachers—not to mention the poverty, disease, ignorance, and hunger that are their social concomitants—no one denies that such a country has had all it can handle to provide the most rudimentary learning for its children.

Certainly, too, when one compares the educational programs of other countries in the Caribbean with Puerto Rico's, one quickly appreciates its relative superiority. One returns from a visit to the public schools of Haiti, Jamaica, and Cuba, for example, with a sense of appreciation—indeed, of awe—that this most overpopulated of all underdeveloped cultures south of the United States could have achieved so much in so little time.

And yet, as we and our respondents evaluate the educational situation, most or all of us would agree that it is not enough to compare Puerto Rican education with still poorer systems. As seen in our study of cultural goals, the aspirations and norms of the people are high. It is by these rather than by lower ones that such an evaluation should be made. Without further consideration, then, of the most obvious needs (though no less imperative for that fact), let us review, in a kind of cross section of all levels, some of the less obtuse but ultimately still more crucial needs stressed in this work. We select aspects that we ourselves judge especially noteworthy.[1]

Take the *curriculum* first. Among the weaknesses most heavily criticized are its "bookishness"—its continued inclusion of too many subject matters divorced from the interests and problems of young Puerto Ricans—and, by the same token, its exclusion of direct stimulating contact with many of the resources of community life and the natural environment. The dearth of vocational courses integrated with liberal-arts courses in the high schools is a serious instance of the same deficiency.

The challenge to vitalize the curriculum does not mean that solid content and high standards should be neglected. An example to the contrary is the need for much better library facilities. Another: better study of Puerto Rican history—history, however, interpreted in relation to wider cultural forces and, on the secondary as well as higher levels, to such searching problems as prediction and progress. Likewise, many recommended more time for the study of English and science. Relatively new contents, too, should be included—sex education, comparative religion, international relations, and critical examination of such controversial issues as communism being cases in point. Meanwhile, other subjects should be greatly expanded and improved, including art education in all its main forms. Pervading many of these needs is the evasive but fundamental one of dealing more thoroughly with the nature of the Puerto Rican culture itself—with its class structure, say, or the complex phenomenon of acculturation, or the whole difficult area of traditional versus emerging values.

Take next the area of *learning*. Here the single most chronic problem seemed to various respondents—as it does to us—to be the widespread perpetuation of practices such as memorization, mechanical testing, passive recitations, and other rote methods adjudged to be psychologically dubious. Meager give-and-take between teacher and student, still more meager critical-mindedness, and only rare utilization of functional techniques such as group dynamics—these weaknesses were often lamented.

Better teacher training is indispensable if learning in turn is to be improved. The problem is acute not only because so many Puerto Rican teachers enter upon their duties with a minimum of professional preparation, but because the training they do receive often perpetuates the weaknesses already illustrated. For example, many teachers of teachers in Puerto Rico, although they pay lip service to something vaguely considered to be "progressive education," do not themselves exemplify modern methods in their classrooms. Also, they frequently encourage a middle-class outlook which may shatter many of the values of young teachers who come from and are later assigned to rural areas with resultant feelings of conflict. Lack of direct experience in the problems of local community life, either during or after the training, tends to widen further the dualism of school and environment. Equally serious is an overemphasis on pedagogical techniques at the expense of either subject-matter fields or a sense of deep dedication to education as a profession. One of many results is minimal understanding by teachers of the emotional problems of children. Another is complacency or insensitivity, reflected especially in young people, toward the cultural transformations occurring both within the Island and the world beyond. Still another is the habit of regarding teaching as little more than a routine way to obtain a modest income and security.

Take, third, the area of educational *control*. The line-staff, highly centralized administrative structure generates the problem of how to translate verbal allegiance to democratic principles into daily educational practice. Parent acquiescence in or indifference to school policies; intimidation of teachers by supervisors and other "higher-ups"; rigid classroom patterns; the lack of effective student councils or other forms of participation; an Island-wide professional organization circumscribed both by narrowness of educational conception and over-concentrated leadership; and endless red tape in providing resource materials for the individual teacher—these are among the difficulties remaining unresolved.

The problems thus far reviewed in the three areas of curriculum, learning, and control are by no means exhaustive. Nor do they apply equally to all schools, all teachers, all administrators, all parents, or all students. They do stem in considerable part from a fourth and still more fundamental need—that of a well-thought-out, well-articulated, widely accepted and implemented philosophy of Puerto Rican education.

This weakness is indicated by the high ratio of disagreement in the superintendents' questionnaire; by symbolic confusions emphasized among our own respondents as widespread in the culture; by disparities prevailing between ideological and configurational patterns of belief concerning, say, democracy, morality, religion, and science; and, finally, by far-reaching disagreements among top-ranking educators who are themselves not only aware of the philosophic issues involved but of the equally far-reaching consequences for Puerto Rican culture that their respective positions entail.

Turn, then, to a brief consideration of educational philosophy itself.

RECONSTRUCTING THE PHILOSOPHY OF PUERTO RICAN EDUCATION

If any one postulate has governed this entire work, it has been that education in Puerto Rico, as everywhere else, is both product and agent of the culture. Philosophy, in turn, is regarded in this context as the expression of the meanings inherent in culture and in education.

There are innumerable ways to examine the network of relations of culture, education, and philosophy. In this study we have tried to do so by means of a theory of culture developed with the help of leading anthropologists, enriched by philosophers of history and other thinkers, and crystallized in terms of our own orientation. The kinds of problems we have raised with respondents have, of course, been governed by our conceptions of culture, education, and philosophy as these interfuse. An interpreter with a different conception would deal with different problems and thus obtain different reactions to the issues confronting Puerto Rico.

Few would be likely to deny, however, that the issues we have raised are fundamental or that the reactions to them are symptomatic of the kind of culture that Puerto Rico has been in the past, of the kind it is today, and of the kind it could or should become in the years and decades ahead. Our purpose now is to select and recapitulate in philosophic terms some of the most significant of these issues and reactions and to appraise them quite frankly from our point of view.[2] We must necessarily be general. The substance is provided by all of our pages thus far.

The culture of Puerto Rico, again like all cultures, is characterized by a triadic relationship of order, processes, and goals—each "angle" of which depends in many complex ways upon both of the others. Any philosophy of education constructed from the postulate we have indicated must therefore take all three angles into continuous account. Let us consider each in turn.

1. From the evidence we have presented within the first of these great categories—*order*—we conclude that the culture possesses a wholeness that may be described in both "spatial" and "temporal" terms. It possesses a "horizontal" and "vertical" structure that may be depicted in the form of various models or maps that cut across regional "boundaries" (such as subcultures), as well as up and down through ascending and descending strata of class and status. Equally, it can be viewed in time: here cultural order in Puerto Rico proves to be accelerating, and attention may focus upon this fact while one or more of its various spatial dimensions are, for the moment, subordinated. The cultural concept that perhaps best embraces both the spatial and temporal in their most comprehensive and often elusive aspects is

configuration—the spatiotemporal way of life which, for any culture, expresses and integrates its most indigenous qualities through many kinds of symbols and many kinds of behavior.

The philosophy of Puerto Rican education should try to translate into everyday school programs all of these aspects of the order of its culture. Granting that the task is gigantic, we have nevertheless been able to record steps that are already being taken, and many more that remain to be taken in the future. In some ways, the most difficult yet imperative of these steps is the last discussed in Part II—that is, the articulation and maturation of Puerto Rico's national character.

The key to this problem has been suggested by the term syncretic. By this we have meant, and many of our respondents have suggested in varying terminology, that the Island is developing a pattern, or patterns, the uniqueness of which centers in its amalgam of two principal streams of cultural influence: the Hispanic and North Ameriican. The fact that other cultures (the Mexican and Cuban, perhaps most) are likewise experiencing this amalgam, and that other powerful cultural forces have played upon the Puerto Rican culture (the whole of Western civilization, as well as the African and aboriginal Indian), is not overlooked. Nevertheless, the concomitance of two great "caravans of culture" is the primary fact. It produces distinctive if also subtle cultural effects. And educational philosophy should take these effects into serious, sensitive account.

How may it do so? Of many suggestions, two may be reemphasized. First, the schools should consciously and deliberately deal, though perhaps pervasively and indirectly oftener than in the form of "courses," with Puerto Rico's own cultural style. Provocative concepts such as non-nationalism that throw light upon the problem should be examined and discussed until they achieve greater refinement than is now the case. As teachers are made aware of the importance of the task, as courses of study begin to raise relevant questions concerning it, the ambiguities and confusions that still remain are likely to decrease. Thereby young citizens should gradually acquire greater clarity of mind and feeling about their culture and thus of themselves as at once its creatures and its makers. This objective, in turn, requires less artificial superimposition of *either* Continental *or* European-based educational philosophies than is still habitual.

Second, education on all levels should at the same time face those difficult questions arising from configurational and metacultural expressions of the Puerto Rican order. Here the need of critical habits of inquiry—above all, scientific method—cannot begin to develop too soon. The schools, beginning in the grades, should become forums through which discrepancies and hypocrisies between ideological creed and everyday behavior are revealed openly and frankly, no matter what sensitive issue is at stake. Democracy, for example, remains a sham in the degree that authoritarianism in administrative and pedagogical routines prevails over sharing, free discussion, and mutual decision-making. Incompatibilities between moral code and moral practice, between ritualistic dogmatism and religious dedication, between superstition and scientific approaches to problems of health and happiness, should be exposed and combated as ruthlessly as any other diseases of the body politic. The aim is maximum compatibility of symbol and experience. For only thus can Puerto Rico (or any other culture) eventually achieve that wholeness and stability of character without which it remains vulnerable to the forces of destruction from within and from without.

A philosophy of education appropriate to contemporary Puerto Rico should come to grips, too, with such urgent problems of order as family, class, and history. As elsewhere in the world, the Puerto Rican family is the core institution. To protect it from degenerating influences, it is not enough to teach units or carry on research projects on population or kinship patterns, say, invaluable though these are. Education has the far more solemn responsibility of helping children, fathers, and mothers to understand and cope with the myriad tensions, bewilderments, and conflicts of family life today. This responsibility becomes a central obligation of the Division of Community Education, of the elementary and secondary schools, of the University's Colleges of Education, General Studies, Humanities, Social Sciences, Law, and of all other private or public institutions concerned in any way with general education. Sex, both in its physiological and moral aspects, should be dealt with forthrightly, with due regard for levels of maturation. The search for norms that can both preserve the intrinsic qualities of loyalty and love in the traditional family, yet move forward to more democratic, harmonious, and satisfactory experience for all its members—this is the primary but far from clarified objective. It is pivotal to the needed philosophy of education.

Education's responsibility toward the class structure is also a double one. On the one hand, it is to provide opportunity in the social studies and elsewhere for critical analysis of the overt and covert conflicts that this structure generates. (Color prejudice is one insidious factor here, but still more crucial may be the disparities of economic interest between owner-manager and worker.) On the other hand, it is to consider the kind of vertical order that ought, as far as possible, to be developed in the future.

For many citizens, the answer to the latter problem lies in the hope of a "middle-class society" with the bottom and top strata less and less pronounced. Even now, though perhaps for the most part unconsciously, teachers tend to emphasize middle-stratum practices and values with minimum awareness of the conflicts they help to induce between their own beliefs and attitudes and those of typical children in their charge. Here, too, the impact of United States culture, with its middle-class orientation, generates confusions and maladjustments which it is education's business to face.

We ourselves question more than do some of our respondents the unqualified desirability of this present trend. To aspire quite legitimately toward a middle-level standard of living for all citizens is one thing; to imperil thereby the more enduring values of the rural and urban common people who constitute the great traditional majority is another thing. The ideas embodied in Operation Serenity, as we understand it, are a preliminary recognition of the dangers inherent in the class problem as it now emerges.

The temporal model of cultural order embraces the philosophic problem of the place that the future as well as the past and present should occupy in the educational program. While agreeing with the stress of our resource panels upon more competent, sustained attention to the Island's past, still more fundamental is the question of whether the whole conception of general education is not in need of reexamination in order to bring both temporal and spatial dimensions into more unified relationship.

History, for example, should be regarded not so much as a discipline studied in a separate compartment of the humanities as a necessary concomitant of any fruitful interpretation of the problems that Puerto Rico faces today. In the course of such interpretation, basic approaches such as the ecological hypothesis utilized in the Steward work, the "great man" theory (that leaders are the principal cause of cultural change), the Marxian view of class struggle and historical materialism, and others should operate as alternative instruments of interpretation. Examination of such issues as progress, causation, and prediction should be integrated with this kind of study—special attention being given the historical relations of the Island with the course of Western civilization in general and of Latin America in particular.

With a minority of our respondents, we agree too that the future should become in a profound sense the guiding temporal principle of general education. This is not to neglect either the past or present. It is to anticipate the goals of the culture, as they crystallize from wants and hopes of the people.

2. To achieve these goals or ends, it is necessary, however, for education to be concerned centrally with ways or means—that is, with the *process* by which every culture transmits and modifies the patterns and structures, the spatial and temporal dimensions, of the all-inclusive order.

We have found that the dynamics of Puerto Rican life are, without exception, germane to its educational tasks. Yet with many of our informants, especially on the national level, we support the indictment that school programs are not thus far effectively meshed with cultural change in other major spheres. Accordingly, the almost fervent conviction of vast numbers of people that education is the master key to their own growth and welfare (a conviction which the Hatt and Tumin studies underscore) is somewhat anachronous. Despite the "cultural lag" so often emphasized, Puerto Rican education does act, in some ways, as a potent agency of change—especially of upward mobility—and this remarkable fact should be fully recognized by the required educational philosophy. But such a philosophy should go further: it should adopt the guiding principle that education is *not* the mere transmitter of the cultural heritage, however important this obligation may be. It is also and even more crucially remaker of the heritage.

This magnetic objective can be approached only if and as education functions in continuous relation with all other cultural processes. Up to now, though the philosophy underlying community education is vulnerable in some respects (it is, we think, too nondirective in its group processes, and hence inadequately goal-centered), yet this

Division more closely approximates such a relationship than any other ongoing program. Particularly is it effective in implementing what we have called the concept of focus. Concerned as it is with the meaningful needs of people, and motivating them to cope with their concrete problems through organized effort and intelligence, the Division should be an example to the entire system. Thus far it remains much too separated not only from the public schools but from other adult agencies concerned with education.

We are not suggesting that all education should be *immediately* of this practical kind. Thorough attention should be paid to long-range theoretical, historical, scientific, humanistic, and still other questions of cultural change that may have no direct utility for years or even decades. One of these problems, or rather a multitude of them, requires understanding and application of the concepts of process themselves—assimilation, nativism, and innovation, among others.

Equally basic to the whole of our second angle is the clarification and implementation of a modern theory of learning. That teachers as well as laymen remain confused in their attitudes toward, for example, the central process of enculturation is not only a commentary upon the need for better professional training in educational psychology; it bears fundamentally upon the entire matter of personality development in relation to cultural change.

In this respect, Puerto Rican personalities are no different from personalities anywhere else. They are largely, though not of course wholly, the product of cultural learnings—in school and out—to which they are exposed from the moment of birth. Education has the task of making sure that young personalities will develop that are as healthy and unified as the behavioral sciences can assure. The task is magnified on the Island by disharmony between what we have found to be strongly "negative" as well as "positive" traits—such negative traits as insecurity and often unconscious hostility vying with such positive ones as self-respect and generosity.

The proposed philosophy of education should, in our judgment, advocate ways of learning and teaching broadly harmonious with the functionalistic viewpoint, and subordinate those that are not. This means gradual elimination of rote learning and of authoritarianism in home and school alike. It also means experimentation with core curricula, stimulation of aesthetic and emotional experience as well as purely "rational" kinds, active and continuous sharing in both school and community planning; Island-wide utilization of classroom television and other audio-visual instruments as everyday affairs; and encouragement of critical thinking and democratic action from the nursery school up. At the same time, we believe that the syncretic character of Puerto Rico provides a milieu for the development of a richer, more mature kind of learning than has been typical of Continental schools where functionalistic processes have been stressed. What we have in mind is symoblized in a greater balance between *becoming* and *being,* the former term pointing directly to such processes, the latter to a widening sense of unity and socialized responsibility in the relations of teachers to children and of children to one another.

The teaching of English—the pedagogical issue that has plagued Puerto Rican education more incessantly than any other—italicizes many of the problems that center in the learning process. Despite advancements made possible by the effort to place such teaching on a "scientific" basis, despite the plausibility of a policy that regards English as a second language, we do not find anything like adequate concern for functionalistic principles. Thus, even were teachers much better trained in "structural linguistics," we question whether proficiency in English will advance at nearly the rate that it could were it to be taught more effectively in terms of those functionalistic principles. Even more fundamental, if that is possible, is the need for a philosophy of language and learning that could contribute to the reduction of symbolic confusions by enabling citizens to achieve a clearer sense of "cultural self-identity."

Meanwhile, just as Spanish is likely to remain the first language for a long time to come, so the Puerto Rican personality, expressed so richly through its native tongue, could not easily and certainly should not change in important aspects. Our evidence has revealed, on the contrary, how much there is to preserve and to build upon. Yet the processes of the culture could be much more effectively channeled if the ordinary citizen, who shares and in a sense ultimately directs these processes, could be purged of his deepest discords and rigidities and helped through education to release his maximum potentialities in behalf both of his own and the culture's maximum fulfillment.

3. To speak of "maximum fulfillment" is to speak of the third

of our three angles. The *goals* of the Puerto Rican culture are the apex of its educational philosophy.

Our study of this problem has produced a body of materials with which to meet a unique opportunity—to create a goal-centered, future-centered policy and program that could inspire not only the people of the Island but of many other countries. Education in the United States, certainly, is weak in this regard: the widespread influence of the progressivist philosophy reflects a historical period of social, economic, and political life concerned much more to glorify utilitarian means, processes, and practices—the "becomings" of experience—than the definitive ends and goals of the culture. It is an influence that should be viewed critically by the Island's educators at the same time that psychological and other contributions of that philosophy are in many respects incorporated into experience at all levels of learning.

It is not, however, only progressivist theory that should be viewed critically. It will be remembered that some respondents on the national level considered the general studies program of the University of Puerto Rico to be based heavily on another imported theory—namely, the perennialist philosophy of education. This philosophy is very much concerned with the ends of education—though not with explicit cultural ends. In its own terms, moreover, it is more definite about them than is progressivism: it locates them both in the potential rationality of man and in the perfectibility of the universe itself. The roots of perennialist doctrine lie in the classical humanist tradition which extends back to ancient Greece.

We have made careful perusal of authoritative formulations (considered to be representative by members of the faculty with whom we have conferred) of the University's philosophy of general education. We are led to conclude, not only with some of our own informants but with others regarded as educational authorities in Puerto Rico, that the influence of the perennialist orientation, under whatever label, has been potent indeed.[3] To be sure, as other informants pointed out, this influence is not without many modifications and even concessions to progressivist theory. Certainly it is not a mere transplantation of the so-called Chicago plan, nor is it solely a "great books" curriculum. Nevertheless, it borrows much from both—altogether too much, in our judgment, to provide a suitable guide either for general studies themselves or for the over-all philosophy of Puerto Rican education.

Anything like an adequate critique of the present policy is impossible here. In the degree that it is governed by perennialist premises, readers are referred to our contention, documented and argued at length elsewhere,[4] that these premises lead to conclusions in practice as well as theory inimical to the needs and purposes of any culture committed, as Puerto Rico is committed, to democratic means and ends.

In terms of the philosophy of education that emerges from this study, the central difficulty with the general studies program is that it is neither geared directly enough with the cultural order of Puerto Rico nor does it share actively enough in cultural processes (through, for example, functionalistic learnings) that could and should lead to the fruition of indigenous cultural goals. There is little by implication in some of its important formulations, moreover, that would be unacceptable to a theorist of Aristotelian-Thomist persuasion—indeed, even the style of some of these formulations reverberates with the dialectics of a Scholastic tract.[5]

At the same time, we would not leave the impression that the program is without admirable features. Study of original sources, respect for standards of scholarship, attempts to practice the Socratic method of critical inquiry, involvement of the faculty in curriculum making, recognition of the importance attached to integrated study, above all the devotion and ability of its directors—these are among the qualities that all Puerto Rican education ought to emulate. Nor, as some critics seem to suppose, is the progressivist philosophy that dominates courses in theory taught by the College of Education the sole alternative to the philosophy underlying the current general studies program. The point is that, though education on the Island may learn much from both, *neither is satisfactory.*

More specifically in terms of the problem of values and goals we suggest, again, that a much more rewarding approach is provided by the behavioral sciences, and thus by increasing analysis and interpretation of the multidimensional characteristics of the Puerto Rican culture itself. Even now, despite an almost total lack of Insular research in the field of values that could compare in thoroughness with research in, say, the nature of the family, it is possible to project directions. The conspicuous values enunciated with the aid of our respondents afford one important direction: they help to provide both description and prescription of the human qualities most widely prized by Puerto Ricans. And they tend to show that the latter are both tolerant of cultures with values different from their own and appreciative of universal or near-universal similarities.

That discords prevail and that a number of values now emerging generate disturbances is to be expected in a culture undergoing swift evolution. Thus, in religion we have found radically different notions of what its ultimate valuational significance is or ought to be. Also, Puerto Rican youth reflect current fluctuations. Even political goals remain unclear—particularly whether Commonwealth status or statehood should be the future permanent choice.

Yet, deeper down, some value commitments are already firm. The conspicuous values embodied in the modal personality are not only real; they are accepted as guiding norms. Nonsectarian Christian values such as brotherhood are equally accepted. Most impressive of all is the strength of commitment to human freedom—freedom defined not as a cliché but as the goal of self-expression synchronized with the rights of others, and as the privilege of sharing and democratic planning in terms of the widest possible welfare of the largest possible group.

Puerto Rican education has a double responsibility with regard to cultural goals. On the one hand, it ought to provide abundant opportunities for direct, critical study of the whole range of problems embracing human values—and this includes such controversial issues as religion, politics, and sex. On the other hand, it ought to provide equally abundant opportunities for students of all ages—*without indoctrination from above*—to achieve uncoerced commitments to whatever goals they may agree upon. Nor are these obligations to be carried out merely in general terms: since values and goals become embodied in institutional arrangements, it is the duty of democratic education to help student citizens determine for themselves and to experience whatever the policies may be that govern these arrangements.

Should a culturally oriented educational philosophy itself give allegiance to clear institutional goals? Our conviction is that it most assuredly should. In an age of crisis, old shibboleths of "impartiality" and "objectivity" in public education prove to be as outmoded as they are often spurious. Indeed, Western history is already ahead of the ideologies that these shibboleths connote. Just as the vast majority of people on this Island are becoming committed to freedom, so their schools should become committed in deed and symbol both to self-expression for every personality and to building democratic institutions that alone make self-expression meaningful. Nor are democratic institutions always equated with traditional forms of economic life. Actually, the people of Puerto Rico, if our panels speak for them, are more than sympathetic to economic patterns that increasingly vary from those forms.

By the same token, we cannot assume a one-to-one correlation of democratic institutions with established political arrangements. Certainly it is not national sovereignty that distinguishes such institutions. Nor, for that matter, is it necessarily either Commonwealth or statehood. Final commitment to one or the other, we suggest, is not as yet essential. This issue may soon enough be superseded by the larger, more crucial one of Puerto Rico's place in a whole network of inter-national-political relations. Many already believe that enforceable world order must eventually replace the chaos of competing nations. The schools could help through critical study and discussion to build an informed public judgment on this most vital question—very soon to be, perhaps, a question of life or death.

Meanwhile, as a policy of widening democratic socialization and designed, decentralized "garden communities" expresses the interests of the great majority, and as the objective of international government becomes congenial to that majority, these should be embodied in Puerto Rico's educational philosophy. We urge the necessity of such embodiment. It is one of the best guarantees against those demagogic dangers which respondents properly feared.

But let us be equally forthright in the insistence that commitment to cultural, including socioeconomic and political, goals does not exempt them from searching criticism. As a number of respondents insisted, dissent is itself an axiom of democratic freedom. The ex-perimental practices of, say, the welfare state *require* constant vigil-ance—a responsibility that education, rightly understood, should be more competent to exercise than any other agency. So, too, with all other goals of the Puerto Rican order. Commitment in terms of public policies is entirely compatible not only with the right to criticize or deviate, but even to repudiate those policies should a minority of critics succeed in persuading the majority of their own persuasions. Here is a risk that freedom demands.

This outline of a proposed educational philosophy is far from complete. Many ingredients could be added that have been discussed in this book, others that have not. Obviously, too, it does not pretend to reflect all the views of every respondent; clearly this would be impossible if only because none agrees wholly with any of the others.

What the outline does offer is, we hope, a prolegomenon to the kind of philosophy of education to which a large and widening share of the people should be, if they are not already, dedicated. It is not a philosophy derived from ready-made, transplanted theories; it is derived from as full an appreciation of the Island culture as the behavioral sciences, working with philosophy, are able to produce within the boundaries imposed upon our efforts.

Despite such boundaries, it provides, we believe, a norm by which to measure day-by-day accomplishments in the direction of Puerto Rican goals. The agenda it implies cannot be accomplished "overnight" or, indeed, ever perfectly. It allows room for healthy disagreement and amendment. It supports democratic efforts already under way.* It stresses the need for personal fulfillment in and out of classrooms. It tries to recognize the stubborn resistances that always lie in the path of cultural change. It provides room for the vigorous material means symbolized by an Operation Bootstrap; equally it provides for the spiritual ends symbolized by an Operation Serenity. But it also builds the framework of a cultural order that both means and ends must serve.

The question remaining is whether the many proposals for "action research," whether the many criticisms that we have recorded, and whether the philosophy that begins to emerge from our study are to receive the critical attention that they ought to receive. One of the weaknesses in Puerto Rican life that many persons have noted is the habit of investing heavily in projects of this kind and then, when

---

* Perhaps the most dramatic has been the "Inquiry of the People," instituted after our research was completed. This was an Island-wide project to stimulate local communities in the discussion of their educational needs. The author, who shared in its planning, urges that it be followed by further "Inquiries" held perhaps biannually.

completed, relegating them to the filing cabinet or library shelf. A culture the quintessence of which is its spirit of renewal can ill afford such waste.

We therefore plead with citizens to return to the first section of this chapter. *Try out these and other proposals and experiments.* Involve students, teachers, and parents in their planning and execution at every possible point. Take into consideration the readiness of some groups for some kinds of experimentation more than of other groups or other kinds. Certainly the propensity to avoid or drop such ventures whenever they are criticized (a propensity considered by some respondents to be accentuated by the personality trait of oversensitivity) cannot be justified. If an experiment fails, education has learned by that experience, too. If it succeeds, it can be widened and improved for the benefit of thousands. Thereby it will be dramatizing and testing educational philosophy as well.

A FINAL WORD

Our respondents, the real authors of this study, should have a final word.

When they were asked to look back upon their long hours of conversation with us, and to crystallize at the end their central ideas of what education on the Island both is and should be, their answers tended to reflect, above all, a hopeful and regenerative mood. Yet it is a mood tempered by tough-mindedness and frank reservations.

Consensus was widest on the national level in holding that Puerto Rican education ought to be a major agent of social, economic, aesthetic, personal, and other kinds of cultural change. Therefore it should be regarded, not just as a follower of conscious or unconscious dictates imposed by custom, habit, or the implicit level of configurational behavior and belief, but as a creative leader—a pointer of the way.

How is this possible? The single most frequently stressed recommendation was also our own at the close of the preceding section— the necessity to experiment. Two leaders singled out for reemphasis the proposal for an experimental junior college that could serve as a clearinghouse and laboratory for the testing of many new ideas. Such a college, one insisted again, should borrow from but not imitate Continental structures. Preferably it should provide four years of education and, most important, be free to try curriculum proposals without restriction of entrance requirements imposed by the higher learning.

Another chose to stress once more the problem of English education, and the necessity of moving more rapidly by way of new techniques toward maximum bilingualism—a goal which, he held, has already been attained in Switzerland, Holland, and Denmark to a greater degree than in Puerto Rico. Here the proposal of an enlarged program of exchange teachers received reiteration.

Still another leader was convinced that the single most urgent task is that of experimentation with the control of overpopulation and of such consequences as migration. The educational suggestions outlined in the Hill-Stycos-Back study earlier reviewed would illustrate his kind of concern.

An interesting afterthought of one contributor was that the several summer camps for students, sponsored by the University, prove the fruitfulness of unorthodox ways of departing from classroom routines. Curiously, no one had earlier mentioned these ventures. Yet they help to prove that one of the most reiterated needs—namely, an active partnership of community and school—can be satisfied in Puerto Rico because, in modest ways, it has already worked. For at least one other leader, such a partnership remains the foremost educational task.

Aside from experimentation as such, other leaders underscored more democratic sharing by all those involved in school operations and, by the same token, a radical revision of the hierarchical pattern of control. Poor channels of communication between, say, the University and other public agencies were lamented as one effect of this pattern. Yet three informants were convinced that the University already leads the culture to a greater degree than any other section of Insular education.

Additional reemphases were these: the need to encourage disagreement (private schools here perform an important role); the need to shift emphasis in teacher training from methodology to critical study of problems such as human values; the need to reorganize second-unit schools; the need to highlight emotional factors in human relations; the need to train more thoroughly in the three R's; the need for much improved vocational and agricultural preparation; the need for less complacency and more vigorous self-criticism; the need to broaden the idea of education to include *much more* than schools; the need for a special commission to provide imaginative short-range and long-range educational designs; the need for Puerto Ricans to understand themselves *as* Puerto Ricans (and of course, related to this, the need for more sustained attention to the nature of their culture); finally, embracing many of the others, the need to enlist schools in the whole national effort to plan for maximum freedom without indoctrination of anyone's plan.

Does education already serve more to advance than to retard the satisfaction of such needs? Here we find for a final time that disagreements continued to prevail. (They were quite consistent with parallel disagreements expressed in Chapter 10.) Four leaders were sure that, by and large, the schools today function more as a "brake" than as an "accelerator." A larger number disagreed: either they felt that it was impossible to choose in these terms or they were persuaded that with all its limitations education does serve to advance more than to retard cultural development.

The skeptical respondents inclined to regard Puerto Rican education as a follower and drifter on a "lazy stream." One bemoaned the ambivalence between overtraining for some kinds of positions and undertraining for others (electrical engineering, say). Another went so far as to accuse current education of being more of a "disintegrative" than an "integrative" force. More broadly, still others were sure that it remains insensitive both to the processes and goals of the culture. It lives too much in its own "ivory tower."

Others were more generous. Puerto Rican education, one said, has helped to build efficient government, to develop technology, and to create awareness of the meaning of democracy in such crucial respects as equality of race. Another felt that it has given new confidence to people that they can change and shape their lives—that they need not acquiesce in the forces of "fate." As a peer put it amusingly, the schools are "geared" to the culture even if they don't yet have enough gasoline.

Nor, said others, is it fair to be too critical. Granting that the profession of teaching leaves much to be desired, let us remember that the cause lies not so much in the profession itself as in social conditions unable thus far to afford a better one. Even so, Puerto Ricans can already be moderately proud of the quantitative achievements of their schools—the growing numbers in attendance, say—despite many qualitative weaknesses.

The fact, still others argued, that education by and large is not an innovator is not surprising either. Where is it otherwise? Actually, we should not ask too much of education. It is, after all, but one institution within the totality of culture. It cannot move too fast, and when it does move, implementers should be sure first to reflect upon what they do and where they want to get. Above all, the schools should guide always *within* the present culture and not be swayed by goals that lie too far beyond.

Despite these precautionary notes, the central emphasis was clear. Granting that the schools are by no means vigorous enough, nevertheless they hold tremendous latent power. Indeed, only one leader was emphatic in his rejection of the principle that education should concern itself directly with political and other kinds of reconstruction. For him, a chief purpose of education—especially of the general studies—is to develop rational and creative leadership. Social reform may result from this kind of education. But it is an *indirect* result.

The majority of our grassroots panel would no more agree with such a perennialist-influenced viewpoint than would the majority on the national level. The schools, they held, should share *directly* in leading the culture. But several were explicit in asserting, too, that it must be concerned with transmission as well as modification of established patterns.

Yet, again like the national panel, many were critical of the effectiveness with which schools now perform a leadership role. True, the belief was not unheard that they already do so; one respondent cited the dramatic instance of a factory being established in his subculture because, he said, students had taken the initiative in circulating petitions and arousing the community. Another held that the University is efficacious in serving as a vanguard. More largely, however, the opinion was expressed that education has not kept pace with the rate of cultural change. As one spokesman put it, only an informed public interest and wider knowledge would enable it to do so.

Let us close with two last comments heard at the grassroots—one from a principal, another from a teacher, both of whom have served their schools for many years. There is tremendous need, the first said, to try experiments at the local level, and to have *autonomía* in the course of trying them. Equally tremendous is the need, the other said, to develop in the young a clear sense of the norms that should guide the Puerto Rican people.

These norms, we have found, are grounded in the cultural configuration. Yet they are growing too—growing toward the goals of a democratic order that possesses both distinctiveness and deep affinity with human beings everywhere on earth.

APPENDIXES

I

NOTES ON METHODOLOGY

THE PROFESSIONAL student of cultural and educational research or theory may be interested in further comments on the methodology utilized in the present work. As indicated in Chapter 2, this methodology is only partially anthropological—at least in any orthodox sense. It is, rather, interdisciplinary because it tries to look upon the Puerto Rican culture from a unified viewpoint encompassing the behavioral sciences, philosophy, and education.

BACKGROUND

The first step toward instrument construction in the present study was taken about five years before any field work was attempted. This consisted of the study of culture theory earlier referred to.[1] As it neared completion, opportunity arose to spend an academic year in Puerto Rico with the expectation that some examples could be included that would enrich the theoretical treatment.

Only a few weeks of experience in Puerto Rico were needed to determine that such examples would be unsatisfactory because superficial and piecemeal. The mistake that so many visitors make in reacting to a strange culture—that of forming snap judgments from limited observations and then publicizing them as authoritative pronouncements—was a mistake that we resolved to avoid as far as possible. Instead, it was proposed to devote two to three years to the task of understanding Puerto Rico, publishing nothing on the subject meanwhile, but trying as patiently as possible to examine the culture in different perspectives with as much guidance from competent persons as could be obtained.

This interest gradually took the form of a hypothesis—namely, that *a fruitful interpretation of a given culture may be developed by systematically operating upon it with an antecedently formulated set of basic concepts derived from culture theory.* Anthropologists may argue that there is nothing original about such a hypothesis, that this is what they have always tried to do. But there are important differences between the typical approach of anthropologists and the approach undertaken here. Although increasing attention is given to theory in their professional training, one may still contend that their major concern and major skills have been concentrated in empirical research—in firsthand experience "in the field."

Some of the most distinguished anthropologists, moreover, have contributed originally to theory only after they have worked for many years with particular cultures. One result of this sequence is that, thus far, culture theory is disjointed and often confusing even to them—a situation that has its salutary aspects, for no one can accuse this young science of rigidity or complacency. But it is also a situation that sometimes produces research deficient in significance because deficient in clarification of premises and purposes.

Whatever the merits and demerits of anthropology as now usually practiced, it was impossible for the present study to be conducted by orthodox research procedures. For better or worse, the author's own training and experience have been primarily in philosophy, with special regard for the philosophic bases of education and the social sciences. In undertaking to study Puerto Rican culture, he accordingly had no choice but to proceed from prolonged immersion in theory to the level of practice rather than in the opposite order. The theoretical interpretation of culture which had been his chief preoccupation for a considerable period could not be discarded when it was decided to study a living culture, even had it been desirable to do so. Instead, the obvious course was to try to utilize this interpretation as deliberately as possible—to try to prove that one can, with careful planning, throw fresh light upon such a culture by utilizing the conceptual tools one has already hammered out. Chapter 2 presented brief working definitions of the main concepts utilized in this study.

The entire first year was devoted to cultural orientation. Travel around the Island to obtain an overview of its geography, principal occupations, and urban and rural patterns was followed by interviews with political and educational leaders, visits to some twenty elementary and secondary schools in town and country, and intensive study of books and articles on the family life, history, geography, economics, politics, art, and education of Puerto Rico.

Particular stimulation was obtained from first meetings with Governor Luis Muñoz Marín; Chancellor Jaime Benítez; Deans Oscar Porrata, Ramón Mellado, and Angel Quintero; Professors Efraín Sánchez Hidalgo (now Secretary of Education), Eugenio Fernández Méndez, and Luz M.

Torruellas Correa; Mr. Ramón Colón-Torres, Mr. and Mrs. Rafael Cordero, Mr. and Mrs. Fred Wale, President Ronald Bauer, and Dr. Rexford Tugwell; and from a series of meetings with official representatives of public housing agencies, economic development, recreation, cooperatives, and organized labor. Special trips were also arranged to rural and urban housing projects, to community education programs, to art exhibits, ballets, and social events.

Returning to Puerto Rico for a second year (the general proposal for a research study meanwhile having been approved for sponsorship by the College of Education, University of Puerto Rico, with the cooperation of the Social Science Research Center), the following four months were devoted to filling in background that could be translated into field research during the second semester. Work began immediately with a visit sponsored by the Division of Community Education to the south coast area, which had just been devastated by a hurricane.

A trip then followed to the Dominican Republic, Haiti, Jamaica, and Cuba in order to gain greater perspective on Puerto Rico. In the Dominican Republic, it was possible to obtain almost no useful impressions during the brief stay there. In Haiti, where the greatest time was spent, ethnologists at the University of Haiti, as well as officials of the Ministry of Education, scheduled visits to two rural communities and a number of rural and urban schools, and made possible brief observations of the rituals and mores of the people. In Jamaica, social workers arranged two long trips into the country. Both private and public schools of various urban types as well as the University College of the West Indies were visited, and conferences were held with both social scientists and leaders of Jamaican education. In Cuba, following a quick survey of Camaguey, several days were spent in Havana, where opportunity was provided by professors at the University of Havana to visit classes, to meet the Chancellor and other leaders, to inspect several public and private schools, and to see a cross section of life in the city.

Upon returning from the Caribbean trip, the next step was the construction of a research design. In this effort, the guidance and aid of the following were indispensable: Dr. Millard Hansen and Mr. Howard Stanton of the Social Science Research Center; Ricardo E. Alegría, Director of the Institute of Puerto Rican Culture; Professors Laguerre, Fernández Méndez, and Ismael Rodríquez Bou; Dean Hiram Cancio; and Acting Commissioner of Education Francisco Collazo. During trips to the Continent, conferences were held with Professor Clyde Kluckhohn of Harvard University and Dr. Margaret Mead of the American Museum of Natural History. Dr. Sol Tax of the University of Chicago further advised us while he was in Puerto Rico. All three of these distinguished anthropologists helped to clarify research methodology, such as interviewing techniques. Guidance was also obtained from three of the anthropologists responsible for *The People of Puerto Rico*[2]—the director of the study, Dr. Julian Steward of the University of Illinois, Dr. Eric Wolf of the University of Virginia, and Dr. Sidney Mintz of Yale University.

It will be remembered that the Steward study, as we have called it, provides more substantial research background for our own study than any other available. Students are urged to acquaint themselves intimately with it. Besides a wealth of information concerning the historical and contemporary life of the Puerto Rican people, it is based upon several theoretical principles of great importance to us. Three of the most relevant principles may be epitomized as follows: first, every culture—including small and compact ones such as Puerto Rico itself—is made up of subcultures that possess many of the characteristics of the whole culture, yet have their distinctive characteristics; second, every culture possesses an ecology (the relations of organism to environment), the most fundamental feature of which is manifested in the relations of its productive processes to the physical and biological environment; and third, every culture consists of levels of organization, from national to local, each of which again has both similarities to and differences from other levels. Steward has developed these and other concepts germane to the Puerto Rican study more fully in his book, *Theory of Culture Change*[3]—a work which has influenced our own theoretical interpretation of culture.

RESEARCH TECHNIQUES IN THE SUBCULTURES

The methodology of selecting and interviewing respondents on both levels is controversial. The question that may be raised most frequently by anthropologists is whether it is possible to obtain respondents of the quality needed for fruitful results by democratic group selection. The process common to anthropological research requires, of course, that the investigator make his own selection after prolonged acquaintance with the respective culture or subculture.

Much has been written in defense of this process, perhaps the most obvious but important point being that only the trained investigator is in a position to know from what kind of person or persons he is most likely to evoke the data he desires. As Steward points out, six months of field work is a minimum requisite for such research; preferably it should continue for several years. Selection of respondents must be made sometime in the interim, however, so that in actual practice the investigator is often far from intimately acquainted with his resource persons at the time of choosing them.

But field work cannot always be stretched even to six months. Shall we then, if less time is available, rule out any attempt to do research at all? Clearly the answer is "no." Anthropology is not an exact science and it is still undergoing rapid development. In every project, the significant question is not: "What can the investigator achieve according to ideal standards?" Rather it is: "What can he hope to achieve within the limits of his resources?" If he accomplishes his aim, he will claim no less and no more than his evidence and his guiding theory allow.

Our study of Puerto Rico required that field work be extended to three subcultural groups, each of which could be intensively and systematically cultivated for only a few weeks. This does not mean that any one of the three was approached "from scratch." It must be remembered that well over a year had previously been devoted to orientation, including contact with many citizens of various backgrounds and positions. Nor should it be forgotten that the Steward study, among others, was constantly presupposed as a foundation upon which our work was built. Given these advantages as well as restrictions, the question of how to obtain the most knowledge within the confines of our schedule seemed to justify the expectation that respondents could be at least as effectively selected by their peer groups as by us.

We did not assume that such selection could succeed without guidance. In each of the meetings arranged for the election of subcultural respondents, anywhere from one to three hours were devoted to explaining what the project involved, what its aims were, and how the respective group could best participate through a representative in whom it had confidence. These meetings were conducted primarily in Spanish, the superintendent of schools or some other local administrator sharing leadership with our research associate, Professor Rosado. Frequently members of the group raised searching, even skeptical questions concerning the project. Invariably they were urged to give consideration to candidates who were familiar with the community from long residence, who were earnestly concerned with education, and who were able to speak competently not only for themselves but for the group they would represent. It will also be remembered, however, that we did not insist upon exclusively elected representatives: of the twenty respondents, six were chosen by ourselves and our local educational advisers for what seemed at the time to be legitimate reasons.

In addition to the practical factors of limited time and association, three more fundamental reasons may be offered in theoretical support of our procedure. The *first* reason follows from the purpose of the study as "applied" research: because we depart from "pure" research by offering ways of improving the educational policy and program of Puerto Rico (in this sense, as one critic pointed out, our study reflects the "reformist" mood of the culture itself), we frankly wanted respondents who could help us most in this task. We saw no good reason why community groups would not already know who such representatives might be. Parents active in educational affairs, for example, are ordinarily well known in a community. Students and teachers who express a serious interest in their own schools are frequently recognized as such by their fellow teachers and fellow students.

It is true that persons of status and prestige, who were likely to be selected when this criterion is emphasized, are by no means always the most sensitive or intelligent representatives who might be found. It was, indeed, to reduce their undue influence in the process of election that the secret ballot was utilized in most cases, and that in all meetings electors were urged to choose persons who would be critical of their community and schools. In some cases, at least, our request was apparently respected. Especially interesting is the fact that none of the three student respondents were school leaders in a "popular" sense; they were prominent neither in extracurricular activities nor did they hold upper-level social status in their communities. Two came from lower-lower families, the third from the middle level. All three, however, were evidently admired by their peers for outstanding scholastic records—perhaps their most similar attribute.

Persons of prestige had other possible values to us. They might, for example, succeed in obtaining more information from their groups than less dominant or less respected representatives. Again, having been involved in the study, they might later help to implement its recommendations in their own subcultures. And even from the point of view of "pure" research, is it not important to learn what evidence can be derived from this kind of respondent? Whether such evidence is less or more significant than that derived from other kinds of respondents could, of course, be determined only by a controlled experiment—a difficult undertaking indeed. Yet the Steward findings (obtained, we recall, from respondents in two of the same subcultures by more conventional methods) already afford some basis of comparison with ours. Chapter 18 has examined these findings partly with such a question in mind and has found that, while they do not differ markedly, each study does contribute some evidence that the other does not. As would be expected from their different aims, metacultural evidence, for example, is more pronounced in our study, ecological evidence more so in the Steward work.

The *second* justification for our methodology of selection brings us back to the philosophy of education which it presupposes, and still more specifically to the role of experts. Granting that all the expertness possible is as much needed in anthropological types of inquiry as in other kinds, it re-

mains a debatable question whether in some research situations the judgments of nonexperts are not at least equally legitimate. One of these
situations, we believe, is education—or certainly the kind of education
that is accepted in principle by a democratic country such as Puerto Rico.

For, in such a country, educational policies are not finally established by
experts; in the degree that they are democratic, they are established by the
majority of people with due regard for minority dissent. Of course those
persons especially equipped by training to clarify the issues involved are,
during the process of establishment, indispensable to popular enlighten-
ment. Also, once policies are decided by the majority, other experts competent to translate them into workable instruments of rule and practice
are equally indispensable. But no democratic people, as long as it remains
democratic, ever relinquishes its powers to decide all public policies.

Education is an apt instance of this contention because it includes nearly
all citizens some of the time, and because it either enhances or stultifies
part, if not most, of their deepest values all of the time. Learning, for
example, is not something remote from the average individual; on the contrary, it is as intimately a part of his own experience as his skin. Experts,
to be sure, can greatly help the average individual to understand the ways
he learns and how he could learn better. But he himself, on the basis of his
experience and his knowledge, must ultimately decide (along with other
average individuals) what policies about learning he wishes to support.

The implications of this viewpoint are complex, for they go to the roots
of social and political philosophy. Elsewhere,[4] we have tried to examine
these implications with more care than is possible here. Our own position
is epitomized in the well-known argument of Harold Laski and others that,
while it takes an expert to make a pair of shoes, only the wearer can
finally tell whether or not they pinch him.

We are by no means saying that only the immediate feelings of a citizen
must be relied upon in determining policy. He needs to *inform* his feelings,
too, and one of the reasons why public schools in Puerto Rico and other
democracies so often tolerate outmoded practices concerning, say, learning, is precisely that he is not well informed. Yet, even if a maximum of
reliable information is obtained, it is he who must approve the policies
that do or do not perpetuate those practices. And such approval properly
involves his own familiarity with and intimate reactions to them.

The method of choosing most subcultural respondents in our study
rested in part, then, upon a theory of policymaking as it should function in
any democratic order and in any school system within that order. Spokesmen for such a system should be representative, and those whom they
represent should be at least as able to select them (though of course they

may err) as are those whom they do not represent—in this case, the "experts" in this study.

At the same time, it should not be forgotten that our panel of grass-roots spokesmen was by no means always lacking in its own competencies. Teacher respondents were certainly better informed than average citizens of their communities; so, for that matter, were most of the other respondents. And in all cases, they were interested in and concerned about Puerto Rican schools. In these respects, indeed, they were perhaps not (according to our own assumptions) representative enough. That is, we should have gone farther, if anything, with our democratic methodology rather than only as far as we did.

The *third* argument, related to the second, centers in what we have termed the concept of "social consensus." By this we mean a fundamental way of achieving agreement about truth and value—a way to which culture theorists, among others, have only begun to pay attention. Like our first and second arguments, this one is too involved to allow adequate treatment in a few paragraphs.[5] Its essential elements, however, are four in number: any social consensus worthy to be called true or good or even beautiful must provide for (1) the presentation of all evidence relative to the problem at issue; (2) unrestricted, full communication (in some cases, nonverbal as well as verbal) of that evidence; (3) maximum agreement among those who have considered and communicated the evidence (this may or may not be unanimous); (4) action, whenever appropriate, to test the agreement obtained. Like most of the concepts utilized in this study, social consensus is operational.

Aside from the question of whether it is also inherent even in the highly objective and exact truth-seeking processes of natural scientists (we hold, given certain qualifications, that it is), the contention here is that social consensus is certainly inherent in all processes involving the democratic interrelations of human beings—and therefore in all potentially or actually democratic cultures. For the same reason that democratic policies concerning, say, learning practices require not only the informed guidance of experts but the involvement of actual learners, so consensus in operation requires not only the most reliable evidence and communication available but a sharing of and reaction to these by whoever may be concerned with the human issue at stake.

The concept is, of course, normative. Evidence in any such issue is rarely if ever complete if only because human relations are themselves elusive, mobile, and often as yet beyond scientific understanding. Communication, because it so frequently involves emotion, and because even the most graphic symbols rarely convey the full measure of any human meaning, may be equally deficient. Agreements may be impulsive or subtly coercive even during the most conscientious effort to maintain a dispassionate, juridical atmosphere; often, too, they are partly or wholly opposed by dissenting individuals or groups. Finally, the actions that follow may be hasty, careless, or otherwise inadequate to test fairly the agreements reached.

Granting, then, that social consensus seldom if ever functions perfectly (for that matter, alternative ways of truth and value seeking seldom do, either), yet we believe that it affords a fresh and productive approach to such domains of human experience as those encompassed by the present study. Operation with the concept demands all four of the required steps as far as possible. We ourselves, aided by evidence from other research, have tried to follow the first three steps both in the subcultures and on the national level. The consensuses obtained, in the degree that these steps have been taken, are on our assumptions and in terms of our methodology therefore approximations of both what is true and what is valuable. But this is not to contend that such approximations are either invulnerable or established once and for all. As in every scientific endeavor, they are subject to criticism, improvement, or even rejection in the light of additional examination. For this, they especially require the fourth step in consensus building—namely, action—a step that we and our respondents have repeatedly urged in our pleas for experimental effort.

To summarize the rationale of our subcultural methodology, we have held that, given practical limitations of time and contact, field work may profitably utilize respondents selected by participating groups. Three theoretical contentions are offered in further support: first, that the status persons likely to be chosen by this process themselves have strategic as well as other values; second, that certainly in some research situations, such as one involving democratic education, the choices of groups may be at least as fruitful and reliable as those of outside experts; and third, that the judgments reached by respondents so chosen may be approximately true or valuable or both in so far as the concept of social consensus has operated during their participation.

Specific techniques of interviewing subcultural respondents on the basis of these theoretical contentions may now be reviewed. The first interview was devoted primarily to restating the method and purpose of the study, establishing the beginnings of rapport, and learning something of the life and personality of the respondent. The rule was emphasized that nothing told us would be identified with the individual spokesman. The immediate aim, by no means always fully achieved, was to win his confidence, and to give him self-assurance as well as a sense of sharing in a cooperative enterprise that might eventually benefit his community and the Island. In retrospect it may be said that, in general, the respondents did gain in these qualities—several rapidly and markedly, two or three relatively little. Only two seemed insecure throughout, possibly even suspicious of our motives. (Both were teachers extremely deficient in the use of English.) Several said they were "honored" to be chosen as participants.

In San José, the interviews following the "get-acquainted" period developed a sequence that proved useful enough to be adapted—although very flexibly—in Hermosa and Cañamelar. The second, third, and fourth sessions tended to move outward from the personal life of the respondent and his family to the local community and its schools, then to the Island as a whole and its relations with the United States and other countries, and finally back to the respondent's personal life and more intimate attitudes. Some effort was made from the beginning, however, to draw respondents into the theoretical framework in the background of every session.

But it was not till about the fifth session that the specific problems contained within this framework were raised in a deliberate way. By the time they were raised, most of the subcultural respondents seemed to have gained enough confidence and enough motivation so that they appeared readier to come to grips with them.

Here the most fruitful technique in the subcultures proved to be that of the "hypothetical question"—a technique suggested to us by Professor Kluckhohn and the Harvard Values Study Project,[6] but modified by the utilization of imaginary role playing. The respondent was asked to imagine two or three friends sitting in the room with us. One of the friends—"Señor Sánchez," let us say—would be quoted: "I am sure that . . ." Then, in vigorous tones and often in the colloquial Spanish in which our research associate was adept, he would express his viewpoint on the topic under discussion, sometimes citing an instance drawn from the respective subculture. Another friend—"Señor Rodríguez" was a favorite name—would next, with equal vigor, express a sharply different viewpoint. Sometimes a third or even fourth imaginary friend would differ from the others. The respondent would then be asked whether he inclined to agree more with one than another of the disputants.

Regularly during such role-playing sessions he would be reminded that he need not agree with any one of them. It was interesting to note that, while he often did take sides, he would on occasion say that he agreed only partly with one, or equally with both (if there were two "friends" discussing), or with none of them. In the latter case, he would either express a still different viewpoint or say that he could not decide. As a rule, whatever answer he gave would be followed by effort on our part to discover his reasons; often he would give emphatic ones, revealing that he had probably thought about the matter before.

Although emphasized, this technique was not invariably utilized, partly because some of the topics did not lend themselves to it as much as others, partly because it becomes tedious if practiced too steadily. Also, the flexible pattern of interviews encouraged unanticipated lines of questioning. Nevertheless, the device proved successful if judged by indications of interest and by the capacity of respondents to grasp the meaning of questions which, stated more abstractly, might have been more greatly distorted or missed entirely.

In addition to interviewing, two other resources have been utilized in the subcultures (see Appendix, III and IV):

1. We have said earlier that the choice of an area for study of the middle class was made somewhat arbitrarily. The question remained whether it could be justified on more objective grounds. To answer this question in part, the assistance of Professor José M. Zapata Muñoz of the College of Education was enlisted. A brief questionnaire prepared with his help was submitted to about forty Hermosa families of children in the elementary school who lived in the surrounding neighborhood, the families being chosen at random by the principal. The questionnaires were administered in the homes by teams of University students under Professor Zapata's direction. They were unsigned.

In the Hermosa senior high school nearby, members of the social-studies faculty were asked to conduct a similar survey, and 136 families answered a questionnaire modified slightly from that used for the elementary school families.

The results of these two surveys, while by no means invulnerable to error, seemed sufficiently useful to justify comparable surveys in San José and Cañamelar, even though we were not interested in their middle classes as such. In both, the surveys were directed by social-studies teachers of the senior high schools, forty-six families being canvassed in San José, thirty-four in Cañamelar.

2. To throw additional light upon data gathered in the three subcultures, the superintendent of schools in each was asked to answer forty-five questions in brief paragraphs, most of which had already been considered in some form by the respective subcultural respondents. Each superintendent was assured that his answers would not be identified as his, and each was invited to consult with an assistant superintendent in preparing his answers.

RESEARCH TECHNIQUES ON THE NATIONAL LEVEL

The use of a single national-level jury to elect the panel of leaders was perhaps less defensible in our theoretical terms than the use of local groups. Certainly no one will deny that the resulting ratio of experts in various aspects of Puerto Rican culture was much higher than on the grass-roots panel.

Also, interviews with the sixteen leaders were more structured, and almost no time was taken to establish confidence or rapport by inviting them to talk about themselves. In the first meeting, the plan and purpose of the project were briefly reviewed; in addition, respondents were told of the companion work which provides the framework of the interviews. They were invited to respond spontaneously to each of our questions (see Appendix, II) as fully or as briefly as they wished. Though less consistently than on the subcultural level, these were often illustrated by familiar examples and were accompanied by subquestions, many of which had been prepared in advance, others of which arose in the course of a particular interview. Usually, each major question together with all its subquestions would be read before the leader responded.

Despite the reservations just noted, some critics may insist that the guiding questions (they of course reflect our theoretical viewpoint) were too general or abstract to be meaningful. Here we are confronted with issues that extend into the semantics of cultural communication. Although our study cannot possibly be judged on the basis of these questions alone, it may be asked whether one can obtain reliable knowledge of any culture by utilizing high-level symbols in cultural research. Our own view is that one can. Not all research deals with meticulous detail; there are many kinds of research according to various aims and methods. As a matter of fact, the question may even be raised (as it was by one critic of our manuscript) whether the guiding questions were not at some points too specific rather than too general in terms of our objectives.

At any rate, philosophic or metacultural research, which this study heavily stresses, is just as legitimately based upon, say, synoptic questions as conventional empirical research is not. People hold and articulate many beliefs about culture in general as well as in specific terms; what they believe in comprehensive terms has its own strengths and weaknesses in the same way that typical fact-finding research has other kinds of strengths and weaknesses. What the former provides by way, for example, of a perspectival view of a culture (as in national-character research) it often lacks in specificity. But what the latter provides by way of minute empirical data it often lacks in perspective. Thus far, social science, including anthropology, is weaker in its generalizing contributions than its particularizing ones. There is need today for greater balance.

Nor can it be argued that only the conductor of a research study concerned, as is ours, with generalizing contributions is qualified to draw them as inferences from the data. Certainly it is his business to do so as far as he is able, but so, too, should it be the business of those who already belong to and represent a culture. Chapters 6 and 7, on the implicit and explicit culture, is one of several that support our contention that interviewees themselves, guided of course by the interviewer, are able to contribute directly to the explication of more or less implicit and configurational beliefs—a contribution not wholly confined, moreover, to the best-educated spokesmen.

We must, indeed, be wary of those who too zealously criticize cultural research concerned with general types of belief. Push them far enough and they will have to admit that no cultural research expressed in symbols— especially verbal symbols—is defensible at all. For all communication above the level of individual grunts and gestures demands, as Alfred Korzybski has shown, greater or lesser degrees of abstraction.[7] The ultimate conclusion from this kind of criticism, though commonly made by pedestrian researchers, is anti-intellectual and anti-scientific.

A memorandum prepared about halfway through the sixteen interviews is reproduced here to throw further light on the premises and procedures of our national-level research:

1. It is assumed that spontaneous answers (no previous knowledge of questions) are significant because (a) they indicate whether the respondent has already thought out opinions; (b) they can be set against his later judgments (since he is provided opportunity to correct or amend) ; (c) they help to indicate the degree to which his total viewpoint is consistent; (d) they help to show whether he possesses a sophisticated background in the theory and practice of culture.

2. Some of the questions raise closely parallel issues to test consistency.

3. It is assumed that once the general viewpoint of a respondent is established, answers will move faster. This has usually been the case, although possibly part of the acceleration is due to (a) a desire to complete the interview as it approaches the end (both the respondent and questioner may share this desire, perhaps unconsciously) ; and (b) the fact that the material overlaps so much that later material is already anticipated by earlier answers.

4. Many of the answers are opinions, although the degree to which they are qualified by various respondents varies sharply. How many of the opinions can already be verified by confirmable fact (such as research evidence) is unknown, although it is expectable that the large majority cannot. Nevertheless, the expressed opinions are of great importance whether as yet confirmable; they represent the judgments of

leaders who, in considerable degree, establish and support policies based upon them.

5. The questions asked are all derived from the author's companion volume and usually, though not always, follow the same order. But in some cases, it is not possible to formulate questions derived from the theoretical study that would be particularly helpful or meaningful, even though all the concepts seemed important when included in that study. By the pragmatic test, it might be contended that some of the concepts should not have been included in the first place, although this perhaps could not have been known at the time.

6. Formulation of the questions has involved the effort to make them meaningful for leaders living in a real culture. Therefore, the questions usually have explicit regard for their applicability to Puerto Rico. At the same time, they are kept fairly abstract and technical, on the assumption that the leaders are well-educated persons who are prepared to understand such questions without "watering down."

7. Respondents are not held to a strict time schedule or a series of "yes-or-no" type questions and answers. Respondents have differed widely in the degree to which their answers are ramified and unfocused, but only rarely have they obviously misunderstood the question (and in these cases, the English language was probably in part responsible).

8. Each respondent has produced new insights and opened new issues which produced fresh subquestions. At the end of the second completed interview, the original set of questions was slightly modified in the light of experience thus far, and again at about the halfway point in the whole series. But no new major questions have been added for two reasons: (a) it would be impractical to add them as long as comparisons between all respondents are to be made; (b) no new major questions have been raised by the respondents, although numerous subquestions have been introduced, a few of which thereafter were included as regular subquestions.

9. After the first few interviews, leaders were given a choice between note taking and tapes. A minority have requested the former (one reason: answers are more spontaneous); the majority have been indifferent. Eight interviews were recorded entirely in notes taken by Mrs. Brameld; five were entirely on tape; three were a combination. Notes and transcriptions have been approved by respondents with only minor changes, indicating a fair degree of satisfaction with their original replies even after a lapse of time. (Subcultural interviews were all taken in on-the-spot notes.)

SOME CRITICAL REACTIONS TO OUR METHODOLOGY

Few research workers in the field of culture, we imagine, have ever come to the completion of a study without the wish to start over. In our case, this wish is acute; we have learned so much by our mistakes that only now, in retrospect, do we feel partially ready to begin.

Bearing in mind that we are concerned here with a methodological evaluation (our principal substantive evaluation has been presented in Chapter 19), let us first note weaknesses in our ways of selecting respondents. On the grassroots level, it would have been preferable to preplan our meetings with community groups more carefully than we did. Particularly helpful would have been advance practice by means of role-playing sessions. The author's inadequate grasp of Spanish was also a handicap not only in evaluating these meetings but in the interviews themselves. Though immeasurably aided by the expert ability of his Puerto Rican associate to translate and interpret meanings in terms familiar both to interviewer and interviewee, inevitably some meanings were lost or distorted. The fact, too, that a minority of respondents were not elected by groups but chosen by the staff turned out to be unfortunate: three of these six were less satisfactory than all but two of the fourteen who were elected—a further commentary, perhaps, on the value of the latter process.

Also, the grassroots panel was far from completely representative of the three subcultures. The panel was made up of predominantly middle-status persons whose education was well above average—a bias that could and does often result, however, from conventional anthropological methods as well.

By way of further extenuation, it should be noted that about half of the group originally came from lower-lower or upper-lower strata, that only four of the twenty had urban rather than rural upbringings, and that seventeen were "natives" of their own subcultures. In one community, moreover, twenty-two of the thirty-three teachers who elected their representative were also born in that municipality and graduated from its high school—a ratio that would probably have been similar at least in a second of the three communities. In this connection, we may recall that no respondent was expected to speak only for himself; on the contrary, he was often requested to consult with his group before answering certain questions and to incorporate their reactions into his own responses. On several occasions, respondents investigated factual questions in documents or like sources concerning the local situation, which they then reported to us. Finally, the fact that a majority of grassroots respondents had achieved middle status was by no means entirely unfavorable to our interest: we have found that Puerto Rico may be moving in the direction of a middle-class culture. The need to describe, evaluate, and anticipate the significance of this trend is therefore a pressing one—especially so since relatively little research hitherto has focused upon it.

We incline to be more critical of our method of choosing the national panel. Members of the jury which elected it were themselves chosen too hastily, with too little preliminary spelling out of their own qualifications, and with too brief orientation provided them in the aims and techniques of our project. In turn, the jury appeared to make its nominations too casually. While we were gratified with the caliber of the nominees, those familiar with Puerto Rican leadership will at once recognize serious omissions and imbalances. The absence of women, labor leaders, journalists, bankers, historians, religious leaders, and artists other than writers is especially glaring. Two outstanding labor leaders were, to be sure, nominated in the first round, but both failed to accept our invitation. A brilliant Puerto Rican historian, nominated by a large majority, accepted but then withdrew before interviews could begin. Others in the above categories were named on the original list compiled by the jury but were eliminated by insufficient votes. One critic of the manuscript considered about two-thirds of the panel to be "pro-American."

To be counted on the favorable side is the fact that social scientists and educators—both of primary importance to us—were well represented. That Popular party leaders were prominent may also be considered helpful in the same way that middle-class respondents were helpful on the subcultural panel: both reflected a large actual or potential proportion of the population. Also, labor was represented by one local leader on the grassroots panel, organized religion by another local leader, and women by five informants. Strong industrial if not banking interests of Insular scope were represented by at least one political leader on the national panel.

The difficulty of perfectly satisfying anyone about the best possible group of leaders is exemplified by conflicting comments from two critics. The first held that the principal trouble with the panel was that it contained too few bona fide "intellectuals." (There was only one, he contended.) The second objected for an opposite reason: there were too few leaders of "practical" fields such as business.

Methods of interviewing on both levels were deficient on several scores. Lack of time, of language facility, of intimate familiarity with metacultural and other subtle aspects of the Puerto Rican culture, of dexterity in ferreting out meanings, and of sufficient insight concerning many of these meanings adds up to a heavy total deficit. Undoubtedly some answers were distorted by what a respondent thought we wanted him to say, others by our own predilections as to what we hoped he would say, still others by guesswork or sheer misinformation.

We particularly regret not having oftener pursued openings provided by the flexible, informal mood of our conversations. Rather often we succeeded in returning to these openings for further examination of the questions raised, but at other times we failed to do so. As any careful reader of our study has noted, a great number of points are recorded that invite fuller treatment by way of criticism and elaboration. Also, despite our effort to maintain flexibility, the interviews were more structured than they should have been by anthropological standards.

At the same time, the informal relationship between interviewers and interviewees produced unequally fruitful material. Some respondents were, as anyone would anticipate, more articulate, better informed, and readier to volunteer information and opinions than others. One result is that there are gaps in the total material that make it more difficult to generalize than might have been the case had the interviews been still more parallel.

Critics of the manuscript differed again, however, on some of these difficulties. One was convinced that no individual not identified with the culture over a period of many years is equipped either to ask the right questions—especially concerning the configuration of Puerto Rico—or to follow through to the right answers. Another was equally convinced that *only* an outsider could do so, because only he would have sufficient perspective to observe or articulate the taken-for-granted beliefs and attitudes of lifelong citizens. Something is to be said for both views, but of necessity we have pursued the latter course.

Nor was the fact that our research schedule required us to move fairly rapidly from one resource to another entirely unrewarding. What the orthodox anthropologist (who usually attaches himself to one fairly narrow area and group) gains in depth he may miss in breadth.[8] The impressions derived from sequential immersion in three subcultures and one culture-wide level could conceivably enrich the total understanding of a culture in ways that complement the ways of, for example, the Steward team.

More basic are the criticisms that could be made of the theory underlying our methodology. For example, a group of Puerto Rican educators now influential in the higher learning could hardly be expected to endorse such principles as democratic policy making and social consensus while at the same time supporting, though under various labels and in different degrees, what we have called the perennialist viewpoint. We recognize and respect the strength of this viewpoint; it should be examined with care. But we do not believe that such a comparison, if conscientiously accomplished, will undermine our own philosophic viewpoint; on the contrary, we contend that it will eventually lead to a repudiation of perennialism and its allied doctrines as contrary and even dangerous to the widening experimental and democratic mood of the culture today.[9]

Meanwhile, further comments are called for concerning the key principle of social consensus as we have sought to operate with it. Despite the welter of deviations and conflicts among respondents, consensuses of greater or lesser importance do clearly emerge. They are not, of course, consensuses to be judged in any quantitative way, nor were they ever achieved by mere "counting of noses." We reiterate that such terms as "majority" and "minority" are utilized in this study only to suggest the direction and strength or weakness of the reported agreements and disagreements. Such greater or lesser consensuses as were obtained are entirely *qualitative* in significance.

We have also said that the theory of social consensus, to the extent that it fulfills its own requirements, provides certain kinds of truths and values. In this study, no truth or value has been perfectly demonstrated because the criteria of the theory were far from perfectly fulfilled. Nevertheless, each has been approached at various points and in various degrees: first, in so far as consensuses of leader and grassroots respondents reinforced each other; second, in so far as judgments of experts (from, say, the national level) tended to be reciprocally supported by judgments of nonexperts (from, say, the subcultural level); third, in so far as evidence from other research studies strengthened our own.

More true and more desirable consensuses might have been obtained had it been possible for us to search more persistently into the dissenting and deviating reactions of individual respondents. Some of these reactions were doubtless the effect of inadequate symbolic clarification of configurational and metacultural meanings—an inadequacy due at least as much to our own insensitivities as to pressures of time. The stress we placed at several points upon conflicting beliefs and attitudes may not, therefore, indicate as unusual or significant a phenomenon as we tended to suggest. Probably any culture, were it approached as we approached Puerto Rico, would reveal disparate, even contradictory, reactions to the types of questions we posed.

Also, in technical philosophic terms, we would criticize the relatively sparse attention paid to the ontological and cosmological as compared with the epistemological and axiological spheres. Doubtless because of our own biases, we have learned less of the way Puerto Ricans view nature and the universe than we have of how, for instance, they view their own conduct.

And yet, as we moved forward in our explorations toward goals and other problems with axiological implications, it sometimes seemed increasingly difficult to obtain clear and firm consensuses. This is not hard to explain. Despite the inescapability and centrality of values in every aspect of cultural life, they are perhaps the most elusive and least clearly demonstrated of human phenomena. Moreover, in Puerto Rico as elsewhere, less careful research has been conducted in the area of goals than in the area of either order or process. An ironic paradox thus emerges: *the greater the need for reliable social consensuses* (after all, the whole public policy and program depend upon sound collective value judgments), *the less careful, sustained effort seems to have been exerted to establish them.* Not only does conventional social science shy away from such axiological effort; so, even, does public education.

What we have said of the imperfect operation of the consensus principle applies, indeed, to our entire philosophy of culture and education. This philosophy, as noted elsewhere,[10] is far from complete or satisfactory. In the present volume, its many imperfections appear most frequently in the endeavor to apply an abstract theory to a concrete situation. Among these imperfections we select four for reemphasis. First, the scope of our study, which reflects our philosophic interest in the comprehensive and general, inevitably results in lack of precision—of sufficient analytical detail. Second, the fact that our data are overwhelmingly symbolic produces not only distortions and ambiguities but neglects some of the more directly observable behaviors prevailing in cultural experience. Third, the deliberate projection of a fairly definite point of view upon a culture also selects and colors some of the material. Fourth, the influence of the pluralistic propensities of contemporary culture theory upon our own theory produces at times more of an eclectic and possibly disunified impression than, say, the Steward volume, which, in turn, is vulnerable for the opposite reason. (The latter, though concerned with differences among subcultures, tends to oversimplify and overunify by interpreting these differences primarily in terms of one hypothesis.)

To all of these criticisms we counter with but a single point of defense —namely, the *consequences* that have followed and will, we hope, follow from our theory in general and our methodology in particular. Those consequences that have followed thus far are the subject matter presented in preceding pages. They speak for themselves. Those that will follow are the educational-cultural experiments and resultant changes for which our Puerto Rican friends must themselves assume chief initiative and responsibility.

Among these friends, we express our deep appreciation especially to the individuals hitherto mentioned in this Appendix; to our respondents in the subcultures whose names we must regretfully omit to protect their anonymity; to our sixteen national-level respondents listed in Chapter 2; to the many other individuals, such as the school administrators of the three subcultures, who offered their hospitality and cooperation during our field work; and to those on the faculty of the University of Puerto Rico and on the staff of the Department of Education who advised and otherwise helped us.

We also thank the following members of the University of Puerto Rico faculty for having read from one to many chapters of the manuscript and for having offered incisive criticisms and suggestions: Professors Antonio J. Colorado Capella and Millard Hansen, Associate Professors Joseph Kavetsky and Carlos Albizu Miranda, Assistant Professors E. Seda Bonilla and Jaime Toro Calder, and, in addition, Dean Porrata, Mr. Charles Rosario Merrick (Director of the Division of Extension Programs), and Mr. Howard Stanton (Assistant Director, Family Life Project). Four North Americans familiar with Puerto Rico also reacted helpfully to parts of the manuscript: Professor Melvin Tumin, Princeton University; Professor Thomas C. Cochran, University of Pennsylvania; and Professor and Mrs. Harold Rugg, Woodstock, New York.

Finally, we are indebted to the administration of the School of Education, New York University, for having authorized leaves of absence to carry on our study; to the *Harvard Educational Review* and *School and Society* for permitting the inclusion of some material that first appeared in their pages; and especially to Dr. Paul Fejos, Research Director, Wenner-Gren Foundation for Anthropological Research, for having arranged additional grants for travel and compilation.

II

GUIDING QUESTIONS FOR NATIONAL-LEVEL LEADERS

I. ORDER

1. Which, if either, of the following beliefs do you consider the *more* influential among the Puerto Rican people today?
   —A. Culture determines what men are.
   —B. Men make culture whatever it is.
   —Is either of these attitudes now developing more rapidly than the other?
   —Does the history of Puerto Rico help to explain why one or the other of these attitudes has been the more dominant?
   —Do science and technology have any fundamental effect on these attitudes among Puerto Ricans?
   —Is it your impression that education is sensitizing people to the import of these ways of looking at culture?
   —Can you suggest any practical ways by which education could more strongly affect one or the other, or both, of these ways of looking at culture?

2. Can Puerto Rican culture be "typed" so that it assumes some kind of fairly whole character, distinguishable from other cultures?
   —If so, could you describe this character?
   —Is it more difficult to effect such a characterization in the case of Puerto Rico than of some other cultures?
   —Do you believe that, because of Puerto Rican history, its cultural character is somewhat ambivalent or at least lacking in a sense of wholeness?
   —Do the schools tend to encourage an awareness of Puerto Rican national character?
   —If you believe they should do so more deliberately, could you suggest ways?

3. What is the structure of the "typical" family with regard to the relationship of its members and lines of authority?

—Is there any marked difference here between rural and urban families?

—Is there any marked difference between families of different statuses or classes?

—Is there a marked tendency toward changing the traditional family structure?

—Is the *compadre* tradition changing markedly?

—Would you like to see any fundamental changes in the typical family structure?

—Can you suggest any practical ways in which education might deal with family patterns and problems more deliberately?

—How, if at all, should adult education concern itself with this problem?

4. How would you describe and appraise the class structure of Puerto Rico?

—Which class, if any, would you say is growing most rapidly today?

—Is the top level differentiated primarily according to wealth, prestige, or some other primary outstanding characteristic?

—Are *americanos* freely admitted to this top level?

—Is the top level also the most powerful class? If not, then which?

—Are *americanos* welcome in middle-class circles? In lower classes?

—Is there a strong sense of conflict between the "haves" and the "have-nots"?

—Does organized labor tend to regard the "haves" more as its opponents or as its allies in the effort to attain prosperity for all?

—Do the upper levels tend to regard the lower levels as inferior in intelligence and ability?

—Do the lower levels tend to regard the upper levels as superior in intelligence and ability?

—Are people of colored skin generally regarded by others as inferior? If so, in social class primarily or in race primarily?

—Where would you place the bulk of teachers in their social class?

—Is it your impression that teachers pay adequate attention to the practices and values of social classes other than their own?

—Would you favor the affiliation of teachers with organized labor?

—What is your judgment of the effect of private schools upon the class structure?

5. Do the explicitly stated beliefs of Puerto Ricans (e.g., about religion, democracy, and morality) fairly well coincide with their more deeply cherished, more implicit beliefs?

—Do you think that Puerto Ricans are greatly concerned over the instability of world conditions?

—Do they feel insecure as a result of the world situation?

—Some anthropologists have contended that the "symbolic systems" of many cultures are today confused, with resulting conflict. Would you say that Puerto Rico is among these cultures? Do people find trouble in making clear to each other what they mean? (In the arts as well as language?)

—The fight against poverty has been central in recent Puerto Rican history. Would Puerto Ricans, in a serious crisis, be willing to sacrifice their democratic privileges for the promise of economic security?

11. Is there a sense of fatalism pervading the culture?

—If so, would you attribute this to its historical experience?

—Is there a marked difference between classes on this question?

—Lewis Mumford speaks of the sense of "renewal" in culture. Do you believe that Puerto Ricans have any such deep feeling?

—Does education play any important role in generating either fatalism or renewal?

—Could you suggest ways in which it could do so more vitally?

12. Since it is said that cultures achieve continuity through learning, what *kinds* of learning should be encouraged in Puerto Rican education, formally and informally?

—Could you say that the average student learns more in or out of school?

—Would you agree with the contention sometimes made that education has the responsibility of inculcating the rules and skills of culture in the learner's early years, and then in the later years emphasizing critical thinking, cooperative experience, and other more functional ways of learning?

—Do you think Puerto Rican education has been overinfluenced by North American education, especially in methods?

—Is it your impression that teachers strongly encourage individuality, creative expression, etc., in children?

—Would you like to see more stress placed upon learning the three R's through exercise and drill?

—Do you feel that teachers are sensitive to the emotional dimensions of learning?

—What improvements could you suggest for the educational program so far as methods of learning and teaching are concerned?

—Where do you think the best teaching takes place in Puerto Rico today—on the elementary, secondary, university, or adult levels?

—What is your impression of the role of radio and television, present and future, as an instrument of learning?

13. Is the Puerto Rican personality changing significantly, or is it likely to change? If so, toward what characterization?

—Can some of its present outstanding characteristics be stated in positive terms and some in negative terms?

—Is there any truth in the opinion sometimes expressed that the Puerto Rican is often suspicious, defensive, and hypersensitive?

—Can Puerto Rican types be distinguished according to class or status?

—Are there any marked differences between rural and urban types?

—As the symbol of the Populars, is the *jíbaro* in any real sense a Puerto Rican archetype?

—Is there any truth in the opinion sometimes expressed that the Spaniard who has recently come from Spain is disliked?

—Are there are significant differences between Puerto Rican personality types according to sex?

—Do you think that the family structure has played a more important role in typing the Puerto Rican personality than any other factor?

—Would you say that neurotic tendencies are increasing or decreasing today? Is the migration pattern an important factor in considering this problem?

—Is education doing anything important by way of reducing emotional disturbances and enhancing mental health?

—Is education doing more to stabilize or to destabilize the Puerto Rican personality type, if such exists?

—Could you suggest practical ways by which education might more directly enable personalities to cope with and advance cultural changes?

III. GOALS

14. Could you say that Puerto Rico has any distinctive values, or, if not distinctive, at least definitive?

—Are Puerto Ricans more competitive than cooperative, or vice versa?

—Are aesthetic values central in the culture?

—Would you say that Puerto Ricans are tolerant of values different from their own?

—Do you think that they tend to regard their own basic goals as pretty similar to those of people in far-removed parts of the world?

—Do the values of subcultures differ in any important ways?

—Would you say that education is helping children to become value-conscious?

—Could you suggest ways by which it might help more than it does?

—What major values of Puerto Ricans would you like to see stressed in Puerto Rican education?

15. How fundamental do you think religious values are in Puerto Rican culture?

—How would you define any such values?

—Would you like to see more stress placed upon religious values in education?

—Would you favor teaching comparative religion in the schools?

—Governor Muñoz has recently popularized the term "Operation Serenity." Is this in any sense a religious goal?

16. Do you approve of the values to which young people in Puerto Rico are most devoted today?

—Is the teen-ager more concerned to gain the approval of his peers than of his parents?

—Are the values of sex and marriage undergoing important change among them?

—Would you support a program of sex education in the schools?

—Do the ambitions of Puerto Rican young people tend to be more modest than those of North American young people?

—Is there much concern among young people with the values of other cultures and subcultures?

—Is there any marked sense of world-mindedness or international order as an ideal among young people?

—Would you recommend more attention to these last two questions by the schools?

17. Are Puerto Ricans in the process of developing *new* values and goals?

—Do you think that they know where they want to go?

—Do you personally agree with the goals of Puerto Rican culture?

—Is education strongly involved in the effort to clarify and struggle for Puerto Rican goals?

—Would you suggest ways in which education could become more strongly involved?

18. Do you think that Puerto Ricans place a high value on freedom?

—How would you personally define this value?

—Some North Americans would say that the "welfare state" constricts freedom in the long run. How do you react to this argument in the case of Puerto Rico?

—In your opinion, does education play an important role in developing a meaningful, experienced freedom?

—Is the typical discipline of teachers in conflict with the freedom of children?

—In the United States, the schools are sometimes criticized for developing freedom as a means but not as an end. Does this criticism have meaning for you with regard to Puerto Rican schools?

—Do Puerto Ricans think much of freedom as a world-wide goal?

19. What is your over-all judgment as to the extent to which education is geared to the culture?

—Does it serve as a brake?

—Does it serve as an accelerator?

—Can you reasonably contend that education is not only a creature but a creator of culture?

—Should education take an active part in political and economic reform?

—Can you suggest any practical ways by which any remaining gap between Puerto Rican education and culture may be narrowed?

III

SOCIOLOGICAL SURVEY

1. Number of persons in household_____
   Age of father_____ age of mother_____
   Number of children_____ males_____ ages_____ females_____
   ages_____
   Members other than parents or children_____

2. Occupations
   Of mother_____
   Of father_____
   Of members other than children in school_____
   _____
   Children in school: year in elementary_____ private_____ public_____
   　　　　　　　　　　　” 　　secondary_____ private_____ public_____
   　　　　　　　　　　” college or university_____
   Other members now studying_____ nature of study_____
   _____

3. Residence
   owner_____
   renter_____
   house or apartment_____
   number of bedrooms_____ living room_____ dining room_____
   garage_____

4. Modern commodities
   automobile_____ make_____ year_____
   radio_____ how many_____
   TV_____ automatic washer_____
   family library?_____

5. Reading
   Books, fiction_____ novels_____ scientific_____ others_____
   Newspapers, which?_____

Magazines, which?_____

Nature of newspaper articles you prefer, sports_____ political_____
international_____ economic_____ labor_____ others_____

6. Religious affiliation
   Denomination_____
   How often father attends? weekly_____ daily_____ occasionally_____
     "   "   mother   "   weekly_____ daily_____ occasionally_____
     "   "   children "   weekly_____ daily_____ occasionally_____
   Parents married by priest_____ minister_____ judge_____

7. Associations
   Parents belong to
   Casino de Puerto Rico_____ Casa de España_____ Caparra Country
     Club_____ Rotary_____ Lions_____ Masonic Lodge_____ Knights
     of Columbus_____ Women's Civic Club_____ sorority_____ frater-
     nity_____ alumni association_____ Others_____
   _____

8. Migration
   Number of household members who have been in U.S._____
   Close relatives in U.S. now: father_____ mother_____ children_____
   Number of members who have worked in U.S._____
   Number of members who have studied in U.S._____

9. Activities
   Average number of hours that children watch TV daily_____
   TV program preferred_____
     by children_____
     by grown-ups_____
   Radio program preferred
     by children_____
     by grown-ups_____
   Number of members who attend movies_____
     weekly_____ occasionally_____
   Number of members who attend baseball games_____
     often_____ occasionally_____ never_____
   Number of members who attend races_____
     weekly_____ occasionally_____ never_____
   Purchase of lottery tickets by parents
     often_____ occasionally_____ never_____
   Number of members who attend cockfights_____
     often_____ occasionally_____ never_____

Number of members who attend social dances_____
often_____ occasionally_____ never_____

10. Household income
Monthly income of father_____ of mother_____ of others_____

11. Language in household
Spanish spoken entirely_____ usually_____ seldom_____ never_____
English spoken entirely_____ usually_____ seldom_____ never_____

12. Hours at home during day
Father_____ mother_____ children_____
If parents are both away during day, is anyone at home while children
are not in school? yes_____ no_____
If yes, who_____

13. Political status
Number of members who voted in 1956_____
Party preference_____
Did any household member change party preference between 1952 and
1956?_____ how many?_____

IV

SUPERINTENDENTS' QUESTIONNAIRE

1. In general, do you feel that the present English-language program is successful? If not, what major changes would you make?
2. Do you think that the present policy is, in general, satisfactory with regard to the teaching of religion in the public schools? If not, what major changes would you make?
3. Do you think that children should be given sex education? If so, what recommendations do you have?
4. Are you, in general, in accord with the present structure of authority in the educational system? If not, what changes would you make of a major nature?
5. Would you approve of a more extensive program in art and music? If so, what would you emphasize as a policy?
6. What major improvements, if any, would you recommend for playground and recreational facilities in the schools?
7. Are you reasonably satisfied with the standards of sanitation in your schools? If not, what changes would you make?
8. Do you think that the quality and quantity of parent participation in school affairs are about right? If not, what changes would you propose?
9. Do you think that children should participate more than they now do in planning curricula, school rules, etc.? If so, in what ways?
10. Do you favor the present policy with regard to school dances in private quarters? Why or why not?
11. Do you favor the encouragement of dancing and dating between high school students of white and dark complexion?
12. Do you think that, in general, the schools of your jurisdiction utilize the resources of the community fairly adequately? If not, would you care to suggest how they might do so?
13. Are you, in general, satisfied with the services of the Department in supplying books, materials, audio-visual aids, etc.? If not, what improvements would you suggest?
14. Are you, in general, satisfied with the quality and quantity of attention

paid in the curriculum to Puerto Rican history and traditions? If not, what changes would you suggest?

15. Would you support higher taxes if the added funds were utilized for education?

16. How would you react to the proposal of teaching home economics to boys as well as girls?

17. Are the schools, in general, doing a fairly good job in helping young people prepare for family life? If not, what would you propose by way of policy?

18. Do you think that parents would attend adult courses dealing with community problems, political and economic issues, etc.? If so, would you favor the establishment of such courses?

19. Are you, in general, reasonably satisfied with the way that various subjects in the curriculum are interrelated—e.g., Spanish and social studies, science and mathematics? If not what would you propose?

20. Do you think that, when the average person graduates from high school, he understands and utilizes the scientific method in dealing with his own problems?

21. Assuming that teachers are largely middle class, or at least lower middle, do you think they are sufficiently sensitive to and appreciative of the attitudes and values of other classes? If not, do you see any problem here that deserves further attention?

22. Are you satisfied, in general, with the enforcement of school attendance? If not, what improvements would you suggest?

23. In general, do you think that teachers are quite sensitive to the emotional aspects of learning? If not, what improvements?

24. Do you think that mental hygiene receives fairly adequate attention in teacher training? If not, what improvements?

25. Would you favor greater participation in political affairs by teachers and/or students?

26. Would you favor the affiliation of teachers with the American Federation of Teachers (AFL-CIO)? Why or why not?

27. In general, are you satisfied with the present program of vocational education? If not, what changes of policy would you propose?

28. Where do you think the best teaching takes place today—on the elementary, secondary, university, or adult level?

29. Do you think that, in general, people today learn more inside school or outside school?

30. In general, are you satisfied with the kinds of discipline exercised by teachers? If not, what changes would you suggest?

31. In general, do you think that children have sufficient opportunity for

self-expression in the average classroom? If not, what would you propose?

32. Where do you think the emphasis should lie in the curriculum—in understanding the social heritage, in dealing with present problems, in planning for the future?

33. Could you say that it is more important for education to help people how to make a good living than it is to build good character, or vice versa?

34. Do you favor the sudy of controversial issues—e.g., communism, race relations, the political status of Puerto Rico? If so, on what level(s)?

35. Would you favor the establishment of a consumer cooperative in some of your schools? Why or why not?

36. Would you feel that high school students are mature enough to deal with such problems of the philosophy of history as causation, prediction, and the meaning of progress?

37. In general, do you think the schools of your jurisdiction are paying adequate attention to problems of culture change? If not, would you suggest what could be done?

38. What is your general opinion of television here? Would you care to suggest any ways in which it might be utilized educationally?

39. In general, are you fairly satisfied with the teaching of the three Rs? If not, what changes would you propose in policy?

40. In general, do you think that teachers help their students to become conscious of the goals of their culture? If not, what changes?

41. In general, are teachers and/or students sufficiently international-minded? If not, what changes?

42. In general, do you believe that the schools must follow the patterns already established by the culture, or can they play an important role in creating those patterns?

43. What do you consider the most serious single problem confronting the schools of your jurisdiction?

44. What do you consider their single greatest achievement as of now?

45. In general, do you think there is any serious gap between the program of the schools and the program of the culture? If so, what would be one step toward narrowing that gap that you consider imperative?

REFERENCES

NOTE: The references below are not a bibliographical guide to Puerto Rico. For the latter, consult Maria Stella O'Neill, *Bibliografía Puertorriqueña* (Rio Piedras [P.R.]: Social Science Research Center, University of Puerto Rico, 1958); Julian H. Steward *et al.*, *The People of Puerto Rico* (Urbana: University of Illinois Press, 1956), pp. 516 ff.

CHAPTER ONE: PUERTO RICAN PROFILE

1. For helpful overviews of contemporary Puerto Rico, consult Earl Parker Hanson, *Transformation—The Story of Modern Puerto Rico* (New York: Simon and Schuster, 1955); "Puerto Rico—A Study in Democratic Development," *The Annals of the American Academy of Political and Social Science*, Vol. 285, 1953, pp. 1 ff.; "Puerto Rico: The Bard of Bootstrap," *Time*, Vol. 71, No. 25, 1958, pp. 30 ff. For somewhat older studies, consult Rexford Guy Tugwell, *The Stricken Land—The Story of Puerto Rico* (Garden City [N.Y.]: Doubleday and Co., 1947); Earl S. Garver and Ernest B. Fincher, *Puerto Rico— Unsolved Problem* (Elgin [Ill.]: Elgin Press, 1945); Wenzell Brown, *Dynamite on Our Doorstep—The Puerto Rican Paradox* (New York: Greenberg, 1945); Paul Blanshard, *Democracy and Empire in the Caribbean* (New York: The Macmillan Co., 1947); Vincenzo A. Petrullo, *Puerto Rican Paradox* (Philadelphia: University of Pennsylvania Press, 1947); C. Wright Mills, Clarence Senior, and Rose K. Goldsen, *The Puerto Rican Journey* (New York: Harper & Brothers, 1950); Clarence Senior, *Strangers and Neighbors—The Story of Our Puerto Rican Citizens* (New York: Anti-Defamation League, 1952). Three books that have appeared since the completion of this work deal on different levels with the Puerto Rican migrant and his background: Christopher Rand, *The Puerto Ricans* (New York: Oxford University Press, 1958); Elena Padilla, *Up From Puerto Rico* (New York: Columbia University Press, 1958; Dan Wakefield, *Island in the City—The World of Spanish Harlem* (Boston: Houghton Mifflin Co., 1959). Other sources relevant to this chapter include William H. Stead, *Fomento—The Economic Development of Puerto Rico* (Washington: National Planning Association, 1958); publications of the Puerto Rican Planning Board; of the Chancellor's Office, University of Puerto Rico; and of the Departments of Health, Labor, and Education, Commonwealth of Puerto Rico.
2. Cf. "Puerto Rico Hurt by U.S. Recession," *The New York Times*, Feb. 16, 1958, p. 77.

CHAPTER TWO: FOCUSING ON THE PUERTO RICAN CULTURE

1. Cf. Theodore Brameld, *Cultural Foundations of Education—An Interdisciplinary Exploration* (New York: Harper & Brothers, 1957).
2. Cf. Theodore Brameld, *Toward a Reconstructed Philosophy of Education* (New York: Dryden Press, 1956); *Philosophies of Education in Cultural Perspective* (New York: Dryden Press, 1955); *Ends and Means in Education—A Midcentury Appraisal* (New York, Harper & Brothers, 1950).
3. Brameld, *Cultural Foundations of Education*, p. 153.
4. Cf. Steward *et al.*, *The People of Puerto Rico*.
5. Cf. W. Lloyd Warner and P. S. Lunt, *The Social Life of a Modern Community* (New Haven: Yale University Press, 1941).

CHAPTER FOUR: THE CLASS STRUCTURE OF PUERTO RICO

1. Cf. Brameld, *Toward a Reconstructed Philosophy of Education*, pp. 61 ff.
2. "Puerto Rico: The Bard of Bootstrap," *loc. cit.*, p. 31.
3. Cf. *Harvard Educational Review*, Vol. 23, 1953, pp. 149 ff., for a critical review of research studies.
4. For elaboration and qualified support, cf. Gordon K. Lewis, "Puerto Rico: A Case Study of Change in an Underdeveloped Area," *Journal of Politics*, Vol. 17, 1955, pp. 614 ff.

CHAPTER FIVE: HOW DO PUERTO RICANS LOOK UPON THEIR HISTORY?

1. For a concise summary of some of these events, cf. Adolfo de Hostos, in *Polémica sobre Boorstin* (Hato Rey [P.R.]: Editorial del Departamento de Instrucción Publica, 1956), pp. 39 ff. Cf. also Antonio S. Pedreira, *Insularismo* (San Juan: Biblioteca de Autores Puertorriqueños, 1946); Eugenio Fernández Méndez (ed.), *Crónicas de Puerto Rico* (San Juan: Estado Libre Asociado de Puerto Rico, Ediciones del Gobierno, 1957); and Tomás Blanco, *Prontuario Histórico de Puerto Rico* (San Juan: Editorial Biblioteca de Autores Puertorriqueños, 1946).
2. Perhaps the most controversial and widely discussed argument of this kind was precipitated by Daniel J. Boorstin in his article, "Self-Discovery in Puerto Rico," *Yale Review*, Vol. 45, 1955, pp. 229 ff. Cf. the series of replies by Puerto Rican scholars in de Hostos, *op. cit.*
3. Cf. Brameld, *Philosophies of Education in Cultural Perspective*, pp. 89 ff.
4. Cf. Brameld, *Toward a Reconstructed Philosophy of Education*, pp. 69 ff., 169 ff.
5. Cf. Brameld, *Philosophies of Education in Cultural Perspective*, pp. 203 ff.

6. For an example, cf. *Economic Report to the Governor* (San Juan: Puerto Rico Planning Board, 1957), pp. 56 ff.

CHAPTER SIX: EXPLICIT AND IMPLICIT CULTURE IN PUERTO RICO: DEMOCRACY, RELIGION, AND MORALITY

1. Parts of this chapter were first presented before the American Anthropological Association, Chicago, December, 1957, and have benefited by the reactions received there.
2. Cf. Henry Wells, "Ideology and Leadership in Puerto Rican Politics," *American Political Science Review*, Vol. 49, 1955, pp. 22 ff.

CHAPTER SEVEN: EXPLICIT AND IMPLICIT CULTURE IN PUERTO RICO: SCIENCE

1. Parts of this chapter were first presented before the Philosophy of Education Society, Indianapolis, April, 1958, and have benefited by the criticisms obtained.
2. Cf. Pierre Lecomte du Noüy, *Human Destiny* (New York: Longmans, Green & Co., 1947).

CHAPTER EIGHT: TOWARD THE "NATIONAL CHARACTER" OF PUERTO RICO

1. John Gillín, "Ethos Components in Modern Latin American Culture," *American Anthropologist*, Vol. 57, 1955, pp. 488 ff. Cf. also his "Modern Latin American Culture," *Social Forces*, Vol. 25, 1947, pp. 243 ff.
2. Luis Muñoz Marín, in "Puerto Rico—A Study in Democratic Development," *loc. cit.*, p. 1.

CHAPTER NINE: A CULTURE IN DYNAMIC FLUX

1. Cf. F. P. Thieme, "The Geographic and Racial Distribution of ABO and Rh Blood Types and Tasters of PTC in Puerto Rico," *American Journal of Human Genetics*, Vol. 4, 1952, pp. 94 ff.
2. Cf. Ricardo E. Alegría, "The Fiesta of Santiago Apostol (St. James the Apostle) in Loíza, Puerto Rico," *Journal of American Folklore*, Vol. 69, 1956, pp. 123 ff.

CHAPTER TEN: EDUCATION'S ROLE IN THE DYNAMICS OF PUERTO RICAN CULTURE

1. Cf. Brameld, *Philosophies of Education in Cultural Perspective*, pp. 89 ff.
2. Cf. *Ibid.*, pp. 287 ff.

CHAPTER TWELVE: LEARNING, PERSONALITY, AND THE CULTURAL PROCESS

1. Cf. Brameld, *Toward a Reconstructed Philosophy of Education*, pp. 282 ff.
2. Cf. *Ibid.*, pp. 189 ff.

CHAPTER THIRTEEN: LANGUAGE AS A CULTURAL PROCESS
IN PUERTO RICO

1. The material in this section is derived principally from two sources: Juan José Osuna, *A History of Education in Puerto Rico* (Rio Piedras [P.R.]: Editorial de la Universidad de Puerto Rico, 1949), and Pedro A. Ceballero, *A School Language Policy for Puerto Rico* (Puerto Rico: Baldrich, no date).
2. In Osuna, *op. cit.*, pp. 376 f.
3. Cf. Ernst Cassirer, *An Essay on Man* (New Haven: Yale University Press, 1944); *Language and Myth* (New York: Harper & Brothers, 1946).
4. Cf. Charles C. Fries, *Teaching and Learning English as a Foreign Language* (Ann Arbor: University of Michigan Press, 1949); *The Teaching of English* (Ann Arbor: George Wahr Publishing Co., 1949); *English Word Lists* (Washington, D.C.: American Council on Education, 1940); *American English Grammar* (New York: D. Appleton-Century Company, 1940); *The Structure of English* (New York: Harcourt, Brace & Company, 1952); "American Linguistics and the Teaching of English," *Language Learning*, Vol. 6, 1955, pp. 1 ff.
5. Cf. Alfred Korzybski, *Science and Sanity* (Lancaster [Pa.]: Science Press, 1933); Cassirer, *op. cit.*; George Herbert Mead, *Mind, Self, and Society* (Chicago: University of Chicago Press, 1934); Kurt Lewin, *A Dynamic Theory of Personality* (New York: McGraw-Hill Book Company, 1935); Gardner Murphy, *Personality* (New York: Harper & Brothers, 1947).

CHAPTER FIFTEEN: PUERTO RICO AND RELIGIOUS VALUES

1. Cf. Arnold J. Toynbee, *An Historian's Approach to Religion* (New York: Oxford University Press, 1956).
2. Cf. Lincoln K. Barnett, *The Universe and Dr. Einstein* (New York: William Sloane Associates, 1948).
3. Cf. Brameld, *Toward a Reconstructed Philosophy of Education*, pp. 303 ff.

CHAPTER SEVENTEEN: FREEDOM AS THE GOAL OF PUERTO
RICAN CULTURE

1. Cf. José Ortega y Gasset, *The Revolt of the Masses* (New York: New American Library, 1950).
2. Cf. Lewis Mumford, *The Culture of Cities* (New York: Harcourt, Brace and Co., 1938).

CHAPTER EIGHTEEN: COMPARISONS WITH OTHER EVIDENCE:
SOCIAL SCIENCE

1. Cf. Steward *et al.*, *op. cit.*
2. *Ibid.*, p. 223.
3. *Ibid.*, p. 261.

4. *Ibid.*, p. 408.
5. *Ibid.*, p. 412.
6. Cf. E. Seda Bonilla, "The Normative Patterns of the Puerto Rican Family in Various Situational Contexts" (unpublished doctoral dissertation, Columbia University, 1957); Howard Stanton, "Puerto Rico's Changing Families," *Transactions of the Third World Congress of Sociology*, Vol. 4, 1956, pp. 101 ff.
7. Cf. Paul K. Hatt, *Backgrounds of Human Fertility in Puerto Rico* (Princeton: Princeton University Press, 1952).
8. *Ibid.*, p. 465.
9. Cf. J. Mayone Stycos, *Family and Fertility in Puerto Rico* (New York: Columbia University Press, 1955).
10. Cf. Reuben Hill, Kurt Back, and J. Mayone Stycos, *The Family and Population Control: A Puerto Rican Experiment in Social Change* (unpublished manuscript, subsequently published; Chapel Hill: University of North Carolina Press, 1959).
11. Cf. David Landy, "Culture, Family, and Childhood" (unpublished doctoral dissertation, Harvard University, 1957).
12. Cf. Lydia J. Roberts and Rosa L. Stefani, *Patterns of Living in Puerto Rican Families* (Rio Piedras: University of Puerto Rico, 1949).
13. Cf. Reuben Hill, "Impediments to Freedom of Mate Selection in Puerto Rico," in Eugenio Fernández Méndez (ed.), *Portrait of a Society* (Rio Piedras: University of Puerto Rico, 1956, mimeographed), pp. 55 ff.
14. Cf. Melvin M. Tumin, "A Study of Stratification and Social Mobility" (unpublished manuscript). Cf. Melvin M. Tumin and Arnold S. Feldman, "Status, Perspective, and Achievement: Education and Class Structure in Puerto Rico," *American Sociological Review*, Vol. 21, 1956, pp. 464 ff.
15. Tumin and Feldman, *op. cit.*
16. Cf. Thomas C. Cochran, "Business and Culture in Puerto Rico: An Historical Perspective" (unpublished manuscript).
17. Cf. Carlos Albizu, "The Concept of Self from a Selected Sample of Puerto Rican Subjects" (unpublished manuscript).
18. Cf. Kathleen L. Wolf, "Growing Up and Its Price in Three Puerto Rican Subcultures," in Fernández Méndez (ed.), *op. cit.*, pp. 211 ff.
19. Cf. Peter Bachrach, "Actitud de los Estudiantes Hacia la Autoridad," *Revista de Ciencias Sociales*, Vol. 1, 1957, pp. 321 ff.
20. Cf. Melvin M. Tumin and Arnold S. Feldman, "The Miracle at Sabana Grande," in Fernández Méndez (ed.), *op. cit.*, pp. 299 ff.

CHAPTER NINETEEN: COMPARISONS WITH OTHER EVIDENCE: EDUCATION

1. Cf. Steward *et. al.*, *op. cit.*, pp. 418 ff.
2. Cf. C. Wright Mills, *White Collar* (New York: Oxford University Press, 1953).

3. Cf. Roberts and Stefani, *op. cit.*, p. 288.
4. Cf. Ramón A. Mellado, *Culture and Education in Puerto Rico* (New York: Bureau of Publications, Teachers College, Columbia University, 1947).
5. Cf. Rosa Luisa Stefani, "An Exploratory Study of Values and Practices in Child Rearing among Urban Laboring Class Families in Puerto Rico" (unpublished doctoral dissertation, Cornell University, 1955).
6. Cf. Ramón Ramírez López, "A Comparative Study of the Values of Teachers, Students of Education, and Other University Students in Puerto Rico" (unpublished doctoral dissertation, University of Texas, 1957).
7. Cf. Oscar E. Porrata, *A Suggested Policy for the Administration and Control of Public Education in Puerto Rico* (Hato Rey: Bureau of Publications, Puerto Rico Teachers Association, 1949).
8. Cf. Aida A. de Vergne, "Improving In-Service Education for Beginning Teachers in Elementary Schools in Puerto Rico" (unpublished doctoral project, Teachers College, Columbia University, 1951).
9. Cf. Herminia Vazquez, "The Role of the College of Education in the Reorientation of Secondary Education in Puerto Rico" (unpublished doctorial project, Teachers College, Columbia University, 1953).
10. Cf. Marion Garcia de Ramírez, "The Guidance of the Normal Student —Proposals for a Program of Staff Participation at the College of Education of the University of Puerto Rico" (unpublished doctoral project, Teachers College, Columbia University, 1953).
11. Cf. José A. Cáceres, "Proposed Modification of Courses in the Social Foundations of Education at the University of Puerto Rico" (unpublished doctoral project, Teachers College, Columbia University, 1956).
12. Cf. Cecelia G. Dávila, "A Proposal for Community Education in Selected Resettlements of Puerto Rico" (unpublished doctoral project, New York University, 1955).
13. Cf. *The Use of Social Research in a Community Education Program* (Paris: Unesco, no date); Charles F. Cannell, Fred G. Wale, and Stephen B. Withey (eds.), "Community Change: An Action Program in Puerto Rico," *The Journal of Social Issues*, Vol. 9, 1953, pp. 1 ff.; *La Ciudad que Rebaso Sus Murallas* (San Juan: Unidad de Análisis, División de Educación de la Communidad, 1957).
14. Cannell, Wale and Withey (eds.), *op. cit.*, p. 51.
15. Cf. *A Survey of the Public Educational System of Porto Rico* (New York: Bureau of Publications, Teachers College, Columbia University, 1926); *Public Education and the Future of Puerto Rico* (New York: Bureau of Publications, Teachers College, Columbia University, 1950).
16. Cf. Charles Morris, *Varieties of Human Value* (Chicago: University of Chicago Press, 1956).
17. Cf. *Ibid.*
18. Cf. Ralph L. Beals and Norman D. Humphrey, *No Frontier to Learn-*

ing—The Mexican Student in the United States (Minneapolis: University of Minnesota Press, 1957). The author is indebted to this book for the term "syncretic" utilized in Chapter 8 above. The term would seem still more appropriate to Puerto Rico than to Mexico.

19. Cf. Morris, *op. cit.*

CHAPTER TWENTY:
NEXT STEPS FOR PUERTO RICAN EDUCATION

1. The organization of educational problems into the three categories of curriculum, learning, and control is derived from Brameld, *Philosophies of Education in Cultural Perspective.*
2. Documentation of and other support for this point of view are provided by the author's books cited in Chapter 2.
3. Cf., e.g., Jaime Benítez, *Education for Democracy on a Cultural Frontier* (Rio Piedras: University of Puerto Rico Bulletin, no date), p. 26 (Chancellor Benítez frequently cites Hutchins in support of his views); Angel Quintero, "A Theory of General Education," *Journal of General Education,* Vol. 3, 1949, pp. 203 ff.; Ramón Mellado, "Problemas de la Educación en Puerto Rico" (mimeographed), the latter a sharp critique of what its author regards as a dominantly perennialist philosophy of education in the University.
4. Cf. Brameld, *Philosophies of Education in Cultural Perspective,* pp. 347 ff.
5. Cf. Joseph J. Schwab, *Eros and Education (The Problem of Education)* (Rio Piedras: Faculty of General Studies, University of Puerto Rico, 1958), especially Chapter 5; cf. also Joseph J. Schwab, "On the Conception of Education by Psychology," *Ethics,* Vol. 68, 1957, pp. 39 ff.

APPENDIX, I

1. Cf. Brameld, *Cultural Foundations of Education.*
2. Cf. Steward *et al., op. cit.*
3. Julian H. Steward, *Theory of Culture Change* (Urbana: University of Illinois Press, 1955).
4. Cf. Brameld, *Toward a Reconstructed Philosophy of Education,* pp. 123 ff., 286 ff.
5. Cf. *Ibid.,* pp. 92 ff., 274 ff., 348 ff.
6. Cf. Evon Z. Vogt and John M. Roberts, "A Study of Values," *Scientific American,* Vol. 195, 1956, pp. 25-31, for a summary of the Harvard University Values Study Project.
7. Cf. Korzybski, *op. cit.*
8. For an earlier attempt to engage more in "breadth" than "depth" research, cf. Theodore Brameld, *Minority Problems in the Public Schools* (New York: Harper & Brothers, 1946).
9. Cf. George D. Spindler (ed.), *Education and Anthropology* (Stanford: Stanford University Press, 1955), pp. 216 ff.
10. Cf. Brameld, *Cultural Foundations of Education,* p. xix.

INDEX